CELTS AND GERMANS

THE EARLY LITERARY EVIDENCE

Other books by V.S.White

	ISBN
The Cock & Pye: St. Albans: Deeds [1515 to 1678]	978 0 9540129 1 5
The Ships of Tarshish: The Phoenicians	978 0 9540129 2 2
Names 1451 – 1500: St. Albans: Hertfordshire	978 0 9540129 3 9
Wheathampstead Manor, Hertfordshire: Account Roll 1406	978 0 9540129 5 3
Atlantic Sailings Prior to 1492	978 0 9540129 6 0

CELTS
AND
GERMANS

THE EARLY
LITERARY EVIDENCE

A set of quotations with linking commentary relating to the characteristics of the Celtic and Germanic peoples taken from translations into English of classical texts.

Compiled by V.S.White

For
Sophie Spencer
and
Andrew Spencer
and
John Henry White

First published 2009
by V.S.White
13 Garden Court,
Wheathampstead, Hertfordshire. AL4 8RE

ISBN   978 0 9540129 7 7

Printed in Great Britain by
Q3 Print Project Management Ltd,
Loughborough,
Leicestershire.

CONTENTS

Contents

SECTION 3 – HETEROGENEOUS ELEMENTS

Contents

Continental Celtic silver coin
  Obverse: Possibly offset head looking left, perhaps with a diadem.
  Reverse: A warrior with a shield.
The figure of the coin is much enlarged, the coin's maximum diameter is 15 mm.

INTRODUCTION

Characteristics of both Celt and German are sprinkled among tomes of the classical world. In the literature of archaeology reference is made to the content of these passages, on occasion without giving the text. In this volume the texts, in translation, from a number of authors are brought together as a convenient compendium of such literary evidence.

The geographical position occupied by a tribe or peoples was transient. The technology and mores of their culture were fluid. Hence the individual statements and opinions of historic authors represent a cut through time and not an everlasting truth.

In Europe, as a generalisation, the peoples moved westwards from a springboard in the steppes of southern Russia. Tribes then spilled over to the south when circumstances allowed. Each wave of migrants was promoted as more fearsome than those who had come before and in some way lost their edge. The situation was much influenced by a pressing weight of numbers and was interposed with instances of technological innovation. The possession of iron weapons is an example of such an advantage that was enjoyed by the Celts when they entered Western Europe in the decades surrounding 850 BC. Homo Sapiens Sapiens has been in Western Europe for above 40,000 years. Thus, the many and various local cultures also must be expected to have influenced the gene pool, technology and cultural values. Not least among them those adventurers probing from the south and the groups edging along the Atlantic coastline.

The Celts had attacked Rome in 390 BC and Delphi in 279 or 278 BC. The Celts of northern Italy were subject to Rome by 222 BC and those of Spain by 179 BC.

Julius Caesar conquered Gaul in the years 58 BC to 55 BC. The defeat of Vercingetorix in 52 BC sealed the fate of the continental Celts until the fall of the Western Roman Empire in the fifth century AD. Following on from the Claudian invasion of 43 AD, the subsequent conquest of southern England and the subjugation of tribes in Wales and the north; in Western Europe only the Celtic tribes within Scotland beyond Hadrian's Wall, in Ireland and those living in the northern isles remained outside the grip of the Roman Empire. A group of Celts entered the Bible as the Galatians.

Having marched through the Celts, the Roman army came upon an old enemy who became known to history as the Germani. In the first century AD the German tribes lived in general north of the River Rhine up to the boundary of the North Sea. The Romans had met and fought with German tribes in 101 BC.

The Celts adopted the Greek alphabet and indeed put epistles to the dead on funeral pyres of others. The Greek alphabet gave way to Latin letters in the fullness of time as a medium within which to record the sounds of the Celtic language. A few authors from the classical world were of Celtic origin but their writings are perceived as those of Roman citizens rather than free Celtic spirits.

Ogham has been promoted as a secret script of the Druids though this proposal has more than one sceptic. The script is associated with the post Roman Celts of Britain and Ireland. Previously its use may have been more widespread in Europe.

A further source of the Celtic written word is their inscribed coinage. On some issues an abbreviated personal name or place-name is found in the title and legend. The Celts favoured the staters of Philip II of Macedonia which on their reverse depicted two horses pulling a chariot. The staters were first circulated about 350 BC. The Celtic nations were prone to copy this design with zestful style both on the Continent and in Southern Britain until the native coinage was displaced by that of Rome.

From evidence drawn from the expensive artefacts of archaeology it has been deduced that the Celts valued wine, horses and women, in that order. From the evidence of literature, fighting presents itself as their first love.

The Belgae, living on the north west border of the continental Celts, were identified by Caesar as having a language that differed from that of the Celts. In the opinion of other commentators they were an admixture of Germani who had moved south and Celts. The German tribes were treated as part of the Celtic nation by more than one author.

According to the sources used by Tacitus, the manner in which the name 'Germani' entered common usage was as follows. *"The word Germany is held to be of modern addition. In support of this hypothesis, they tell us that the people who first passed the Rhine, and took possession of a canton in Gaul, though known at present by the name of Tungrians, were, in that expedition, called Germans, and thence the title assumed by a band of emigrants, in order to spread a general terror in their progress, extended itself by degrees, and became, in time, the appellation of a whole people."*

The Germanic tribes developed the writing format known as Runic. They were not subject to the particular priesthood of the Druids though like the Celts they counted by nights and were at least as warlike, boasting champions of awesome valour. The Germanic peoples infiltrated the northern boundaries of the Roman Empire and in time settled within its borders. They were instrumental in over running the empire, precipitating its fall and subjugating or displacing some people of Celtic stock.

The layout of this volume is such that substantial passages from Caesar's *Gallic War* and Tacitus are reproduced in the opening section, since between them they contain the bulk of what is known from classical texts of the Celtic and Germanic peoples. The authors are then taken in approximate date order. The third section of this volume contains a motley set of data considered relevant to the topic in hand. It begins at chapter 16 with the description of the structure of the Roman army written by Polybius together with the notes on Roman army camps and the order of the army on the march supplied by Josephus. Appendix 1 contains the short account by Cassius Dio of the Claudian invasion of Britain. The sections in the *Annals of Tacitus* which particularly refer to Britain are reproduced in Appendix 2. These comprise the rebellion of the Iceni and events of 48 AD to 54 AD, Boudicca and 61 AD. Passages in the *Agricola* which refer to Britain are given in Appendix 3. The report by Julius Caesar of his invasions of Britain in 55 BC and 54 BC are reproduced in Appendix 4. Giraldus visited Ireland at the end of the twelfth century. His synopsis of Irish mythological history is placed in Appendix 5. Appendix 6 contains *The Germania* of Tacitus. To sate curiosity aroused by Diodorus directing attention to a nineteen year lunar / solar cycle followed in an *"island in the ocean over against Gaul, (as big as Sicily) under the arctic pole"*, quotations concerning the Hyperborei are gathered together in Appendix 7.

Use of the horse is central to the cultures of Celt and German in Western Europe. The European wild horses show subtle differences in their genetic codes between areas. It is not yet decided whether the taming of horses arose independently in more than one area or alternatively that the idea of domestication migrated across the continent.

The greater part of topics examined herein are set out in the table below. In a good number of the extracts it is not evident whether the authors, when sourcing their data, were quoting from another book and perpetuating a fact or a falsehood, from information freshly supplied or from their own experience. The page number shown is where the relevant passage begins.

SOME SOURCE DATA COVERED BY THIS VOLUME

Celts

			Page
Gaul = Belgae, Aquitani, Celti.	Caesar GW	1.1	17
Garonne was Celt / Aquitani frontier.	Caesar GW	1.1	17
Marne and Seine were Celt / Belgae frontier.	Caesar GW	1.1	17
Celts in Pyrenees, Gauls north of these but Romans call them all Gauls.	Diodorus	5.2	50
Tall muscular white skin, blond [not red] hair bleached, moustaches, shaving, Gauls.	Diodorus	5.2	50
Converse with few words and in riddles, boasters, Gauls.	Diodorus	5.2	50
Women match men in stature & courage.	Diodorus	5.2	50
Celtic women rain punches.	Ammianus	15.12	103
Tall, fair, ruddy, fierce eyes, quarrelsome, overbearing, clean and neat, courageous.	Ammianus	15.12	103
Gauls and Germans kinsmen, similar nature and government, prone to migrate.	Strabo	4.4.2	67
Galatians of Bible, the Tectosages.	Strabo	4.1.13	65

Celts, general data

Celtiberians? boats of tanned leather, 2nd century BC.	Strabo	3.3.7	64
Barley beer, Zythos. Wash honeycombs, Gauls.	Diodorus	5.2	50
Wine without moderation, exchange jar [hogshead] for a slave, Gauls.	Diodorus	5.2	50
Greedy for wine, continual drunkenness, Gauls.	Ammianus	15.12.4	103
Sleep with 2 catamites though wives comely.	Diodorus	5.2	50
Young men prodigal charms, Celts.	Strabo	4.4.6	67
Bards, instruments like lyres and lyric poets, Gauls.	Diodorus	5.2	50
Bards, Vates (diviners) & Druids among Gauls.	Strabo	4.4.4	67
Musical skill, Ireland.	Gerald, Ire	3.11	119

Celtic dress

Dyed embroidered shirts, breeches, striped [or basketwork] coats, Gauls.	Diodorus	5.2	50
Wear 'sagum', tight breeches, sleeved tunic, Gauls.	Strabo	4.4.3	67
Celtiberians wear rough black cloaks.	Diodorus	5.2	50
Hoods to shoulder, mantles, trousers, black sheep. Ireland.	Gerald, Ire	3.10	119
Dignitaries garments dyed and sprinkled with gold, Gauls.	Strabo	4.4.5	67

SOME SOURCE DATA COVERED BY THIS VOLUME

Celtic custom and law

			Page
Plead in chains, Helvetii, Celts.	Caesar GW	1.4	17
Commonality almost slaves, Celts.	Caesar GW	6.13	20
Land allocated annually by neighbours of Celtiberians.	Diodorus	5.2	50
Children do not approach father in public, Celts.	Caesar GW	6.18	20
Dowry, husband adds equal portion, Celts.	Caesar GW	6.19	20
Life and death, husband over wife and child, Celts.	Caesar GW	6.19	20
Rumour reported to council only, Celts.	Caesar GW	6.20	20
Cut cloak of hecklers in assembly, Gauls.	Strabo	4.4.3	67
Knights and Druids only orders of rank, Celts.	Caesar GW	6.13, 6.15	20
Reckon by nights, keep birthdays and months, Celts.	Caesar GW	6.18	20
Day of 5th day of moon was 1st of month, 30 year unit, Gauls.	Pliny Nat H	16.95	82
Open house to strangers, Gauls.	Diodorus	5.2	50
Open house, offered water to wash if staying, Wales.	Gerald, Wales	1.10	128

Celtic superstition and cult practice

Superstitious, Celts.	Caesar GW	6.16	20
Large figures filled with men set afire, convicts then innocents, Celts.	Caesar GW	6.16	20
Prisoners kept 5 years, captives, burnt in large pyres, Gauls.	Diodorus	5.2	50
Straw colossus with men and animals, Gauls.	Strabo	4.4.5	67
Brennus laughs in Greek temple, 279 BC.	Diodorus	22.9	56
Worship Mercury, Apollo, Mars, Jupiter, Minerva; Celts.	Caesar GW	6.17	20
Castor & Pollux (argonauts) venerated by Celts.	Diodorus	4	48
Celtiberians and north sacrifice at new moon in front of houses.	Strabo	3.4.16	64
Hailing moon means healing all things, Gauls.	Pliny Nat H	16.95	82
Soul immortal, commence new life, Gauls.	Diodorus	5.2	50
Soul immortal, fire and water prevail.	Strabo	4.4.4	67
Priestesses re-roof temple, tear to pieces one of their own.	Strabo	4.4.6	67
Crumbs & crows, decision on disputes.	Strabo	4.4.6	67
Kill captured animals, pile booty, left untouched, Celts.	Caesar GW	6.17	20
Dis, Gauls descended from say Druids.	Caesar GW	6.18	20
Wife questioned when noble dies, Celts.	Caesar GW	6.19	20
Funerals; favourite items, creatures, and once people burnt, Celts.	Caesar GW	6.19	20
Letters to dead on pyre, Gauls.	Diodorus	5.2	50
Cannibals in north reported, Gauls.	Diodorus	5.2	50
White mare and kingship rite, Ireland.	Gerald, Ire	3.25	120

Celtic arms and warfare

Gauls once excelled Germans in prowess.	Caesar GW	6.24	28
Wagons and chariots drawn up, Celts.	Polybius	2.28	45
Chariots, 2 horse, shield bearers, single combat, Gauls.	Diodorus	5.2	50
Fought naked, some Gaesatae, Celts.	Polybius	2.28	45
Din trumpets, war cries, torques, armlets, Celts.	Polybius	2.29	45
Trousers and light cloaks, Celts.	Polybius	2.28	45
Gold bracelets for gods left untouched, Celts.	Diodorus	5.2	50
Heads of foes taken, stored, not sold even for weight in gold.	Diodorus	5.2	50
Heads boasted about, nailed to houses, Gauls.	Diodorus	5.2	50
Foes heads on necks of horses, ornaments, Gauls + north.	Strabo	4.4.5	67
Armour and weapons, trumpets like barbarians use, Gauls.	Diodorus	5.2	50
Gallic arms.	Strabo	4.4.3	67
Celtiberians bury iron to rust, then fashion weapons.	Diodorus	5.2	50
Single combat even at meals, warriors portion, Gauls.	Diodorus	5.2	50
War mad, Gallic race.	Strabo	4.4.2	67
War leader was chosen by people, Gauls.	Strabo	4.4.3	67
Poisoned arrows, Celts.	Strabo	4.4.6	67
Gallic Walls.	Caesar GW	7.23	23

Druids

Druids conduct sacrifices, disputes. One supreme.	Caesar GW	6.13	20
Druids, Gauls assemble in Carnutes land at fixed times.	Caesar GW	6.13	20
Druids, supposed devised in Britain, go there to study.	Caesar GW	6.13	20
Druids, verses to memory, not writing, 20 years training.	Caesar GW	6.14	20
Druids write Greek characters in transactions.	Caesar GW	6.14	20
Druids teach souls pass to another body after death, disregard fear of death.	Caesar GW	6.14	20
Druids granted sole knowledge, soul immortal. Warriors courage to face death.	Lucan Civ W	1, 445 to 470	74
Druids teach stars and nature of things.	Caesar GW	6.14	20
Women in black, Druids, cover altar with captives blood, Anglesey in 61 AD.	Tac. Annals	14.30	33
Human sacrifice only if Druids present, Druids can stop wars.	Diodorus	5.2	50
Human sacrifice, Druids.	Strabo	4.4.4	67
Mistletoe sacred, possible Druid from Greek word oak.	Pliny Nat H	16.95	82

Iberians

Turdetanians have alphabet and history in verse.	Strabo	3.1.6	64
Fawn of Sertorius.	Plutarch, Lives		92

SOME SOURCE DATA COVERED BY THIS VOLUME

British Isles   Page

Inland Britons born there.	Caesar GW	5.12	18
Britons original inhabitants.	Diodorus	5.2	48
Caledonians, red hair, large limbs, thus German origin.	Tac. Agricola	11	31, Ap3
Silurians, swarthy faces mostly curly hair, thus Iberian.	Tacitus Agric	11	31, Ap3
Southern Britons similar to coastal Gauls including religion and language.	Tacitus Agric	11	31, Ap3
Kent most civilised, similar to Gauls.	Caesar GW	5.14	18
Belerium, people work tin, hospitable, Britons. Ictis (St. Michael's mount) tin market, overland to Med.	Diodorus	5.2	48
Belgae settled south coast Britain.	Caesar GW	5.12	18
Britons taller than Celts, not so yellow haired.	Strabo	4.5.2	69
Exports grain, gold, silver, iron, hides, slaves, dogs.	Strabo	4.5.2	69
Iron and brass as money in Britain.	Caesar GW	5.12	18
Hare, Cock and Goose kept not eaten in Britain.	Caesar GW	5.12	18
Blue dye on bodies when fighting, Britons.	Caesar GW	5.14	18
Stained bodies, inland tribes, Britain.	Mela D S Orb	3.6	88
Long hair, moustache shave rest; Britons.	Caesar GW	5.14	18
Wives in common, Britons.	Caesar GW	5.14	18
Inland Britain, no corn, live on milk, flesh, clad in skins.	Caesar GW	5.14	18
Store corn ears, Britons.	Diodorus	5.2	48
Some make no cheese but have milk.	Strabo	4.5.2	69
Returned shipwrecked Roman soldiers AD 16 to 19.	Tacitus Ann	2.24	Ap2
Sacrifices like those in Samothrace to Demeter and Core (Ceres and Proserpine).	Strabo	4.4.6	67
Divination by Hare by Boudicca, outrages, goddess Andraste, sacrifice captives.	Dio Rom H	62.6 62.7	99
Iceni revolt, AD 48 to 54, Silures, Caractacus to Rome, Rivers Sabrina (Severn) Antona border.	Tacitus Ann	12.31 to 12.40	Ap2
Boudicca AD 61 sacked Colchester, London, St Albans, Women prophesied in frenzy.	Tacitus Ann	14.29 to 14.39	Ap2
Boudicca, a description.	Dio Rom H	62.2	99
Seneca's loan re Iceni uprising.	Dio Rom H	62.2	100
55 BC. Caesar's 1st invasion Britain, 7th and 10th legions.	Caesar GW	4.20 to 4.38	Ap4
54 BC Caesar's 2nd invasion Britain, Cassivellaunus, 5 legions and 2000 cavalry.	Caesar GW	5.1 to 5.24	Ap4
Infantry strength, some tribes use chariots, Britain.	Tacitus Agric	12	31
Chariots, Britons.	Diodorus	5.2	48
Chariots as do some Celts, Britons.	Strabo	4.5.2	69
Chariots called 'Covines' set with scythes, Britain.	Mela D S Orb	3.6	88
Cassivellaunus in command.	Caesar GW	5.11	Ap4

Wales

Open house, offered water to wash, harp playing, Wales.	Gerald, Wales	1.10	128
Singing in parts, Britons, Wales.	Gerald, Wales	1.13	128
Soothsayers 'awenddyon' among Britons, Wales.	Gerald, Wales	1.16	128

Ireland

Ireland, people differ little from Britain, merchants trade.	Tacitus Agric	24	32
Hoods to shoulder, mantles, trousers, black sheep, into battle without armour, pastoral people, Ireland.	Gerald, Ire	3.10	119
Musical skill, Ireland.	Gerald, Ire	3.11	119
Cannibals, the Britons who live in Ireland are reported.	Diodorus	5.2	50
More savage than Britons, man-eaters? Ireland.	Strabo	4.5.4	70
Void of godliness, cattle country, Ireland.	Mela D S Orb	3.6	88
White mare and kingship rite, Ireland.	Gerald, Ire	3 25	120

Germans

Germans beyond Rhine.	Caesar GW	1.1	17
Rhine and Danube separate from Gaul, Raetia, Pannonia.	Tac. Germania	1	33
Amalchian Sea (frozen), Morimarusa (Dead Sea is Cimbrian name) beyond is Cronian Sea.	Pliny Nat H	4.27	77
5 German races; Vandili, Ingaevones, Istaevones, Hermiones, Peucini (Basternae).	Pliny Nat H	4.28	77
Wilder, taller than Celts but similar. Germani means genuine in Latin, genuine Galatae.	Strabo	7.1.2	70
Indigenous no admixture, Germans.	Tacitus Ger	2	33
Fierce blue eyes, red hair, large frames, Germans.	Tacitus Ger	4	33
Cimbrians, were they the Cimmerians?	Diodorus	5.2	50

German custom and law

Small temporary huts, flocks, migrate, Germans.	Strabo	7.1.3	70
Chaste, bathe promiscuously in rivers (mixed and naked?), use skins and deerhide cloaks, Germans.	Caesar GW	6.21	28
Food largely milk, cheese, flesh, Germans.	Caesar GW	6.22	28
Land allocated annually, Germans.	Caesar GW	6.22	28
Lay waste land round them for security and pride, Germans.	Caesar GW	6.23	28
Guests, open house, Germans.	Caesar GW	6.23	28
Songs sole history, founders Tuisto and Mannus, Germans.	Tacitus Ger	2	33
Wine renders men effeminate, Germans.	Caesar GW	4.2	29

German superstition and cult practice

No Druids, not great regard to sacrifices, Germans.	Caesar GW	6.21	28
Gods instruments the sun, fire, moon, Germans.	Caesar GW	6.21	28
Priestesses of Cimbri human sacrifice, beat wagon hides.	Strabo	7.2.3	70
Foreknowledge in women, Germans.	Tacitus Ger	8	34
Human sacrifice, Germans.	Tacitus Ger	9	34
Isis, symbol galley, part of Suebi sacrifice to, Germans.	Tacitus Ger	9	34

German arms and warfare

Banditry encouraged to sharpen youth, Germans.	Caesar GW	6.23	28
War, magistrates elected to preside, Germans.	Caesar GW	6.23	28
Military art and hunting occupy Germans.	Caesar GW	6.21	28
Shield songs, broken roar, Germans.	Tacitus Ger	3	33

Divitiacus
Dumnorix
Ariovistus
Elitovius
Cassivellaunus

Vortigern
Calgacus
Cingetorix
Carvilius
Boudicca
Liscus
Taximagulus
Prasutagus
Segonax
Commius
Vercingetorix
Hengis
Venutius
Horsa
Tasciovanus
Cartimandua
Cunobelin
Orgetorix
ODIN
Dubnovellaunus
Verica
Caratacus
Addedomarus
Epaticcus
Cichorius
Mandubratius
Ambigatus
Bellovesus
Boeorix
Vosenos
Sigovesus
Imanuentius
Eppillus
Amminus
BRENNUS
Tincommius
Elitovius
Armimius

Lygdamis
DIS

CELTI Iverne Demetae INGAEVONES Suevi ISTAEVONES
Brigantes Caledonii Ambriani Hassi Sitones Morini Eborones
Iceni Ordivices Veneti Burgundiones Frisii
Scotti Epidii Dumnoni Parisi Meatae Osismi Ambibari Cherusci
Durotriges Cornovii Vercones Taezali Caltes Pictones Bellovaci
Atrebates Novantae Pretani
BELGAE AQUITANI Ambivareti Arveni VANDELI
Regni Cantii Selgovae Decantae Aedui Erdini Batavi Robogii
Catuvellauni Damnonii Carnonacae Voluntii Eblanii Cordiondi
Creones
Silures Otadini Vacomagni Chausi Smertae Venniconii
Dobuni Horesti Ancalites Cassi Usdiae Manapii Caereni Darini
Trinovantes Segontiaci Carnutes Cornovii Cangi Cauci Bibroci
PECHTIS Cenomagni Orci HERMIONES Lugi BASTERNAE

CAESAR AND TACITUS

2   JULIUS CAESAR

Caesar's *Gallic War* embraced the years 58 BC to 52 BC. It is generally held that Caesar dictated his account contemporary with or close after the events recorded. He was assassinated on 15th March 44 BC, then aged between 56 and 58. The last part of the *Gallic War* is believed to have been written by the person acting as Caesar's secretary for the main text. The translation used is that of W.A.McDevitte, of Trinity College Dublin, completed in 1848 and published in the Bohn's Classical Library *"in conjunction with W.S.Bohn, the publisher's eldest son"* in 1851. The quotations come from the 1919 edition. The McDevitte translation was re-published in the Everyman's Library series in 1915.

Celts and Belgae

Caesar: Gallic War book 1, chapters 1 to 4 [McDevitte]
"1. All Gaul is divided into three parts, One of which the Belgae inhabit, the Aquitani another, those who in their own language are called Celts, in ours Gauls, the third. All these differ from each other in language, customs and laws. The river Garonne separates the Gauls from the Aquitani; the Marne and the Seine separate them from the Belgae. . . the Germans who dwell beyond the Rhine . . . .
3. . . . the Helvetii were the most powerful of the whole of Gaul; . . .
4. When the scheme was disclosed to the Helvetii by informers, they, according to their custom, compelled Orgetorix to plead his cause in chains; it was the law that the penalty of being burned by fire should await him if condemned."(1.1)

Caesar: Gallic War book 4, chapter 5 [McDevitte]
"5. Caesar, when informed of these matters, fearing the fickle disposition of the Gauls, who are easily prompted to take up resolutions, and much addicted to change, considered that nothing was to be entrusted to them; for it is the custom of that people to compel travellers to stop, even against their inclination, and inquire what they may have heard, or may know, respecting any matter; and in towns the common people throng around the merchants and force them to state from what countries they come, and what affairs they know of there. They often engage in resolutions concerning the most important matters, induced by these reports and stories alone; of which they must necessarily instantly repent, since they yield to mere unauthorised reports; and since most people give to their questions answers framed agreeably to their wishes."(1.2)

Caesar: Gallic War book 5, chapters 11 and 12 [McDevitte]
"11. . . . the chief command and management of the war having been entrusted to Cassivellaunus, whose territories a river, which is called the Thames, separates from the maritime states at about eighty miles from the sea. At an earlier period perpetual wars had taken place between him and the other states; but greatly alarmed by our arrival, the Britons had placed him over the whole war and the conduct of it.
12. The interior portion of Britain is inhabited by those of whom they say that it is handed down by tradition that they were born in the island itself: the maritime portion by those who had passed over from the country of the Belgae for the purpose of plunder and making war; almost all of whom are called by the names of those states from which being sprung they went thither, and having waged war, continued there and began to cultivate the lands. The number of people is countless, and their buildings exceedingly numerous, for the most part very much like those of the Gauls: the number of cattle is great. They use either brass or iron rings, determined at a certain weight, as their money. Tin is produced in the midland regions; in the maritime, iron; but the quantity of it is small: they employ brass, which is imported. There, as in Gaul, is timber of every description, except beech and fir. They do not regard it lawful to eat the hare, and the cock, and the goose; they, however, breed them for amusement and pleasure. The climate is more temperate than in Gaul, the colds being less severe."(1.3)

Caesar: Gallic War book 5, chapter 14 [McDevitte]
"14. The most civilised of all these nations are they who inhabit Kent, which is entirely a maritime district, nor do they differ much from the Gallic customs. Most of the inland inhabitants do not sow corn, but live on milk and flesh, and are clad with skins. All the Britons, indeed, dye themselves with wood, which occasions a bluish colour, and thereby have a more terrible appearance in fight. They wear their hair long, and have every part of their body shaved except their head and upper lip. Ten and even twelve have wives common to them, and particularly brothers among brothers, and parents among their children; but if there be any issue by these wives, they are reputed to be the children of those whom respectively each first espoused when a virgin."(1.4)

In any culture where men's lives are daily at risk, wives' in common helps ensure the well being of the children.

The routine explanation for warriors colouring their bodies with blue dye is it enables them to appear more fearsome or to gain supernatural protection. A further aspect of this practice could have been to be less clear-cut at a distance, especially under low light conditions, and to more easily dissolve into the background vegetation.

Caesar invaded Britain in 55 BC. His record of events is given in Appendix 4. It is accompanied by comment to the effect that the first invasion was a disaster. A small degree of support for this viewpoint is found in a letter from Cicero in the year 55 BC to Trebatius. Trebatius was a lawyer who achieved success in later life.

Cicero: Letter to Trebatius (A.U.699) - letter 12, book 2 [Melmoth]
"I am glad, for my sake, as well as yours, that you did not attend Caesar into Britain: as it has not only saved you the fatigue of a very disagreeable expedition, but me likewise that of being the perpetual auditor of your wonderful exploits."(2.1)

Cicero: Letter to Trebatius (A.U.700) - letter 15, book 3 [Melmoth]
"If it were not for the compliments you sent me by Chrysippus, the freedman of Cyrus the architect, I should have imagined I no longer possessed a place in your thoughts. . . . Perhaps, however, you may have forgotten the use of your pen, and so much the better, let me tell you, for your clients; as they will lose no more causes by its blunders. But if it is myself only that has escaped your remembrance, I must endeavour to refresh it by a visit, before I am worn out of your mind beyond all power of recollection. After all, is it not the apprehensions of the next summer's campaign, that has rendered your hand too unsteady to perform its office? If so, you must e'en play over again the same gallant stratagem you practised last year in relation to your British expedition, and frame some heroic excuse for your absence."(2.2)

Cicero had written to Trebatius before the first invasion giving a glimpse of a world where a Roman officer had half an eye to the hope of becoming rich on the spoils of war.

Cicero: Letter to Trebatius (A.U.699) - letter 9, book 2 [Melmoth]
"I never write to Caesar or Balbus, without taking occasion to mention you in the advantageous terms you deserve: . . . But more of this another time: in the mean while, let me advise you, who know so well how to manage securities for others, to secure yourself from the British charioteers."(2.3)

Cicero: Letter to Trebatius (A.U.699) - letter 10, book 2 [Melmoth]
" . . . I am informed there is neither gold nor silver in all Britain. If that should be the case, I would advise you to seize one of the enemy's military cars, and drive back to us with all expedition. But if you think you shall be able to make your fortune without the assistance of British spoils, by all means establish yourself in Caesar's friendship. To be serious; . . "(2.4)

The rumour and reports circulating among Caesar's contemporaries in Rome, whilst often malicious, were not as well honed to enhance his public image as those from his own hand.

Cicero: Letter from [Marcus] Coelius (A.U.702) - letter 25, book 3 [Melmoth]
"Agreeably to my promise when we parted, I have sent you a full account of every event that has happened since you left Rome. . . . As to Caesar, we have frequent, and no very favourable reports concerning him: however, they are at present, nothing more than rumours. Some say he has lost all his cavalry; and I believe this is the truth of the case: others, that the seventh legion has been entirely defeated, and that he himself is surrounded by the Bellovaci, that he cannot possibly receive any succours from the main body of his army. But this news is not publicly known; on the contrary, it is only the whisper of a party which I need not name, and who mentioned it with great caution; particularly Domitius, who tells it in your ear with a most important air of secrecy."(2.5)

A footnote identifies Lucius Domitius Aenobarbus as one of Caesar's enemies at Rome and the Bellovaci as a people of Belgic Gaul.

The translation of the letters of Cicero was by William Melmoth (1710 - 1799). The quotations are from the edition published in 1804.

The relative size in terms of population of the Celtic tribes of continental Europe who were still free to rally to Vercingetorix may be indicated by the forces levied from each state in 52 BC. The data is drawn from the account of Julius Caesar. As ever, the absolute values could be interpreted as flattering the victorious commander and his army.

Caesar: Gallic War book 7, chapter 75 [McDevitte]
"75. . . . They demand thirty-five thousand men from the Aedui and their dependants, the Segusiani, Ambivareti, and Aulerci Brannovices; an equal number from the Arveni; twelve thousand each from the Senones, Sequani, Bituriges, Santones, Ruteni, and Carnutes; ten thousand from the Bellovaci; the same number from the Lemovici; eight thousand each from the Pictones, and Turoni, and Parisii, and Helvii; five thousand each from the Suessiones, Ambiani, Mediomatrici, Petrocorii, Nervii, Morini, and Nitiobriges; the same number from the Aulerci Cenomani; four thousand from the Atrebates; three thousand each from the Bellocassi, Lexovii, and Aulerci Eburovices; thirty thousand from the Rauraci, and Boii; six thousand from all the states together which border on the Atlantic, and which in their dialect are called Armoricae (in which numbers are comprehended the Curisolites, Rhedones, Ambibari, Caltes, Osismii, Lemovices, Veneti, and Unelli). Of these the Bellovaci did not contribute their number, as they said that they would wage war against the Romans on their own account, and at their own discretion, and would not obey the orders of any one: however, at the request of Commius, they sent two thousand in consideration of a tie of hospitality which subsisted between him and them."(1.5)

This description of the Gauls was produced by Caesar after waging war against the Celts over a number of seasons and living among them. Some authorities reject this supposition that Druidism was devised in Britain. They deduce it arrived with the Celts, moving from east to west, and retained a strong foothold in barbarous Britain when on the wane elsewhere. A small step from Caesar's account is that Druidism originated or blossomed in a pre-Celtic Britain and was adopted by the Celts after they had entered Western Europe. Oak and mistletoe, beloved of the Druids, must have been indigenous flora where the Druid religion flowered. If a Druid origin in the British Isles is not found admissible then, allowing for a modest climatic variation over the centuries, it remains plausible that the detail of the religion was assimilated either after the migration to the west began or before the archaic era when proto Celts moved into the Steppes and the land of wild horses.

Caesar: Gallic War book 6, chapter 13 to 20 [McDevitte]
"13. Throughout all Gaul there are two orders of those men who are of any rank and dignity: for the commonality is held almost in the condition of slaves, and dares to undertake nothing of itself and is admitted to no deliberation. The greater part, when they are pressed either by debt, or the large amount of their tributes, or the oppression of the more powerful, give themselves up in vassalage to the nobles, who possess over them the same rights without exception as masters over their slaves. But of these two orders, one is that of the Druids, the other that of the knights. The former are engaged in things sacred, conduct the public and the private sacrifices, and interpret all matters of religion. To these a large number of young men resort for the purpose of instruction, and they are in great honour among them.

For they determine respecting almost all controversies, public and private; and if any crime has been perpetrated, if murder has been committed, if there be any dispute about inheritance, if any about boundaries, these same persons decide it; they decree rewards and punishments if anyone, either in a private or public capacity, has not submitted to their decision, they interdict him from the sacrifices. This among them is the most heavy punishment. Those who have been thus interdicted are esteemed in the number of the impious and the criminal: all shun them, and avoid their society and conversation, lest they receive some evil from their contact; nor is justice administered to them when seeking it, nor is any dignity bestowed on them. Over all these Druids one presides, who possesses supreme authority among them. Upon his death, if any individual among the rest is pre-eminent in dignity, he succeeds; but, if there are many equal, the election is made by the suffrages of the Druids; sometimes they even contend for the presidency with arms. These assemble at a fixed period of the year in a consecrated place in the territories of the Carnutes, which is reckoned the central region of the whole of Gaul. Hither all, who have disputes, assemble from every part, and submit to their decrees and determinations. This institution is supposed to have been devised in Britain, and to have been brought over from it into Gaul; and now those who desire to gain a more accurate knowledge of that system generally proceed thither for the purpose of studying it."

A question can be posed as to whether this annual convocation with its supreme authority in the territory of the Carnutes truly represented all Druids or alternatively those in a confederation of tribes which included the Carnutes. Did Druids from Albion and Iverne submit to the authority of the assembly held in the middle of Celtic Gaul?

"14. The Druids do not go to war, nor pay tribute together with the rest; they have an exemption from military service and a dispensation in all matters. Induced by such great advantages, many embrace this profession of their own accord, and are sent to it by their parents and relations. They are said there to learn by heart a great number of verses; accordingly some remain in the course of training twenty years. Nor do they regard it lawful to commit these to writing, though in almost all other matters, in their public and private transactions, they use Greek characters. That practice they seem to me to have adopted for two reasons; because they neither desire their doctrines to be divulged among the mass of the people, nor those who learn, to devote themselves the less to the efforts of memory, relying on writing; since it generally occurs to most men, that, in their dependence on writing, they relax their diligence in learning thoroughly, and their employment of the memory. They wish to inculcate this as one of their leading tenets, that souls do not become extinct, but pass after death from one body to another, and they think that men by this tenet are in a great degree excited to valour, the fear of death being disregarded. They likewise discuss and impart to the youth many things respecting the stars and their motion, respecting the extent of the world and of our earth, respecting the nature of things, respecting the power and the majesty of the immortal gods."

If the matters of Druidical doctrine and practice evolved before its practitioners assimilated the use of the written word, then a verbal data base was the only option available to carry information down the generations, and the tradition continued.

"15. The other order is that of the knights. These, when there is occasion and any war occurs (which before Caesar's arrival was for the most part wont to happen every year, as either they on their part were inflicting injuries or repelling those which others inflicted on them), are all engaged in war. And those of them most distinguished by birth and resources have the greatest number of vassals and dependants about them. They acknowledge this sort of influence and power only.

16. The nation of all the Gauls is extremely devoted to superstitious rites; and on that account they who are troubled with unusually severe diseases and they who are engaged in battles and dangers, either sacrifice men as victims, or vow that they will sacrifice them, and employ the Druids as the performers of those sacrifices; because they think that unless the life of a man be offered for the life of a man, the mind of the immortal gods cannot be rendered propitious, and they have sacrifices of that kind ordained for national purposes. Others have figures of vast size, the limbs of which formed of osiers they fill with living men, which being set on fire, the men perish enveloped in the flames. They consider that the oblation of such as have been taken in theft, or in robbery, or any other offence, is more acceptable to the immortal gods; but when a supply of that class is wanting, they have recourse to the oblation of even the innocent.

17. They worship as their divinity, Mercury in particular, and have many images of him, and regard him as the inventor of all arts, they consider him the guide of their journeys and marches, and believe him to have very great influence over the acquisition of gain and mercantile transactions. Next to him they worship Apollo, and Mars, and Jupiter, and Minerva; respecting these deities they have for the most part the same belief as other nations: that Apollo averts diseases, that Minerva imparts the invention of manufactures, that Jupiter possesses the sovereignty of the heavenly powers; that Mars presides over wars. To him when they have determined to engage in battle, they commonly vow those things they shall take in war. When they have conquered, they sacrifice whatever captured animals may have survived the conflict, and collect the other things into one place.

[Footnote. Athenaeus remarks "that the Gauls sacrifice their captives to the Gods."]

In many states you may see piles of these things heaped up in their consecrated spots; nor does it often happen that anyone, disregarding the sanctity of the case, dares either to secrete in his house things captured, or take away those deposited; and the most severe punishment, with torture, has been established for such a deed.

18. All the Gauls assert that they are descended from the god Dis, and say that this tradition has been handed down by the Druids. For that reason they compute the divisions of every season, not by the number of days, but of nights; they keep birthdays and the beginnings of months and years in such an order that the day follows the night. Among the other usages of their life, they differ in this from almost all other nations, that they do not permit their children to approach them openly until they are grown up so as to be able to bear the service of war; and they regard it as indecorous for a son of boyish age to stand in public in the presence of his father."

Pliny, whose writing post dates Caesar's by a century, was aware of the importance of mistletoe to the Druids, the Celtic month commencing at the fifth day (night) of the moon and the thirty-year cycle (Pliny *Nat. Hist.* book 16.95). In general, the name 'Dis' is accepted as being the Celtic name for their deity. Some authorities interpret 'Dis' as a Roman founding figurehead who had an equivalence with the Celtic Sucellos.

"19. Whatever sums of money the husbands have received in the name of a dowry from their wives, making an estimate of it, they add the same amount out of their own estates. An account is kept of all this money conjointly, and the profits are laid by: whichever of them shall have survived, to that one the portion of both reverts, together with the profits of the previous time. Husbands have power of life and death over their wives as well as over their children: and when the father of a family, born in a more than commonly distinguished rank, has died, his relations assemble, and, if the circumstances of his death are suspicious, hold an investigation upon the wives in the manner adopted towards slaves; and if proof is obtained, put them to severe torture, and kill them. Their funerals, considering the state of civilisation among the Gauls, are magnificent and costly; and they cast into the fire all things, including living creatures, which they suppose to have been dear to them when alive; and, a little before this period, slaves and dependants, who were ascertained to have been beloved by them, were, after the regular funeral rites were completed, burnt together with them.

20. Those states which are considered to conduct their commonwealth more judiciously, have it ordained by their laws, that, if any person shall have heard by rumour and report from neighbours anything concerning the commonwealth, he shall convey it to the magistrate and not impart it to any other; because it has been discovered that inconsiderate and inexperienced men were often alarmed by false reports and driven to some rash act, or else took hasty measures in affairs of the highest importance. The magistrates conceal those things which require to be kept unknown; and they disclose to the people whatever they determine to be expedient. It is not lawful to speak of the commonwealth, except in council."(1.6)

The description by Caesar of the method whereby Gallic Walls were constructed and their advantages is important. It is of use when interpreting the archaeological record and when thinking through plausible models for Celtic defensive earthworks.

Caesar: Gallic War book 7, chapter 23 [McDevitte]
"23. But this is usually the form of all the Gallic walls. Straight beams, connected lengthwise and two feet distant from each other at equal intervals, are placed together on the ground; these are mortised on the inside, and covered with plenty of earth. But the intervals which we have mentioned are closed up in the front by large stones. These being thus laid and cemented together, another row is added above, in such a manner, that the same interval may be observed, and that the beams may not touch one another, but equal spaces intervening, each row of beams is kept firmly in its place by a row of stones. In this manner the whole wall is consolidated, until the regular height of the wall be completed. The work, with respect to appearance and variety, is not unsightly, owing to the alternate rows of beams and stones, which preserve their order in right lines; and, besides, it possesses great advantages as regards utility and the defence of cities; for the stone protects it from fire, and the wood from the battering ram, since it [the wood] being mortised in the inside with rows of beams, generally forty feet in length, can neither be broken through nor torn asunder."(1.7)

Cicero was defending Marius Fonteius against accusations of lining his own pocket by placing an arbitrary tax on wine when praetor of Gallia Narbonensis. Part of the defence was to blacken the name of these civilised Gauls by attributing to them an affinity with the behaviour of those still free of domination and secondly by recalling selected deeds of their ancestors. This near contemporary oration reinforces Caesar's account of human sacrifice. The text was translated by C.D.Yonge and the quotation is taken from the 1877 edition published in Bohn's Library series.

Cicero: on behalf of Marcus Fonteius [Yonge]
" . . . That after this the Gauls would drink their wine more diluted, because they thought that there was poison in it. . . . . Do you think that those nations are influenced in giving their evidence by the sanctity of their oath, and by the fear of the immortal gods, which are so widely different from other nations in their habits and natural disposition? For other nations undertake wars in defence of their religious feelings; they wage war against the religion of every people: other nations when waging war beg for sanction and pardon from the immortal gods; they have waged war with the immortal gods themselves.

10. These are the nations which formerly marched to such a distance from their settlements, as far as Delphi, to attack and pillage the Pythian Apollo, and the oracle of the whole world. By these same nations, so pious, so scrupulous in giving their evidence, was the Capitol besieged, and that Jupiter, under the obligations of whose name our ancestors decided that the good faith of all witnesses should be pledged. Lastly, can anything appear holy or solemn in the eyes of those men, who, if ever they are so much influenced by any fear as to think it necessary to propitiate the immortal gods, defile their altars and temples with human victims? So that they cannot pay proper honour to religion itself without first violating it with wickedness. For who is ignorant that, to this very day, they retain that savage and barbarous custom of sacrificing men! What, therefore, do you suppose is the good faith, what the piety of those men, who think that even the immortal gods can be most easily propitiated by the wickedness and murder of men? Will you connect your own religious ideas with these witnesses?"(3.1)

Marcus Tullius Cicero was born to Helvia at Arpinum, the son of a Roman knight descended from the kings of the Sabines - who are better remembered on account of their nubile women. He studied philosophy under Philo, law under Mutus Scaevola and during military service his commander was Sylla. Well received in Sicily as quaestor, he subsequently survived an assassination attempt initiated by Catiline. For a period, he found himself banished from Rome by Clodius. Cicero, a celebrated orator, served a term as pro-consul in Cilicia. He was assassinated aged 63 years in December 43 BC on the orders of Marc Anthony (4). His brother, Quintus, was Caesar's lieutenant in Gaul.

Among the 'fragments' published in Reference 1 is a statement by Servius that Caesar was captured during an encounter when in Gaul!

Fragments The Journals: Servius, Virgil, Ae. 11, 743 [McDevitte]
"When Julius Caesar was carrying on one of his campaigns in Gaul, he was taken prisoner by the enemy and hurried along, when one of them recognising him ran up and insultingly said, Cecos Caesar, which signifies in the Gallic language, let him go; and thus it occurred that he escaped. Caesar himself says this in one of his journals where he records his good fortune.

The quotation above is included for completeness whilst aware its content may not be true. Honoratus Maurus Servius, who flourished in the fourth century AD, wrote commentaries on the work of Virgil. His data would require corroboration by other authors before it could gain any stature, as he wrote significantly after the event. There was a Servius whose works are lost who was a contemporary of Cicero (4). A modicum of support comes from a passage in Plutarch's life of Caesar that reads as follows: *"But he seems to have some check at first, for the Arveni still show a sword suspended in one of their temples, which they declare was taken from Caesar."* The quotation relates to the battle at Alesia. On balance, it is judged unrealistic for Plutarch to have made a statement on the sword being in the temple in his own lifetime (50 AD to 125 AD) without some foundation. If wrong his critics would have pounced upon the error.

A man named Divitiacus has several entries among the pages of Caesar's *Gallic War*. He was an acquaintance of Caesar and close to being a friend. Divitiacus the Aeduan obtained a pardon for his brother Dumnorix from Caesar (*GW* book 1.16 to 1.20), complained of the cruelty of the German tribes under Ariovistus (*GW* 1.31), created a diversionary action against the Belgic Bellovaci to Caesar's advantage (*GW* 2.10), then interceded on their behalf with Caesar (*GW* 2.14), and travelled to Rome to be refused a request for aid against the German tribes (*GW* book 6.12). It is received wisdom that Divitiacus was an Arch-Druid and known to Cicero (Cicero: *De Divinatione*, book 1.41; see Ap.4.4). Against this background the description of Druid activity supplied by Caesar is given credit for particular accuracy. This interface with the Aedui was associated with Caesar's first Gallic campaign in 58 BC. It continued into subsequent years. The Germanic Suebi lead by Ariovistus had overcome the Aedui by 71 BC. The plea by Divitiacus to the senate at Rome is placed in the year 61 BC.

The intended migration from Switzerland to lands between the River Garonne and the Pyrenees by the Celtic Helvetii brought about by the incursion of the superior forces of German tribes is 'tentatively' dated to 28th March 58 BC. The implication of a Helvetii migration was that the German tribes would be a real and immediate threat to the Roman province of Narbonesis Gallia.

Caesar: Gallic War book 1, chapter 16 to 18 [McDevitte]
"16. . . . The Aedui . . . - having called together their chiefs, of whom he had a great number in his camp, among them Divitiacus, and Liscus who was invested with the chief magistracy, (whom the Aedui style the Vergobretus, and who is elected annually, and has power of life and death over his countrymen,) he severely reprimands them. . . . .
17. . . .
18. Caesar perceived that, by this speech of Liscus, Dumnorix, the brother of Divitiacus, was indicated; . . .

He [Caesar] makes inquiries on the same points privately of others, and discovers that it is all true; that 'Dumnorix is the said person, a man of the highest daring, in great favour with the people on account of his liberality, a man eager for revolution: that for a great many years he has been in the habit of contracting for the customs and all the other taxes of the Aedui at a small cost, because when he bids, no one dares to bid against him. By these means he has both increased his own private property, and amassed great means for giving largesse; that he maintains constantly at his own expense and keeps about his own person a great number of cavalry, and that not only at home, but even among the neighbouring states, he has great influence, and for the sake of strengthening this influence has given his mother in marriage among the Bituriges to a man the most noble and most influential there; that he has himself taken a wife from among the Helvetii, and has given his sister by the mother's side and his female relations in marriage into other states; that he favours and wishes well to the Helvetii on account of this connection; and that he hates Caesar and the Romans, on his own account, because by their arrival his power was weakened, and his brother's Divitiacus, restored to his former position of influence and dignity: that, if anything should happen to the Romans, he entertains the highest hope of gaining the sovereignty by means of the Helvetii, but that under the government of the Roman people he despairs not only of royalty, but even of that influence which he already has. "(1.9)

This insight into the manner whereby the business of taxing the tribe to fund its organisation and defence was bid for can be supposed as not particular to the Aedui and hence commonplace among the neighbouring Celtic tribes, if not beyond.

The intervention by Divitiacus on behalf of the Bellovaci occurred in 57 BC. During the same year, according to Caesar, unco-operative members of the aristocracy of that tribe moved to Britain.

Caesar: Gallic War book 2 chapter 10 to 15 [McDevitte]
"10. . . . The enemy . . . . Together with other causes, this consideration also led them to that resolution, viz.: that they had learnt that Divitiacus and the Aedui were approaching the territories of the Bellovaci. And it was impossible to persuade the latter to stay any longer, or to deter them from conveying succour to their own people.
11. . . .
12. . . .
13. . . . In like manner, when he had come up to the town, and there pitched his camp, the boys and the women from the wall, with outstretched hands, after their custom, begged peace from the Romans.
14. For these Divitiacus pleads (for after the departure of the Belgae, having dismissed the troops of the Aedui, he had returned to Caesar). 'The Bellovaci had at all times been in the alliance and friendship of the Aeduan state; that they had revolted from the Aedui and made war upon the Roman people, being urged thereto by their nobles, who said that the Aedui, reduced to slavery by Caesar, were suffering every indignity and insult. That they who had been the leaders of that plot, because they perceived how great a calamity they had brought upon the state, had fled into Britain. That not only the Bellovaci, but also the Aedui, entreated him to use his [accustomed] clemency and lenity towards them [the Bellovaci]: . . . '
15. Caesar said that on account of his respect for Divitiacus and the Aeduans, he would receive them into his protection,"(1.10)

A speech was put into the mouth of Divitiacus the Aeduan at the time of Caesar's first campaign in Gaul. The year was 58 BC. These words are a window through which to appreciate the power of the expansion by Germanic tribes thrusting into new territory westwards across the Rhine at the expense of the warlike and populous holders of that land. The Germanic Cimbri had wrought havoc at the frontiers of the Roman provinces in 101 BC. A generation later by 71 BC the Suebi were threatening the well being of the Roman state.

Caesar: Gallic War book 1 chapter 31
"31. . . . For these Divitiacus the Aeduan spoke and told him:- 'That there were two parties in the whole of Gaul; that the Aedui stood at the head of one of these, the Arverni of the other. After these had been violently struggling with one another for the superiority for many years, it came to pass that the Germans were called in for hire by the Arverni and the Sequani. That about 15,000, of them [i.e. of the Germans] had at first crossed the Rhine: but after that these wild and savage men had become enamoured of the lands and the refinement and the abundance of the Gauls, more were brought over, that there were now as many as 120,000 of them in Gaul that with these the Aedui and their dependants had repeatedly struggled in arms,- that they had been routed, and had sustained a great calamity - had lost all their nobility, all their senate, all their cavalry. And that broken by such engagements and calamities, although they had formerly been very powerful in Gaul, both from their own valour and from the Roman people's hospitality and friendship, they were now compelled to give the chief nobles of their state, as hostages to the Sequani, and to bind their state by an oath, that they would neither demand hostages in return, nor supplicate aid from the Roman people, nor refuse to be for ever under their sway and empire. That he was the only one out of all the state of the Aedui, who could not be prevailed upon to take the oath or to give his children as hostages. On that account he had fled from his state and had gone to the senate at Rome to beseech aid, as he alone was bound neither by oath nor hostages. But a worse thing had befallen the victorious Sequani than the vanquished Aedui, for Ariovistus, the king of the Germans, had settled in their territories, and had seized upon a third of their land, which was the best in the whole of Gaul, and was now ordering them to depart from another third part, because a few months previously 24,000 men of the Harudes had come to him, for whom room and settlements must be provided. The consequence would be, that in a few years they would all be driven from the territories of Gaul, and all the Germans would cross the Rhine; for neither must the land of Gaul be compared with the land of the Germans, nor must the habit of living of the latter be put on a level with the former. Moreover, [as for] Ariovistus, no sooner did he defeat the forces of the Gauls in a battle, which took place at Magetobria, than [he began] to lord it haughtily and cruelly, to demand as hostages the children of all the principal nobles, and wreak on them every kind of cruelty, if everything was not done at his nod or pleasure; that he was a savage, passionate, and reckless man, and that his commands could no longer be borne. Unless there was some aid in Caesar and the Roman people, the Gauls must all do the same thing that the Helvetii have done [viz] emigrate from their country, and seek another dwelling place, other settlements remote from the Germans, and try whatever fortune may fall to their lot."(1.11)

Germans

Caesar: Gallic War book 6, chapter 21 to 24 [McDevitte]

"21. The Germans differ much from these usages, for they have neither Druids to preside over sacred offices, nor do they pay great regard to sacrifices. They rank in the number of the gods those alone whom they behold, and by whose instrumentality they are obviously benefited, namely, the sun, fire, and the moon; they have not heard of the other deities even by report. Their whole life is occupied in hunting and in the pursuits of the military art; from childhood they devote themselves to fatigue and hardships. Those who have remained chaste for the longest time, receive the greatest commendation among their people: they think that by this the growth is promoted, by this the physical powers are increased and the sinews are strengthened. And to have had knowledge of a women before the twentieth year they reckon among the most disgraceful acts; of which matter there is no concealment, because they bathe promiscuously in the rivers and only use skins or small cloaks of deers' hides, a large portion of the body being in consequence naked.

22. They do not pay much attention to agriculture, and a large portion of their food consists in milk, cheese, and flesh; nor has anyone a fixed quantity of land or his own individual limits; but the magistrates and the leading men each year apportion to the tribes and families, who have united together, as much land as, and in the place in which, they think proper, and the year after compel them to remove elsewhere. For this enactment they advance many reasons - lest seduced by long-continued custom, they may exchange their ardour in the waging of war for agriculture; lest they may be anxious to acquire extensive estates, and the more powerful drive the weaker from their possessions; lest they construct their houses with too great a desire to avoid cold and heat; lest the desire of wealth spring up, from which cause divisions and discords arise; and that they may keep the common people in a contented state of mind, when each sees his own means placed on an equality with the most powerful.

23. It is the greatest glory to the several states to have as wide deserts as possible around them, their frontiers having been laid waste. They consider this the real evidence of their prowess, that their neighbours shall be driven out of their lands and abandon them, and that no one dare settle near them; at the same time they think that they shall be on that account the more secure, because they have removed the apprehension of a sudden incursion. When a state either repels war waged against it, or wages it against another, magistrates are chosen to preside over that war with such authority, that they have power of life and death. In peace there is no common magistrate, but the chiefs of provinces and cantons administer justice and determine controversies among their own people. Robberies which are committed beyond the boundaries of each state bear no infamy, and they avow that these are committed for the purpose of disciplining their youth and of preventing sloth. And when any of their chiefs has said in an assembly 'that he will be their leader, let those who are willing to follow, give in their names'; they who approve of both the enterprise and the man arise and promise their assistance and are applauded by the people; such of them as have not followed him are accounted in the number of deserters and traitors, and confidence in all matters is afterwards refused them. To injure guests they regard as impious; they defend from wrong those who have come to them for any purpose whatever, and esteem them inviolable; to them the houses of all are open and maintenance is freely supplied.

24. And there was formerly a time when the Gauls excelled the Germans in prowess, ...
but their proximity to the Province and knowledge of commodities from countries beyond
the sea supplies to the Gauls many things tending to luxury as well as civilisation.
Accustomed by degree to be overmatched and worsted in many engagements, they do not
even compare themselves to the Germans in prowess."(1.12)

Caesar's regard for the Germani was approaching that of admiration. Who can know whether it was formulated from his personal experience, the reports of merchants and travellers to the hinterland or the books of authors with whom he was familiar?

The Germani of 50 BC by implication had a dearth of woven textiles and produce which took more than one season to mature, thus excluding most cultivated fruits. A matter of conjecture is that either the Germanic tribes took prisoners and made slaves during their migrations, thus assimilating the populations which they over ran, or they put all in their path to the sword and annihilated the peoples and cultures who previously occupied the land. The post Roman Norse and Anglo-Saxon societies utilised slave labour and were more firmly based upon a settled agriculture.

Caesar: Gallic War book 4, chapters 1 to 3 [McDevitte]
"1. . . . The nation of the Suevi is by far the largest and the most warlike nation of all the
Germans. They are said to possess a hundred cantons, from each of which they yearly
send from their territories for the purpose of war a thousand armed men: the others who
remain at home, maintain themselves and those engaged in the expedition. The latter
again, in their turn, are in arms the year after: the former remain at home. Thus neither
husbandry nor the art and practice of war are neglected. But among them there exists no
private and separate land; nor are they permitted to remain more than one year in one
place for the purpose of residence. They do not live much on corn, but subsist for the
most part on milk and flesh, and are much in hunting; which circumstance must, by the
nature of their food, and by their daily exercise and the freedom of their life (for having
from boyhood been accustomed to no employment, or discipline, they do nothing at all
contrary to their inclination), both promote their strength and render them men of vast
stature of body. And to such a habit have they brought themselves, that even in the
coldest parts they wear no clothing whatever except skins, by reason of the scantiness of
which a great portion of their body is bare, and besides they bathe in open rivers.
2. Merchants have access to them rather that they may have persons to whom they may
sell those things which they have taken in war, than because they need any commodity to
be imported to them. Moreover, even as to labouring cattle, in which the Gauls take the
greatest pleasure, and which they procure at a great price, the Germans do not employ
such as are imported, but those poor and ill-shaped animals which belong to their
country; these, however, they render capable of the greatest labour by daily exercise. In
cavalry actions they frequently leap from their horses and fight on foot; and train their
horses to stand still in the very spot on which they leave them, to which they retreat with
great activity when there is occasion; nor, according to their practice, is anything
regarded as more unseemly, or more unmanly, than to use housings. Accordingly, they
have the courage, though they be themselves but few, to advance against any number
whatever of horse mounted with housings. They on no account permit wine to be
imported to them, because they consider that men degenerate in their powers of enduring
fatigue, and are rendered effeminate by that commodity.

3. They esteem it their greatest praise as a nation that the lands about their territories lie unoccupied to a very great extent, inasmuch as that by this circumstance is indicated that a great number of nations cannot withstand their power;"(1.13)

The name of Julius Caesar is known to all (but a few) people whose background is the culture of Western Europe. His name has survived two thousand years though the reality of his life has been much coloured by a single play from the pen of Shakespeare rather than the myriad words of other authors.

Lempriere's Dictionary contains the following definition. *"Caesar, a surname given to the Julian family at Rome, either because one of them kept an elephant, which bears the same name in the Punic tongue, or because one was born with a thick head of hair. This name, after it had been dignified in the person of Julius Caesar and of his successors, was given to the apparent heir of the empire, in the age of the Roman emperors."(4)*

The son of L.Caesar and Aurelia the daughter of Cotta, Gaius Julius Caesar was born between 102 BC and 100 BC. He was assassinated on the 15th March, 44 BC after becoming a perpetual dictator. The inclusion of Brutus among the assassins was recognised as being of especial significance. The background of contemporary hearsay whispered that Julius Caesar was the natural father of Brutus, who was fifteen or sixteen years his junior. Caesar was undoubtedly well acquainted with the mother of Brutus in later life and dallied in her company on occasion. His legitimate daughter, Julia, had married Pompey but died in childbirth about the time of the second invasion of Britain in 54 BC. His son, Caesarion, born to Queen Cleopatra of Egypt was proclaimed king of Cyprus and Egypt when aged 13 by Anthony and subsequently put to death 5 years after by Augustus. See Suetonius, *Augustus* 17 and *Caesar* 52 (4).

His critics would have it that he indulged in homosexual practice from time to time, whereas Suetonius identified the young Caesar's stay at the court of king Nicomedes of Bithynia as the only serious charge of unnatural practice against him. *"In his private character, Caesar has been accused of seducing one of the vestal virgins, and suspected of being privy to Catiline's conspiracy; and it was his fondness for dissipated pleasures which made his countrymen say, that he was the husband of all the women at Rome, and the woman of all men."(4).* Suetonius attributed the 'every woman's husband' quotation to the Elder Curio.

Plutarch described Caesar as being of a slender build, fair and with an epileptic condition. Suetonius added brown eyes and early hair loss.

3 TACITUS

Tacitus lived in the years AD 55 to AD 120. He wrote in AD 97 - 98 on the exploits of his father-in-law Agricola, who, as a Roman Governor, was in Britain from the summer of AD 78. Agricola had previously held a military post in Britain.

An account of the campaigns of the Roman army in Northern Britain was given by Tacitus in his *Life of Agricola*. This account included an expedition into Caledonia and the battle of Mons Graupius, see Appendix 3.

The translation of the *Agricola* and *Germania* by Arthur Murphy (1727-1805) was first published in 1793. The quotations are taken from the edition republished in the Everyman's Library series.

Celts

Tacitus: Agricola chapters 11, 12 [Murphy]
"*XI. Whether the first inhabitants of Britain were natives of the island, or adventitious [sic] settlers, is a question lost in the mists of antiquity. The Britons, like other barbarous nations, have no monuments of their history. They differ in the make and habit of their bodies, and hence various inferences concerning their origin. The ruddy hair and lusty limbs of the Caledonians indicate a German extraction. That the Silures were at first a colony of Iberians is concluded, not without probability, from the olive tincture of their skin, the natural curl of their hair, and the situation of the country, so convenient to the coast of Spain. On the side opposite to Gaul the inhabitants resemble their neighbours on the continent; but whether that resemblance is the effect of one common origin, or of the climate in contiguous nations operating on the make and temperament of the human body, is a point not easy to be decided. All circumstances considered, it is rather probable that a colony from Gaul took possession of a country so inviting by its proximity. You will find in both nations the same religious rites, and the same superstition. The two languages differ but little. In provoking danger they discover the same ferocity, and in the encounter, the same timidity. The Britons, however, not yet enfeebled by a long peace, are possessed of superior courage. The Gauls, we learn from history, were formerly a warlike people; but sloth, the consequence of inactive times, has debased their genius, and virtue died with expiring liberty. Among such of the Britons, as have been for some time subdued, the same degeneracy is observable. The free and unconquered part of the nation retains at this hour the ferocity of the ancient Gauls.*
XII. The strength of their armies consists in infantry, though some of their warriors take the field in chariots. The person of highest distinction guides the reins, while his martial followers, mounted in the same vehicle, annoy the enemy. The Britons were formerly governed by a race of kings: at present they are divided into factions under various chieftains; and this disunion, which prevents their acting in concert for a public interest, is a circumstance highly favourable to the Roman arms against a warlike people, independent, fierce, and obstinate. A confederation of two or more states to repel the common danger is seldom known: they fight in parties, and the nation is subdued."(5.1)

Tacitus: Agricola chapter 24 [Murphy]
Ireland is less than Britain, but exceeds in magnitude all the islands of the Mediterranean. The soil, the climate, the manners and genius of the inhabitants, differ little from those of Britain. By the means of merchants resorting thither for the sake of commerce, the harbours and approaches to the coast are well known."(5.2)

An extract from the *Annals* of Tacitus describing events in Britain is given in Appendix 2. The *Annals* record the delivery of the British leader Caractacus (also translated as Caratacus) in chains to the Romans by Cartimandua, queen of the Brigantes, nine years after the beginning of the war in Britain. Caractacus was subsequently paraded through Rome and then pardoned by the emperor Claudius.

Attached to the wake of this Roman triumph is a story of the early introduction of Christianity to Britain. It is claimed that 'Bran the blessed', the father of Caractacus, was taken to Rome among the captives. While there, Bran was introduced to Christianity by fellow inmates of the prisons in Rome; he adopted the faith and returned to Britain. Tacitus lists Caractacus, his wife, daughter and brothers as transported to Rome. If Bran (Brennus) was a name given to outstanding war leaders then the father, or father-in-law, of Caractacus may have had such a distinction and a good number in the retinue of Caractacus would have survived to return to Britain. Otherwise, it is a judgement whether there is a kernel of truth in this story of an early basis for the Celtic Church or whether it is an example of the Celtic storyteller's art. Elsewhere, Cassius Dio lists Caractacus as the son of Cymbeline; Cunobelinus being dead by 43 AD.

A more widely retold tale connecting the Celts in Britain and the early Christian Church is the romantic tradition that Joseph of Arimathea, in whose tomb Christ had been laid to rest, visited the Glastonbury region of Somerset in the West of England. The legend tells that Joseph of Arimathea, with his twelve companions and the cup used at the last supper among his possessions, at some stage in his travels visited England and was given land by Prince Aviragus on the Isle of Avalon in the Somerset marshes where Joseph founded a church. Joseph pushed his staff into the ground to mark the spot where his journey had ended and the staff took root and grew into a tree which flowers each year at Christmas-tide. The subtlety of this tale is that by selecting Joseph, who was a minor figure in the biblical events, it adds credibility to the whole; whereas a piece of propaganda might be anticipated to have embraced a more prominent personage for a role to enhance the standing of Glastonbury.

A wider interpretation of Joseph of Arimathea is that he was a merchant who was a relative, perhaps an uncle, of Mary, the mother of Christ, and as such was accustomed to trade with that Celtic part of England. This line of reasoning leads to his being accompanied on some trips by members of his family, a perception later incorporated in the poetry of William Blake *'And did those feet in ancient time walk upon England's mountains green'*. Thus a vision of Jesus visiting British shores before he set out on his ministry is kept alive. If the word read as 'grail' was intended to convey the meaning of the person of Jesus Christ, the tale of the Glastonbury visit would gain in stature.

The *Annals* of Tacitus as translated by Alfred John Church and William Jackson Brodribb was first published in 1869. The quotations are taken from the reprint in 1888 published by Macmillan and Company, London (6).

The Roman army under Suetonius Paulinus attacked Anglesey in 61 AD.

Tacitus: Annals book 14 chapters 29, 30. [Church and Brodribb]
"29. . . . He therefore prepared to attack the island of Mona . . .
30. On the shore stood the opposing army with its dense array of armed warriors, while between the ranks dashed women, in black attire like the Furies, with hair dishevelled, waving brands. All around, the Druids, lifting up their hands to heaven, and pouring forth dreadful imprecations, scared our soldiers by the unfamiliar sight, ... A force was next set over the conquered, and their groves, devoted to inhuman superstitions, were destroyed. They deemed it indeed a duty to cover their alters with the blood of captives and to consult their deities through human entrails."(6.1)

Germans

Tacitus: Germania chapters 1 to 4 [Murphy]
I. The whole vast country of Germany is separated from Gaul, from Rhaetia, and Pannonia, by the Rhine and the Danube; from Dacia and Sarmatia, by a chain of mountains, and, where the mountains subside, mutual dread forms a sufficient barrier. The rest is bounded by the ocean, embracing in its depth of water several spacious bays, and islands of prodigious extent, whose kings and peoples are now, in some measure, known to us, the progress of our arms having made recent discoveries. . . .
II. The Germans, there is reason to think, are an indigenous race, the original natives of the country, without any intermixture of adventitious settlers from other nations. . . . In all songs and ballads, the only memorials of antiquity amongst them, the god Tuisto, who was born of the Earth, and Mannus, his son, are celebrated as the founders of the German race. Mannus, it is said, had three sons, from whom the Ingaevones, who bordered on the sea-coast; the Hermiones, who inhabit the midland country; and the Istaevones, who occupy the remaining track, have all respectively derived their names. Some indeed, taking advantage of the obscurity that hangs over remote and fabulous ages, ascribe to the god Tuisto a more numerous issue, and thence trace the names of various tribes, such as the Marsians, the Gambrivians, the Suevians, and the Vandals. The ancient date and authenticity of those names are, as they contend, clearly ascertained.
The word Germany is held to be of modern addition. In support of this hypothesis, they tell us that the people who first passed the Rhine, and took possession of a canton in Gaul, though known at present by the name of Tungrians, were, in that expedition, called Germans, and thence the title assumed by a band of emigrants, in order to spread a general terror in their progress, extended itself by degrees, and became, in time, the appellation of a whole people. They have a current tradition that Hercules visited those parts. When rushing to battle, they sing, in preference to all other heroes, the praises of that ancient worthy.
III. The Germans abound with rude strains of verse, the reciters of which, in the language of the country, are called BARDS. With this barbarous poetry they inflame their minds with ardour in the day of action, and prognosticate the event from the impression which it happens to make on the minds of the soldiers, who grow terrible to the enemy, or despair of success, as the war-song produces an animated or a feeble sound. Nor can their manner of chanting this savage prelude be called the tone of human organs: it is rather a furious uproar; a wild chorus of military virtue. The vociferation used upon these occasions is uncouth and harsh, at intervals interrupted by the application of their bucklers to their mouths, and by the repercussion bursting out with redoubled force.

An opinion prevails among them, that Ulysses, in the course of those wanderings which are so famous in poetic story, was driven into the Northern Ocean, and that, having penetrated into the country, he built, on the banks of the Rhine, the city of Asciburgium, which is inhabited at this day, and still retains the name given originally by the founder. It is further added, that an altar dedicated to Ulysses, with the name of Laertes, his father, engraved upon it, was formerly discovered at Usciburgium. Mention is likewise made of certain monuments and tombstones, still to be seen on the confines of Germany and Rhaetia, with epitaphs or inscriptions in Greek characters. But these assertions it is not my intention either to establish or to refute; the reader will yield or withhold his assent, according to his judgment [sic] or his fancy.

IV. I have already acceded to the opinion of those, who think that the Germans have hitherto subsisted without intermarrying with other nations, a pure; unmixed, and independent race, unlike any other people, all bearing the marks of a distinct national character. Hence, what is very remarkable in such prodigious numbers, a family likeness throughout the nation; the same form and feature, stern blue eyes, ruddy hair, their bodies large and robust, but powerful only in sudden efforts. They are impatient of toil and labour; thirst and heat overcome them; but, from the nature of their soil and climate, they are proof against cold and hunger.

V. The face of the country, though in some parts varied, presents a cheerless scene, covered with the gloom of forests, or deformed with wide-extended marshes; towards the boundaries of Gaul, moist and swampy; on the side of Noricum and Pannonia, more exposed to the fury of the winds. Vegetation thrives with sufficient vigour. The soil produces grain, but is unkind to fruit-trees; well stocked with cattle, but of an under-size, and deprived by nature of the usual growth and ornament of the head. The pride of a German consists in the number of his flocks and herds: they are his only riches, and in these he places his chief delight. Gold and silver are withheld from them; is it by the favour or the wrath of Heaven? I do not, however, mean to assert that in Germany there are no veins of precious ore; for who has been a miner in those regions? Certain it is, they do not enjoy the possession and use of those metals with our sensibility. There are, indeed, silver vessels to be seen amongst them, but they were presents to their chiefs or ambassadors; the Germans regard them in no better light than common earthenware. It is, however, observable, that near the borders of the empire, the inhabitants set a value upon gold and silver, finding them subservient to the purposes of commerce. The Roman coin is known in those parts, and some of our specie is not only current, but in request. In places more remote, the simplicity of ancient manners still prevails: commutation of property is their only traffic. Where money passes in the way of barter, our old coin is the most acceptable, particularly that which is indented at the edge, or stamped with the impression of a chariot and two horses, called the SERRATI and BIGATI. Silver is preferred to gold, not from caprice or fancy, but because the inferior metal is of more expeditious use in the purchase of low-priced commodities."(5.3)

Tacitus: Germania chapters 8 to 14 [Murphy]
VIII. . . . . There is, in their opinion, something sacred in the female sex, and even the power of foreseeing future events. Their advice is, therefore, always heard; they are frequently consulted, and their responses are deemed oracular. . . .
IX. Mercury is the god chiefly adored in Germany. On stated days they think it lawful to offer to him human victims. They sacrifice to Hercules and Mars such animals as are usually slain in honour of the gods.

In some parts of the country of the Suevians, the worship of Isis is established. To trace the introduction of ceremonies, which had their growth in another part of the world, were an investigation for which I have no materials: suffice it to say, that the figure of a ship (the symbolic representation of the goddess) clearly shows that the religion was imported into the country. Their deities are not immured in temples, nor represented under any kind of resemblance to the human form. To do either, were, in their opinion, to derogate from the majesty of superior beings. Woods and groves are the sacred depositories; and the spot being consecrated to those pious uses, they give to that sacred recess the name of the divinity that fills the place, which is never profaned by the steps of man. The gloom fills every mind with awe; revered at a distance, and never seen but with the eye of contemplation."

Isis was a goddess of Egypt, a motherhood figure. She was given the head of a cow after her own head was cut off by her son when she interfered in a fight between him and Set. If not depicted with the head of a cow, she was often shown with horns. As an alternative, the Norse goddess Frigg had a dimension associated with the sea.

"X. Their attention to auguries, and the practice of divining by lots, is conducted with a degree of superstition not exceeded by any other nation. Their mode of proceeding by lots is wonderfully simple. The branch of a fruit-tree is cut into small pieces, which, being all distinctly marked, are thrown at random on a white garment. If the question of public interest be depending, the priest of the canton performs the ceremony; if it be nothing more than a private concern, the master of the family officiates. With fervent prayers offered up to the gods, his eyes devoutly raised to heaven, he holds up three times each segment of the twig, and as the marks rise in succession, interprets the decrees of fate. If appearances prove unfavourable, there ends all consultation for that day: if, on the other hand, the chances are propitious, they require, for greater certainty, the sanction of auspices. The well-known superstition, which in other countries consults the flight and notes of birds, is also established in Germany; but to receive intimation of future events from horses is a peculiar credulity of the country. For this purpose a number of milk-white steeds, unprofaned by mortal labour, are constantly maintained at the public expense, and placed to pasture in the religious groves. When occasion requires, they are harnessed to a sacred chariot, and the priest, accompanied by the king, or chief of the state, attends to watch the motions and the neighing of the horses. No other mode of augury is received with such implicit faith by the people, the nobility, and the priesthood. The horses, upon these solemn occasions, are supposed to be the organs of the gods, and the priests their favoured interpreters. They have still another way of prying into futurity, to which they have recourse, when anxious to know the issue of an important war. They seize, by any means in their power, a captive from the adverse nation, and commit him in single combat with a champion selected from their own army. Each is provided with weapons after the manner of his country, and the victory, wherever it falls, is deemed a sure prognostic of the event.
XI. In matters of inferior moment the chiefs decide; important questions are reserved for the whole community. Yet even in those cases where all have a voice, the business is discussed and prepared by the chiefs. The general assembly, if no sudden alarm calls the people together, has its fixed and stated periods, either at the new or full moon. This is thought the season most propitious to public affairs. Their account of time differs from that of the Romans; instead of days they reckon the number of nights.

Their public ordinances are so dated; and their proclamations run in the same style. The night, according to them, leads the day. Their passion for liberty is attended with this ill consequence: when a public meeting is announced, they never assemble at the stated time. Regularity would look like obedience: to mark their independent spirit, they do not convene at once, but two or three days are lost in delay. When they think themselves sufficiently numerous, the business begins. Each man takes his seat, completely armed. Silence is proclaimed by the priests, who still retain this coercive authority. The king, or chief of the community, opens the debate: the rest are heard in their turn, according to age, nobility of descent, renown in war, or fame for eloquence. No man dictates to the assembly: he may persuade, but cannot command. When anything is advanced not agreeable to the people, they reject it with a general murmur. If the proposition pleases, they brandish their javelins. This is their highest and most honourable mark of applause; they assent in a military manner, and praise by the sound of their arms.

XII. In this council of state, accusations are exhibited, and capital offences prosecuted. Pains and penalties are proportioned to the nature of the crime. For treason and desertion, the sentence is to be hanged on a tree: the coward and such as are guilty of unnatural practices, are plunged under a hurdle into bogs and fens. In these different punishments, the point and spirit of the law is, that crimes which affect the state may be exposed to public notoriety: infamous vice cannot be too soon buried in oblivion. He who is convicted of transgressions of an inferior nature, pays a mulct of horses, or of cattle. Part of that fine goes to the king or the community, and part to the person injured or to his family. It is in these assemblies that princes are chosen and chiefs elected to act as magistrates in the several cantons of the state. To each of these judicial officers, assistants are appointed from the body of the people, to the number of a hundred, who attend to give their advice, and strengthen the hands of justice.

XIII. A German transacts no business, public or private, without being completely armed. The right of carrying arms is assumed by no person whatever, till the state has declared him duly qualified. The young candidate is introduced before the assembly, where one of the chiefs, or his father, or some near relation, provides him with a shield and javelin. This, with them, is the manly gown: the youth from that moment ranks as a citizen; till then he was considered as part of the household; he is now a member of the commonwealth. In honour of illustrious birth, and to mark the sense men entertain of the father's merit, the son, though yet of tender years, is called to the dignity of a prince or chief. Such as are grown up to manhood, and have signalised themselves by a spirit of enterprise, have always a number of retainers in their train. Where merit is conspicuous, no man blushes to be seen in the list of followers, or companions. . . .

XIV. . . . If, in the course of a long peace, the people relax into sloth and indolence, it often happens that the young nobles seek a more active life in the service of other states engaged in war."(5.4)

Tacitus: Germania chapters 31 to 37 [Murphy]
XXXI. A custom, known, indeed, in other parts of Germany, but adopted only by a few individuals of a bold and ardent spirit, is with the Cattians a feature of the national character. From the age of manhood they encourage the growth of their hair and beard; nor will any one, till he has slain an enemy, divest himself of that excrescence, which by a solemn vow he has devoted to heroic virtue. Over the blood and spoils of the vanquished, the face of the warrior is, for the first time, displayed.

The Cattian then exults; he has now answered the true end of his being, and has proved himself worthy of his parents and his country. The sluggard continues unshorn, with the uncouth horrors of his visage growing wilder to the close of his days."

Among the few references to the Franks grudgingly made by Gregory of Tours in his *History of the Franks*, the Bructeri, Chamavi, Amsivari and Chatti were identified as Frankish tribes and the (or some) Frankish kings were described as long haired. Thus, it follows that long hair became a sign of nobility in time, regardless of what it had represented to the informants of Tacitus. Gregory died in 594 AD. Elsewhere in Gregory's history, a band of Saxons, as a sign of an oath they had jointly sworn, vowed to cut neither hair nor beard until they had achieved vengeance.

"The men of superior courage and uncommon ferocity wear also an iron ring, in that country a badge of infamy, and with that, as with a chain, they appear self-condemned to slavery, till by the slaughter of an enemy they have redeemed their freedom. With this extraordinary habit, the Cattians are in general much delighted. They grow grey under a vow of heroism, and by their voluntary distinctions render themselves conspicuous to their friends and enemies. In every engagement the first attack is made by them: they claim the front of the line as their right, presenting to the enemy an appearance wild and terrible. Even in the time of peace they retain the same ferocious aspect; never softened with an air of humanity. They have no house to dwell in, no land to cultivate, no domestic care to employ them. Wherever chance conducts them, they are sure of being maintained. Lavish of their neighbours' substance, and prodigal of their own, they persist in this course, till towards the decline of life their drooping spirit is no longer equal to the exertions of a fierce and rigid virtue.

XXXII. The Usipians and Tencterians border on the Cattians. Their territory lies on the banks of the Rhine, where that river, still flowing in one regular channel, forms a sufficient boundary. In addition to their military character, the Tencterians are famous for the discipline of their cavalry. Their horse is no way inferior to the infantry of the Cattians. . . . With their goods and valuable effects their horses pass as part of the succession, not however, by the general rule of inheritance, to the eldest son, but, in a peculiar line, to that son who stands distinguished by his valour and his exploits in war.

XXXIII. In the neighbourhood of the last-mentioned states formerly occurred the Bructerians, since that time dispossessed of their territory, and, as fame reports, now no longer a people. The Chamavians and Angrivarians, it is said, with the consent of the adjacent tribes, invaded the country, and pursued the ancient settlers with exterminating fury."

As the Bructeri were named by Gregory of Tours, they were not annihilated.

"XXXIV. At the back of the states, which I have now described, lie the Dulgibinians and the Chasuarians, with other nations of inferior note. In front occurs the country of the Frisians, divided into two communities, called, on account of their degrees of strength, the Greater and the Lesser Frisia. Both extend along the margin of the Rhine as far as the ocean, . . .

XXXV. We have hitherto traced the western side of Germany. From the point where we stop, it stretches away with a prodigious sweep towards the north.

In this vast region, the first territory that occurs is that of the Chaucians, beginning on the confines of the Frisians, and, though at the extremity bounded by the sea-shore, yet running at the back of all the nations already described, till, with an immense compass, it reaches the borders of the Cattians. Of this immeasurable tract it is not sufficient to say that the Chaucians possess it: they even people it. Of all the German nations, they are, beyond all question, the most respectable. Their grandeur rests upon the surest foundation, the love of justice; wanting no extension of territory, free from avarice and ambition, remote and happy, they provoke no wars, and never seek to enrich themselves by rapine and depredation. Their importance among the nations round them is undoubtedly great; but the best evidence of it is, that they have gained nothing by injustice. Loving moderation, yet uniting to it a warlike spirit, they are ever ready in a just cause to unsheathe the sword. Their armies are soon in the field. In men and horses, their resources are great, and even in profound tranquillity their fame is never tarnished.

XXXVI. Bordering on the side of the Chaucians, and also of the Cattians, lies the country of the Cheruscans; . . . The downfall of the Cheruscans drew after it that of the Fosi, a contiguous nation, in their day of prosperity never equal to their neighbours, but fellow-sufferers in their ruin. . . .

XXXVII. In the same northern part of Germany we find the Cimbrians on the margin of the ocean; a people at present of small consideration, though their glory can never die. Monuments of their former strength and importance are still to be seen on either shore. Their camps and lines of circumvallation are not yet erased. From the extent of ground which they occupied, you may even now form an estimate of the force and resources of the state, and the account of their grand army, which consisted of such prodigious numbers, seems to be verified. It was in the year of Rome six hundred and forty, in the consulship of Caecilius Metellus and Papirius Carbo, that the arms of the Cimbrians first alarmed the world. If from that period we reckon to the second consulship of the emperor Trajan, we shall find a space of near two hundred and ten years: so long has Germany stood at bay with Rome! "(5.5)

The experience of the Roman armies at the hands of the Cimbri and the eventual defeat of the Cimbri in 101 BC by an army lead by Marius, newly returned from fighting in North Africa, were highlighted by Plutarch in his life of Marius.

Tacitus: Annals book 1 chapter 61 [Church and Brodribb]
"In the centre of the field were the whitening bones of men, as they had fled, or stood their ground, strewn everywhere or piled in heaps. Near, lay fragments of weapons and limbs of horses, and also human heads, prominently nailed to trunks of trees. In the adjacent groves were the barbarous altars, on which they had immolated tribunes and first-rank centurions."(6.2)

These were the remains of the army of Varus. In 9 AD the Germans slaughtered his army. It had comprised three Legions. P.Quinctilius Varus had been the Roman commander in Germany from 6 AD. Varus reached the Visurgis and then turned his troops back into the Teutoburgiensis Saltus (Teutoburger Wold) in Northern Germany, a place of hills, swamps and forest. The forces under his command were annihilated by the German tribe of the Cherusci lead by their chief Arminius. Prior to this battle, Arminius is reported to have visited Rome and to have been granted Roman citizenship.

In due course of time the Roman army fell back to the Rhine as its frontier and abandoned the strategy of a frontier consolidated along the River Elbe. Suetonius in his *Twelve Caesars* recorded that Tiberius (later emperor) visited the region after the event and laid the blame squarely on the leadership of Varus.

C. Cornelius Tacitus, born in the reign of Nero, was the son of a Roman knight who had sometime been the governor of Belgic Gaul. This biographic data is given in *Lempriere's Classical Dictionary* (4) whereas other reference books are less precise on his origin and family.

Tacitus, a long standing friend of Pliny the Younger, enjoyed the early patronage of Vespasian and in time achieved the rank of consul in 97 AD. A senator, he served a term as the provincial governor of Western Anatolia. The summary in Lempriere's Dictionary reads *"Tacitus wrote a treatise on the manners of the Germans, a composition admired for the fidelity and exactness with which it is executed, though some have declared that the historian delineated manners and customs with which he was not acquainted, and which never existed. His life of C. Julius Agricola, whose daughter he had married, . . . "(4)*.

The *Histories* covered the period from the death of Nero in 68 AD to the end of the reign of Domitian and this comprised 12 or 14 books of which 5 books survive (one not intact). The *Annals* began at the death of Augustus with the reign of Tiberius in 14 AD and ended with the death of Nero in 68 AD. Sixteen books of the *Annals* are extant. Thus, parts of 21 books survive from an original total of 30. The first modern edition of his surviving works was published at Rome in 1515 AD (4) and all modern editions, it is reported, stem from parts of two codices that came to light in the fourteenth or fifteenth centuries and found their way to Florence. A surviving *Dialogue on Famous Orators*, that examines the decline in oratory, is argued as having been written by Tacitus.

Lempriere continues *"It is said that the emperor Tacitus, who boasted in being one of the descendants of the historian, ordered the works of his ancestor to be placed in all public libraries, and directed that 10 copies, well ascertained for accuracy and exactness, should be yearly written, that so great and so valuable a work should not be lost." (4)*. The namesake emperor Tacitus reigned in 275 to 276 AD. His action supports a modest expectation that additional fragments of the works of Tacitus await discovery.

Pliny the Younger wrote to his great friend Tacitus on the circumstances of the death of his mother's brother, Pliny the Elder.

Pliny the Elder had written *The Wars in Germany* (now lost), which reasonably it can be supposed was available to Tacitus together with the volumes of notes made by the industrious Pliny and all his works. The view of Germany through the hand of Tacitus was based upon the firm rock of Pliny's half century old first hand observations modified with the anecdotes of those returning from army service.

There is an unresolved question whether Tacitus, on leaving Rome in 89 AD, became governor of Gallic Belgica. Otherwise, historians envisage no opportunity when an interlude existed in which he could have visited the frontier with Germany. Tacitus had little need to visit the region in person to obtain fresh information since there could have been no shortage of data on German frontier tribes available in Italy.

Tacitus has been criticised for contrasting the ideal of the noble savage, exemplified by the German tribes, with the vice-ridden, luxuriant excesses of the despotism within which he lived, and what was wrong with that?

A letter from Pliny the Younger to Macer supplied the titles of the following works written by Pliny the Elder. The order below approximates to the order in which the works of Pliny were finished though not necessarily begun, see Reference 17 volume 1.

Works of Pliny the Elder

1.	On the use of the Javelin by Cavalry.	1 book	lost
2.	Life of Q.Pomponius Secundus. A friend of Pliny.	2 books	lost
3.	The Wars in Germany.	20 books	lost
4.	The Student. In 6 volumes because of size. Contains instructions for the training of the orator, from the cradle to his entrance on public life.	3 books	lost
5.	On Difficulties in the Latin Language. [Footnote. 'De Dubia Sermone.' A few scattered fragments of it still survive.]	8 books	
6.	Continuation of the History of Aufodius Bassus.	31 books	lost
7.	Natural History.	37 books	
Also	160 volumes of notes. [Footnote. 'Electorum Commentarii.']		

The library of Pliny, his works and notes must have been available to Tacitus through his friendship with Pliny the Younger.

Pliny the Younger (61/63 to 112/113 AD) was born Caius Caecilius. His father died and he and his widowed mother were taken under the roof of Pliny - Caius Plinius Secundus, surnamed the elder. Pliny adopted him as his son and heir. Caius Caecilius changed his name to Caius Plinius (Caecilius?) Secundus, surnamed the younger (4).

SECTION 2

CLASSICAL TEXTS

4   HERODOTUS

Referred to by Cicero as the father of Greek history, Herodotus of Halicarnassus was born between 490 BC and 480 BC and travelled widely. Herodotus had less reading matter available to consult than later historians but his library did include the works of the sixth century BC author Hecataeus of Miletus, to whom Herodotus refers.

The quotations are from the translation by George Rawlinson that was first published in 1858. An edition of Rawlinson was published by the Everyman's Library in 1910.

The earliest published translation of Herodotus into English comprised the first two books and this was produced in 1584 under the initials B R. The first complete, though criticised, translation of Herodotus into English was that of Isaac Littlebury in 1709. The second translation was by William Beloe in 1791. J. Lempriere, the Jersey schoolmaster better remembered for his Classical Dictionary (4), published a translation of the first three books in 1792. *De Legibus 1.5* supplies the father of history quotation. The initials B R are attributed to Barnaby Rich, see *TLS* June 27 2008.

Darius I, son of Hystaspes, is described as king of the Persians and the whole continent. Darius had fought a combination of Greeks at the celebrated battle of Marathon in 490 BC and died in about 486 BC. The reported beliefs of the Getae show an affinity with those of the Druids.

Herodotus: book 4, chapters 93 to 96 [Rawlinson]
"93. Before arriving at the Ister, the first people whom he subdued were the Getae, who believe in their immortality. . . . gave themselves up to Darius without a struggle; but the Getae obstinately defending themselves, were forthwith enslaved, notwithstanding that they are the noblest as well as the most just of all the Thracian tribes.
94. The belief of the Getae in respect of immortality is the following. They think that they do not really die, but that when they depart this life they go to Zalmoxis, who is called also Gebeleizis by some among them. To this god every five years they send a messenger, who is chosen by lot out of the whole nation, and charged to bear him their several requests. Their mode of sending him is this. A number of them stand in order, each holding in his hand three darts; others take the man who is to be sent to Zalmoxis, and swinging him by his hands and feet, toss him into the air so that he falls upon the points of the weapons. If he is pierced and dies, they think that the god is propitious to them; but if not, they lay the fault on the messenger, who (they say) is a wicked man: and so they choose another to send away. The messages are given while the man is still alive. The same people, when it lightens and thunders, aim their arrows at the sky, uttering threats against the god; and they do not believe that there is any god but their own.
95. I am told by the Greeks who dwell on the shores of the Hellespont and the Pontus, that this Zalmoxis was in reality a man, that he lived at Samos, and while there was the slave of Pythagoras son of Mnesarchus.

41

After obtaining his freedom he grew rich, and leaving Samos, returned to his own country. The Thracians at that time lived in a wretched way, and were a poor ignorant race; Zalmoxis, therefore, who by his commerce with the Greeks, and especially with one who was by no means their most contemptible philosopher, Pythagoras to wit, was acquainted with the Ionic mode of life and with manners more refined than those current among his countrymen, had a chamber built, in which from time to time he received and feasted all the principal Thracians, using the occasion to teach them that neither he, nor they, his boon companions, nor any of their posterity would ever perish, but that they would all go to a place where they would live for aye in the enjoyment of every conceivable good. While he was acting in this way, and holding this kind of discourse, he was constructing an apartment underground, into which, when it was completed, he withdrew, vanishing suddenly from the eyes of the Thracians, who greatly regretted his loss, and mourned over him as one dead. He meanwhile abode in his secret chamber three full years, after which he came forth from his concealment, and showed himself once more to his countrymen, who were thus brought to believe in the truth of what he had taught them, such is the account of the Greeks.
96. I for my part neither put entire faith in this story of Zalmoxis and his underground chamber, nor do I altogether discredit it: but I believe Zalmoxis to have lived long before the time of Pythagoras. Whether there was ever really a man of the name, or whether Zalmoxis is nothing but a native god of the Getae, I now bid him farewell."(7.1)

Thrace was west of the Black Sea and to the north east of Greece. This cynical story of the Greeks serves to highlight a degree of similarity between the views of Pythagoras and the beliefs, as reported to Herodotus, held in the fifth century BC by the Getae.

A footnote states *"The identity of the Getae with the Goths of later times is more than a plausible conjecture."* However, the Getae may have moved on by the time the Goths reached prominence. It occurred to the translators of Caesar's *Gallic War* that Pythagoras's teaching on the transmigration of souls at death into a new body had its origin in the beliefs of the Druids rather than vica versa.

Translators Footnote to Reference 1.6, Caesar's Gallic War. [McDevitte]
"Because Pythagoras is said by Diogenes Laertius to have visited not only the Greek, but likewise the Barbarian schools in pursuing his study of Sacred Mysteries, it has been thought that he derived his Metempsychosis from the Druids. But, though there is in another writer the additional record that Pythagoras had heard the Druids, the conjecture above stated will not be readily received.
Between the Druidical and the Pythagorean Metempsychosis there was this difference, that the latter maintained the migration of the soul into irrational animals, while the former restricted the dogma to the passage of the soul from man to man."(1.6)

Original thought on the concept of transmigration of souls is also identified with the fifth century BC Sicilian born philosopher Empedocles, who died on Mount Etna after jumping into the crater with the intention of proving his theory. A passing similarity between the death of Empedocles and the romantic death of Pliny the Elder, brought about by the volcanic activity of Vesuvius, was noted by H.T.Riley, see Reference 17.

Elsewhere, Herodotus adopted a minimalist approach to the Celts. The Celts had not poured over the Alpes Maritimes by his lifetime and did not feature in his history.

Herodotus: book 2 chapter 33 [Rawlinson]
"The Celts live beyond the pillars of Hercules, and border on the Cynesians, who dwell at the extreme west of Europe."(7.2)

5   XENOPHON

Xenophon: Hellenica book 7, chapter 1.19 to 1.22 [Dakyns]
369 BC. Second Theban Invasion.
" At the date of the above transactions the Lacedaemonians were cheered by the arrival of a naval reinforcement from Dionysius, consisting of more than twenty warships, which conveyed a body of Celts and Iberians and about fifty cavalry. . . ."
369 or 368 BC.
"After this the Thebans remained only a few more days and then turned back homewards; and the rest likewise to their several homes. Thereupon the troops sent by Dionysius attacked Sicyon. Engaging the Sicyonians in the flat country, they defeated them, killing about seventy men and capturing by assault the fortress of Derae. After these achievements this first reinforcement from Dionysius re-embarked and set sail for Syracuse."(8.1)

The Thebans in this encounter were attacking the city of Corinth. This Dionysius was the elder son of Hermocrates, Tyrant of Syracuse. He also had a son called Dionysius and there was a general of Athens of the same name alive in 387 BC. Syracuse was a Greek settlement in Sicily. Lacedaemonians are known as Spartans, whereas strictly the term Spartan originally applied to the inhabitants of the city of Sparta.

Dionysius *"made a subterraneous cave in a rock, said to be still extant, in the form of a human ear, which measured 80 feet in height and 250 in length. It was called the ear of Dionysius. The sounds of this subterraneous cave were all necessarily directed to one common tympanum, which had a communication with an adjoining room, where Dionysius spent the greatest part of his time to hear whatever was said by those whom his suspicion and cruelty had confined in the apartments above. The artists that had been employed in making this cave were all put to death by order of the tyrant, for fear of their revealing to what purposes a work of such uncommon construction was to be appropriated."(4).* Thus, the pre-radar, aircraft approach warning sonar collection devices set up on the south coast of Britain in the 1930's were pre-dated by twenty four centuries!

It is customary to interpret the second reinforcement from Dionysius to have included Celtic warriors.

Xenophon: Hellenica book 7 chapter 1.27 to 1.32. 368 or 367 BC [Dakyns]
"Whilst these matters were still pending, the second reinforcement from Dionysius arrived. . . . Archidamus, debouching upon a flat space of ground where the roads to Eutresia and Medea converge, drew up his troops and offered battle. . . . Presently, when Archidamus led the advance, a few only of the enemy cared to await them at the spear's point, and were slain; the mass of them fled and fleeing fell. Many were cut down by the cavalry, many by the Celts."(8.2)

The immediate point of embarkation of the Celts and Iberes in the first instance is placed in Sicily or southern Italy. In general, historians are content to assume these Celts were an offshoot of those who remained after that influx into Italy whose warriors had stormed Rome in 390 BC. If not a transcribing error, the arrival of Iberians coupled with a body of Celts leads some authors to look for a home port towards the coast of France or Spain and the area of conflict where Greek influence gave way to Carthaginian. The novelty of receiving pay to fight could have induced the Celts to cross over a sea and take part in a foreign war.

According to the writings of Diogenes Laertius (third century? AD) who was quoting from Demetrius Magnes (i.e. of Magnesia, alive in 55 BC), Xenophon *"He was the author of something like forty books, divided differently by different editors, ..."*

Xenophon was born between 450 BC and 428 BC. His death, it is argued, occurred in 354 BC or soon after. He spent his early years in Athens, during his middle age lived in Sparta and by tradition died at Corinth. In that robust period of Greek history, politics, writing and warfare filled his life.

The quotations are from the translation by H.G.Dakyns published by Macmillan in 1892. In his introduction, H.G.Dakyns informs us that the source manuscripts known to him are as follows. *"The earliest that we possess are not older than the twelfth century (that famous epoch). These are Vaticanus (1335) of uncertain date, and Marcianus (511), 1166 AD. The earliest printed Xenophon is the Latin edition of Filelfo, Mediol: 1467 AD: the first Greek edition, the Hellenica, published by Aldo in 1503, which was followed by the Juntine, 1516 AD."*

In practice an Iberian presence would ostensibly predate the evolution of Greek and Roman civilisations on the southern shores of Europe. Iberians could well have been a widespread physical type that was subsumed into later developing societies whilst they retained their own identity in areas away from the melting pot that was the Mediterranean. The fifth century BC Athenian leader and historian Thucydides identified a people living in Sicily as Iberian. Thucydides died in 391 BC aged 79 or 80 years. His history of the Peloponnesian war comprised 8 books, the last of which has been attributed to his daughter.

The quotations are taken from the translation of Thucydides by Henry Dale published in the 1888 edition of the Bohn's Classical Library series.

Thucydides: The Peloponnesian War book 6.1 to 6.2 [Dale]
"2 Now it was settled originally in the following manner, and these were all the nations that occupied it. The earliest people said to have lived in any part of the country are the Cyclopes and Laestrygones; with regard to whom, I can neither tell their race, nor whence they came into it, nor whither they departed out of it: but let that suffice which has been said by the poets, and which every body in any way knows of them. The Sicanians appear to have been the first who settled in it after them; indeed, as they themselves assert, even before them, as being the aboriginal population; but as the truth is found to be, they were Iberians, and were driven from the river Sicanus, in Iberia, by the Ligurians. And it was from them that the island was at that time called Sicania, having previously been called Trinacria; and still, even to this day, they inhabit Sicily in its western districts. But on the capture of Troy, some of the Trojans, having escaped the Greeks, came in vessels to Sicily, and having settled in the neighbourhood of the Sicanians, they were all together called Elymi and their cities, Eryx and Segesta. . . .

The Sicels, again, went over into Sicily from Italy, ... and being victorious in battle over the Sicanians, they compelled them to remove to the southern and western parts of it, and caused the island to be called Sicily, instead of Sicania, and occupied the best parts of the land; having held them, after they crossed over, nearly three hundred years before any Greeks came into Sicily;"(9.1)

A speech by Alcibiades on events surrounding 415 BC shows his intention to hire Iberian soldiers in Sicily.

Thucydides: The Peloponnesian War book 6.90 [Dale]
"90. . . . . We sailed to Sicily, in the first place, to subdue the Siceliots, if we could; after them, again, the Italiots; and then also to make an attempt on the dominion of the Carthaginians, and on their own city. If either all or most of these schemes proved successful, then we intended to attack the Peloponnese, after bringing here the united force of the Greeks that had joined us in those parts, taking many barbarians into our pay - both Iberians and others of those nations, confessedly the most warlike barbarians at the present day - and building many triremes in addition to what we have, (since Italy contains timber in abundance)."(9.2)

6   POLYBIUS

Polybius, a Greek whose life spanned the years c.206 BC to c.124 BC, was a sometime prisoner of war in Rome, a friend of Scipio and an explorer in his own right.

The quotations are taken from the translation by W.R.Paton in the Loeb Classical Library series published by William Heinemann Ltd. in 1923.

The clash between the Celts and the Roman armies described below occurred about 225 BC in Northern Italy. This clash arose during the lull in active hostilities between the Carthaginians and Romans from the end of the first Punic War in 241 BC to the beginning of the second in 218 BC. This information supplied by Polybius on Celtic dress and behaviour did not come directly from his own observations.

The Histories of Polybius includes a summary of the unexpected inroad by Celts into Northern Italy. The version of such events selected herein is that which flowed from the pen of Livy, see chapter 8 below.

Polybius: History book 2, chapters 28 to 33 [Paton]
"28. The Celts had drawn up facing their rear, from which they expected Aemilius to attack, the Gaesatae from the Alps and behind them the Insubres, and facing in the opposite direction, ready to meet the attack of Gaius' legions, they placed the Taurisci and the Boii from the right bank of the Po. Their wagons and chariots they stationed at the extremity of either wing and collected their booty on one of the neighbouring hills with a protecting force round it. This order of the Celtic forces, facing both ways, not only presented a formidable appearance, but was well adapted to the exigencies of the situation. The Insubres and Boii wore their trousers and light cloaks, but the Gaesatae had discarded these garments owing to their proud confidence in themselves, and stood naked, with nothing but their arms, in front of the whole army, thinking that thus they would be more efficient, as some of the ground was overgrown with brambles which would catch in their clothes and impede the use of their weapons. . . .

45

In this action Gaius the Consul fell in the mellay fighting with desperate courage, and his head was brought to the Celtic kings; . . .

29. . . . . The Romans, however, were on the one hand encouraged by having caught the enemy between their two armies, but on the other they were terrified by the fine order of the Celtic host and the dreadful din, for there were innumerable horn-blowers and trumpeters, and, as the whole army were shouting their war-cries at the same time, there was such a tumult of sound that it seemed that not only the trumpets and the soldiers but all the country round had got a voice and caught up the cry. Very terrifying too were the appearance and the gestures of the naked warriors in front, all in the prime of life, and finely built men, and all in the leading companies richly adorned with gold torques and armlets. . . .

30. But when the javelineers advanced, as is their usage, from the ranks of the Roman legions and began to hurl their javelins in well-aimed volleys, the Celts in the rear ranks indeed were well protected by their trousers and cloaks, but it fell out far otherwise than they had expected with the naked men in front, and they found themselves in a very difficult and helpless predicament. For the Gaulish shield does not cover the whole body; . . . The Roman shields, it should be added, were far more serviceable for defence and their swords for attack, the Gaulish sword being only good for a cut and not for a thrust. . . .

31. About forty thousand Celts were slain and at least ten thousand taken prisoners, among them the king Cincolitanus. The other king, Aneroestes, escaped with a few followers to a certain place where he put an end to his life and to those of his friends. The Roman Consul collected the spoils and sent them to Rome, returning the booty of the Gauls to the owners. With his legion he traversed Liguria and invaded the territory of the Boii, from whence, after letting his legions pillage to their heart's content, he returned at their head in a few days to Rome. He sent to ornament the Capitol the standards and necklaces (the gold necklets worn by the Gauls), but the rest of the spoil and the prisoners he used for his entry into Rome and the adornment of his triumph."

Polybius went on to state the edge of the Gauls' swords were easily bent and blunted. He gave this as a not wholly convincing argument as to why, as a change of tactic when fighting Gauls, the front rank of a Roman legion was equipped with spears. Could it be they urgently needed to find a counter to the opening charge of the Celtic infantry? At a later date when describing an earlier event, Plutarch, in his life of Camillus, commented upon the way the Gaulish swords were blunted with use when the Gauls were beaten by the forces under Camillus in about 377 BC.

"Thus were destroyed these Celts during whose invasion, the most serious that had ever occurred, all the Italians and especially the Romans had been exposed to great and terrible peril. This success encouraged the Romans to hope that they would be able entirely to expel the Celts from the plain of the Po and both the Consuls of the next year, Quintus Fulvius and Titus Manlius, were sent against them with a formidable expeditionary force. They surprised and terrified the Boii, compelling them to submit to Rome, but the rest of the campaign had no practical results whatever, owing to the very heavy rains, and an epidemic which broke out among them.

32. Next year's consuls, however, Publius Furius and Gaius Flaminius, again invaded the Celtic territory, through the country of the Anares who dwelt not far from Marseilles. Having admitted this tribe to their friendship, they crossed into the territory of the Insubres, near the junction of the Po and the Adda. Both in crossing and in encamping on the other side, they suffered some loss, and at first remained on the spot, but later made a truce and evacuated the territory under its terms. After a circuitous march of some days, they crossed the river Clusius and reached the country of the Cenomani, who were their allies, and accompanied by them, again invaded from the district at the foot of the Alps the plains of the Insubres and began to lay the country waste and pillage their dwellings.

The chieftains of the Insubres, seeing that the Romans adhered to their purpose of attacking them, decided to try their luck in a decisive battle. Collecting all their forces in one place, they took down the golden standards called "immovable" from the temple of Minerva, and having made all other necessary preparations, boldly took up a menacing position opposite the enemy. They were about fifty thousand strong. The Romans, on the one hand, as they saw the enemy were much more numerous than themselves, were desirous of employing also the forces of their Celtic allies, but on the other hand, taking into consideration Gaulish fickleness and the fact that they were going to fight against those of the same nation as these allies, they were wary of asking such men to participate in an action of such vital importance. Finally, remaining themselves on their side of the river, they sent the Celts who were with them across it, and demolished the bridges across the stream, firstly as a precaution against their allies, and secondly to leave themselves no hope of safety except in victory, the river, which was impassable, lying in their rear. After taking these measures they prepared for battle.

33. The Romans are thought to have managed matters very skilfully in this battle, their tribunes having instructed them how they should fight, both as individuals and collectively. For they had observed from former battles that Gauls in general are most formidable and spirited in their first onslaught, while still fresh, and that, from the way their swords are made, as has been already explained, only the first cut takes effect; after this they at once assume the shape of a strigal, being so much bent both length-wise and side-wise that unless the men are given leisure to rest them on the ground and set them straight with the foot, the second blow is quite ineffectual. The tribunes therefore distributed among the front lines the spears of the triarii who were stationed behind them, ordering them to use their swords instead only after the spears were done with.

They then drew up opposite the Celts in order of battle and engaged. Upon the Gauls slashing first at the spears and making their swords unserviceable the Romans came to close quarters, having rendered the enemy helpless by depriving them of the power of raising their hands and cutting, which is the peculiar and only stroke of the Gauls, as their swords have no points. . . . (10.1)

The structure of the Roman army was recorded by Polybius in book 6 of *The Histories*. This account by Polybius is given in chapter 16 together with the report contained in *The Wars of the Jews* by Josephus that includes a description of the order of the Roman army when on the march.

7   DIODORUS

The quotations are taken from the translation of the Greek by G.Booth published in 1814 and printed by W.McDowall of Pemberton Row, Gough Square, Fleet Street, for J.Davis, Military Chronicle Office, Essex Street, Strand in London (11).

Diodorus Siculus was so called because he was born at Argyra in Sicily. He was born in the first century BC. Diodorus was an historian who spent thirty years producing forty volumes of which fifteen are extant. His text implies that he travelled widely in Asia and Europe and that he spent time in Rome. Diodorus is not held in much esteem by some people for his own work, whereas, the compilations of other authors to be found in his works are considered to be of value (4).

Diodorus tells us the historian Timaeus was of the opinion that the argonauts, having taken the golden fleece and believing that Pontus was blockaded against them, made their escape from the Black Sea up the River Don, carried their boat across land to another river which flowed into the ocean and found their way back to Greece through the straits of Gibraltar. The twins Castor and Pollox, also known as the Dioscori, were on board the Argosy with Jason. The thirty day pack-horse route for Cornish tin across France to the mouth of the Rhone may be ancient.

Diodorus: Histories book 4, chapter 3 [Booth]
" . . . Many, both of the antient [sic] and modern writers, (amongst whom is Timaeus), report that the Argonauts (after the carrying away of the golden fleece) coming to understand that Aeetes had blocked up the mouth of Pontus with his fleet, to prevent their return, performed that which was wonderfully remarkable: for it is said, they sailed up to the head of the river Tanais, and there drew the ship a considerable way over, and into another river that ran into the ocean, and so fell down that way into the sea; and then bending their course from the north to the west, leaving the continent on their left hand side, they at length entered our sea near Gades: and to confirm this, they use these arguments –

First, that the Celts, the inhabitants near the ocean, do adore Castor and Pollox above all the rest of the gods; for among these Celts there is an ancient tradition, that these gods appeared, and came to them out of the ocean: and they affirm, that there are several places near the sea, that had their names from the Argonauts and the Dioscuri, which remain still to this day; and that within the continent beyond Gades, there are apparent marks and signs of the return of the Argonauts: for sailing by Tyrrhenia, and arriving at a certain island called Aethalia, there is a spacious haven, called by them Argo, from the name of their ship, which name the port retains to this day: and that there is another harbour in Etruria, eight hundred furlongs from Rome, which they named Telamon, and that the port at that city Formiae into Italy they called Aetes, which is now named Caieta.
They further say . . . "(11.1)

Diodorus: Histories book 5, chapter 2 (Britain) [Booth]
"CHAP.II.   Of Madeira, Britain, Gallia, Celtiberia, Iberia, Tyrrhenia, and of the inhabitants, and their laws and customs.

Since we have gone through the islands lying eastwards, on this side within the pillars of Hercules, we shall now launch into the main ocean to those that lie beyond them; for over against Africa, lies a very great island in the vast ocean, of many days sail from Libya, westwards. The soil here is very fruitful, a great part whereof is mountainous, . . .

. . . For over against the French shore, opposite to the Hercynian mountains (which are the greatest of any in Europe) there lie in the ocean many islands, the greatest of which is that which they call Britain, which antiently [sic] remained untouched, free from all foreign force; for it was never known that either Bacchus, Hercules, or any of the antient [sic] heroes or princes, ever made any attempt upon it by force of arms: but Julius Caesar in our time (who by his great achievements gained the title of Divine) was the first (that any author makes mention of) that conquered that island, and compelled the Britons to pay tribute. But these things shall be more particularly treated of in their proper time; we shall now only say something concerning the island, and the tin that is found there.

In form it is triangular, like Sicily, but the sides are unequal. It lies in an oblique line, over against the continent of Europe; so that the promontory called Cantium, next to the continent (they say) is about a hundred furlongs from the land: here the sea ebbs and flows: but the other point, called Belerium, is four days sail from the continent.”

The English Channel is *à peu près* 22 miles wide i.e. about 176 furlongs. This is a greater distance than 100 stades. It is a surprise that Diodorus did not have a better estimate of the distance at his disposal. A misread 200 stades in the document chain suggests itself.

“The last, called Horcas, or Orcades, runs out far into the sea. The least of the sides facing the whole continent is seven thousand and five hundred furlongs in length; the second, stretching out itself all along from the sea to the highest point, is fifteen thousand furlongs; and the last is twenty thousand: so that the whole compass of the island is forty-two thousand five hundred furlongs. The inhabitants are the original people thereof, and live to this time after their own antient manner and custom; for in fights they use chariots, as it is said the old Greek heroes did in the Trojan war. They dwell in mean cottages, covered for the most part with reads or sticks. In reaping of their corn, they cut off the ears from the stalk, and so house them up in repositories under ground; thence they take and pluck out the grains of as many of the oldest of them as may serve them for the day, and, after they have bruised the corn, make it into bread. They are of much sincerity and integrity, far from the craft and knavery of men among us; contented with plain and homely fare, strangers to the excess and luxury of rich men. The island is very populous, but of a cold climate, subject to frosts, being under the Arctic pole. They are governed by several kings and princes, who, for the most part, are at peace and amity one with another. But of their laws, and other things peculiar to this island, we shall treat more particularly when we come to Caesar's expedition into Britain.

Now we shall speak something of the tin that is dug and gotten there. They that inhabit the British promontory of Belerium, by reason of their converse with merchants, are more civilized and courteous to strangers than the rest are. These are the people that make the tin, which with a great deal of care and labour they dig out of the ground; and that being rocky, the metal is mixed with some veins of earth, out of which they melt the metal, and then refine it; then they heat it into four-square pieces like to a dye, and carry it to a British isle near at hand, called Ictis. For at low tide, all being dry between them and the island, they convey over in carts abundance of tin in the meantime. But there is one thing peculiar to these islands which lie between Britain and Europe: for at full sea they appear to be islands, but at low water for a long way, they look like so many peninsulas. Hence the merchants transport the tin they buy of the inhabitants to France; and for thirty days journey, they carry it in packs upon horses backs through France, to the mouth of the River Rhone.

But thus much concerning tin. Now something remains to be said of amber.

Over against Scythia above Gaul, in the ocean, lies an island called Basilea, upon which there is cast, by the working of the sea, abundance of amber, not to be found in any other part of the world.

. . . For amber is gathered in this island before mentioned, and transported by the inhabitants into the opposite continent, from whence it is brought over to us in these parts as is before declared.

After this account given of the western islands, we conceive it is not impertinent, if we briefly relate some things which were omitted in the former books concerning the neighbouring nations in Europe.

In Celtica (they say) once ruled a famous man, who had a daughter of a more tall and majestic stature than ordinary, . . . It happened that Hercules at the time he was engaged in the war against Gallia, marched into Celtica, . . . Of this lady he begat Galatae, . . . he called his country subjects after his own name, Galatians, and the country Galatia, Gaul.

Having shewn [sic] the original of the name, something is to be said of the country itself. Gaul is inhabited by several nations, but not all alike populous: the greatest of them have in them two hundred thousand men, the least but fifty thousand. Of these there is one that has been an antient [sic] ally of the Romans, and continues so to this day.

In regard it lies for the greatest part under the Arctic pole, it is very . . ."(11.2)

Diodorus: Histories book 5, chapter 2 (Gauls, Celts) [Booth]
" . . . This excessive cold and immoderate temper of the air, is the cause why the earth in these parts produces neither wine nor oil; and therefore the Gauls, to supply their want of these fruits, make a drink of barley, which they call Xythus: they mix likewise their honeycombs with water, and make use of that for the same purpose. They are so exceedingly given to wine, that they guzzle it down as soon as it is imported by the merchant, and are so eager and inordinate, that making themselves drunk, they either fall dead asleep, or become stark mad. So that many Italian merchants (to gratify their own covetousness) make use of the drunkenness of the Gauls to advance their own profit and gain. For they convey the wine to them both by navigable rivers, and by land in carts, and bring back an incredible price: for in lieu of a hogshead of wine, they receive a boy, giving drink in truck for a servant.

In Gaul there are no silver mines, but much gold, with which the nature of the place supplies the inhabitants, without the labour or toil of digging in the mines. For the winding course of the river washing with its streams the feet of the mountains, carries away great pieces of golden ore, which those employed in this business gather, and then grind and bruise these clods of golden earth: and when they have so done, cleanse them from the gross earthly part, by washing them in water, and then melt them in a furnace; and thus get together a vast heap of gold, with which not only the woman, but the men deck and adorn themselves. For they wear bracelets of this metal about their wrists and arms, and massy chains of pure and beaten gold about their necks, and weighty rings upon their fingers, and crosslets of gold upon their breasts.

The custom observed by the higher Gauls in the temples of their gods, is admirably remarkable; for in the oratories and sacred temples of this country, in honour of their gods they scatter pieces of gold up and down, which none of the inhabitants (their superstitious devotion is such) will in the least touch or meddle with, though the Gauls are of themselves most exceeding covetous.

For stature they are tall, but of a sweaty and pale complexion, red-haired, not only naturally, but they endeavour all they can to make it redder by art. They often wash their hair in a water boiled with lime, and turn it backward from the forehead to the crown of the head, and thence to their very necks, that their faces may be more fully seen, so that they look like satyrs and hobgoblins. By this sort of management of themselves, their hair is as hard as a horse's mane. Some of them shave their beards; others let them grow a little. The persons of quality shave their chins close, but their mustachios they let fall so low, that they even cover their mouths; so that when they eat, their meat hangs dangling by their hair; and when they drink, the liquor runs through their mustachios as through a sieve. At meal-time they all sit, not upon seats, but upon the ground, and instead of carpets, spread wolves or dogs skins under them. Young boys and girls attend them, such as are yet but mere children. Near at hand they have their chimnies [sic], with their fires well furnished with pots and spits full of whole joints of flesh meat; and the best of the fairest joints (in a way of due honour and regard) they set before the persons of best quality: as Homer introduces the Grecian captains entertaining of Ajax, when he returned victor from his single combat with Hector, in this verse –

> *But Agamemnon as a favouring sign,*
> *Before great Ajax set the lusty chine.*

They invite likewise strangers to their feasts, and after all is over, they ask who they are, and what is their business. In the very midst of feasting, upon any small occasion, it is ordinary for them in a heat to rise, and without any regard of their lives, to fall to it with their swords. For the opinion of Pythagoras prevails much amongst them, that men's souls are immortal, and that there is a transmigration of them into other bodies, and after a certain time they live again; and therefore in their funerals, they write letters to their friends, and throw them into the funeral pile, as if they were to be read by the deceased."

Thus, the Gauls used the medium of writing! Blond haired is preferred to red haired in other translations of book 5.2 above. The word *truck* takes the meaning of to exchange, to barter, to pay in goods, to traffic. The word *battalia* in the quotation below takes the meaning of order of battle, the main body of an army in array. (*Chambers Dictionary*).

The selection of a champion's portion of meat would easily slip into the folk tales from the period of Irish heroes, as would the hospitality shown to strangers and combat among warriors for no good reason without any regard for their own lives.

Chariot warfare was the subject of particular comment when encountered by Caesar in Britain. Diodorus in book 5.2 observed the British use of chariots preserved a more ancient manner of life (11.2). An explanation for the two differing pieces of information is that Diodorus, when describing Gauls in 5.2 below, was copying from a different author from a separate age to his source for 5.2 above describing Britain.

" In their journeys and fights they use chariots drawn with two horses, which carry a charioteer and a soldier, and when they meet horsemen in the battle, they fall upon their enemies with their saunians [Footnote – a kind of dart.]; then quitting their chariots, they do it with their swords. There are some of them that so despise death, that they will fight naked, with something only about their loins. They carry along with them to the wars for their servants, libertines, chosen out of the poorer sort of people, whom they make use of for waggoners, and pedees.

When the army is drawn up in battalia, it is usual for some of them to step out before the army, and to challenge the stoutest of their enemy to a single combat, brandishing their arms to terrify their adversary. If any comes forth to fight with them, then they sing some song in commendation of the valiant acts of their ancestors, and blazon out their own praises: on the contrary they vilify their adversary, and give forth slighting and contemptuous words, as if he had not the least courage. When at any time they cut off their enemies heads, they hang them about their horses' necks.

They deliver their spoils to their servants, all besmeared with blood, to be carried before them in triumph, they themselves in the meantime singing the triumphant paean. And as the chief of their spoils, they fasten those they have killed, over the doors of their houses, as if they were so many wild beasts taken in hunting. The heads of their enemies that were the chiefest [sic] persons of quality, they carefully deposit in chests, embalming them with the oil of cedars, and shewing them to strangers, glory and boast how that some of their ancestors, their fathers, or themselves, (though great sums of money have been offered for them), yet have refused to accept them.

Some glory so much on this account, that they refuse to take for one of these heads its weight in gold; in this manner exposing their barbarous magnanimity. For it is brave and generous indeed not to sell the ensigns of true valour; but to fight with the dead bodies of those that were men like ourselves, resembles the cruelty of wild beasts."

This description of nailing up heads has a parallel in Strabo 4.4.4 (15.6) *"Posidonius says he witnessed this in many different places"*. Posidonius is a candidate for being the common source of the data.

It is possible that techniques for making articles and shoes from birch bark were practiced in Northern Europe, for example in Poland, up until the twentieth century.

" Their garments are very strange; for they wear party coloured coats, interwoven here and there with divers sorts of flowers; and hose which they call Bracae. They make likewise their cassocks of basket-work joined together with laces on the inside, and chequered with many pieces of work like flowers; those they wear in winter are thicker, those in summer more slender.

Their defensive arms are a shield, proportionable to the height of a man, garnished with their own ensigns. Some carry the shapes of beasts in brass, artificially wrought, as well for defence as ornament. Upon their heads they wear helmets of brass, with large pieces of work raised upon them for ostentation sake, to be admired by the beholders; for they have either horns of the same metal joined to them, or the shapes of birds and beasts carved upon them. They have trumpets after the barbarian manner, which in sounding make a horrid noise, to strike a terror fit and proper for the occasion. Some of them wear iron breast-plates, and hooked [sic-front to back?]; but others, content with what arms nature affords them, fight naked. For swords, they use a long and broad weapon called Spatha, which they hang across their right thigh by iron or brazen chains. Some gird themselves over their coats with belts gilt with gold or silver. For darts they cast those they call Lances, whose iron shafts are a cubit or more in length, and almost two hands in breadth.

For their swords are as big as the saunians of other people, but the points of their saunians are larger than those of their swords; some of them are strait [sic], others bowed and bending backwards, so that they not only cut, but break the flesh; and when the dart is drawn out, it tears and rents the wound most miserably.

These people are of a most terrible aspect, and have a most dreadful and loud voice. In their converse they are sparing of their words, and speak many things darkly and figuratively. They are high and hyperbolical in trumpeting out their own praises, but speak slightly and contemptibly of others. They are apt to menace others, self opiniated [sic], grievously provoking, of sharp wits, and apt to learn.

Among them they have poets that sing melodious songs, whom they call bards, who to their musical instruments like unto harps, chant forth the praises of some, and the dispraises of others.

There are likewise among them philosophers and divines [sic], whom they call Saronidae [Footnote. Druids; for Saronidae, or Saronids, are of the same signification with Druids, the one of an oak, the other of an hollow oak.], are held in great veneration and esteem. Prophets likewise they have, whom they highly honour, who foretell future events by viewing the entrails of the sacrifices, and to these soothsayers all the people generally are very observant.

When they are to consult on some great and weighty matter; they observe a most strange and incredible custom; for they sacrifice a man, striking him with a sword near the diaphragm, cross over his breast, who being thus slain, and falling down, they judge of the event from the manner of his fall, the convulsion of his members, and the flux of blood; and this has gained among them (by long and ancient usage) a firm credit and belief.

It is not lawful to offer any sacrifice without a philosopher; for they hold that by these, as men acquainted with the nature of the deity, and familiar in their converse with the gods, they ought to present their thank-offerings, and by these ambassadors to desire such things as are good for them. These Druids and Bards are observed and obeyed, not only in times of peace, but war also, both by friends and enemies.

Many times these philosophers and poets, stepping in between two armies near at hand, when they are just ready to engage, with their swords drawn, and spears presented one against another, have pacified them, as if some wild beasts had been tamed by enchantments. Thus rage is mastered by wisdom, even amongst the most savage barbarians, and Mars himself reverences the Muses.

And now it will be worth while to declare that which multitudes are all together ignorant of. Those who inhabit the inland parts beyond Massilia [Footnote. Marseilles.], and about the Alps, and on this side the Pyrenean mountains, are called Celts; but those that inhabit below this part called Celtica, southwards to the ocean and the mountain Hyreinus, and all as far as Scythia, are called Gauls. But the Romans call all these people generally by one and the same name, Gauls.

The women here are both as tall and as courageous as the men. The children, for the most part, from their very birth are grey-headed; but when they grow up to men's estate, their hair changes in colour like to their parents. Those towards the north, and bordering upon Scythia, are so exceeding fierce and cruel, that (as report goes) they eat men, like the Britains that inhabit Iris [Footnote. Some part of Britain, then so called. Steph.]"

Chapter 5.2 confirms the indications elsewhere in his work that Diodorus did not differentiate between German and Celt; he referred to them all as Gauls. The clothing, as described, induces a picture in the mind's eye of having been made from a tartan fabric; though was the basket-work cassock of birch bark? Under the Bear meant under that star constellation and hence well to the north. Iris was the island of Ireland.

" They are so noted for a fierce and warlike people, that some have thought them to be those that antiently overran all Asia, and were then called Cimerians, and who are now (through length of time) with a little alteration, called Cimbrians.

Antiently they gave themselves to rapine and spoil, wasting and destroying other countries, and slighted and despised all other people. These are they that took Rome, and robbed the temple at Delphos. These brought a great part of Europe and Asia under tribute, and possessed themselves of some of the countries of those they subdued. Because of their mixture with the Grecians, they were at last called Gallo-Grecians. They often routed and destroyed many great armies of the Romans."

The Cimbrians, a Germanic confederation, caused havoc in Italy around 100 BC. These may well have been one and the same peoples as those who had entered Greece as marauders in the seventh century BC.

" According to their natural cruelty, they are as impious in the worship of their gods; for malefactors, after that they have been kept close prisoners five years together, they impale upon stakes, in honour to the gods, and then, with many other victims, upon a vast pile of wood, they offer them up as a burnt sacrifice to their deities. In like manner they use their captives also, as sacrifices to the gods. Some of them cut the throats, burn, or otherwise destroy both men and beasts that they have taken in time of war: though they have very beautiful women among them, yet they little value their private society, but are transported with raging lust to the filthy act of sodomy; and lying upon the ground on beast's skins spread under them, they tumble together, with their catamites lying on both sides of them: and that which is the most abominable is, that without any sense of shame, or regard to their reputation, they will readily prostitute their bodies to others upon every occasion. And they are so far from looking upon it to be any fault, that they judge it a mean and dishonourable thing for any thus caressed to refuse the favour offered them."

Peoples who had overcome the might of Greece and Rome were painted in a bad light by Diodorus of Sicily.

A footnote from the translation of the Greek by C.H.Oldfather published in the Loeb Classical Library says that the Greek word translated as catamite may mean, 'with concubines of both sexes'; but Athenaeus (13.603 A) states that the Celts were accustomed to sleep with two boys.

"Having spoken of the Celts, we shall now give an account of their neighbours the Celtiberians. The two nations of Celts and Iberians, heretofore breaking forth into a war about the boundaries of their countries, at length agreed to inhabit together promiscuously, and so marrying one with another, their issue and posterity (they say) afterwards were called Celtiberians. Two potent nations being thus united, and possessed likewise of a rich and fertile country, these Celtiberians became very famous and renowned; so that the Romans had much ado to subdue them after long and tedious wars with them. These Celtiberians bring into the field not only stout and valiant horsemen, but brave foot, both for strength and hardiness able to undergo all manner of labour and toil. They wear black rough cassocks made of wool, like to goat's hair. Some of them are armed with the Gaulish light shields, others with bucklers as big as shields, and wear greaves about their legs made of rough hair, and brazen helmets upon their heads, adorned with red plumes.

They carry two-edged swords exactly tempered with steel, and have daggers beside, of a span long, which they make use of in close fights. They make weapons and darts in an admirable manner; for they bury plates of iron so long under the ground, till the rust hath consumed the weaker part, and so the rest becomes more strong and firm. Of this they make their swords and other warlike weapons; and with these arms, thus tempered, they so cut through every thing in their way, that neither shield, helmet, nor bone can withstand them. And because they are furnished with two swords, the horse, when they have routed the enemy, alight and join with the foot, and fight to admiration [sic].

There is another strange and wonderful custom they have amongst them; for, though they are very nice and curious in their diet, yet they have a very sordid and filthy practice, to wash their whole bodies over with urine, and rub their very teeth with it, which is counted a certain means of health to their bodies. As to their manners, they are very cruel towards their enemies and other malefactors, but very courteous and civil to strangers; for to all such, from what place soever they come, they readily and freely entertain them, and strive who shall perform the greatest office of kindness and respect. Those who are attended upon by strangers they commend and esteem them as friends of the gods. They live upon all sorts of flesh in great plenty, and their drink is made of honey, their country abounding therewith: but they buy wine also of the merchants that traffic thither.

Of those that border upon them, the most civilized nations are the Vaccaei [Footnote. People of the higher province of Spain.], who every year divide the lands among them, and then till and plough it, and after the harvest, distribute the fruits, allotting to every one their share; and therefore it is death to steal, or underhandedly to convey away any thing from the husbandman. Those they call Lusitanians [Footnote. Portuguese.] are the most valiant of all the Cimbri [Iberians in Oldfather's trans.-compiler]. These, in times of war, carry little targets made of bowel strings, so strong and firm, as completely to guard and defend their bodies. In fights they manage these, so nimbly whirling them about here and there, that with a great deal of art they avoid and repel every dart that is cast at them.

They use hooked saunians made all of iron, and wear swords and helmets like to those of the Celtiberians. They throw their darts at a great distance, and yet are sure to hit their mark, and wound deeply: being of active and nimble bodies, they can easily fly from, or pursue their enemy, as there is occasion: but when they are under hardships, they cannot endure near so much as the Celtiberians. In time of peace, they have a kind of a light and airy way of dancing, which requires great agility and nimbleness of the legs and thighs. In time of war they march observing time and measure; and sing the paeans when they are just ready to charge the enemy."(11.3)

The habit of allocating land annually was also taken note of as prevalent among the Germans in Caesar's *Gallic War*, 6.2.2.

A large number of Celts invaded Greece in 279 BC (2nd year of the 125th Olympiad) and were repulsed and returned to Asia according to Pausanias (book 10.23.14) writing in the second century AD. During this episode Brennus, the leader of the Celts, entered a Greek temple at the shrine at Delphi.

Diodorus: Histories book 22 [Booth]

" . . . *Brennus, king of the Gauls, made an inroad into Macedonia with a hundred and forty thousand targeteers, and ten thousand horse, and a great multitude of other foreign rabble, and many merchants, together with two thousand carts and carriages. He made great havock [sic] and slaughter, with a design to ruin them utterly. At last he broke into Greece, and fully purposed to rifle the temple at Delphos. By frequent engagements Brennus lost myriads of his men, and he himself received three desperate wounds. Being near his end, he called his army together, and made a speech to the Gauls, and advised them to kill both him and the rest of the wounded men, to burn their carriages, and return home with all speed, and make Cichorius their king. Brennus at length, after he had drunk freely of wine, ran himself through the body. Cichorius, so soon as he had buried Brennus, knocked all the wounded men on the head, those at least that were likely to be starved with hunger or perished by the cold, to the number of twenty thousand; and then returned with the remainder the same way they came. But the Grecians, who lay in ambush in the strait [sic] and narrow passages, cut off all their rear, and took most of their baggage. Marching forward to Thermopylae, they there left behind them twenty thousand more for want of food. At length, as they were passing through the country of the Dardanians, they all perished; and not one man returned to his own country."(11.4)*

The report that, to a man, the army once led by Brennus all perished is taken with a pinch of salt.

The Ludovic Dindorf / Charles Muller edition of Diodorus published in Paris in 1855 adds a further fragment. Reliqueae Libri XXII, 6 – 9 page 438 contains a Latin translation of the Greek fragment identified by the reference Esc.Vatican. p.46, 47.

Diodorus: Histories book 22 [Dindorf, Muller]

"*(4) (Junge cum [Paragraph character] 1.) Brennus, Gallorum rex, templum ingressus nullum vidit aureum argenteumive donarium, s[?]ed lapidaeas tantum igneasque statuas deprehendens, Graeci[?] irrisit, quod deos, quos humana specle praeditos existinarent[?], ligneos atque lapideos statuissent.*

[Rough translation. Brennus, king of the Gauls, entering the temple, saw no gold and silver in the temple treasure chamber [donarium], but he perceived only stone and wooden statues. He derided [scoffed at] them [the Greeks] that they supposed the gods were endowed with human form, in statues of wood and stone.]"(12.1)

In truth, was it Brennus or Diodorus himself who chided the Greeks for representing the gods in their own likeness?

The religion of the Celts is here shown as not including the images of its deities. Other sources supply evidence that such images had a role to play. For example the images equated with Mercury by Caesar [*Gallic War* 6.17 (1.6)] and the wooden figurines and occasional sculptures in stone coming to light during archaeological excavation. The enigma that was the priesthood of the Druids, thought by Caesar to have had their centre in Britain, is the third strand. To accommodate these diverse dimensions there is scope to envisage more than one denomination in the religion of the various peoples collectively known as the Celts, whether identified by tribe or within the hierarchical structure of Celtic society.

On occasion the Celtic attack on Delphi is referred to as being contained within *the Hymn of Delos*, but the lines are of little help in describing the actions of the Celts. Callimachus was the librarian at Alexandria between 260 BC and 240 BC. A poet, he was said by Strabo (book 17.3) to be a member of the house of Cyrene, the Battiadae, named after its founder Battus and hence he was called Battiades by Ovid (Ib.53). He may have had a nephew with the same name of whom Lucan was aware. The translation and information is taken from the book written by the Reverend J. Banks, the headmaster of Ludlow school, published in 1876 (13). Delos was a Greek island of the Cyclades.

Callimachus: The Hymn of Delos, about 161 - 175.
"At some future time, too, at last shall come to us a common struggle, whensoever, having raised up the barbarian sword and Celtic warfare against the Greeks, the giants of-a-later-brood shall rush-on from the farthest West, like unto snows, or equal in number to the stars, when they pasture thickest in the air."
[Footnote. "The allusion here is to the struggle against an immense host of Celts, who had invaded Macedon and Thrace, and the north of Greece, when Ptolemy Ceraunus, brother and rival of Philadelphus, was slain by the invaders. A second invasion penetrated as far as Delphi, BC 279, attracted by the fame of the treasures, when the god vindicated his sanctuary, as he did when it was attacked by the Persians. Brennus and his Gauls were routed with great loss. Cf Just xxiv.6; Pausin. X.xxiii.; "](13.1)

8   LIVY
Titus Livius was born at Padua, lived most of his working life at Naples and Rome and spent time at the court of Augustus. He died in 17 AD aged about 67. Livy wrote a *History of Rome* from its foundation up to the time of the death of Drusus in Germany. The work comprised 140 books of which 35 survive. Some sections of his work are assessed as having drawn directly upon Polybius (4).

The translation is that of D. Spillan in the Bohn's Library series.

Whilst allowing for errors and mis-information in the detail available to Livy, this statement establishes that the widespread movement of Celts into Cisalpine Gaul occurred in the years immediately preceding 390 BC. A coincident expansion northwards, where discerned in the archaeological record, invites a tentative placement in the same decade.

Livy: History of Rome book 5 chapters 34 to 39 [Spillan]
AUR 364.
34. Concerning the passage of the Gauls into Italy we have heard as follows. In the reign of Tarquinius Priscus at Rome, the supreme government of the Celts, who compose a third part of Gaul, was in the hands of the Biturigians: they gave a king to the Celtic nation. This was Ambigatus, one very much distinguished by his merit, and both his great prosperity in his own concerns and in those of the public: for under his administration Gaul was so fruitful and so well peopled, that so very great a population appeared scarcely capable of being restrained by any government.

He being now advanced in years, and anxious to relieve his kingdom of so oppressive a crowd, declares his intention to send his sister's sons, Bellovesus and Sigovesus, two enterprising youths, into whatever settlements the gods should grant them by augury: that they should take out with them as great a number of men as they pleased, so that no nation might be able to obstruct them in their progress. Then to Sigovesus the Hercynian forest was assigned by the oracle: to Bellovesus the gods marked out a much more cheering route into Italy. He carried out with him from the Biturigians, the Arvenians, the Senonians, the Aeduans, the Ambarrians, the Carnutians, and the Aulercians, all that was superfluous in their population. Having set out with an immense force of horse and foot, he arrived in the country of the Tricastinians. Next the Alps were opposed [to their progress], and I am not surprised that they should seem impassable, as they had never been climbed over through any path as yet, as far at least as tradition can extend, unless we are disposed to believe the stories regarding Hercules. When the height of the mountains kept the Gauls there penned up as it were, and they were looking around [to discover] by what path they might pass into another world between the summits, which joined the sky, a religious scruple detained them, it having been announced to them that strangers in search of land were attacked by the nation of the Salyans. These were the Massilians, who had come by sea from Phocaea. The Gauls considering this an omen of their own fortune, assisted them in fortifying the ground which they had taken possession of on their first landing, covered with spacious woods. They themselves crossed the Alps through the Taurinian and pathless forests; and having defeated the Etrurians not far from the Ticinus, on hearing that the land in which they had posted themselves was called Insubria, the same name as the Insubres, a canton of the Aedui: embracing the omen of the place, they built a city there, and called it Mediolanum.

35. Some time after another body, consisting of Cenomanians, having followed the tracks of the former under the conduct of Elitovius, crossed the Alps through the same forest, with the aid of Bellovesus, and settled themselves where the cities of Brixia and Verona now stand (the Libuans then possessed these places). After these came the Salluvians, who fix themselves near the ancient canton of the Ligurians called Laevi, inhabiting the banks of the Ticinus. Next the Boians and Lingonians, having made their way over through the Penine pass, all the tract between the Po and the Alps being occupied, crossed the Po on rafts, and drove out of the country not only the Etrurians, but the Umbrians also: they confined themselves however within the Apennines. Then the Senonians, the latest of these emigrants, took possession of the track [extending] from the Utens to the Aesis. I find that it was this nation that came to Clusium, and thence to Rome; whether alone, or aided by all the nations of the Cisalpine Gauls, is not duly ascertained. . .

37. . . Already all places in front and on each side were crowded with the enemy, and this nation, which has a natural turn for causeless confusion, by their harsh music and discordant clamours, filled all places with a horrible din."

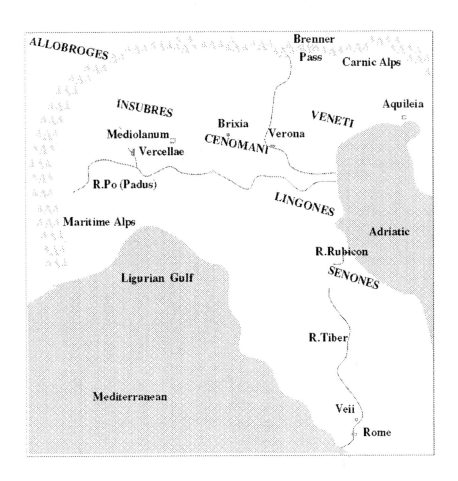

ITALY: 390 BC CELTIC ADVANCE

"AUR 365

38. . . . For Brennus, the chieftain of the Gauls . . .

39. The miraculous attainment of so sudden a victory held even the Gauls in a state of stupefaction. And at first they stood motionless with panic, as if not knowing what had happened; then they apprehended a stratagem; at length they began to collect the spoils of the slain, and to pile up the arms in heaps, as is their custom. Then, at length, when no appearance of any thing hostile was any where observed, having proceeded on their journey, they reach the city of Rome not long before sun-set:" (14.1)

The capture of Rome by Gauls lead by Brennus, the ransoming of the Capitol and subsequent welshing on the deal for payment by the Romans, were recorded by Livy in the best light he could put on an event that he found unpalatable. Although writing in the age of Augustus and Tiberius, it is probable that Livy relied on a text written closer to the events of 390 BC. The tale of the geese raising the alarm when the Capitol was under attack comes from this engagement.

Livy: History of Rome book 5, chapters 47, 48, 49 [Spillan]
"47. Whilst these things were going on at Veii, in the meanwhile the citadel and Capitol of Rome were in great danger. For the Gauls either having perceived the track of a human foot where the messenger from Veii had passed, or having of themselves remarked the easy ascent by the rock at the temple of Carmentis, on a moonlight night, after they had at first sent forward an unarmed person, to make trial of the way, delivering their arms, whenever any difficulty occurred, alternately supported and supporting each other, and drawing each other up, according as the ground required, they reached the summit in such silence, that they not only escaped the notice of the sentinels, but of the dogs also, an animal extremely wakeful with respect to noises at night. The notice of the geese they did not escape, which, as being sacred to Juno, were spared though they were in greatest scarcity of food. Which circumstance was the cause of their preservation. . . .
48. . . . at length not only food but hope also failing, and their arms weighing down their debilitated bodies, whilst the guards were being relieved, insisted that there should be either a surrender, or that they should be bought off, on whatever terms were possible, the Gauls intimating in rather plain terms, that they could be induced for no very great compensation to relinquish the siege. Then the senate was held and instructions were given to the military tribunes to capitulate. Upon this the matter was settled between Quintus Sulpicius, a military tribune, and Brennus, the chieftain of the Gauls, and one thousand pounds' weight of gold was agreed on as the ransom of a people, who were soon after to be the rulers of the world. To a transaction very humiliating in itself, insult was added. False weights were brought by the Gauls, and on the tribune objecting, his sword was thrown in in addition to the weight by the insolent Gaul, and an expression was heard intolerable to the Romans, 'Woe to the vanquished!'
49. But both gods and men interfered to prevent the Romans from living on the condition of being ransomed; for by some chance, before the execrable price was completed, all the gold being not yet weighed in consequence of the altercation, the dictator comes up, and orders the gold to be removed, and the Gauls to clear away. When they, holding out against him, affirmed that they had concluded a bargain, he denied that the agreement was a valid one, which had been entered into with a magistrate of inferior authority without his orders, after he had been nominated dictator; and he gives notice to the Gauls to get ready for battle. . . . The Gauls, thrown into confusion by the unexpected event, take up arms, and with rage, rather than good judgement, rushed upon the Romans. . . . At the first encounter, therefore, the Gauls were routed"(14.2)

The newly appointed dictator who arrived with an army was Camillus. Brennus, the leader of the Gauls who attacked Rome in 390 BC, shared the same name with Brennus the leader of the Celts who attacked Greece in about 279 BC.

A battle at the bridge at Anio between the Romans and a party of Gauls occurred in the year that Titus Quinctius Pennus was dictator.

This episode supplies an example of a period when battles could be decided by a champion from each side. Also it provides a snapshot of the Gaul sticking out his tongue as an insult at that level of mortal combat.

Livy: History of Rome book 7 chapters 9, 10 [Spillan]
"9. . . . There were frequent skirmishes for the possession of the bridge; nor could it be clearly determined who were masters of it, the superiority being so indecisive. A Gaul of very large stature advanced on the bridge, then unoccupied, and says with as loud a voice as he could exert, 'Let the bravest man that Rome now possesses come forward here to battle, that the event of an engagement between us both may show which nation is superior in war.'
10. . . . Titus Manlius . . . When armed and equipped, they lead him out against the Gaul, who exhibited stolid exultation, and (for the ancients thought that also worthy of mention) thrust out his tongue in derision. They then retire to their station; and the two being armed, are left in the middle space, more after the manner of a spectacle, than according to the law of combat, by no means well matched, according to those who judged by sight and appearance. The one had a body enormous in size, glittering in a vest of various colours, and in armour painted and inlaid with gold; the other had a middle stature, as is seen among soldiers, and a mien unostentatious, in arms fit for ready use rather than adapted for show. He had no song, no capering, nor idle flourishing of arms,"(14.3)

400 A.U.C., ab urbe condita, from the founding of the city, the city understood as Rome, translates to 353 BC when using the traditional estimate of 753 BC for the founding of Rome.

A further example of individual combat between a Gaul and a victorious Roman soldier, on this occasion Marcus Valerius, was supplied by Livy under the year Appius Claudius Crassus was consul, which is estimated as between 349 BC and 347 BC. A contemporary of Livy would have been aware of the symbolism implied by the crow in this anecdote. It is less clear at this distance from events.

Livy: History of Rome book 7, chapters 18 to 26 [Spillan]
"18. On the four hundredth year after the building of the city of Rome, and the thirty fifth after its recovery from the Gauls, the consulship being taken away from the commons after eleven years, consuls, both patricians, entered into office after the interregnum, Caius Sulpicius Peticus a third time, and Marcus Valerius Publicola. . . . Both the consuls elected were patricians, Marcus Fabius Ambustus a third time, Titus Quinctius. In some annals I find Marcus Popilius mentioned as consul instead of Titus Quinctius.
19. . . . Both consulships therefore remained with the patricians. The consuls appointed were Caius Sulpicius Paeticus a fourth time, Marcus Valerius Publicola a second time. . . .
21. At the close of the year a dispute between the patricians and commons suspended the consular elections, . . . matters came to an interregnum. . . . in the election of consuls. To Publius Valerius Publicola, Caius Marcus Rutilus, a plebeian, was assigned as a colleague.
. . .
22. An attempt made at home by the dictator, to have the election of two patrician consuls, brought the government to an interregnum. The two interreges, Caius Sulpicius and Marcus Fabius, . . . The persons elected were, Caius Sulpicius Peticus himself, who first resigned the office of interrex, and Titus Quinctius Pennus. Some attach the name of Kaeso, others that of Caius to Quinctius. . . .

23. Marcus Popillius Laenas was chosen consul on the part of the commons, Lucius Cornelius Scipio on that of the patricians. . . .

24. . . . Lucius Furius Camillus being nominated dictator, Publius Cornelius Scipio being attached as master of the horse, restored to the patricians their former possession of the consulship. He himself being, for that service, elected consul, had Appius Claudius Crassus named as his colleague.

25. . . .

26. Where when they were spending the time in quiet in their quarters, a Gaul, remarkable for his size and the appearance of his arms, came forward; and striking his shield with his spear, after he had procured silence, through an interpreter he challenged any one of the Romans to contend with him with the sword. There was a tribune of the soldiers, a young man, Marcus Valerius, who considering himself not less worthy of that distinction than Titus Manlius, having first ascertained the consul's pleasure, advanced fully armed into the middle space. The human contest was rendered less remarkable by reason of the interposition of the divine power. For just as the Roman was commencing the encounter, a crow settled suddenly on his helmet, facing the enemy, which, as an augury sent from heaven, the tribune at first received with pleasure. Then he prayed that whatever god or goddess had sent him the auspicious bird, would willingly and kindly aid him. Wondrous to relate, the bird not only kept the place it had once taken, but as often as the encounter was renewed, raising itself on its wings, it attacked the face and eyes of the foe with its beak and talons, until Valerius slays him terrified at the sight of such a prodigy, and confounded both in his vision and understanding. The crow soaring out of sight makes towards the east. Hitherto the advanced guards on both sides remained quiet."(14.4)

The Roman authors paint the expansionist Roman state in a benign light whereas the tribes in their path knew well they could only lose their freedom once.

Livy: History of Rome book 8, chapter 37 [Spillan]
"37. . . . The sentence of the Pollian tribe was, that the grown-up males should be beaten and put to death, and their wives and children sold by auction, according to the rules of war."(14.5)

Sub hasta vendo, to sell by auction (*White's Latin Dictionary*), and the English word 'subhastation' for a sale by public auction, have a literal meaning of sell under the lance. A lance was set up by the Romans as a sign that an auction was to be held (*Chambers*). Perhaps the phrase had its origins in army slang.

The battle of Vesuvius near the small River Veseris was fought in 340 BC between the army of Rome and their near neighbours the Latins allied with the peoples of Campania; a peace settlement was made in 338 BC. The component parts of the Roman army at that time were described by Livy some three hundred years later using records available to him. This description together with additional information on the structure of the Roman army at a later date is given in chapter 16.

Elsewhere in the Mediterranean world, battles were being fought on a larger stage. In 334 BC Alexander the Great was declared leader of the combined Greek forces sent against the Persians. Alexander died aged 32 or 33 in 323 BC, having carved out with his adroit generals an empire from Egypt to the frontiers of India.

9   STRABO

Strabo was an Asiatic Greek who lived from 64 or 63 BC to 25 AD. His *Geography* as translated from the Greek by H.C.Hamilton (books 1 to 6) and W.Falconer (the remainder) was included in Bohn's Classical Library and published between 1854 and 1857. William Falconer was the Rector of Bushey in Hertfordshire. Henry G.Bohn stated that this translation was *"the first which has been laid before the English public."*

The following information was obtained from the preface by W.Falconer to his translation (15). In Greek the name 'Strabo' meant squinting and this was a term carried forward into Latin. Nothing is known of his father's family but it is deduced that Strabo's mother came from a family of substance that lived at Cnossus in Crete and whose ancestors were connected with Mithridates Euergetes and Mithridates Eupator, kings of Pontus. Pontus, a country of northern Anatolia, borders the southern side of the Black Sea. The *Geography* of Strabo is not recognised as having been much quoted in either the works of his contemporaries or later authors. Strabo also wrote a *History* in 43 books, now lost, which, it is deduced, continued to the battle of Actium from the point at which the *History* written by Polybius ended. Strabo's *History* was referred to by both Plutarch and Josephus (*History of the Jews* 14.7). Actium (31 BC) was the decisive naval fight in the civil war that ensued Caesar's assassination where Augustus (then Octavius Caesar) beat the forces of Anthony and Cleopatra.

Strabo is regarded as a Stoic. He had studied grammar and rhetoric under Aristodemus at Nysa in Caria, philosophy under Xenarchus of Seleucia, and the philosophy of Aristotle under Boethus of Sidon. In addition he received tuition from the grammarian Tyrannio of Amisus, though perhaps in Rome and not at Amisus. When not travelling, a conventional assumption is that he lived in his native town of Amaseia. He was familiar with Rome and had visited Egypt *"to the frontiers of Ethiopia"* and a number of places in the Mediterranean world. *"He mentions having been in Egypt, the island Gyarus, Populonium near Elba, Comana in Cappadocia, Ephesus, Mylasa, Nysa, and Hierapolis in Phrygia. He visited Corinth, Argos, Athens, and Megara; but on the whole, he does not appear to have seen more of Greece than in passing through it on his way to Brundusium, while proceeding to Rome. Populonium and Luna in Italy were the limit of his travels northwards. It is probable he obtained his information as to Spain, France, Britain, and Germany, while staying in Rome"*(15).

The sets of documents known to Falconer in 1857, upon which knowledge of the *Geography* of Strabo was founded, accompany the preface to volume three of his translation. Falconer states *"The codices or manuscripts which exist of Strabo's work appear to be copies of a single manuscript existing in the middle ages, but now lost."*

A brief note on the biblical Moses was included by Strabo in *Geography* book 16.2.34 and 35. Thus, it was both researched and written in an era concurrent with the lifetime of Jesus. Passages in Strabo's works that give an insight into Strabo's family are found in book 12.3.33 and book 12.3.39. The nature of the report on Moses could raise the fleeting prospect that the text was interfered with at sometime during its first thousand years of existence when being re-copied.

Strabo: Geography book 3, chapter 1.6 [Hamilton]
"From this river the country has received the name of Baetica; it is called Turdetania by the inhabitants, who are themselves denominated Turdetani, and Turduli. . . . These people are esteemed to be the most intelligent of all the Iberians; they have an alphabet, and possess ancient writings, poems, and metrical laws six thousand years old, as they say. The other Iberians are likewise furnished with an alphabet, although not of the same form, nor do they speak the same language."(15.1)

The area of Spain called Baetica contained the port of Tartessus on the Atlantic coast beyond Gibraltar. Tartessus, also known as Gades, was a stronghold of mariners who came originally from the biblical Tyre. Therefore, it is not beyond question that this alphabet was Phoenician in origin. That the laws were not written down until the medium of writing became available is a truism. That the verses had been handed down for many years does evoke images in the mind of a dedicated priesthood as custodians of the oral tradition. Spain was well known at the time of Strabo and so the report of this alphabet should be accepted at face value. It so happens that the Iberian alphabet is also well known from other data. Although the alphabet under discussion was that used by Iberians in Spain rather than the continental Celts or Germans, the information is of general interest. It serves to illustrate that some among the barbarians did keep their laws and history in verse form. A simple verse format is an aid to memory.

Strabo: Geography book 3, chapter 3.7 [Hamilton]
"Up to the time of [the expedition of] Brutus they made use of vessels constructed of skins for crossing the lagoons formed by the tides; they now have them formed out of the single trunk of a tree, but these are scarce."(15.2)

D.Junius Brutus was alive in 136 BC. These curragh using people inhabited the coast of Spain. An assumption is that they were Celtiberians or Iberians.
The Celtiberians occupied a zone in the north and northwest of Spain. They arose from a fusion of Celtic invaders and the peoples who then occupied the area, the Iberes. It has been deduced the Iberes did not speak a language which evolved from the Indo European group of languages and were not of Indo-European stock. — BASQUES

Strabo: Geography book 3, chapter 4.11 to 4.13 and 4.16 [Hamilton]
"11. The side of the Pyrenees next Iberia is covered with forests containing numerous kinds of trees and evergreens, whilst the side next Keltica is bare: in the midst (the mountains) enclose valleys admirably fitted for the habitation of man. These are mainly possessed by the Kerretani, a people of the Iberians. The hams they cure are excellent, fully equal to those of the Cantabrians, and they realize no inconsiderable profit to the inhabitants.
12. Immediately after passing Idubeda, you enter on Keltiberia, a large and irregular country. It is for the most part rugged, and watered by rivers, being traversed by the Guadiana, the Tagus, and many other of the rivers which flow into the western sea, but have their sources in Keltiberia. Of their number is the Doura, which flows by Numantia and Serguntia. The Guadalquiver rises in Orospeda, and after passing through Oretania, enters Baetica. The Berones inhabit the districts north of the Keltiberians, and are neighbours of the Conish Cantabrians. They likewise had their origin in the Keltic expedition.

Their city is Varia, situated near to the passage of the Ebro. They are adjacent to the Bardyitae, now called the Bardyli. To the west (of the Keltiberians) are certain of the Astures, Gallicians and Vacaei, besides Vettones and Carpetani. On the south are the Orcetani, and the other inhabitants of Orospeda, both Bastetani and Edetani, and to the east is Edubeda.

13. Of the four divisions into which the Keltiberians are separated, the most powerful are the Arunci, situated to the east and south, near to the Carpetani and the sources of the Tagus. Their most renowned city is Numantia. They showed their valour in the war of twenty years, waged by the Keltiberians against the Romans; for many armies of the Romans, together with their generals, were destroyed; and in the end the Numantians, besieged within their city, endured the famine with constancy, till, reduced to a very small number, they were compelled to surrender the place. The Lusones are also situated to the east, and likewise border on the sources of the Tagus. Segeda and Pallantia are cities of the Aruaci. Numantia is distant from Caesar Augusta, situated as we have said upon the Ebro, about 800 stadia. Near to Segobriga and Bilbilis, likewise cities of the Keltiberians, was fought the battle between Metellus and Sertorius. Polybius, describing the people and countries of the Vaccaei and Keltiberians, enumerates Segesama and Intercatia amongst their other cities. Posidonius tells us that Marcus Marcellus exacted of Keltiberia a tribute of 600 talents, which proves that the Keltiberians were a numerous and wealthy people, notwithstanding the little fertility of their country. Polybius narrates that Tiberius Gracchus destroyed 300 cities of the Keltiberians. This Posidonius ridicules, and asserts that to flatter Gracchus, Polybius described as cities the towers such are exhibited in the triumphal processions. This is not incredible; for both generals and historians easily fall into this species of description, by exaggerating their doings. Those who assert that Iberia contained more than a thousand cities, seem to me to have been carried away in a similar manner, and to have denominated as cities what were merely large villages; since, from its very nature, this country is incapable of maintaining so many cities, on account of its sterility, wildness, and its out-of-the-way position. Nor, with the exception of those who dwell along the shores of the Mediterranean, is any such statement confirmed by the mode of life or actions of the inhabitants. The inhabitants of the villages, who constitute the majority of the Iberians, are quite uncivilised. Even the cities cannot very easily refine their manners (of their inhabitants), as the neighbouring woods are full of robbers, waiting only an opportunity to inflict injury on the citizens.

14. . . .

15. . . .

16. . . . Some say that the Gallicians are atheists, but that the Keltiberians, and their neighbours to the north, (sacrifice) to a nameless god, every full moon, at night, before their doors, the whole family passing the night in dancing and festival."(15.3)

Strabo: Geography book 4, chapter 1.13 [Hamilton]

"13. But the Tectosages dwell near the to the Pyrenees, . . . dissensions having arisen amongst them, they drove a vast multitude of their number from their homes; and that these men associating with others of different nations took possession of Phrygia, next to Cappadocia, and the Paphlagonians. Of this those who are now called the Tectosages afford us proof, for (Phrygia contains) three nations, one of them dwelling near the city of Aneyra, being called the Tectosages; the remaining two, the Trocmi and Tolistobogii. The resemblance these nations bear to the Tectosages is evidence of their having immigrated from Keltica,"(15.4)

These are the Galatians of the New Testament who were addressed by Paul in one of his letters. The letter, dated to between 48 and 57 AD, was written by Paul for circulation among people of the Christian persuasion living in Galatia. They lived at that time in an area of what is now modern Turkey. The Galatians came into focus again when Strabo described the area they then occupied in Asia Minor. The administrative structure whereby each tribe sent 100 people to the central council possibly reflected a practice that operated among the European Celtic nations in general. The mother goddess 'Agdistis' of the Galatians could have a connection with 'Dis' from whom the Gauls said they were descended, see Caesar *Gallic War* 6.18 (1.6).

Strabo: Geography book 12, chapter 5.1 [Falconer]
"1. To the south of the Paphlagonians are the Galatians of whom there are three tribes; two of them, the Trocmi and the Tolistobogii, have their names from their chiefs; the third, the Tectosages, from the tribe of that name in Celtica. The Galatians took possession of this country after wandering about for a long period, and overrunning the country subject to the Attalic and the Bithynian kings, until they received by a voluntary cession the present Galatia, or Gallo-Graecia, as it is called. Leonnorius seems to have been the chief leader of these people when they passed over into Asia. There were three nations that spoke the same language, and in no respect differed from one another. Each of them was divided into four portions called tetrarchies, and had its own tetrarch, its own judge, and one superintendent of the army, all of whom were under the control of the tetrarch, and two subordinate superintendents of the army. The council of the twelve Tetrarchs consisted of three hundred persons, who assembled at a place called the Drynemetum. The council determined causes relative to murder; the tetrarchs and the judges decided the others. Such, anciently, was the political constitution of Galatia; but, in our times, the government was in the hands of three chiefs, then of two, and at last it was administered by Deiotarus, who was succeeded by Amyntas. . . .
2. The Trocmi occupy the parts near Pontus and Cappadocia, which are the best which the Galatians possess. They have three walled fortresses, Tavium, a mart for the people in that quarter, where there is a colossal statue of Jupiter in brass, and a grove, which is used as a place of refuge; . . .
The Tectosages occupy the parts towards the greater Phrygia near Pessinus, and the Orcaorci. They had the fortress Ancyra, of the same name as the small Phrygian city towards Lydia near Blaudus. The Tolistobogii border upon the Bithynians, and Phrygia Epictetus, as it is called. They possess the fortresses Blacium (Luceium) which was the royal seat of Deiotarus, and Peium, which was his treasure-hold.
3. Pessinus is the largest mart of any in that quarter. It contains a temple of the Mother of the Gods, held in the highest veneration. The goddess is called Agdistis. The priests anciently were a sort of sovereign, and derived a large revenue from their office. At present their consequence is much diminished, but the mart still subsists. The sacred enclosure was adorned with fitting magnificence by the Attalic kings, with a temple and portions of marble. The Romans gave importance to the temple by sending for the statue of the goddess from thence according to the oracle of the Sibyl, as they had sent for that of Asclepius from Epidaurus."(15.5)

Caesar placed the Veneti among those who were called Amoricae in their dialect, *Gallic War* 7.75 (1.6). Elsewhere, Amorican is given no more meaning in Celtic than people who live by the sea.

The hand launched 'piece of wood' principally used to down birds would, it is supposed, have stimulated comment had it returned to the launch point if it made no contact with the prey. Thus, a Celtic boomerang is not envisaged as stemming from this description by Strabo. But did they exist? An oaken object dated to about 300 BC from Velsen in the Netherlands exhibits flight qualities sufficient for a boomerang, see note by Mr Hess, *Antiquity Vol. XLVII No.188 December 1973, page 303.*

Strabo: Geography book 4 chapter 4 [Hamilton]
"1. After the nations mentioned come those of the Belgae, who dwell next the ocean. Of their number are the Veneti, who fought a naval battle with Caesar. . . .
2. The entire race which now goes by the name of Gallic, or Galatic, is warlike, passionate, and always ready for fighting, but otherwise simple and not malicious. If irritated, they rush in crowds to the conflict, openly and without any circumspection; and thus are easily vanquished by those who employ stratagem. . . . Their power consists both in the size of their bodies and also in their numbers. . . . but we have described their customs as we understood they existed in former times, and as they still exist amongst the Germans. These two nations, both by nature and in their form of government, are similar and related to each other. Their countries border on each other, being separated by the river Rhine, and are for the most part similar. . . . Thus it is that they can so easily change their abode. They march in crowds in one collected army, or rather remove with all their families, whenever they are ejected by a more powerful force. . . .
3. Of these they say that the Belgae are the bravest. They are divided into fifteen nations, and dwell near the ocean between the Rhine and the Loire, . . . The Gauls wear the sagum, let their hair grow, and wear short breeches. Instead of tunics they wear a slashed garment with sleeves descending a little below the hips. The wool (of their sheep) is course, but long; from it they weave the thick saga called laines. . . . The equipment (of the Gauls) is in keeping with the size of their bodies; they have a long sword hanging on their right side, a long shield, and lances in proportion, together with a madaris somewhat resembling a javelin; some of them also use bows and slings; they have also a piece of wood resembling a pilum, which they hurl not out of a thong, but from their hand, and to a farther distance than an arrow. They principally make use of it in shooting birds. To the present day most of them lie on the ground, and take their meals seated on straw. They subsist principally on milk and all kinds of flesh, especially that of swine, which they eat both fresh and salted. . . . The people dwell in great houses arched, constructed of planks and wicker, and covered with a heavy thatched roof. They have sheep and swine in such abundance, that they supply saga and salted pork in plenty, not only to Rome but to most parts of Italy. Their governments were for the most part aristocratic; formerly they chose a governor every year, and a military leader was likewise elected by the multitude. At the present day they are mostly under subjection to the Romans. They have a peculiar custom in their assemblies. If any one makes an uproar or interrupts the person speaking, an attendant advances with a drawn sword, and commands him with menaces to be silent; if he persists, the attendant does the same thing a second and third time; and finally, (if he will not obey,) cuts off from his sagum so large a piece as to render the remainder useless.

The labours of the two sexes are distributed in a manner the reverse of what they are with us, but this is a common thing with numerous barbarians."

The sagum was a cloak. According to Polybius sagum was a Celtic word (*White's Dictionary*). In Caesar's account the common people were treated almost as slaves. This passage points to electing a war leader by common consent of an assembly selected from among the warrior aristocracy and freemen. Some readers construe that the custom relating to men and women refers to the geometry when enjoying sex.

"4. Amongst (the Gauls) there are generally three divisions of men especially reverenced, the Bards, the Vates, and the Druids. The Bards composed and chanted hymns; the Vates occupied themselves with the sacrifices and the study of nature; while the Druids joined to the study of nature that of moral philosophy. The belief in the justice (of the Druids) is so great that the decision both of public and private disputes is referred to them; and they have before now, by their decision, prevented armies from engaging when drawn up in battle-array against each other. All cases of murder are particularly referred to them. When there is plenty of these they imagine there will likewise be a plentiful harvest. Both these and the others assert that the soul is indestructible, and likewise the world, but that sometimes fire and sometimes water have prevailed in making great changes.
5. To their simplicity and vehemence, the Gauls join much folly, arrogance, and love of ornament. They wear golden collars round their necks, and bracelets on their arms and wrists, and those who are of any dignity have garments dyed and worked with gold. . . . they have a barbarous and absurd custom, common however with many nations of the north, of suspending the heads of their enemies from their horses' necks on their return from battle, and when they have arrived nailing them as a spectacle to their gates. Posidonius says he witnessed this in many different places, and was at first shocked, but became familiar with it in time on account of its frequency. The heads of any illustrious persons they embalm with cedar, exhibit them to strangers, and would not sell them for their weight in gold. However, the Romans put a stop to these customs, as well as to their modes of sacrifice and divination, which were quite opposite to those sanctioned by our laws. They would strike a man devoted as an offering in his back with a sword, and divine from his convulsive throes. Without the Druids they never sacrifice. It is said they have other modes of sacrificing their human victims; that they pierce some of them with arrows, and crucify others in their temples; and that they prepare a colossus of hay and wood, into which they put cattle, beasts of all kinds, and men, and then set fire to it."

The link between 'plenty' of murder cases and a good harvest is the anticipated proportionate outcome of the number of criminals executed in offerings to their deities. This would then complement Caesar's account that they executed innocent people when the supply of criminals was not sufficient. Reference to a Colossus is found in Caesar's *Gallic War*, book 6.16.

Strabo is not forthcoming as to whether these separate accounts rely upon one literary source or several independent witnesses. There is no reason to disbelieve the character, dress and ritual summarized by Strabo as an accurate record of Celtic practice, aspects of which a consensus among archaeologists interprets as being depicted in a panel on the Gundestrup bowl.

"6. They say that in the ocean, not far from the coast, there is a small island lying opposite to the outlet of the river Loire, inhabited by Samnite women who are Bacchantes, and conciliate and appease that god by mysteries and sacrifices. No man is permitted to land on the island; and when the women desire to have intercourse with the other sex, they cross the sea, and afterwards return again. They have a custom of once a year unroofing the whole of the temple, and roofing it again in the same day before sunset, each one bringing some of the materials. If any one lets her burden fall, she is torn in pieces by the others, and her limbs carried round the temple with wild shouts, which they never cease until their rage is exhausted. (They say) it always happens that some one drops her burden, and is thus sacrificed.

But what Artemidorus tells us concerning the crows, partakes still more of fiction. He narrates that on the coast, washed by the ocean, there is a harbour named the Port of Two Crows, . . . Those who have any disputes come here, and each one having placed a plank for himself on a lofty eminence, sprinkles crumbs thereupon; the birds fly to these, eat up the one and scatter the other, and he whose crumbs are scattered gains the cause. . . . What he narrates concerning Ceres and Proserpine is more credible. He says that there is an island near Britain in which they perform sacrifices to these goddesses after the same fashion that they do in Samo-thrace. The following is also credible, that a tree grows in Keltica similar to a fig, which produces a fruit resembling a Corinthian capital, and which, being cut, exudes a poisonous juice which they use for poisoning their arrows. It is well known that all the Kelts are fond of disputes; and that amongst them paederasty is not considered shameful. . . . they take great care not to become fat or big-bellied, and that if any young man exceeds the measure of a certain girdle, he is punished. Such is our account of Keltica beyond the Alps."(15.6)

The British Isles were not well known to the Roman literate classes of Strabo's day and reports were subject to the imaginative excesses of the unknown. The implied converse of the statement on the act of cheese making in Britain is that the Celts in continental Europe made cheese, if evidence is not otherwise forthcoming from the archaeological record. In reality, the Belgic tribes had influenced Southern Britain from the first century BC - complete with coinage, pottery and agricultural technique. It follows there is a suspicion Strabo's account of Britain relied on sources that terminated with Julius Caesar. Artemidorus of Ephesus was alive in 104 BC (4).

Strabo: Geography book 4, chapter 5.2 [Hamilton]
"2. [Britain] . . . It produces corn, cattle, gold, silver, and iron, which things are brought thence, and also skins, and slaves, and dogs sagacious in hunting; the Kelts use these, as well as their native dogs, for the purpose of war. The men are taller than the Kelts, with hair less yellow; they are slighter in their persons. . . . Their manners are in part like those of the Kelts, though in part more simple and barbarous; insomuch that some of them, though possessing plenty of milk, have not skill enough to make cheese, and are totally unacquainted with horticulture and other matters of husbandry. There are several states amongst them. In their wars they make use of chariots for the most part, as do some of the Kelts. Forests are their cities; for having enclosed an ample space with felled trees, they make themselves huts therein, and lodge their cattle, though not for any long continuance."(15.7)

Strabo: Geography book 4, chapter 5.4 [Hamilton]
"4. There are also other small islands around Britain; but one, of great extent, Ierne, lying parallel to it towards the north, long, or rather, wide; concerning which we have nothing certain to relate, further than that its inhabitants are more savage than the Britons, feeding on human flesh, and enormous eaters, and deeming it commendable to devour their deceased fathers, as well as openly to have commerce not only with other women, but also with their own mothers and sisters. But this we relate perhaps without very competent authority; although to eat human flesh is said to be a Scythian custom; and during the severities of a siege, even the Kelts, the Iberians, and many others, are reported to have done the like."(15.8)

A candidate for his un-trustworthy witness was Pytheas of Marseilles, who is believed to have travelled in British waters at sometime between 350 BC and 300 BC. When looking back to the era inferred by his source document, Strabo did not necessarily view as Celts those people of Iverne who had attracted these curious observations.

Strabo: Geography book 7, chapter 1.2 [Falconer]
"2. Next after the Keltic nations come the Germans who inhabit the country to the east beyond the Rhine; and these differ but little from the Keltic race, except in their being more fierce, of a larger stature, and more ruddy in countenance; but in every other respect, their figure, their customs and manners of life, are such as we have related of the Kelts. The Romans therefore, I think, have very appositely applied to them the name 'Germani,' as signifying genuine; for in the Latin language Germani signifies genuine."(15.9)

Tacitus, at the end of the first century, would have it that Germani was the name of but one tribe that crossed the Rhine. The name Germani gradually gained currency as the name for the whole nation (5.3).

Strabo: Geography book 7, chapter 1.3 [Falconer]
"All these nations easily change their abode, on account of the scantiness of provisions, and because they neither cultivate the lands nor accumulate wealth, but dwell in miserable huts, and satisfy their wants from day to day, the most part of their food being supplied by the herd, as amongst the nomade races, and in imitation of them they transfer their households in wagons, wandering with their cattle to any place which may appear most advantageous."(15.10)

Strabo: Geography book 7, chapter 2.3 [Falconer]
"3. It is reported that the Cimbri had a peculiar custom. They were accompanied in their expeditions by their wives; these were followed by hoary-headed priestesses, clad in white, with cloaks of carbasus fastened on with clasps, girt with brazen girdles, and bare footed. These individuals, bearing drawn swords, went to meet the captives throughout the camp, and having crowned them, led them to a brazen vessel containing about 20 amphorae, and placed on a raised platform, which one of the priestesses having ascended, and holding the prisoner above the vessel, cut his throat; then, from the manner in which the blood flowed into the vessel, some drew certain divinations; while others, having opened the corpse, and inspected the entrails, prophesied victory to their army. In battle too they beat skins stretched on the wicker sides of chariots, which produces a stunning noise."(15.11)

A footnote states that flax and the fabric made from it were called carbasus.

The term Kelto-Scythian, used by early Greek historians, covers a wider variation of peoples than encompassed in later centuries by the term Scythian. When examining information that was ancient history in his own day, it is seen that Strabo was of the opinion the Trojans had crossed the Hellespont from Europe into Asia Minor and that they had moved from an area of Thrace.

At one point in time, Enea was a rival to the name Europe to designate the continent. Enea took its name from Aeneas the Trojan, who in turn may have been named after an older mythological figurehead. The Romans, Franks and British Celts each claimed they were descended from Aeneas and the Trojans. Allowing a little romantic imagination, the mythology is credited with an element of truth in that each of the groups could have sprung from a core nation on the borders of Europe and Asia and, moreover, a nation in which the horse was held in high esteem.

Strabo: Geography book 11, chapter 6.2 [Falconer]
"2. Upon sailing into the Caspian, on the right hand side, contiguous to the Europeans, Scythians and Sarmatians occupy the country between the Tanais and this sea; they are chiefly Nomades, or shepherd tribes, of whom I have already spoken. On the left hand are the Eastern Scythian Nomades, who extend as far as the Eastern sea, and India.
The ancient Greek historians called all the nations towards the north by the common name of Scythians, and Kelto-Scythians. Writers still more ancient than these called the nations living above the Euxine, Danube, and Adriatic, Hyperboreans, Sauromatae, and Arimaspi."(15.12)

Without paying overmuch attention to a phrase of no significant weight in Strabo's eyes, this reference to writers more ancient than the Greeks invites speculation as to who they were and the society of which they were a part. The world of Crete, Phoenicia, Egypt, Persia or the Hittite empire are immediate candidates. It reminds the reader that Strabo had the opportunity of sifting through data that is no longer available in the twenty-first century.

Plutarch in his life of Marius (see chapter 13) posed the question as to whether the Cimmerii, a thorn in the side of the Greeks, became known as the Germanic Cimbri, the bete noir of Roman army commanders.

Strabo: Geography book 11, chapters 2.1 to 2.5 [Falconer]
"1. According to this disposition, the first portion towards the north and the Ocean is inhabited by certain tribes of Scythians, shepherds, (nomades,) and Hamaxoeci (or those who live in waggon-houses). Within these tribes live Sarmatians, who also are Scythians, Aorsi,
[Footnote. The Aorsi and Siraci occupied the country between the Sea of Azov, the Don, the Volga, the Caspian Sea, and the Tetek. May not the Aorsi, says Gossellin, be the same as the Thyrsagetae, Agathursi, Utidursi, Adorsi, Alanorsi of other writers, but whose real name is Thryrsi? The Sirari do not appear to differ from the Soraci or Seraci of Tacitus, (Ann.xii. l5, d.c,) and may be the same as Iyrces afterwards called Turcae.]
and Siraci, extending as far as the Caucasian Mountains towards the south. Some of these are Nomades, or shepherd tribes, others Scenitae, (or dwellers in tents,) and Georgi, or tillers of the ground.

About the lake Maeotis live the Maeote. Close to the sea is the Asiatic portion of the Bosporus and Sindica. Next follow Achaei, Zygi, Heniochi, Cercetae, and Macropogones (or the long-beards). Above these people are situated the passes of the Phtheirophangi (or lice-eaters). After the Heniochi is Colchis, lying at the foot of the Caucasian and Moschic mountains. Having assumed the Tanais as the boundary of Europe and Asia, we must begin our description in detail from this river.

2. The Tanais or Don flows from northern parts. . . . its sources, like those of the Nile, are unknown. . . . We are acquainted with the mouths of the Don, (there are two in the most northerly parts of the Maeotis, distant 60 stadia from each other,) but a small part only of the tract above the mouths is explored, on account of the severity of the cold, and the destitute state of the country; the natives are able to endure it, who subsist, like the wandering shepherd tribes, on the flesh of their animals and on milk, but strangers cannot bear the climate nor the privations. Besides, the nomades dislike intercourse with other people, and being a strong and numerous tribe have excluded travellers from every part of the country which is accessible.

3. Upon the river, and on the lake, stands a city Tanais, founded by the Greeks, who possess the Bosporus; but lately the king Polemon laid it waste on account of the refractory disposition of the inhabitants. It was the common mart both of the Asiatic and of the European nomades, and of those who navigate the lake from the Bosporus, some of whom bring slaves and hides, or any other nomadic commodity; others exchange wine for clothes, and other articles peculiar to a civilised mode of life. . . .

The city Tanais, to those who sail in a direct line towards the north, is distant from the mouth of the Maeotis 2200 stadia, nor is the distance much greater in sailing along the coast (on the east).

4. In the voyage along the coast, the first object which presents itself to those who have proceeded to the distance of 800 stadia from the Tanais, is the Great Rhombites, . . . Then at the distance of 800 stadia more is the lesser Rhombotes, . . .

[Footnote. Strabo makes the distance too great between the two rivers Rhombites.]

From the lesser Rhombites to Tyrambe, and the river Anticeites, are 600 stadia; then 120 to the Cimmerian village whence vessels set out on their voyage along the lake. . . .

5. Cimmerieum was formerly a city built upon a peninsula, the isthmus of which it enclosed with a ditch and a mound. The Cimmerii once possessed great power in the Bosporus, whence it was called the Cimmerian Bosporus. These are the people who overran the territory of the inhabitants of the inland parts, on the right of the Euxine, as far as Ionia. They were dislodged from these places by Scythians, and the Scythians by Greeks, who founded Panticapaeum, and the other cities of the Bosporus."(15.13)

Herodotus recounted versions of the Scythian foundation myths, one of which embraced Hercules. This Scythian interlude arose later than his venture to carry off the cattle of Geryon, see Herodotus book 4.8 to 4.10. Herodotus was more inclined to believe that the Scythians had displaced incumbent Cimmerians.

Herodotus: book 4, chapters 6 to 11 [Rawlinson]
"6. From Leipoxais sprang the Scythians of the race called Auchatae; from Arpoxais, the middle brother, those known as the Catiari and Traspians; from Colaxais, the youngest, the Royal Scythians, or Paralatae. All together they are named Scoloti, after one of their kings: the Greeks, however, call them Scythians.

7. Such is the account which the Scythians give of their origin. They add that from the time of Targitais, their first king, to the invasion of their country by Darius, is a period of one thousand years, neither less nor more. The Royal Scythians guard the sacred gold with most especial care, and year by year offer great sacrifices in its honour. . . . "
[Hercules story.]
"11. There is also another different story, now to be related, in which I am more inclined to put faith than in any other. It is that the wandering Scythians once dwelt in Asia, and there warred with the Massagetae, but with ill success; they therefore quitted their homes, crossed the Araxes, and entered the land of Cimmeria. For the land which is now inhabited by the Scyths was formerly the country of the Cimmerians. On their coming, the natives, who heard how numerous the invading army was, held a council. At this meeting opinion was divided, and both parties stiffly maintained their own view; but the council of the Royal tribe was the braver. For the others urged that the best thing to be done was to leave the country, and avoid a contest with so vast a host; but the Royal tribe advised remaining and fighting for the soil to the last. As neither party chose to give way, the one determined to retire without a blow and yield their lands to the invaders; but the other, . . . resolved not to flee . . . Having thus decided, they drew apart in two bodies, the one as numerous as the other, and fought together. All of the Royal tribe were slain, and the people buried them near the river Tyras, where their grave is still to be seen. Then the rest of the Cimmerians departed, and the Scythians, on their coming, took possession of a deserted land."(7.3)

Equating the Germanic Cimbri and their associate tribes with the Cimmerians of a previous age was a recurring topic with Roman authors. The cache of sacred gold would sit more easily within the bounds of Celtic behaviour and values.

Strabo: Geography book 13, chapter 1.21 [Falconer]
"21. . . . There was also in Lesbos a city called Arisba, the territory belonging to which was possessed by the Methymnaeans. There is a river Arisbus in Thrace, as we have said before, near which are situated the Cabrenii Thracians. There are many names common to Thracians and Trojans, as Scaei, a Thracian tribe, a river Scaeus, a Scaean wall, and in Troy, Scaean gates. There are Thracians called Xanthii, and a river Xanthus in Troja; an Arisbus which discharges itself into the Hebrus, and an Arisbe in Troja; a river Rhesus in Troja, and Rhesus, a king of the Thracians. The poet mentions also another Asius, besides the Asius of Arisbe."(15.14)

Strabo was familiar with the countryside once dominated by Trojan cities. His interpretation, of evidence available to him that the Trojans had crossed from Thrace to Asia Minor, was given without justifying why a reverse emigration had not occurred. The Trojan cities dominated the passage of trade between Asia Minor and Europe across the Dardanelles as they did the seaborne traffic to and fro between the Mediterranean and the Black Sea.

Excavation shows the Trojan cities were settled sites before 3,000 BC whatever the name of the people in their ruling class. There is evidence for the introduction of the potter's wheel after 3,000 BC and the horse between 2,000 BC and 1,500 BC. The cities of Troy flourished prior to the fusion of cultures and peoples which evolved into 'Classical Greece'. 'The poet' was always understood to be Homer.

Strabo showed that he had read Herodotus, though the translator of Herodotus prefers Zalmoxis.

Strabo: Geography book 16, chapter 2.39 [Falconer]
"39. . . . in former times there was Zamolxis, a Pythagorean, who was accounted a god among the Getae;"(15.15)

10   LUCAN

Marcus Annaeus Lucanus was born at Coruba in Spain on 3rd November 39 AD. He was forced to commit suicide on the 30th April 65 AD by the emperor Nero, when implicated in a plot to kill Nero. Lucan was the son of M. Annaeus Mela who himself was a brother of Lucius Annaeus Seneca (Seneca). The event of his death was recorded by Tacitus (*Annals* book 15 chapters 48 to 70).

This description of the Druids was associated with a narrative of the activities of Julius Caesar. The English translation was by Sir Edward Ridley in 1896.

Lucan: Civil War book 1, about lines 445 to 470 [Edward Ridley]
"And those who pacify with blood accursed
Savage Teutates, Hesus' horrid shrines,
And Taranis' altars cruel as were those
Loved by Diana, goddess of the north;
All these now rest in peace. And you, ye Bards,
Whose martial lays send down to distant times
The fame of valorous deeds in battle done,
Pour forth in safety more abundant song.
While you, ye Druids, when the war was done,
To mysteries strange and hateful rites returned:
To you alone 'tis given the gods and stars
To know or not to know; secluded groves
Your dwelling-place, and forests far remote.
If what ye sing be true, the shades of men
Seek not the dismal homes of Erebus
Or death's pale kingdoms; but the breath of life
Still rules these bodies in another age –
Life on this hand and that, and death between.
Happy the peoples 'neath the Northern Star
In this their false belief; for them no fear
Of that which frights all others: they with hands
And hearts undaunted rush upon the foe
And scorn to spare the life that shall return.
Ye too depart who keep the banks of Rhine
Safe from the foe, and leave the Teuton tribes
Free at their will to march upon the world."(16.1)

A translation by J.D.Duff (who identified that his text had been reprinted from the edition of A.E.Houseman) of Lucan's Civil War was published in the Loeb Classical Library. A footnote in the translation by J.D.Duff states the Romans identified Teutates with Mars, Esus with Mercury and Taranis with Jupiter.

Lucan: The Civil War, book 3, about lines 462 to 489 [Edward Ridley]
"Now fell the forests far and wide, despoiled
Of all their giant trunks: for as the mound
On earth and brushwood stood, a timber frame
Held firm the soil, lest pressed beneath its towers
The mass might topple down. There stood a grove
Which from the earliest time no hand of man
Had dared to violate; hidden from the sun
Its chill recesses; matted boughs entwined
Prisoned [sic] the air within. No sylvan nymphs
Here found a home, nor Pan, but savage rites
And barbarous worship, altars horrible
On massive stones upreared; sacred with blood
Of men was every tree. If faith be given
To ancient myth, no fowl has ever dared
To rest upon these branches, and no beast
Has made his lair beneath: no tempest falls
Nor lightnings flash upon it from the cloud.
Stagnant the air, unmoving, yet the leaves
Filled with mysterious trembling; dripped the streams
From coal-black fountains; effigies of gods
Rude, scarcely fashioned from some fallen trunk
Held the mid space; and, pallid with decay,
Their rotting shapes struck terror. Thus do men
Dread most the god unknown. 'Twas said that caves
Rumbled with earthquakes, that the prostrate yew
Rose up again; that fiery tongues of flame
Gleamed in the forests depths, yet were the trees
Unkindled; and that snakes in frequent folds
Were coiled around the trunks. Men flee the spot
Nor dare to worship near: and e'en the priest
Or when bright Phoebus holds the height, or when
Dark night controls the heavens, in anxious dread
Draws near the grove and fears to find its lord."(16.2)

The translation from which these quotations from Lucan are taken is published on the internet by *Project Gutenberg* under EText-No 602, Release Date 1996-07-01. The caveat associated with their use is as follows.

11 PLINY THE ELDER

Pliny the Elder lived from 23 AD to 79 AD. He died at Stabiae when overcome by fumes from the eruption of Vesuvius dated to 24th August AD 79 which destroyed Pompeii. The information is taken from Pliny the Elder's *Natural History* translated by John Bostock and H.T.Riley and published in 1855 by the Bohn Classical Library. The preface to the Bohn publication states *"The only translation of Pliny's Natural History which has hitherto appeared in the English language is that by Philemon Holland, published in the latter part of the reign of Elizabeth."*

During his time spent in the army, between approximately 46 AD and 52 AD Pliny was stationed in Germany and travelled both to the German Ocean and the country of the Belgae. C. Plinius Secundus was made auger in Rome, served as governor of Spain, and became an acquaintance of Vespasian whom it is believed he worked directly for in matters of state when Vespasian was emperor (69 AD to 79 AD).

The death of Pliny at Stabiae was the subject of a letter from Pliny the Younger - the nephew of Pliny the Elder - to Tacitus. Another letter from Pliny the Younger that was addressed to Macer, conveniently, contains a list of the prodigious literary works of Pliny the Elder.

Pliny's *Natural History* comprised 37 books. From the titles given to Titus in the preface by Pliny, it is judged to have been first published in 77 AD. The works written by Pliny that are now lost include *The use of the Javelin by Cavalry* (1 book), *The Life of Q. Pomponius Secundus* (2 books), *The Wars in Germany* (20 books), *The Student* (6 volumes), *On Difficulties in the Latin Language* (8 books of which fragments survive), *Continuation of the History of Aufidius Bassus* (31 books).

The tribes of Dacia and Scythia situated to the north of the Black Sea, as recorded by Pliny in the first century AD, were pressing on the eastern boundary of the Celtic and Germanic peoples that had an interface in the west with the expanding Roman state.

Pliny: Natural History book 4, chapters 25 to 34 [Bostock and Riley]
"Chapter 25. - Dacia - Sarmatia.
On setting out from this spot, all the nations met with are Scythian in general, though various races have occupied the adjacent shores; at one spot the Getae, by the Romans called Daci; at another the Sarmatae, by the Greeks called Sauromatae, and the Hamaxobii"
[Footnote. 'Dwellers in waggons'. These were a Sarmatian tribe who wandered with their waggons along the banks of the Volga. The chief seats of the Aorsi, who seem in reality to have been a distinct people from the Hamaxobi, was in the country between the Tanais, the Euxine, the Caspian, and the Caucasus.]
"or Aorsi, a branch of them, then again the base-born Scythians and descendants of slaves, or else the Troglodytae;"
[Footnote. 'Dwellers in caves'.]
"and then, after them, the Alani and the Rhoxalani. The higher parts again, between the Danube and the Hercynian Forest, as far as the winter quarters of Pannonia at Carnuntium, and the borders of the Germans, are occupied by the Sarmatian Iaxyges, who inhabit the level country and the plains, while the Daci, whom they have driven as far as the river Pathissus,"
[Footnote. The lower Theiss.]

"inhabit the mountain and forest ranges. On leaving the river Marus, whether it is that or the Duria, that separates them from the Suevi and the kingdom of Vannius,"

[Footnote. A chief of the Quadi; who as we learn from Tacitus, was made king of the Suevi by Germanicus, AD 19. Being afterwards expelled by his nephews Vangio and Sicio, he received from the emperor Claudius a settlement in Pannonia. Tacitus gives the name of Suevia to the whole of the east of Germany from the Danube to the Baltic. This passage appears to be in a mutilated state.]

"the Basternae, and, after them, other tribes of the Germans occupy the opposite sides. . . . The name 'Scythian' has extended in every direction, even to the Sarmatae and the Germans; but this ancient appellation is now only given to those who dwell beyond those nations, and live unknown to nearly all the rest of the world.

Chapter 26 - Scythia.

. . . Leaving Taphrae, and going along the mainland, we find in the interior the Aucheta, in whose country the Hypanis has its rise, as also the Neuroe, in whose district the Borysthenes has its source, the Geloni,"

[Footnote. Of the Geloni, called by Virgil 'picti', or 'painted', nothing certain seems to be known: they are associated by Herodotus with the Budini, . . .]

"the Thyssagetae, the Budini, the Basilidae, and the Agathyrsi "

[Footnote. The Agathyrsi are placed by Herodotus near the upper course of the river Maris, in the S.E. of Dacia or the modern Transylvania. Pliny however seems here to assign them a different locality.]

"with their azure coloured hair. Above them are the Nomades, and then a nation of Anthropophagi or cannibals. On leaving Lake Buges, above the Lake Maeotis we come to the Sauromatae and the Essedones. Along the coast, as far as the river Tanais, are the Maeotae, from whom the lake derives its name, and the last of all, in the rear of them, the Arimaspi. We then come to the Riphaean mountains and the region known by the name of Pterophoros, because of the perpetual fall of snow there, the flakes of which resemble feathers; . . .

Behind these mountains, and beyond the region of the northern winds, there dwells, if we choose to believe it, a happy race, known as the Hyperborei, . . . Some writers have placed these people, not in Europe, but at the very verge of the shores of Asia, because we find there a people called the Attacori, who greatly resemble them and occupy a very similar locality. Other writers again have placed them midway between the two suns, at the spot where it sets to the Antipodes and rises to us; a thing however that cannot possibly be, in consequence of the vast tract of sea which there intervenes. . . ."

The list of the tribes of Germany and Gaul supplied by Pliny is given below. It is recognised that it differs in detail and geographical position from that of both Caesar and Tacitus.

"As to the remaining parts of these shores, they are only known from reports of doubtful authority. With reference to the Septentrional or Northern Ocean; Hecataeus calls it, after we have passed the mouth of the river Parapanisus, where it washes the Scythian shores, the Amalchian Sea, the word 'Amalchian' signifying in the language of these races, frozen. Philemon again says that it is called Morimarusa or the 'Dead Sea' by the Cimbri, as far as the Promontory of Rubeas, beyond which it has the name of the Cronian Sea.

Xenophon of Lampsacus tells us that at a distance of three days' sail from the shores of Scythia, there is an island of immense size called Baltia, which by Pytheas is called Basilia. Some islands called Oonae are said to be here, the inhabitants of which live on the eggs of birds and oats; . . .

Leaving these however, we come to the nation of the Ingaevones, the first in Germany; at which we begin to have some information upon which more implicit reliance can be placed. In their country is an immense mountain called Sevo, not less than those of the Riphaean range, and which forms an immense gulf along the shore as far as the Promontory of the Cimbri. This gulf, which has the name of the 'Codanian,' is filled with islands; the most famous among which is Scandinavia, of a magnitude as yet unassertained: the only portion of it at all known is inhabited by the nation of the Hilleviones, who dwell in 500 villages, and call it a second world: it is generally supposed that the island of Eningia is of not less magnitude. Some writers state that these regions, as far as the river Vistula, are inhabited by the Sarmati, the Venedi, the Sciri, and the Hirri, and that there is a gulf there known by the name of Cylipenus, at the mouth of which is the island of Latris, after which comes another gulf, that of Lagnus, which borders on the Cimbri. The Cimbrian Promontory, running out into the sea for a great distance, forms a peninsula which bears the name of Cartris."

[Footnote. The modern Cape of Skagen on the north of Jutland.]

"Passing this coast, there are three and twenty islands which have been made known by the Roman arms: the most famous of which is Burcana, called by our people Fabaria, from the resemblance borne by a fruit which grows there spontaneously. There are those also called Glaesaria by our soldiers, from their amber; but by the barbarians they are known as Austeravia and Actania.

Chapter 28. Germany

The whole of the shores of this sea as far as the Scaldis, a river of Germany, is inhabited by nations, the dimensions of whose respective territories it is quite impossible to state, so immensely do the authors differ who have touched upon this subject. . . .

There are five German races; the

Vandili	*, parts of whom are the Burgundiones, the Varini, the Carini, and the Gutones: the*
Ingaevones	*, forming a second race, a portion of whom are the Cimbri, the Teutoni, and the tribes of the Chauci. The*
Istaevones	*, who join up to the Rhine, and to whom the Cimbri belong, are the third race; while the*
Hermiones	*, forming a fourth, dwell in the interior, and include the Suevi, the Hermunuri, the Chatti, and the Cherusci: the fifth race is that of the Peucini, who are also the*
Basternae	*, adjoining the Daci previously mentioned.*

The more famous rivers that flow into the ocean are the Guttalus, the Vistillus or Vistula, the Albis, the Visurgis, the Amisius, the Rhine, and the Mosa. In the interior is the long extent of the Hercynian range, which in grandeur is inferior to none."

The name Cimbri is listed under two groups [quorum Cimbri]. The translator accepted that it may have been substituted for another name under Istaevones. The translator stated that Gibbon interpreted the name Cimbri to have signified 'robbers'.

"Chapter 29. - Ninety-six Islands of the Gallic Ocean.

In the Rhine itself, nearly 100 miles in length, is the most famous island of the Batavi and the Canninefates, as also other islands of the Frisii, the Chauci, the Frisiabones, the Sturii, and the Marsacii, which lie between Helium and Flevum. These are the names of the mouths into which the Rhine divides itself, discharging its waters on the north into the lakes there, and on the west into the river Mosa. At the middle mouth which lies between these two, the river, having but a very small channel, preserves its own name. . . .

Chapter 30 . . .

Chapter 31 - Gallia Belgica.

The whole of Gaul that is comprehended under the general name of Comata,"

[Footnote. Transalpine Gaul, with the exception of that part of it called Narbonensis, was called Gallia Comata, from the custom of the people allowing their hair to grow to a great length.]

"is divided into three races of people, which are more especially kept distinct from each other by the following rivers. From the Scaldis to the Sequana"

[Footnote. From the Scheldt to the Seine.]

"it is Belgic Gaul; from the Sequana to the Garumna"

[Footnote. From the Seine to the Garonne.]

"it is Celtic Gaul or Lugdunensis;"

[Footnote. Lyonese Gaul, from Lugdunum, the ancient name of the city of Lyons.]

"and from the Garumna to the promontory of the Pyrenaean range it is Aquitanian Gaul, formerly called Aremorica."

[Footnote. Said by Camden to be derived from the Celtic words Ar-mor, 'by the Sea.'].

"Agrippa makes the entire length of the coast of Gaul to be 1800 miles, measured from the Rhine to the Pyrenees: and its length, from the ocean to the mountains of Gebenna and Jura, excluding therefrom Gallia Narbonensis, he computes at 420 miles, the breadth being 318.

Beginning at the Scaldis, the parts beyond are inhabited by the Toxandri, who are divided into various peoples with many names; after whom come the Menapii, the Morini, the Oromarsaci, who are adjacent to the burgh which is known as Gesoriacum [Boulogne], the Britanni, the Ambiani, the Bellovaci, the Hassi, and more in the interior, the Catoslugi, the Atrebates, the Nervii, a free people, the Veromandui, the Suaeuconi, the Suessiones, a free people, the Ulmanetes, a free people, the Tungri, the Sunuci, the Frisiabones, the Betasi, the Leuci, a free people, the Treveri, who were formerly free, and the Lingones, a federal state, the federal Remi, the Mediomatrici, the Sequani, the Raurici, and the Helvetii. The Roman colonies are Equestris and Rauriaca. The nations of Germany which dwell in this province, near the sources of the Rhine, are the Nemetes, the Triboci, and the Vangiones; nearer again, the Ubii, the Colony of Agrippina, the Cugerni, the Batavi, and the peoples whom we have already mentioned as dwelling on the islands of the Rhine.

Chapter 32 - Gallia Lugdunensis.

That part of Gaul which is known as Lugdunensis contains the Lexovii, the Vellocasses, the Galeti, the Veneti, the Abrincatui, the Ossismi, and the celebrated river Ligeris, as also a most remarkable peninsula [Finisterre], which extends into the ocean at the extremity of the territory of the Ossismi, the circumference of which is 625 miles, and its breadth at the neck 125. Beyond this are the Nannetes, and in the interior are the Aedui, a federal people, the Carnuti, a federal people, the Boii, the Senones, the Auderci, both those surnamed Eburovices and those called Cenomanni, the Meldi, a free people, the Parisii, the Tricasses, the Andecavi, the Viducasses, the Bodiocasses, the Venelli, the Cariosvelites, the Diablinti, the Rhedones, the Turones, the Atesui, and the Secusiani, a free people, in whose territory is the colony of Lugdunum.

Chapter 33 - Gallia Aquitanica.

In Aquitanica are the Ambilatri, the Anagnutes, the Pictones, the Siantoni, a free people, the Bituriges, surnamed Vivisci, the Aquitani, from whom the province derives its name, the Sediboviates, the Convenae, who together form one town, the Begerri, the Tarbelli, Quatuorsignani, and Cocosates Sexsignani, the Venami, the Onobrisates, the Belendi, and then the Pyrenaean range. Below these are the Monesi, the Oscidates a mountain race, the Sibyllates, the Componi, the Bercorcates, the Pindedunni, the Lassunni, the Vellates, the Tornates, the Consoranni, the Ausci, the Elusates, the Sottiates, the Oscidates Campestres, the Successes, the Tarusates, the Basabocates, the Vassei, the Sennates, and the Cambolectri Agessinates. Joining up to the Pictones are the Bituriges, a free people, who are also known as the Cubi, and then the Lemovices, the Arveni, a free people, and the Gabales.

Again, adjoining the province of Narbonensis are the Ruteni, the Cadurci, the Nitiobriges, and the Petrocori, separated by the river Tarnis from the Tolosani. The seas around the coast are the Northern Ocean, flowing up to the mouth of the Rhine, the Britannic Ocean between the Rhine and the Sequana, and between it and the Pyrenees, the Gallic Ocean. There are many islands belonging to the Veneti, which bear the name of 'Veneticae,' as also in the Aquitanic Gulf, that of Uliarus.

Chapter 34 - Nearer Spain, Its Coast Along the Gallic Ocean

At the promontory of the Pyrenees Spain begins, more narrow, not only than Gaul, but even than itself in its other parts, as we have previously mentioned, seeing to what an immense extent it is here hemmed in by the ocean on the one side, and by the Iberian Sea on the other. A chain of the Pyrenees, extending from due east to south west, divides Spain into two parts, the smaller one to the north, the larger to the south. The first coast that presents itself is that of Nearer Spain, otherwise called Tarraconensis. On leaving the Pyrenees and proceeding along the coast, we meet with the forest ranges of the Vascones, Olarso, the towns of the Vardali, the Morosgi, Menosca, Vesperies, and the Port of Amanus, where now stands the colony of Flariobriga. We then come to the district of the nine states of the Cantabri,"

[Footnote. According to Ptolemy, the Cantabri possessed the western part of the province of La Montana, and the northern parts of the province of Palencia and Toro.]

"the river Sauga, and the Port of Victoria of the Juliobrigenses, from which place the sources of the Iberus are distant forty miles. We next come to the Port of Blendium, the Orgenomesci, a people of the Cantabri, Vereasueca their port, the country of the Astures, the town of Noega, and on a peninsula, the Paesici. Next to these we have, belonging to the jurisdiction of Lucus,"

[Footnote. Now Lugo in Gallicia.]

"after passing the river Navilubio, the Cibarci, the Egovarri, surnamed Namarini, the Iadoni, the Arrotrebae, the Celtic Promontory, the rivers Florius and Nelo, the Celtici, surnamed Neri, and above them the Tamarici, in whose peninsula are the three altars called Sestianae, and dedicated to Augustus; the Corpori, the town of Noela, the Celtici surnamed Praesamarci, and the Cileni: of the islands, those worthy of mention are Corticata and Aunios. After passing the Celini, belonging to the jurisdiction of the Bracari, we have the Heleni, the Gravii, and the fortress of Tyde, all of them deriving their origin from the Greeks. Also, the islands called Cicae, the famous city of Abobrica, the river Minius,"

[Footnote. The Minho.]

"four miles wide at its mouth, the Leuni, the Seurbi, and Augusta, a town of the Bracari, above whom lies Gallaecia. We then come to the river Limia, and the river Durius, one of the largest in Spain, and which rises in the district of the Pelendones, passes near Numantia, and through the Arevaci and the Vaccaei, dividing the Vettones from Asturia, the Gallaeci from Lusitania, and separating the Turduli from the Bracari. The whole of the region here mentioned from the Pyrenees is full of mines of gold, silver, iron, and lead, both black and white."

[Footnote. Both lead properly so called, and tin.]"(17.1)

The importance of mistletoe to the Druids attracted both Pliny's attention and his scorn. At the present day mistletoe is used as a house decoration at Christmas whilst it is excluded in the decoration of churches. Mistletoe is a parasitic plant more commonly found growing on fruit trees in greater abundance than on oaks in the modern environment.

Pliny: Natural History book 16, chapter 95 [Bostock and Riley]

"Upon this occasion we must not admit to mention the admiration that is lavished upon this plant by the Gauls. The Druids - for that is the name they give to their magicians - held nothing more sacred than the mistletoe and the tree that bears it, supposing always that tree to be the robur. Of itself the robur is selected by them to form whole groves, and they perform none of their religious rites without employing branches of it; so much so, that it is very probable that the priests themselves may have received their name from the Greek name for that tree. In fact, it is the notion with them that everything that grows on it has been sent immediately from heaven, and the mistletoe upon it is a proof that the tree has been selected by God himself as an object of his especial favour.

The mistletoe, however, is but rarely found upon the robur; and when found, is gathered with rites replete with religious awe. This is done more particularly on the fifth day of the moon, the day which is the beginning of their months and years, as also of their ages, which, with them, are but thirty years. This day they select because the moon, though not yet in the middle of her course, has already considerable power and influence; and they call her by a name which signifies, in their language, the all-healing. Having made all due preparation for the sacrifice and a banquet beneath the trees, they bring thither two white bulls, the horns of which are bound then for the first time. Clad in a white robe the priest ascends the tree, and cuts the mistletoe with a golden sickle, which is received by others in a white cloak. They then immolate the victims, offering up their prayers that God will render this gift of his propitious to those to whom he has so granted it. It is the belief with them that the mistletoe, taken in drink, will impart fecundity to all animals that are barren, and that it is an antidote for all poisons. Such are the religious feelings which we find entertained towards trifling objects among nearly all nations."(17.2)

It is a thought, but nothing more, that nuances in the pharmacological properties of mistletoe may rest with the variety of host plant.

No doubt it was the fifth night of the moon that was recognised as the first of the month owing to the Celtic habit of reckoning elapsed time by nights, see also Caesar's, *Gallic War* 6.18. The thirty years is interpreted as a Celtic cycle of time, a 'Celtic century' unit for recording time. A sixty-year cycle is preferred by the Chinese in their longstanding calendar.

The Phoenicians, sailing out of Gades (Cadiz), were among the early traders in Cornish tin. Whilst beyond proof, it is not beyond reason that, at a prior date, merchants serving the market in the Cretan civilisation had established a supply route. The tin was first mined by members of a society in Cornwall which predated the arrival of Celtic peoples and their culture. Whether Iron Age technology was absorbed with or without an accompanying imposition of a Celtic hierarchy is examined in other publications. The language of Cornwall in the post Roman era was Celtic.

Pliny: Natural History book 7, chapter 57 [Bostock and Riley]
Chapter 57.(56.) - The Inventors of Various Things.
" ... Midacritus
[Footnote. We have no account of any individual bearing this name, and it has been proposed by Hardonin to substitute for it 'Midas Phrygius,' who is said, both by Hyginus and by Cassiodorus, to have been the discoverer of lead. -B.]
was the first who brought tin from the island called Cassiteris.
[Footnote. From the accounts of Pliny, B.iv.c.36, as well as of Strabo, and the other ancient geographers, it appears, that he here alludes to the Scilly Isles, including, probably, the western extremity of Cornwall. We are informed by Herodotus, B.iii.c.115, that tin was brought from them, and they were hence named the 'tin islands,' from the Greek word for tin, ...]
The Cyclopes invented the art of working iron.
[Footnote. According to Pausanias, the art of forging iron was discovered by Glancus of Chios. Strabo ascribes it to the Idean Dactyli, and the art of manufacturing utensils of bronze and iron to the Telchines; the former were inhabitants of Crete, the latter of Rhodes. -B.]"(17.3)

One explanation as to why the Cyclops were portrayed with the distinguishing characteristic of apparently having only one eye was because of the head armour which they wore having a single aperture to see through. Alternatively, they could have been archers and got the 'nickname' from their one eyed appearance as a foe. The Cyclops of Greek mythology are said to have occupied Sicily whereas in this instance they were in all probability a peoples of Asia. Pliny is likely to be correct when he records that iron working reached the Mediterranean world from the frontiers of Asia. The Indo-European Hittites who crossed into Asia Minor about 2,500 BC and whose empire collapsed by 1200 BC were users of iron.

The Welsh 'cwrwgle', in English coracle, or perhaps a larger vessel for coastal work had been drawn to the attention of Pliny.

Pliny: Natural History book 7, chapter 57 [Bostock and Riley]
Chapter 57.(56.) - The Inventors of Various Things.
" . . . Danais was the first who passed over in a ship from Egypt to Greece. Before his time, they used to sail on rafts, which had been invented by King Erythras, to pass from one island to another in the Red Sea. There are some writers to be found, who are of the opinion that they were first thought of by the Mysians and the Trojans, for the purpose of crossing the Hellespont into Thrace. Even at the present day, they are made in the British ocean, of wicker-work covered with hides; on the Nile they are made of papyrus, rushes, and reeds."(17.4)

The deliberate mating of dogs with wolves to increase the sharp edge of the dogs must have been in addition to the random mating that took place in areas where wolves were present. As Pliny had spent time in Gaul, this data is assessed as coming from his own observation.

Pliny: Natural History book 8, chapter 61 [Bostock and Riley]
Chapter 61.(40.) - The Qualities of the Dog.
" . . . The Gauls do the same with the wolf and the dog; and their packs of hounds have, each of them, one of these dogs, which acts as their guide and leader. This dog they follow in the chase, and him they carefully obey; for these animals have even a notion of subordination among themselves."(17.5)

The mattresses and embroidered carpets of the Gauls are not in general to be found among the archaeological finds on any excavation. Fortunately they were of sufficient interest to be noted by Pliny as were the British oysters.

Pliny: Natural History book 8, chapter 73 [Bostock and Riley]
Chapter 73.(43.) - The Different Kinds of Wool, and their Colours.
"The thick, flocky wool has been esteemed for the manufacture of carpets from the very earliest times; it is quite clear from what we read in Homer, that they were in use in his time.
[Footnote. Od.B.iv.1.427. 'And to throw on fair coverlets of purple, and to lay carpets upon them.']
The Gauls embroider them in a different manner from that which is practised by the Parthians. Wool is compressed also for making a felt, which, if soaked in vinegar, is capable of resisting iron even; and, what is still more, after having gone through the last process, wool will even resist fire; the refuse, too, when taken out of the vat of the scourer, is used in making mattresses, an invention, I fancy, of the Gauls. At all events, it is by Gallic names that we distinguish the different sort of mattresses at the present day; but I am not well able to say at what period wool began to be employed for this purpose. Our ancestors made use of straw for the purpose of sleeping upon, just as they do at present when at camp."(17.6)

Pliny: Natural History book 9, chapter 79 [Bostock and Riley]
Chapter 79.(54.) - The first Person that Formed Artificial Oyster-Beds
"The British shores had not as yet sent their supplies, at the time when Orata thus ennobled the Lucrine oysters:"(17.7)

It is reassuring that in Pliny's day, as ever, the next generation were portrayed as being softer men than their fathers.

Pliny: Natural History book 10, chapter 27 [Bostock and Riley]
Chapter 27.- Who First Taught Us to Use the Livers of the Goose for Food.
"A second income, too, is also to be derived from the feathers of the white goose. In some places, this animal is plucked twice a year, upon which the feathers quickly grow again. Those are the softest which lie nearest to the body, and those that come from Germany are the most esteemed: the geese there are white, but of small size, and are called gantae. The price paid for their feathers is five denarii per pound. It is from this fruitful source that we have repeated charges brought against the commanders of our auxiliaries, who are in the habit of detaching whole cohorts from the posts where they ought to be on guard, in pursuit of these birds: indeed we have come to such a pitch of effeminacy, that now-a-days, not even the men can think of lying down without the aid of the goose's feathers by way of pillow."(17.8)

The eagle became the predominant emblem of the legions when Rome was emerging as a Mediterranean power. A Caius Marius was first elected consul in 108 BC and for a second time in 104 BC.

Pliny: Natural History book 10, chapter 5 [Bostock and Riley]
Chapter 5.(4.) - When the Eagle was First Used as the Standard of the Roman Legions.
"Caius Marius, in his second consulship, assigned the eagle exclusively to the Roman Legions. Before that period it had only held the first rank, there being four others as well, the wolf, the minotaur, the horse, and the wild boar, each of which preceded a single division. Some few years before his time it had begun to be the custom to carry the eagle only into battle, the other standards being left behind in camp; Marius, however, abolished the rest of them entirely."(17.9)

"All Gaul is divided into three parts, One of which the Belgae inhabit, the Aquitani another, those who in their own language are called Celts, in ours Gauls, the third. . . . The river Garonne separates the Gauls from the Aquitani; the Marne and the Seine separate them from the Belgae. . . . " (Caesar Gallic War 1.1)

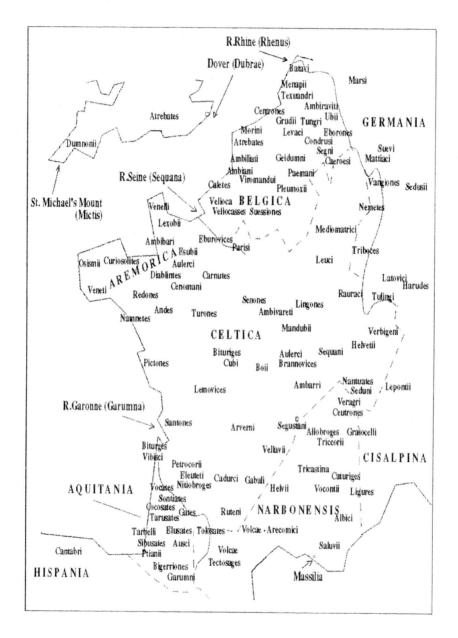

GAUL

"The whole vast country of Germany is separated from Gaul, from Rhaetia, and Pannonia, by the Rhine and the Danube; from Dacia and Sarmatia, by a chain of mountains, and, where the mountains subside, mutual dread forms a sufficient barrier. The rest is bounded by the ocean, . . . " (Tacitus Germania 1.1)

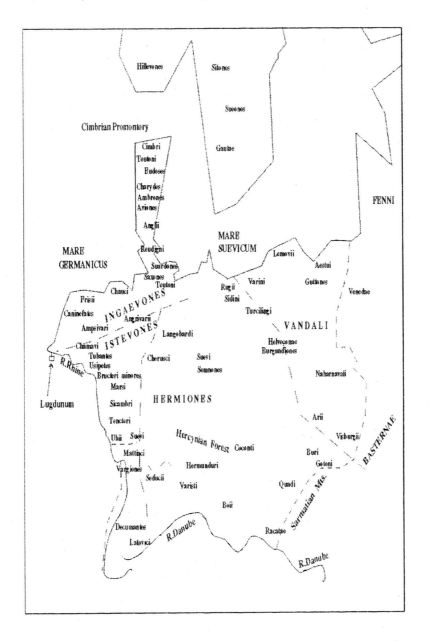

GERMANIA

87

12   MELA

Mela Pomponius was a Spaniard who was alive in 45 AD. He wrote a geography in three books entitled *De Situ Orbis* (4).

The translation was made by Arthur Golding in the sixteenth century.

Mela: On the Situation of the World, book 3, 6. [Arthur Golding]
"On Britain
. . . It beareth Nations, and Kinges of Nations, but they are all uncivill, and the further they be from the mayne Land, so much the more unacquainted with the wealth of other Nations; onely ritch of Cattaell and Land: and (whether it be for to beautifie themselves, or for some other purpose) they be stayned all theyr bodies over. They seeke occassion of Warre, and pick quarrels one with an other from time to time, specially for desire of soueragnitie, and to enlarge those things which they possesse. They fight not onelie on horsebacke and on foote, but also in Wagons and Chariottes, and are armed after the manner of the Galles. They cal those Chariots Couines, which are set with sithes round about the naves.

Above Brittaine is Ireland, almost of like space, but on both sides equall, with shores euelong, of an evyll ayre to rypen things that are sowne, but so aboundant of Grasse which is not onelie rancke but also sweete, that the Cattell may in small parte of the daye fyll themselves, and if they be not kept from feedying, they burste with grazing over-long.

The inhabiters thereof are unnurtured and ignorant of all vertues more than other Nations, but yet have they some knowledge, howbeit altogether voide of godlinesse."(18.1).

13   PLUTARCH

Any scepticism arising in response to the claim of Servius (1.8) that Julius Caesar was captured while in Gaul is tempered by a report that the Arveni had Caesar's sword hanging in their temple. Plutarch included such a claim in his life of Caesar. Also, the information that Caesar employed two secretaries for his correspondence and dictated to them between engagements was supplied by Plutarch. Suetonius stated that, when appropriate, Caesar used a code of replacing a letter of the contemporary Latin 23 (?) letter alphabet with one 4 places lower, thus B became E etc.

Plutarch's Lives: Gaius Julius Caesar [Langhorne]
"When he slept, it was commonly upon a march, either in a chariot or a litter, that rest might be no hindrance to business. In the daytime he visited the castles, cities, and fortified camps, with a servant at his side, whom he employed, on such occasions, to write for him, and with a soldier behind, who carried a sword. By these means he travelled so fast, and with so little interruption, as to reach the Rhone in eight days after his first setting out for those parts from Rome.

He was a good horseman in his early years, and brought that exercise to such perfection by practice that he could sit a horse at full speed with his hands behind him. In this expedition he also accustomed himself to dictate letters as he rode on horseback, and found sufficient employment for two secretaries at once, or, according to Oppius, for more. It is also said, that Caesar was the first to communicate his thoughts by letter to his friends, who were in the same city with him, when any urgent affair required it, and the multitude of business or great extent of the city did not admit of an interview. . . .

Many nations had entered into the league; the principal of which were the Arveni
  [Footnote. The people of Auvergne, particularly those of Clermont and St. Flour.]
and Carnutes.
  [Footnote. The people of Chartres and Orleans.].
  The chief direction of the war was given to Vercingetorix, whose father the Gauls had put to death, for attempting at monarchy. . . But had he stayed a little longer, till Caesar was actually engaged in the civil war, the terrors of the Gauls would not have been less dreadful to Italy now, than those of the Cimbri were formerly. . . .
Thus he went on, till the Edui
  [Footnote. The people of Autun, Lyons, Macon, Chalons upon Sone [sic], and Nevers.]
also revolted, who had styled themselves as brothers to the Romans, and had been treated with particular regard. Their joining the insurgents spread uneasiness and dismay throughout Caesar's army. He, therefore, decamped in all haste, and traversed the country of the Lingones, in order to come into that of the Sequani,
  [Footnote. The district of Besancon.]
who were fast friends, and nearer to Italy than the rest of the Gauls. The enemy followed him thither, and surrounded him. Caesar, without being in the least disconcerted, sustained the conflict, and after a long and bloody action, in which the Germans were particularly serviceable to him, gave them a total defeat. But he seems to have received some check at first, for the Arveni still show a sword suspended in one of their temples, which they declare was taken from Caesar. His friends pointed it out to him afterwards, but he only laughed; and when they were for having it taken down, he would not suffer it, because he considered it as a thing consecrated to the gods."

The clause *"But he seems to have received some check at first"* arouses a suspicion that there was a disaster, and a disaster not prudent to link to the name of the deified Caesar and the reputation of the Roman state, even in 100 AD. Plutarch continued in a vein that showed disbelief at the events surrounding the supposed great victory by the forces under Caesar at Alesia. This victory culminated in the surrender of Vercingetorix to Caesar. It may be that Plutarch was seeking to downgrade the achievements of Caesar. Vercingetorix was exhibited at a triumph in Rome and at a later date killed when in prison. Not so very long after these events at Alesia, Caesar with his forces crossed the River Rubicon, which divides Cisalpine Gaul from Italy, and became embroiled in the civil war.

"Most of those who escaped out of the battle, retired into Alesia
  [Footnote. Caesar calls it Alexia, now Alisc, near Flavigny.]
with their king. Caesar immediately invested the town, though it appeared impregnable, as well on account of the height of the walls, as the number of troops there was to defend it. During the siege he found himself exposed to a danger from without, which makes imagination giddy to think on. All the bravest men in Gaul assembled from every quarter, and came armed to the relief of the place, to the number of three hundred thousand; and there were not less than seventy thousand combatants within the walls. Thus shut up between two armies, he was forced to draw two lines of circumvallation, the interior one against the town, and that without against the troops that came to its succour; for, could the two armies have joined, he had been absolutely lost.

This dangerous action at Alesia contributed to Caesar's renown on many accounts. Indeed, he exerted a more adventurous courage and greater generalship than on any other occasion. But what seems very astonishing, is, that he could engage and conquer so many myriads without, and keep the action a secret to the troops in the town.

[Footnote. Caesar says, that those in the town had a distinct view of the battle.]

It is still more wonderful that the Romans, who were left before the walls, should not know it, till the victory was announced by the cries of the men in Alesia, and the lamentations of the women, who saw the Romans on each side of the town bringing to their camp a number of shields adorned with gold and silver, helmets stained with blood, drinking vessels, and tents of the Gaulish fashion. Thus did this vast multitude vanish and disappear like a phantom, or a dream, the greatest part being killed on the spot."(19.1)

Suetonius confided in his readers that Gnaeus Pompey had divorced Mucia, the mother of three of his children, because of her affair with Caesar. Pompey then married Caesar's daughter Julia. Caesar's wife Cornelia, the mother of Julia, died and in due course he married Pompeia, the daughter of Quintus Pompey and grand-daughter of Sulla. It is noted that the Langhorne translation lists Pompeia as his third wife. The expression 'Caesar's wife must be above suspicion' has a home in this passage from Plutarch, as do a handful of phrases that find an echo in the words of Shakespeare:

"Let me have men about me that are fat;
Sleek headed men and such as sleep at nights;
Yon Cassius has a lean and hungry look;
He thinks too much: such men are dangerous.

. . .

The ides of March are come.
Aye Caesar, but not yet gone."etc.

Caesar divorced Pompeia and married Calpurnia, the daughter of Piso.

Plutarch's Lives: Gaius Julius Caesar [Langhorne]
"It had long been the custom in Rome, for the aged women to have funeral panegyrics, but not the young. Caesar first broke through it, by pronouncing one for his own wife, who died in her prime. . . . When that commission was expired, he took Pompeia to his third wife; having a daughter by his first wife Cornelia, whom he afterwards married to Pompey the Great. . . .

There was a young patrician, named Publius Clodius. . . . This man entertained a passion for Pompeia, Caesar's wife, nor did she discountenance it. . . . Aurelia, Caesar's mother, who was a woman of great virtue and prudence, . . . Aurelia's woman ran up to the lights and the company, crying out she had found a man in the house. . . . At length Clodius was found lurking in the chamber of the maid-servant who had introduced him . . . Caesar immediately divorced Pompeia; yet, when called as an evidence on the trial, he declared he knew nothing of what was alleged against Clodius. As this declaration appeared somewhat strange, the accuser demanded, why, if that was the case, he had divorced his wife: 'Because,' said he, 'I would have the chastity of my wife clear even of suspicion.' . . , Clodius came off clear, . . . , for he [Caesar] was of a slender make, fair, of a delicate constitution, and subject to violent headach[e]s and epileptic fits. He had the first attack of the falling sickness at Corduba. . . .

Cassius perceiving his friend's ambition a little stimulated by these papers, began to ply him closer than before, and spur him on to the great enterprise, for he had a particular enmity against Caesar, for the reasons which we have mentioned in the life of Brutus. Caesar, too, had some suspicion of him, and he even said one day to his friends, 'What think you of Cassius? I do not like his pale looks.' Another time, when Anthony and Dolabella were accused of some designs against his person and government, he said, 'I have no apprehensions from those fat and sleek men; I rather fear the pale and lean ones;' meaning Cassius and Brutus. . . .

What is still more extraordinary, many report, that a certain soothsayer fore-warned him of a great danger which threatened him on the ides of March, and that when the day was come, as he was going to the senate-house, he called to the soothsayer, and said laughingly, 'The ides of March are come;' to which he answered softly, 'Yes; but they are not gone.' . . . The same night, as he was in bed with his wife. . . . Calpurnia in a sleep, uttering broken words and inarticulate groans. . . .

Caesar died at the age of fifty-six, . . ."(19.2)

Suetonius gave Caesar's age at death as 55 years old. This episode with Clodius found its way into a letter from Cicero written in 55 BC.

Cicero: Letter to Lentulus (A.U.699) - letter 17, book 2 [Melmoth]
" . . . But let me entreat you to reflect a moment on the subsequent conduct of my political associates. In the first place, they screened from punishment that infamous intruder on the matron-mysteries, who shewed no more reverence for the awful ceremonies of the goddess in whose honour these sacred solemnities are celebrated, than for the chastity of his three sisters. And thus, by preventing a worthy tribune of the people from obtaining that justice upon Clodius which he endeavoured to procure, they deprived future times of a most salutary example of chastised sedition."(2.6)

Julius Caesar had good reason to entertain the notion he was the teenage father of Brutus.

Plutarch's Lives: Marcus Brutus [Langhorne]
"Brutus . . . his mother Servilia. Cato, the philosopher, was the brother of Servilia . . . .
When Rome was divided into two factions, and Pompey and Caesar were in arms against each other, it was generally believed that Brutus would join Caesar, because his father had been put to death by Pompey. However, he thought it his duty to sacrifice his sentiments to the interest of his country; and judging Pompey's to be the better cause, he joined his party, . . .
Caesar, it is said, had so high an esteem for him, that he ordered his officers by all means to save him, if he would surrender himself; and, if he refused, to let him escape with his life. Some have placed this kindness to the account of Servilia, the mother of Brutus, with whom Caesar had connexions of a tender nature in the early part of his life. Besides, as this amour was in full blow about the time when Brutus was born, Caesar had some reason to believe he might be his son."(19.3)

In 46 BC, Caesar introduced the Julian Calendar.

Plutarch's Lives: Gaius Julius Caesar [Langhorne]
"He completed, however, the regulation of the calendar, and corrected the erroneous computation of time, agreeably to a plan which he had ingeniously contrived, and which proved of great utility. For it was not only in ancient times that the Roman months so ill agreed with the revolution of the year, that the festivals and days of sacrifice, by little and little, fell back into seasons quite the opposite to those of their institution; but even in the time of Caesar, when the solar year was made use of, the generality lived in perfect ignorance of the matter; and the priests, who were the only persons that knew any thing about it, used to add all at once, and when nobody expected it, an intercalary month, called Mercidonius, of which Numa was the inventor. That remedy, however, proved far too weak, and was far from operating extensively enough, to correct the great miscomputations of time; as we have observed in that prince's life."(19.4)

Suetonius stated that Caesar extended the standard year from 355 days to 365 plus one extra day added every fourth year and did away with the short month previously included after February in every second year. In the Roman equivalent of 46 BC, Caesar added an extra two months between November and December in addition to the one inserted that year after February giving a fifteen month year in order to make the next 1st January fall on the correct day. Suetonius need not have grasped the precise reasoning behind the changes implemented by Caesar.

In Plutarch's text there are indications of the methods used by the German women when divining.

Plutarch's Lives: Gaius Julius Caesar [Langhorne]
" . . . Ariovistus [king of the Germans] . . . saw his own troops were disheartened. They were dispirited still more by the prophecies of their matrons who had the care of divining, and used to do it by the eddies of rivers, the windings, the murmurs, or other noise made by the stream. On this occasion they charged the army not to give battle before the new moon appeared."(19.5)

Plutarch, a Greek, lived in the period 50 AD to 125 AD. He wrote in his lives of illustrious men about the life of Sertorius, a Roman who was an opponent of Sulla and was fighting in Spain from 81 BC. Sertorius was assassinated in 69 BC. The tale of the fawn exemplifies the superstitious nature of the Iberians / Celtiberians / Celts. It introduces the prospect that similar animals were kept by priests elsewhere.

Plutarch's Lives: Sertorius [Langhorne]
"And to those advantages he added artiface to amuse and gain the people. That of the hind was none of the least. Spanus, a countryman who lived in those parts, happening to fall in with a hind which had newly yeaned, and which was flying from the hunters, failed in his attempt to take her; but charmed with the uncommon colour of the fawn, which was a perfect white, he pursued and took it. By good fortune Sertorius had his camp in that neighbourhood; and whatever was brought to him taken in hunting, or of the productions of the field, he received with pleasure, and returned the civility with interest.

The countryman went and offered him the fawn. He received this present like the rest, and at first took no extraordinary notice of it. But in time it became so tractable and fond of him, that it would come when he called, follow him wherever he went, and learned to bear the hurry and tumult of the camp. By little and little he brought the people to believe there was something sacred and mysterious in the affair; giving it out that the fawn was a gift from Diana, and that it discovered to him many important secrets. For he knew the natural power of superstition over the minds of the barbarians. In pursuance of his scheme, when the enemy was making a private eruption into the country under his command, or persuading some city to revolt, he pretended the fawn had appeared to him in a dream, and warned him to have his forces ready. And if he had intelligence of some victory gained by his officers, he used to conceal the messenger, and produce the fawn crowned with flowers for its good tidings; bidding the people to rejoice and sacrifice to the gods, on account of some news they would soon hear.

By this invention he made them so tractable that they obeyed his orders in everything without hesitation, no longer considering themselves as under the conduct of a stranger, but the immediate direction of heaven. And the astonishing increase of his power, far beyond all they could rationally expect, confirmed them in that persuasion. - For with two thousand six hundred men . . . he carried on war against four Roman generals, who had a hundred and twenty thousand foot, six thousand horse . . . "(19.6)

The quotations above from the lives of Caesar, Brutus and Sertorius were taken from the translation of Plutarch by J. and W. Langhorne in the edition published in 1859 by Henry G.Bohn. The quotations from the lives of Marius and Sylla, which follow, are taken from the 'Dryden Translation' of Plutarch's Lives as edited by A.H.Clough and published by the Athenaeum Press.

The interaction between the Germanic tribes and the Romans in the years surrounding 100 BC approximates to the following summary of events. In 184 BC the Romans expanded to the north east and the Adriatic, they set up a colony at Aquileia and subsequently annexed Macedonia. In 114 BC, C. Porcius Cato marched the Roman army from Macedonia towards the Danube and they were severely defeated by the Celtic Scordisci; the Romans finally were victorious by 110 BC when M. Minucius reached the Danube where they encountered to their cost the wagon living Germanic Cimbri, 'the Champions'. In 113 BC the Cimbri were known to be at the Carnic Alps, near Aquileia, and they totally defeated the Romans under Cn. Papirius Carbo and then moved over to Jura, north of the Romanised province of Narbonne. Here they were attacked by M. Junius Silanus in 109 BC and again the Romans were crushed.

In 105 BC, the Cimbri under their leader Boiorix, or Boeorix, moved towards Italy, routed the Romans under M. Aurelius Scaurus on the banks of the River Rhone, then routed another army under the command of Caepio at Arausio (Orange) followed by the Roman army under consul Cn. Mallius (or Manlius) Maximus on or about the sixth of October 105 BC. The Roman armies were slain.

The Cimbri then turned aside from Italy into Spain and were there opposed by the Celt Iberians. By 103 BC the Cimbri had moved northwards along the coast of the Atlantic Ocean and English Channel where around the area of the River Seine, or further north, they met up with the Teutones and other German tribes.

At some juncture a group of the Cimbri again moved south to the Carnic Alps. At the same time members of the Teutones and Ambrones approached Italy from the west and were defeated by a Roman army under Marius at Sextiae (Aix on Seilles in Provence) in 102 BC. The Cimbri, perhaps intermixed with Celtic Helvetii, crossed the Brenner Pass and broke the Roman legions in the area of the River Po in Northern Italy, but were themselves later well beaten at the battle of Vercellae in 101 BC by Roman armies under the command of Marius (in his 5th consulship) and Catulus.

The section in 'Dryden' on the life of Marius was translated by Miles Stapleton. Plutarch was writing at the turn of the first century AD but can be expected to have had available histories written closer to the dates at which the actions occurred. As the Roman armies were eventually victorious in defending their own territory there was no need for Plutarch to undervalue the prowess of their foe, though exaggeration might appear inappropriate when describing the German tribes. It would seem that the heat of the day was to the significant advantage of the Roman army in the battle against the Cimbri at Vercellae.

Plutarch's Lives: Caius Marius [Dryden]
"Jugurtha's apprehension was only just known, when the news of the invasion of the Teutones and Cimbri began. The accounts at first exceeded all credit, as to the number and strength of the approaching army; but in the end the report proved much inferior to the truth, as they were three hundred thousand effective fighting men, besides a greater number of women and children. They professed to be seeking new countries to sustain their great multitudes, and cities where they might settle and inhabit, in the same way as they had heard the Celti before them had driven out the Tyrrhenians, and possessed themselves of the best part of Italy. Having had no commerce with the southern nations, and travelling over a wide extent of country, no man knew what people they were, or whence they came, that thus like a cloud burst over Gaul and Italy; yet by their grey eyes and the largeness of their stature, they were conjectured to be some of the German races dwelling by the northern sea; besides that, the Germans call plunderers Cimbri.

There are some that say, that the country of the Celti, in its vast size and extent, reaches from the farthest sea and the arctic regions to the lake Maeotis eastward, and to that part of Scythia which is near Pontus, and that there the nations mingle together; that they did not swarm out of their country all at once, or on a sudden, but advancing by force of arms, in the summer season, every year, in the course of time they crossed the whole continent. And thus, though each party had several appellations, yet the whole army was called by the common name Celto-Scythians. Others say that the Cimmerii, anciently known to the Greeks, were only a small part of the nation, who were driven out upon some quarrel among the Scythians, and passed all along from the lake Maeotis to Asia, under the conduct of one Lygdamis; and that the greater and more warlike part of them still inhabit the remotest regions lying upon the outer ocean. These, they say, live in a dark and woody country hardly penetrable by the sunbeams, the trees are so close and thick, extending into the interior as far as the Hercynian forest: and their position on the earth is under that part of heaven, where the pole is so elevated, that by the declination of the parallels, the zenith of the inhabitants seems to be but little distance from it; and that their days and nights being almost of an equal length, they divide their year into one of each. This was Homer's occasion for the story of Ulysses calling up the dead,"

94

Lake Maeotis is identified as the Sea of Azov, a north north east enclave of the Black Sea into which flows the River Don. In this context, Pontus, Pontus Euxinus in full, was the Black Sea. The Hercynian Forest was a name given to a swathe of land extending across central and northern Europe that was largely unknown territory to the Greeks and the Romans. The action of 'Lygdamis' leading the Germanic tribes west from Asia is similar to that of Odin within Nordic mythology.

> " [Footnote. When Ulysses bade Circe fulfil her promise, and send him on his way, she told him he must first visit the home of the dead and consult Tiresias; crossing the ocean, he would come to a shore and to the woods of Persephone. Accordingly, 'through the whole day the sails of the ship, travelling through the seas, were stretched; and the sun set and all ways were darkening, and she came to the ends of the deep-flowing ocean; there is the people and town of the Cimmerians, hidden in mist and cloud; the shining sun never looks on them with his rays, either when he climbs the starry heaven, or when he turns again from heaven to earth; darkness is spread over unhappy mortals. There we brought our ship to shore.']
> and from this region the people, anciently called Cimmerii, and afterwards, by an easy change, Cimbri, came into Italy. All this, however, is rather conjecture than an authentic history.
> Their numbers, most writers agree, were not less, but rather greater than reported. They were of invincible strength and fierceness in their wars, and hurried into battle with the violence of a devouring flame; none could withstand them; all they assaulted became their prey. Several of the greatest Roman commanders with their whole armies, that advanced for the defence of Transalpine Gaul, were ingloriously overthrown, and, indeed, by their faint resistance, chiefly gave them the impulse of marching towards Rome. . . . The Romans, being from all parts alarmed with this news, sent for Marius to undertake the war, . . . Thus it was decided; and Marius, bringing over his legions out of Africa on the very first day of January, which the Romans count the beginning of the year, . . . "

The first day of the Roman year is said to have been moved from March to January by Numa, see Plutarch's *Life of Numa*. Numa was among the earliest leaders in Rome following after Romulus. The Julian calendar was adhered to in the lifetime of Plutarch.

The theatrical use by Marius of the prophetess Martha was later echoed by the fawn of Sertorius.

> "Does the defeat of Carbo and Caepio who were vanquished by the enemy, affright him? Surely they were much inferior to Marius . . . And, in fact, he used solemnly to carry about in a litter, a Syrian woman, called Martha, a supposed prophetess, and to do sacrifice at her directions. . . . When she went to sacrifice, she wore a purple robe lined and buckled up, and had in her hand a little spear trimmed with ribbons and garlands. This theatrical show made many question, whether Marius really gave any credit to her himself, or only played the counterfeit, when he showed her publicly, to impose upon the soldiers. . . .

Thus they marched till they came to the place called Sextillius's Waters. . . . pointing to a river that ran near the enemy's camp. Now a great company of their boys and camp-followers, having neither drink for themselves nor for their horses, went down to that river; some taking axes and hatchets, and some, too, swords and darts with their pitchers, resolving to have water though they fought for it. These were the first encountered by a small party of the enemies; for most of them had just finished bathing, and were eating and drinking, and several were still bathing, the country thereabouts abounding in hot springs; so that the Romans partly fell upon them whilst they were enjoying themselves, and occupied with the novel sights and pleasantness of the place. Upon hearing the shouts, greater numbers still joining in the fight, it was not a little difficult for Marius to contain his soldiers, who were afraid of losing the camp-servants; and the more warlike part of the enemies, who had overthrown Manlius and Caepio, (they were called Ambrones, and were in number, one with another, above thirty thousand,) taking the alarm, leaped up and hurried to arms.

These, though they had just been gorging themselves with food, and were excited and disordered with drink, nevertheless did not advance with an unruly step, or in mere senseless fury, nor were their shouts mere inarticulate cries; but clashing their arms in concert, and keeping time as they leapt and bounded onward, they continually repeated their own name, 'Ambrones !' either to encourage one another, or to strike the greater terror into their enemies. . . . The river disordered the Ambrones; before they could draw up all their army on the other side of it, the Ligurians presently fell upon the van, and began to charge them hand to hand. The Romans, too, coming to their assistance, and from the higher ground pouring upon the enemy, forcibly repelled them, and the most of them (one thrusting another into the river) were there slain, and filled it with their blood and dead bodies. Those that got safe over, not daring to make head [Not venturing to face about – Stewart and Long], were slain by the Romans, as they fled to their camp and wagons where the women meeting them with swords and hatchets, and making a hideous outcry, set upon those that fled as well as those that pursued, the one as traitors, the other as enemies; and, mixing themselves with the combatants, with their bare arms pulling away the Roman shields, and laying hold on their swords, endured the wounds and slashing of bodies to the very last, with undaunted resolution. Thus the battle seems to have happened at that river rather by accident than by the design of the general."

Although these events were dressed up as a great Roman victory, an alternative scenario is that the Romans had stumbled upon a party of Ambrones who were enjoying a recreational swim, largely without clothes or a full complement of weapons. The Romans had also attacked some nearby wagons where the women were going about their daily business. At this juncture the Teutones had already "determined to march forward, hoping to reach the other side of the Alps without opposition, and, packing up their baggage, passed securely by the Roman camp"(20). They were leaving the area.

If the report is true that the Ambrones chanted their name when going to fight, then Ambrones could have been derived from the name of their special deity, thus leaving open the option that they had a different name for themselves.

"After the Romans were retired from the great slaughter of the Ambrones, night came on; but the army was not indulged, as was the usual custom, with songs of victory, drinking in their tents, and mutual entertainments, and (what is most welcome to soldiers after successful fighting) quiet sleep, but they passed that night, above all others, in fears and alarm. For their camp was without either rampart or palisade, and there remained thousands upon thousands of their enemies yet unconquered; to whom were joined as many of the Ambrones as escaped. There were heard from these, all through the night, wild bewailings, nothing like the sighs and groans of men, but a sort of wild-beastlike howling and roaring, joined with threats and lamentations rising from the vast multitude, and echoed among the neighbouring hills and hollow banks of the river. The whole plain was filled with hideous noise, insomuch that the Romans were not a little afraid, . . ."

The Cimbri were defeated at Vercellae by the Roman armies under the command of Marius and Catulus.

". . . passing the river Po, he endeavoured to keep the barbarians out of that part of Italy which lies south of it. . . . Marius answered, that the Romans never consulted their enemies when to fight; however, he would gratify the Cimbri so far; and so they fixed upon the third day after, and for the place, the plain near Vercellae, . . . Sylla, who was present at the fight, gives this account; . . . The infantry of the Cimbri marched quietly out of their fortifications, having their flanks equal to their front; every side of the army taking up thirty furlongs. Their horse, that were in number fifteen thousand, made a very splendid appearance. They wore helmets, made to resemble the heads and jaws of wild beasts, and other strange shapes, and heightening these with plumes of feathers, they made themselves appear taller than they were. They had breastplates of iron, and white glittering shields; and for their offensive arms, every one had two darts, and when they came hand to hand, they used large and heavy swords. . . .
whom Sylla says he was; adding that the Romans had great advantage of the heat and the sun that shone in the faces of the Cimbri. For they, well able to endure cold, and having been bred up, (as we observed before,) in cold and shady countries, were overcome with the excessive heat; they sweated extremely, and were much out of breath, being forced to hold their shields before their faces; for the battle was fought out not long after the summer solstice, or, as the Romans reckon, upon the third day before the new moon of the month now called August, and then Sextilis. . . . Here the greatest part and the most valiant of the enemies were cut to pieces; for those that fought in the front, that they might not break their ranks, were fast tied to one another, with long chains put through their belts. But as they pursued those that fled to their camp, they witnessed a most fearful tragedy; the women, standing in black clothes on their wagons, slew all that fled, some their husbands, some their brethren; others their fathers; and strangling their little children with their own hands, threw them under the wheels, and the feet of the cattle, and then killed themselves. They tell of one who hung herself from the end of the pole of a wagon, with her children tied dangling at her heels. The men, for want of trees, tied themselves, some to the horns of the oxen, others by the neck to their legs, that so pricking them on, by the starting and springing of the beasts, they might be torn and trodden to pieces. Yet for all they thus massacred themselves, above sixty thousand were taken prisoners, and those that were slain were said to be twice as many."(20.1)

Lucian Cornelius Sylla was set down as a contrast with Lysander in Plutarch's lives. The translation of 'Sylla' in the 'Dryden' edition was made by William Davies. The text refers to the memoirs which Sylla wrote in twenty two volumes. The content of these memoirs might have been used by Plutarch to enrich Plutarch's description of events. Sylla is painted as a brave but obnoxious character who rose to the rank of consul. This brief diversion is included as an example to demonstrate that not all leading Romans were noble. The removal of the library containing books written by Aristotle attracted the attention of Strabo in his *Geography*, book 13.1.54.

Plutarch's Lives: Sylla [Dryden]
"His general appearance may be known by his statues; only his blue eyes, of themselves extremely keen and glaring, were rendered all the more forbidding and terrible by the complexion of his face, in which white was mixed with rough blotches of fiery red. Hence, it is said, he was surnamed Sylla, and in allusion to it one of the scurrilous jesters at Athens made the verse upon him, 'Sylla is a mulberry sprinkled with meal'. . . .

Sylla imposed on Asia in general a tax of twenty thousand talents, and despoiled individually each family by the licentious behaviour and long residence of the soldiery in private quarters. For he ordained that every host should allow his guest four tetredrachms each day, and moreover entertain him, and as many friends as he should invite, with a supper; that a centurion should receive fifty drachmas a day, together with one suit of clothes to wear within doors, and another when he went abroad.

Having set out from Ephesus with the whole navy, he came the third day to anchor in the Piraeus. Here he was initiated in the mysteries, and seized for his use the library of Apellicon the Teian, in which were most of the works of Theophrastus and Aristotle, then not in general circulation. When the whole was afterwards conveyed to Rome, there, it is said, the greater part of the collection passed through the hands of Tyrannion the grammarian, and that Andronicus the Rhodian, having through his means the command of numerous copies, made the treatises public, and drew up the catalogues that are now current. . . . During Sylla's stay about Athens, his feet were attacked by a heavy benumbing pain, which Strabo calls the first inarticulate sounds of gout. . . . Notwithstanding this marriage, he kept company with actresses, musicians, and dancers, drinking with them on couches night and day. His chief favourites were Roscius the comedian Sorex the arch mime, and Metrobius the player, for whom, though past his prime, he still professed a passionate fondness. By these courses he encouraged a disease which had begun from some unimportant cause; and for a long time he failed to observe that his bowels were ulcerated, till at length the corrupted flesh broke out into lice. . . . Sylla not only foresaw his end, but may be also said to have written of it. For in the two and twentieth book of his Memoirs, which he finished two days before his death, . . . And the very day before his end, it being told him that the magistrate Granius deferred the payment of a public debt, in expectation of his death, he sent for him to his house, and placing his attendants about him, caused him to be strangled; but through the straining of his voice and body, the impostume breaking, he lost a great quantity of blood. Upon this, his strength failing him, after spending a troublesome night, he died, . . . "(20.2)

This account of Boudicca, elsewhere called Boadicea, was written around 200 AD, some four generations after the events of 61 AD. The physical description of her was either taken from an eyewitness report written at an earlier date or painted with imagination and a knowledge of Celtic dress.

Cassius Dio: Roman History book 62, chapter 2 [Herbert Baldwin Foster].
" But the person who most stirred their spirits and persuaded them to fight the Romans, who was deemed worthy to stand at their head and to have the conduct of the entire war, was a British woman, Buduica, of the royal family and possessed of greater judgement than often belongs to women. It was she who gathered the army to the number of nearly twelve myriads [A Greek myriad was ten thousand. – Chambers Dictionary.] and ascended a tribunal of marshy soil made after the Roman fashion. In person she was very tall, with a most sturdy figure and a piercing glance; her voice was harsh; a great mass of yellow hair fell below her waist and a large golden necklace clasped her throat; wound about her was a tunic of every conceivable colour and over it a thick chlamys [A short cloak worn by men in ancient Greece. – Chambers Dictionary.] had been fastened with a broach. This was her constant attire. She now grasped a spear to aid her in terrifying all beholders and spoke as follows:- "(21.1)

Chambers Dictionary defines a Greek *myriad* as ten thousand and a *chlamys* as a short cloak worn by men in ancient Greece.

Cassius Dio then put a rousing speech into the mouth of Boudicca and continued as follows, clearly showing he held Boudicca a better man than her contemporary, the emperor Nero.

Cassius Dio: Roman History book 62, chapter 6 and 7 [Herbert Baldwin Foster].
"6. At these words, employing a species of divination, she let a hare escape from her bosom, and as it ran in what they considered a lucky direction, the whole multitude shouted with pleasure, and Buduica raising her hand to heaven, spoke: 'I thank thee, Andraste, and call upon thee, who are a woman, being myself also a woman that rules not burden-bearing Egyptians like Nitocris, nor merchant Assyrians like Semiramis (of these things we have heard from the Romans), nor even the Romans themselves, as did Messalina first and later Agrippina; - at present their chief is Nero, in name a man, in fact a woman, as is shown by his singing, his playing the cithara, his adorning himself: - but ruling as I do men of Britain that know not how to till the soil or ply a trade yet are thoroughly versed in the arts of war and hold all things common, even children and wives; whereof the latter possess the same valo[u]r as the males: being therefore queen of such men and such women I supplicate and pray thee for victory and salvation and liberty against men insolent, unjust, insatiable, impious, - if, indeed we ought to term those creatures men who wash in warm water, eat artificial dainties, drink unmixed wine, anoint themselves with myrrh, sleep on soft couches with boys for bedfellows (and past their prime at that), are slaves to a zither-player, yes, an inferior zither-player. Wherefore may this Domitia-Nero woman reign no more over you or over me: let the wench sing and play the despot over the Romans. They surely deserve to be in slavery to such a being whose tyranny they have patiently borne already this long time. But may we, mistress, ever look to thee alone as our head.'

7. After an harangue of this general nature Buduica led her army against the Romans. The latter chanced to be without a leader for the reason that Paulinus their commander had gone on an expedition to Mona [Anglesey], an island near Britain. This enabled her to sack and plunder two Roman cities, and, as I said, she wrought indescribable slaughter. Persons captured by the Britons underwent every form of most frightful treatment. The conquerors committed the most atrocious and bestial outrages. For instance, they hung naked the noblest and most distinguished women, cut off their breasts and sewed them to their mouths, to make the victims appear to be eating them. After that they impaled them on sharp skewers run perpendicularly the whole length of the body. All this they did to the accompaniment of sacrifices, banquets, and exhibitions of insolence in all of their sacred places, but chiefly in the grove of Andate, - that being the name of the personification of Victory, to whom they paid the most excessive reverence."(21.2)

When reading these translations it comes to mind that *Andraste* and *Andate* may once have been written as the same word in the original document of Cassius Dio.

As during the war-torn years from the invasion of 43 AD until 61 AD there was not the opportunity for many Roman women of noble birth to have ventured to Britain, a case exists that the atrocities were reserved by the Celtic women for those Celtic women and camp-followers who embraced too readily the company of the new Roman conquerors. Moreover, the retribution as reported by Cassius Dio largely took place under the auspices of a Celtic goddess. Stemming from Tacitus *"For it was not on making prisoners and selling them, or on any of the barter of war, that the enemy was bent, but on slaughter, on the gibbet, the fire and the cross, like men soon about to pay the penalty, and meanwhile snatching at instant vengeance."*; it has been suggested the odious behaviour of the Celts in some way was to be a retribution for the atrocities that they unconsciously knew would be metered out to themselves following their inevitable defeat. A less analytic view is that they and their society were painted by Dio as sadistic and depraved.

Events belie a first hand description of proceedings having an origin in a member of the Romanised society of the occupying force. A number could have witnessed the rotting, pecked, bitten debris when edging back to the urban centres in the aftermath. Any soul with an ounce of sense would have fled London and crossed south of the Thames on news that Colchester was laid waste, the merchant ships putting out on the next tide. Tacitus estimated seventy thousand citizens and allies were slaughtered during the uprising of 61 AD; Colchester, London and St Albans being left in ruins, see Appendix 2. Indeed, charcoal layers at Silchester may bear witness to the rout.

Ahead of his description of Boudicca, Cassius Dio apportions some blame for the uprising on Seneca. The word *lacuna* indicates that a section of the text is missing.

Cassius Dio: Roman History book 62, chapter 2 [Herbert Baldwin Foster].
"2. The causus belli lay in the confiscation of the money which Claudius had given to the foremost Britons, - Decianus Catus, governor of the island, announcing that this must now be sent back. This was one reason (Lacuna) and another was that Seneca had lent them on excellent terms as regards interest a thousand myriads that they did not want, and had afterwards called in this loan all at once and levied on them for it with severity."(21.3)

Seneca the Younger had been the tutor of Nero. Thus, Seneca was in part implicated by Dio in that significant slaughter of 70,000 citizens and allies of the Roman Empire.

Boudicca was the wife and, by 61 AD, the widow of Prasutagus, king of the Iceni, a tribe who occupied the northern end of East Anglia. A possibility, if only remotely so, is that Iceni was composed from the name Ceni with the prefix 'I' indicating their relative compass point, size or importance. This would then match the reference to the Cenimagni by Caesar when in Britain, *Gallic War* 5.21 (1.14). Although Boudicca was queen of the Iceni, she need not have been from the tribe of the Iceni. She could have been the daughter of a noble family of an associate tribe. Because Boudicca held such sway over an army which doubtless included many raised from outside the borders of the Iceni (and her original tribe), it is supposed that as a reasonable explanation she was a Druidess of importance or a priestess from the senior echelon of a parallel cult.

The administrative centre for the Iceni during the Roman occupation has long been suspected as laying to the south of Norwich at Caistor St Edmond. Field work in 2007 led by members of Nottingham University revealed the street grid of a substantial complex. The nature of pre Roman activity at the site is yet to be established.

The translation of Cassius Dio from the Greek is taken from the book by Herbert Baldwin Foster published in 1905 by Pafraets Book Company, Troy, New York.

Cassius Dio was a Greek by birth who lived from about 163 AD to 235 AD. He became a Roman senator and rose to the rank of consul. He served a term as the governor of Pannonia and another of Dalmatia.

It is axiomatic that the coin producing, wine-loving tribe of the Catuvellauni centred at Welwyn, Wheathampstead and Verulam sought the goods of the Mediterranean. They would not have been content with a commerce reliant upon the ports of entry controlled by the men of Kent or the trading centres set up to serve their Trinovantian rivals at Colchester. For the site of their emporium the geography points to Hertford and higher up the River Lea, or the north bank of the Thames above the outfall of the Lea at Blackwall (south of Bromley by Bow) inland to Staines where the River Colne joins the Thames. The Ver is a tributary of the Colne and the oppidum at Wheathampstead overlooks the Lea. A trading ship's captain would have felt more at ease with the confluence of the Lea and Thames as it avoided the need to pass upstream around the Isle of Dogs and did not compromise his escape route to an unnecessary degree. Nonetheless, if willing he could come up on the tide to a port at Putney Bridge at least.

As a hypothesis it is proposed that the Thames was bridged at London before the arrival of the Legions, and Roman London of 'the square mile' was a green field site adjacent to the trading town and on balance down stream of it. The reference by Cassius Dio to a Thames bridge at the time of the Claudian invasion of 43 AD is unambiguous. The implied speed of the follow through attack on the Britons and the flow of the text are in keeping with the use of an existing bridge rather than one quickly constructed. A Thames bridge downstream of London is difficult to accommodate on account of the river width (prior to the modern embankment) and progressive tidal effects. For operational reasons, the port would have been downstream of the bridge - thus, ships sailing on the tide were neither encumbered by the height of the bridge nor restricted from slipping away in times of difficulty.

If and when a bridge was built in the Roman period across from the Roman city to Southwark then, in consequence, it is envisaged the port migrated down stream to beyond the bridge while remaining upstream of the position now occupied by the Tower.

Cassius Dio: Roman History, book 60.20 [Herbert Baldwin Foster].
" Thence the Britons retired to the river Thames at a point near where it empties into the ocean and the latter's flood-tide forms a lake. This they crossed easily because they knew where the firm ground in this locality and the easy passages were; but the Romans in following them up came to grief at this spot. However, when the Celtae [Other translators give Germans – Compiler.] swam across again and some others had traversed a bridge a little way up stream, they assailed the barbarians from many sides at once and cut down large numbers of them. In pursuing the remainder incautiously they got into swamps from which it was not easy to make one's way out, and in this way lost many men."(21.4 and Appendix 1)

The name Londinium was recorded by Tacitus in connection with the uprising of Boudicca in 61 AD.

Tacitus: Annals book 14 chapter 33
"33. Suetonius, however, with wonderful resolution, marched amid a hostile population to Londinium, which though undistinguished by the name of a colony, was much frequented by a number of merchants and trading vessels."(6.5 and Appendix 2)

If the town had been initiated by the Romans then it would be expected that a recognisable Roman name or connection with or an embodiment of a local tribal name was evident in the name of Londinium, and this has not been established to date. Lud of Ludgate Hill is never far below the surface whereas Gog a' Magog, the two giants who defend London, have no part to play in its name.

The first medieval stone bridge at London was begun in 1176, taking 33 years in the building. The engineer driving the project was Peter, a curate in the city church of St Mary Colechurch in the Cheap, see *London for ever The Sovereign City* written by Colonel Robert J. Blackham published some time ago by Sampson Low, Marston. Historical evidence for a wooden London bridge extends back to the tenth century.

The construction of wooden causeways and bridges to artificial islands is attested by archaeology to have been practised in the Bronze Age within the British Isles. The concept and wherewithal did not await the arrival of the Romans.

The establishment position is that London was founded after the Roman occupation begun in 43 AD.

The short description by Cassius Dio of the Claudian invasion of Britain is given in Appendix 1. The information in the Annals of Tacitus relating to Boudicca and the year 61 AD is reproduced in Appendix 2.

15   AMMIANUS MARCELLINUS

Books 14 to 31 inclusive, covering as they do the period from after the death of the usurper Magnentius in 353 AD to the death of Valens in 378 AD, are the extant history written by Ammianus. A Greek, he was a soldier and an acquaintance of Julian who was emperor between 360 AD and 363 AD (4).

The surviving text relies on a manuscript dated to the ninth century. The translation from the Latin by C.D.Yonge was published in the Bohn Classic Library series.

Ammianus: History book 15, chapters 9 to 12 [Yonge]
Written with events of year 355 AD.
"Chapter 9
1. Now then, since, as the sublime poet of Mantua has sung, 'A greater series of incident rises to my view; in a more arduous task I engage,' - I think it a proper opportunity to describe the situation and different countries of the Gauls, lest, among the narration of fiery preparations and the various chances of battles, I should seem, while speaking of matters not understood by every one, to resemble those negligent sailors, who, when tossed about by dangerous waves and storms, begin to repair their sails and ropes which they might have attended to in calm weather.
2. Ancient writers, pursuing their investigations into the earliest origin of the Gauls, left our knowledge of the truth very imperfect; but at a later period, Timagenes, a thorough Greek both in diligence and language, collected from various writings facts which had long been unknown, and guided by his faithful statements, we, dispelling all obscurity, will now give a plain and intelligible relation of them.
3. Some persons affirm that the first inhabitants over seen in these regions were called Celts, after the name of their king, who was very popular among them, and sometimes also Galatae, after the name of his mother. For Galatae is the Greek translation of the Roman term Galli. Others affirm that they are Dorians, who following a more ancient Hercules, selected for their home the districts bordering on the ocean.
4. The Druids affirm that a portion of the people was really indigenous to the soil, but that other inhabitants poured in from the islands on the coast, and from the districts across the Rhine, having been driven from their former abodes by frequent wars, and sometimes by inroads of the tempestuous sea."

This statement points to Druids having had an existence in Western Europe before the Celts arrived. But was the data freshly taken by Ammianus or from his library?

"5. Some again maintain that after the destruction of Troy, a few Trojans fleeing from the Greeks, who were then scattered over the whole world, occupied these districts, which at that time had no inhabitants at all."

The tradition that a subgroup among the Celts were descended from Trojan stock had a pedigree established before the post Roman Welsh bards wrote down their mythological histories.

"6. But the natives of these countries affirm this more positively than any other fact (and, indeed, we ourselves have read it engraved on their monuments), that Hercules, the son of Amphitryon, hastening to the destruction of those cruel tyrants, Geryon and Tauriscus, one of whom was oppressing the Gauls, and the other Spain, after he had conquered both of them, took to wife some women of noble birth in those countries, and became the father of many children; and that his sons called the districts (of which they became the kings) after their own names.

7. Also an Asiatic tribe coming from Phocaea in order to escape the cruelty of Harpalus, the lieutenant of Cyrus the king, sought to sail to Italy.

[Footnote. This story of the Phocaeenses is told by Herodotus, i, 166, and alluded to by Horace, Epod. xv, 10.]

And a part of them founded Velia, in Lucania, others settled a colony at Marseilles, in the territory of Vienne; and then, in subsequent ages, these towns increasing in strength and importance, founded other cities. But we must avoid a variety of details which are commonly apt to weary.

8. Throughout these provinces, the people gradually becoming civilised, the study of liberal accomplishments flourished, having been first introduced by the Bards, the Eubages,

[Footnote. The Eubages, or 'Ovateis' as Strabo calls them, appear to have been a tribe of priests.]

and the Druids. The bards were accustomed to employ themselves in celebrating the brave achievements of their illustrious men, in epic verse, accompanied with sweet airs on the lyre. The Eubages investigated the system and sublime secrets of nature, and sought to explain them to their followers. Between these two came the Druids, men of loftier genius, bound in brotherhoods according to the precepts and example of Pythagoras; and their minds were elevated by investigations into secret and sublime matters, and from the contempt which they entertained for human affairs they pronounced the soul immortal.

Chapter 10 . . .

Chapter 11

1. In former times, when these provinces were little known, as being barbarous, they were considered to be divided into three races, namely, the Celtae, the same who are also called Galli; the Aquitani, and the Belgae: all differing from each other in language, manners, and laws.

2. The Galli, who, as I have said, are the same as the Celtae, are divided from the Aquitani by the river Garonne, which rises in the mountains of the Pyrenees; and after passing through many towns, loses itself in the ocean.

3. On the other side they are separated from the Belgians by the Marne and the Seine, both rivers of considerable size, which flowing through the tribes of the Lugdunenses, after surrounding the stronghold of the Parisi named Lutetia, so as to make an island of it, proceed onwards together, and fall into the sea near the camp of Constantius.

4. Of all these people the Belgians are said by ancient writers to be the most warlike, because being more remote from civilisation, and not having been rendered effeminate by foreign luxuries, they have been engaged in continual wars with the Germans on the other side of the Rhine.

5. For the Aquitanians, to whose shores, as being nearest and also pacific, foreign merchandise is abundantly imported, were easily brought under the dominion of the Romans, because their character had become enervated.

6. *But from the time when the Gauls, after long and repeated wars, submitted to the dictator Julius, all their provinces were governed by Roman officers, the country being divided into four portions; one of which was the province of Narbonne; containing the districts of Vienne and Lyons; a second province comprehended all the tribes of the Aquitanians; upper and lower Germany formed a third jurisdiction, and the Belgians a fourth at that period.*

7. *But now the whole extent of the country is portioned out into many provinces. The second (or lower) Germany is the first, if you begin on the western side, fortified by Cologne and Tongres, both cities of great wealth and importance.*

8. *Next comes the first (or high) Germany, in which besides other municipal towns, there is Mayence, and Worms, and Spiers, and Strasburg, a city celebrated for the defeats sustained by the barbarians in its neighbourhood.*

9. *After these the first Belgic province stretches as far as Metz and Treves, which city is the splendid abode of the chief governor of the country.*

10. *Next to that comes the second Belgic province, where we find Amiens, a city of conspicuous magnificence, and Chalons [sur Marne] and Rheims.*

11. *In the province of the Sequani, the finest cities are Basancon and Basle. The first Lyonnese province contains Lyons, Chalons [sur Saone], Sens, Bourges, and Autun, the walls of which are very extensive and of great antiquity.*

12. *In the second Lyonnese province are Tours, and Rouen, Evreux, and Troyes. The Grecian and Penine Alps have, besides other towns of less note, Avenche, a city which indeed is now deserted, but which was formerly one of no small importance, as even now is proved by its half-ruinous edifices. These are the most important provinces, and most splendid cities of the Galli.*

13. *In Aquitania, which looks towards the Pyrenees, and that part of the ocean which belongs to the Spaniards, the first province is Aquitanica, very rich in large and populous cities; passing over others, I may mention as pre-eminent. Bordeaux, Clermont, Saintes, and Poitiers.*

14. *The province called the Nine Nations is enriched by Ausch and Bazas. In the province of Narbonne, the cities of Narbonne, Euses, and Toulouse are the principal places of importance. The Viennese exults in the magnificence of many cities, the chief of which are Vienne itself, and Arles, and Valence; to which may be added Marseilles, by the alliance with and power of which we read that Rome itself was more than once supported in moments of danger.*

15. *And near to these cities is also Aix, Nice, Antibes, and the islands of Ilieres.*

16. *. . . The Rhone . . .*

17. *And thus passing through that lake without any damage, it runs through Savoy and the district of Franche Comte; and, after a long course, it forms the boundary between the Viennese on the left, and the Lyonnese on its right. Then after many windings it receives the Saone, a river which rises in the first Germany, and this latter river here merges its name in the Rhone. At this point is the beginning of the Gauls. And from this spot the distances are measured not by miles but by leagues.*

18. *. . . .*

Chapter 12
1.Nearly all the Gauls are of a lofty stature, fair, and of ruddy complexion; terrible from the sternness of their eyes, very quarrelsome, and of great pride and insolence. A whole troop of foreigners would not be able to withstand a single Gaul if he called his wife to his assistance, who is usually very strong, and with blue eyes; especially when, swelling her neck, gnashing her teeth, and brandishing her sallow arms of enormous size, she begins to strike blows mingled with kicks, as if they were so many missiles sent from the string of a catapult.
2. The voices of the generality are formidable and threatening, whether they are in good humour or angry; they are all exceedingly careful of cleanliness and neatness, nor in all the country, and most especially in Aquitania, could any man or women, however poor, be seen either dirty or ragged.
3. The men of every age are equally inclined to war, and the old man and the man in the prime of life answer with equal zeal the call to arms, their bodies being hardened by their cold weather and by constant exercise, so that they are all inclined to despise dangers and terrors. Nor has any one of this nation ever mutilated his thumb from fear of the toils of war, as men have done in Italy, whom in their district are called Murci.
4. The nation is fond of wine, and of several kinds of liquor which resemble wine. And many individuals of the lower orders, whose senses have become impaired by continual intoxication, which the apophthegm of Cato defined to be a kind of voluntary madness, run about in all directions at random; so that there appears to be some point in that saying which is found in Cicero's oration in defence of Foneius, 'that henceforth the Gauls will drink their wine less strong than formerly,' because forsooth they thought there was poison in it."(22.1)

The Gauls had been part of the Roman Empire for 400 years by the time Ammianus wrote this description. In civil terms the Gauls would also have been disarmed for that time. Ammianus served in Gaul during his career as a soldier. Whatever his prowess in the military, it is plain the Gaulish women left him ill at ease.

The opening account of the Gauls by Ammianus echoed the lines of Caesar. As Ammianus repeated that the Belgae had a different language to that of the Celts following four centuries of familiarity after Caesar, *Gallic War* book 1.1 (1.1), then the statement carries a degree of authority. The metal and pottery remains of the Belgae show them to have been a vigorous blossoming of Celtic craft traditions with positive developments in all aspects of Celtic technology. The options include a dominant survival of a Bronze Age tongue from one of the successful peoples then living in the area, a significant German contribution to the population and language or none of these. According to the Index of Reference 1, "*the name Belgae belongs to the Cymric language, in which, under the form 'Belgiaid', the radical of which is 'Belg', it signifies warlike;*". Caesar's inquiries led him to the conclusion the Belgae were Germanic.

Whether Divitiacus was a personal name or the Latinised title of the chief Druid may be argued either way. What is clear cut is the Druids held sway in some territories of the Belgae before Divitiacus was ousted. Divitiacus was replaced as leader at a time prior to Caesar's campaigns in their country. This is evidence the Druid cult had been accepted among the Germanic Belgae and was not restricted to adherents within the Celtic tribes. It is supposed the Druid cult continued to be practised among the Belgae after the demise of Divitiacus.

Caesar: Gallic War book 2 chapter 3 to 5 [McDevitte]

"3. As he arrived there unexpectedly and sooner than any one anticipated, the Remi, who are the nearest of the Belgae to [Celtic] Gaul, sent to him Iccius and Antebrogius [two of] the principal persons of the state, as their ambassadors: to tell him that they surrendered themselves and all their possessions to the protection and disposal of the Roman people: and that they had neither combined with the rest of the Belgae, nor entered into any confederacy against the Roman people: and were prepared to give hostages, to obey his commands, to receive him into their towns, and to aid him with corn and other things; that all the rest of the Belgae were in arms; and that the Germans, who dwell on this side the Rhine, had joined themselves to them; and that so great was the infatuation of them all, that they could not restrain even the Suessiones, their own brethren and kinsmen, who enjoy the same rights, and the same laws, and who have one government and one magistracy [in common] with themselves, from uniting with them.

4. When Caesar inquired of them what states were in arms and how powerful they were, and what they could do in war, he received the following information: that the greater part of the Belgae were sprung from the Germans, and that having crossed the Rhine at an early period, they had settled there, on account of the fertility of the country, and had driven out the Gauls who inhabited those regions; and that they were the only people who, in the memory of our fathers, when all Gaul was overrun, had prevented the Teutones and the Cimbri from entering their territories; the effect of which was, that, from the recollection of those events, they assumed to themselves great authority and haughtiness in military matters."

It follows from this account the German tribes were in Western Europe and had crossed westward over the Rhine before 100 BC.

"The Remi said, that they had known accurately everything respecting their number, because, being united to them by neighbourhood and by alliances, they had learnt what number each state had in the general council of the Belgae promised for that war. That the Bellovaci were the most powerful amongst them in valour, influence, and number of men; that these could muster 100,000 armed men, [and had] promised 60,000 picked men out of that number, and demanded for themselves the command of the whole war. That the Suessiones were their nearest neighbours and possessed a very extensive and fertile country; that among them, even in our own memory, Divitiacus, the most powerful man in all Gaul, had been king, who had held the government of a great part of these regions, as well as of Britain; that their king at present was Galba; that the direction of the whole war was conferred by the consent of all, upon him, on account of his integrity and prudence: that they had twelve towns; that they had promised 50,000 armed men: and that the Nervii, who are reckoned the most warlike among them, and are situated at a very great distance, [had promised] as many; the Atrebates 15,000; the Ambiani, 10,000; the Morini, 25,000; the Menapii, 9,000; the Celeti, 10,000; the Volocasses and the Veromandui as many; the Aduatuci 19,000; that the Condrusi, the Eburones, the Caeraesi, the Paemani, who are called by the common name of Germans [had promised], they thought, to the number of 40,000.

5. Caesar, having encouraged the Remi, and addressed them courteously, ordered the whole senate to assemble before him, and the children of their chief men to be brought to him as hostages; all which commands they punctually performed by the day [appointed]. He, addressing himself to Divitiacus, the Aeduan, with great earnestness points out how much it concerns the republic and their common security, that the forces of the enemy should be divided, so that it might not be necessary to engage with so large a number at one time. [He asserts] that this might be effected if the Aedui would lead their forces into the territories of the Bellovaci, and' begin to lay waste their country. With these instructions he dismissed him from his presence."(1.15)

Setting aside that the Belgic aristocracy tended to have names and titles showing a Celtic affinity, thoughts flit through the mind as to how intelligible would the language of the man in the street of Claudian London have been to a person speaking early English some four hundred years hence. How close was the Belgic tongue of common man akin to Anglo-Saxon? But then, maybe they would not have understood one word. Such thoughts outside the box are heresy to the Celtic lobby.

HETEROGENEOUS ELEMENTS

16   THE ROMAN ARMY

The nature of warfare was high on the list of relative importance for the Celts up to the time of their subjugation by Rome. For the unconquered Celtic and Germanic tribes it continued unabated through the period of the Western Roman Empire and into the following centuries. The procedures in place within the Roman army were evolved and changed over time. In all likelihood the Celts and the Germans studied the Roman military procedures and modified their own tactics where Roman techniques could be adapted by their own forces to advantage. Furthermore, they would have identified any weakness in the procedures and order of battle of the Roman army that could be exploited by the mode of fighting best suited to their particular assets and topography.

The structure of the Roman army was set down in outline by Polybius writing in the second century BC. The military order in which the army marched was described by Josephus at a time when the Roman army under Vespasian, then a general, was marching towards Galilee between 67 AD and 69 AD. Both Polybius and Josephus were military men and their accounts are relied upon as being wholly accurate.

JOSEPHUS

Josephus: Wars of the Jews, book 3 chapters 5 and 6 [Whiston]
"Chapter V
Description of the Roman armies and Roman camps;
and what the Romans are commended for.
1. Now here one cannot but admire at the precaution of the Romans, in providing themselves of such household servants, as might not only serve at other times for the common offices of life, but might also be of advantage to them in their wars; and indeed, if any one does but attend to the other parts of their military discipline, he will be forced to confess that their obtaining so large a dominion, hath been the acquisition of their valour, and not the bare gift of fortune; for they do not begin to use their weapons first in time of war, nor do they then put their hands first into motion, while they avoided so to do in times of peace; but as if their weapons did always cling to them, they have never any truce from warlike exercise; nor do they stay till times of war admonish them to use them; for their military exercises differ not at all from the real use of their arms, but every soldier is every day exercised, and that with great diligence, as if it were in time of war, which is the reason why they bear the fatigue of battle so easily; for neither can any disorder remove them from their usual regularity, nor can fear affright them out of it, nor can labour tire them; which firmness of conduct makes them to overcome those that have the same firmness; nor would lie he mistaken that should call those their exercises unbloody battles, and their battles bloody exercises.

Nor can their enemies easily surprise them with the suddenness of their incursions; for as soon as they have marched into an enemy's land, they do not begin to fight till they have walled their camp about; nor is the fence they raise rashly made, or uneven; nor do they all abide in it, nor do those that are in it take their places at random; but if it happens that the ground is uneven, it is first levelled: their camp is also four-square by measure, and carpenters are ready, in great numbers, with their tools, to erect their buildings for them.

2. As for what is within the camp, it is set apart for tents, but the outward circumference hath the resemblance of a wall, and is adorned with towers at equal distances, where between the towers stand the engines for throwing arrows and darts, and for slinging stones, and where they lay all other engines that can annoy the enemy, all ready for their several operations. They also erect four gates, one at every side of the circumference, and those large enough for the entrance of the beasts, and wide enough for making excursions, if occasion should require. They divide the camp within into two streets, very conveniently, and place the tents of the commanders in the middle; but in the very midst of all is the general's own tent in the nature of a temple, insomuch that it appears to be a city built on the sudden, with its market-place, and place for handicraft trades, and with seats for the officers, superior and inferior; where, if any differences arise, their causes are heard and determined. The camp, and all that is in it, is encompassed with a wall all round about, and that sooner than one would imagine, and this by the multitude and skill of the labourers; and, if occasion require, a trench is drawn round the whole, whose depth is four cubits, and its breadth equal.

3. When they have thus secured themselves, they live together by companies with quietness and decency, as are all their other affairs managed with good order and security. Each company hath also their wood, and their corn, and their water brought them, when they stand in need of them; for they neither sup nor dine as they please themselves singly, but all together. Their times also for sleeping, and watching, and rising, are notified beforehand by the sound of trumpets, nor is any thing done without such a signal; and in the morning the soldiery go every one to their centurions, and these centurions to their tribunes, to salute them; with whom all the superior officers go to the general of the whole army, who then gives them of course the watch-word and other orders, to be by them carried to all that are under their command; which is also observed when they go to fight, and thereby they turn themselves about on the sudden, when there is occasion for making sallies, as they come back when they are recalled, in crowds also.

4. When they are to go out of their camp, the trumpet gives a sound, at which time nobody lies still, but at the first intimation they take down their tents, and all is made ready for their going out; then do the trumpets sound again, to order them to get ready for the march; then do they lay their baggage suddenly upon their mules and other beasts of burden, and stand, at the place for starting, ready to march; when also they set fire to their camp, and this they do because it will be easy for them to erect another camp, and that it may not ever be of use to their enemies. Then do the trumpets give a sound the third time, that they are to go out in order to excite those that on any account are a little tardy, that so no one may be out of his rank when the army marches. Then does the crier stand at the general's right hand, and asks them thrice, in their own tongue, whether they be ready to go out to war or not. To which they reply as often, with a loud and cheerful voice, saying 'We are ready.' And this they do almost before the question is asked them; they do this as filled with a kind of martial fury, and at the time that they so cry out, they lift up their right hands also.

5. *When, after this, they are gone out of their camp, they all march without noise, and in a decent manner, and every one keeps his own rank, as if they were going to war. The footmen are armed with breast-plates and head-pieces, and have swords on each side; but the sword which is upon their left side is much longer than the other; for that on the right side is not longer than a span. Those footmen also that are chosen out from amongst the rest to be about the general himself, have a lance and a buckler; but the rest of the foot-soldiers have a spear and a long buckler, besides a saw and a basket, a pick-axe and an axe, a thong of leather, and a hook, with provisions for three days; so that a footman hath no great need of a mule to carry his burdens. The horsemen have a long sword on their right sides, and a long pole in their hand: a shield also lies by them obliquely on one side of their horses, with three or more darts that are borne in their quiver, having broad points, and no smaller than spears. They have also head-pieces and breast-plates, in like manner as have all the footmen. And for those that are chosen to be about the general, their armour no way differs from that of the horsemen belonging to other troops; and he always leads the legion forth, to whom the lot assigns that employment.*

6. *This is the manner of the marching and resting of the Romans, as also these are the several sorts of weapons they use.* . . . .

Chapter VI

Placidus attempts to take Jotapata, and is beaten off.

Vespasian marches into Galilee.

1. . . .

2. *But as Vespasian had a great mind to fall upon Galilee, he marched out from Ptolemais, having put his army into that order wherein the Romans used to march. He ordered those auxiliaries which were lightly armed, and the archers, to march first, that they might prevent any sudden insults from the enemy, and might search out the woods that looked suspiciously, and were capable of ambuscades. Next to these followed that part of the Romans who were most completely armed, both footmen and horsemen. Next to these followed ten out of every hundred, carrying along with them their arms, and what was necessary to measure out a camp withal; and after them, such as were to make the road even and straight, and if it were anywhere rough and hard to be passed over, to plane it, and to cut down the woods that hindered their march, that the army might not be in distress, or tired with their march. Behind these he set such carriages of the army as belonged both to himself and to the other commanders, with a considerable number of their horsemen for their security. After these he marched himself, having with him a select body of footmen and horsemen, and pikemen. After these came the peculiar cavalry of his own legion, for there were an hundred and twenty horsemen that peculiarly belonged to every legion. Next to these came the mules that carried the engines for sieges, and the other warlike machines of that nature. After these came the commanders of the cohorts, and tribunes, having about them soldiers chosen out of the rest. Then came the ensigns encompassing the eagle, which is at the head of every Roman legion, the king, and the strongest of all birds, which seems to them a signal of dominion, and an omen that they shall conquer all against whom they march; these sacred ensigns are followed by the trumpeters. Then came the main army in their squadrons and battalions, with six men in depth, which were followed at last by a centurion, who, according to custom, observed the rest. As for the servants of every legion, they all followed the footmen, and led the baggage of the soldiers, which was borne on the mules and other beasts of burden.*

But behind all the legions came the whole multitude of the mercenaries; and those that brought up the rear came last of all for the security of the whole army, being both footmen, and those in their armour also, with a great number of horsemen.

3. And thus did Vespasian march with his army, and came to the bounds of Galilee, . . ."(23.1)

Joseph ben Matthias adopted the name Flavius which was the family name of his benefactor Vespasian. Vespasian was emperor of Rome between AD 69 and AD 79. Flavius Josephus became a Roman citizen and eventually settled in Rome. Josephus (AD 37 – circa AD 93) was a Jew by birth. *The Jewish War* was written by Josephus towards the end of Vespasian's reign.

William Whiston was born in Leicestershire in 1667 and died in 1752. His translation of Josephus was published in 1737: an edition based upon this was produced by Thomas Nelson of Edinburgh in 1843.

POLYBIUS

The methods employed by the Roman Army would have evolved as their circumstances changed. Over time, the use of foreign troops became commonplace, the weapon technology progressed, the nature of their foe altered and the terrain in which they fought became varied.

Polybius: History book 6, chapters 19 to 41 [Paton]

" The Roman Military System

19. After electing the consuls, they appoint military tribunes, fourteen from those who have seen five years' service and ten from those who have seen ten. As for the rest, a cavalry soldier must serve for ten years in all and an infantry soldier for sixteen years before reaching the age of forty-six, with the exception of those whose census is under four hundred drachmae, all of whom are employed in naval service. In case of pressing danger twenty years' service is demanded from the infantry. No one is eligible for any political office before he has completed ten years' service. . . .

20. . . . when the strength of each legion is brought up to 4,200, or in times of exceptional danger to 5,000 . . . the cavalry . . . three hundred are assigned to each legion.

21. . . . When they come to the rendezvous, they choose the youngest and poorest to form the velites; the next to them are made hastati; those in the prime of life principes; and the oldest of all triarii, these being the names among the Romans of the four classes in each legion distinct in age and equipment. They divide them so that the senior men known as triarii number 600, the principes 1,200, the rest, consisting of the youngest, being velites. If the legion consists of more than 4,000 men, they divide accordingly, except as regards the triarii, the number of whom is always the same.

22. The youngest soldiers or velites are ordered to carry a sword, javelins, and a target (parma). The target is strongly made and sufficiently large to afford protection, being circular and measuring three feet in diameter. They also wear a plain helmet, and sometimes cover it with a wolf's skin or something similar both to protect and to act as a distinguishing mark by which their officers can recognise them and judge if they fight pluckily or not. The wooden shaft of the javelin measures about two cubits in length and is about a finger's breadth in thickness; its head is a span long hammered out to such a fine edge that it is necessarily bent by the first impact, and the enemy is unable to return it. If this were not so the missile would be available for both sides.

23. *The next in seniority called hastati are ordered to wear a complete panoply. The Roman panoply consists firstly of a shield (scutum), the convex surface of which measures two and a half feet in width and four feet in length, the thickness at the rim being a palm's breadth. It is made of two planks glued together, the outer surface being then covered first with canvas and then with calf-skin. Its upper and lower rims are strengthened by an iron edging which protects it from descending blows and from injury when rested on the ground. It also has an iron boss (umbo) fixed to it which turns aside the more formidable blows of stones, pikes, and heavy missiles in general. Besides the shield they also carry a sword, hanging on the right thigh and called a Spanish sword. This is excellent for thrusting, and both of its edges cut effactually, as the blade is very strong and firm. In addition they have two pila, a brass helmet, and greaves. The pila are of two sorts - stout and fine. Of the stout ones some are round and a palm's length in diameter and others are a palm square. The fine pila, which they carry in addition to the stout ones, are like moderate size hunting-spears, the length of the haft in all cases being about three cubits. Each is fitted with a barbed iron head of the same length as the haft. This they attach so securely to the haft, carrying the attachment halfway up the latter and fixing it with numerous rivets, that in action the iron will break sooner than become detached, although its thickness at the bottom where it comes in contact with the wood is a finger's breadth and a half; such great care do they take about attaching it firmly. Finally they wear as an ornament a circle of feathers with three upright purple or black feathers about a cubit in height, the addition of which on the head surmounting their other arms is to make every man look twice his real height, and to give him a fine appearance, such as will strike terror into the enemy. The common soldiers wear in addition a breastplate of brass a span square, which they place in front of the heart and call the heart-protector (pectorale), this completing their accoutrements; but those who are rated above 10,000 drachmas wear instead of this a coat of chain-mail (lorica). The principes and triarii are armed in the same manner except that instead of the pila the triarii carry long spears (hastae).*

24. *From each of the classes except the youngest they elect ten centurions according to merit, and then they elect a second ten. All these are called centurions, and the first man elected has a seat in the military council. The centurions then appoint an equal number of rearguard officers (optiones). Next, in conjunction with the centurions, they divide each class into ten companies, except the velites, and assign to each company two centurions and two optiones from among the elected officers. The velites are divided equally among all the companies; these companies are called ordines or manipuli or vexilla, and their officers are called centurions or ordinum ductores. Finally these officers appoint from the ranks two of the finest and bravest men to be standard-bearers (vexillarii) in each maniple. It is natural that they should appoint two commanders for each maniple; for it being uncertain what may be the conduct of an officer or what may happen to him, and affairs of war not admitting of pretext and excuses, they wish the mandiple never to be without a leader and chief. When both centurions are on the spot, the first elected commands the right half of the maniple and the second the left, but if both are not present the one who is commands the whole. They wish the centurions not so much to be venturesome and daredevil as to be natural leaders, of a steady and sedate spirit. They do not desire them so much to be men who will initiate attacks and open the battle, but men who will hold their ground when worsted and hard pressed and be ready to die at their posts.*

25. In like manner they divide the cavalry into ten squadrons (turmae) and from each they select three officers (decuriones), who themselves appoint three rear-rank officers (optiones). The first commander chosen commands the whole squadron, and the two others have the rank of decuriones, all three bear this title. If the first of them should not be present, the second takes command of the squadron. The cavalry are now armed like that of Greece, but in old times they had no cuirasses but fought in light undergarments, the result of which was that they were able to dismount and mount again at once with great dexterity and facility, but were exposed to great danger in close combat, as they were nearly naked. Their lances too were unserviceable in two respects. In the first place they made them so slender and pliant that it was impossible to take a steady aim, and before they could fix the head in anything, the shaking due to the mere motion of the horse caused most of them to break. Next, as they did not fit the butt-ends with spikes, they could only deliver the first stroke with the point and after this if they broke they were of no further service. The buckler was made of ox-hide, somewhat similar in shape to the round bosse cake used at sacrifices. They were not of any use for attacking, as they were not firm enough; and when the leather covering pealed off and rotted owing to the rain, unserviceable as they were before, they now became entirely so. Since therefore their arms did not stand the test of experience, they soon took to making them in the Greek fashion, which ensures that the first stroke of the lance-head shall be both well aimed and telling, since the lance is so constructed as to be steady and strong, and also that it may continue to be effectively used by reversing it and striking with the spike at the butt end. And the same applies to Greek shields, which being of solid and firm texture do good service both in defence and attack. The Romans, when they noticed this, soon learnt to copy Greek arms; for this too is one of their virtues, that no people are so ready to adopt new fashions and imitate what they see is better in others.

26. The tribunes having organised the troops and ordered them to arm themselves in this manner, dismiss them to their homes. When the day comes on which they have all sworn to attend at the place appointed by the consuls – each consul as a rule appointing a separate rendezvous for his own troops, since each has received his share of the allies and two Roman legions – none of those on the roll ever fail to appear, no excuse at all being admitted except adverse omens or absolute impossibility. The allies having now assembled also at the same places as the Romans, their organisation and command are undertaken by the officers appointed by the consuls known as praefecti sociorum and twelve in number. They first of all select for the consuls for the whole force of allies assembled the horsemen and footmen most fitted for actual service, these being known as extraordinarii, that is "select." The total number of allied infantry is usually equal to that of the Romans, while the cavalry are three times as many. Of these they assign about a third of the cavalry and a fifth of the infantry to the picked corps; the rest they divide into two bodies, one known as the right wing and the other as the left.

When these arrangements have been made, the tribunes take both the Romans and allies and pitch their camp, one simple plan of camp being adopted at all times and in all places. I think, therefore, it will be in place here to attempt, as far as words can do so, to convey to my readers a notion of the disposition of the forces when on the march, when encamped, and when in action. For who is so averse to all noble and excellent performance as not to be inclined to take a little extra trouble to understand matters like this, of which when he has once read he will be well informed about one of those things really worth studying and worth knowing?"

The values used in the translation are Roman feet. English values are as follows.

One Acre	= 4840 square yards	= 43,560 square feet	e.g. a chain by a furlong
One Mile	= 1760 yards	= 5280 feet	i.e. 8 furlongs.

"27. *The manner in which they form their camp is as follows. When the site for the camp has been chosen, the position in it giving the best general view and most suitable for issuing orders is assigned to the general's tent (praetorium). Fixing an ensign on the spot where they are about to pitch it, they measure off round this ensign a square plot of ground each side of which is one hundred feet distant, so that the total area measures four plethra. Along one side of this square in the direction which seems to give the greatest facilities for watering and foraging, the Roman legions are disposed as follows. As I have said, there are six tribunes in each legion; and since each consul has always two Roman legions with him, it is evident that there are twelve tribunes in the army of each. They place then the tents of these all in one line parallel to the side of the square selected and fifty feet distant from it, to give room for the horses, mules, and baggage of the tribunes. These tents are pitched with their backs turned to the praetorium and facing the outer side of the camp, a direction of which I will always speak as 'the front.' The tents of the tribunes are at an equal distance from each other, and at such a distance that they extend along the whole breadth of the space occupied by the legions.*

28. They now measure a hundred feet from the front of all these tents, and starting from the line drawn at this distance parallel to the tents of the tribunes they begin to encamp the legions, managing matters as follows. Bisecting the above line, they start from this spot and along a line drawn at right angles to the first, they encamp the cavalry of each legion facing each other and separated by a distance of fifty feet, the last-mentioned line being exactly half-way between them. The manner of encamping the cavalry and the infantry is very similar, the whole space occupied by the maniples and squadrons being a square. This square faces one of the streets or viae and is of a fixed length of one hundred feet, and they usually try to make the depth the same except in the case of the allies. When they employ the larger legions they add proportionately to the length and depth.

29. The cavalry camp is thus something like a street running down from the middle of the tribunes' tents and at right angles to the line along which these tents are placed and to the space in front of them, the whole system of viae being in fact like a number of streets, as either companies of infantry or troops of horse are encamped facing each other all along each. Behind the cavalry, then, they place the triarii of both legions in a similar arrangement, a company next each troop, but with no space between, and facing in the contrary direction to the cavalry. They make the depth of each company half its length, because as a rule the triarii number only half the strength of the other classes. So that the maniples being often of unequal length, the length of the encampments is always the same owing to the difference in depth. Next at a distance of 50 feet on each side they place the principes facing the triarii, and they are turned towards the intervening space, two more streets are formed, both starting from the same base as that of the cavalry, i.e. the hundred-foot space in front of the tribunes' tents, and both issuing on the side of the camp which is opposite to the tribunes' tents and which we decided to call the front of the whole. After the principes, and again back to back against them, with no interval they encamp the hastati. As each class by virtue of the original division consists of ten maniples, the streets are all equal in length, and they break off on the front side of the camp in a straight line, the last maniples being here so placed as to face to the front.

30. *At a distance again of 50 feet from the hastati, and facing them, they encamp the allied cavalry, starting from the same line and ending on the same line. As I stated above, the number of the allied infantry is the same as that of the Roman legions, but from these the extraordinarii must be deducted; while that of the cavalry is double after deducting the third who serve as extraordinarii. In forming the camp, therefore, they proportionately increase the depth of the space assigned to the allied cavalry, in the endeavour to make their camp equal in length to that of the Romans. These five streets having been completed, they place the maniples of the allied infantry, increasing the depth in proportion to their numbers, with their faces turned away from the cavalry and facing the agger and both the outer sides of the camp. In each maniple the first tent at either end is occupied by the centurions. In laying the whole camp out in this manner they always leave a space of 50 feet between the fifth troop and the sixth, and similarly with the companies of foot, so that another passage traversing the whole camp is formed, at right angles to the streets, and parallel to the line of the tribunes' tents. This is called quintana, as it runs along the fifth troops and companies.*

31. *The spaces behind the tents of the tribunes to right and left of the praetorium, are used in the one case for the market and in the other for the office of the quaestor and the supplies of which he is in charge. Behind the last tent of the tribunes on either side, and more or less at right angles to these tents, are the quarters of the cavalry picked out from the extraordinarii, and a certain number of volunteers serving to oblige the consuls. These are all encamped parallel to the sides of the agger, and facing in the one case the quaestor's depot and in the other the market. As a rule these troops are not only thus encamped near the consuls but on the march and on other occasions are in constant attendance on the consul and quaestor. Back to back with them, and looking towards the agger are the select infantry who perform the same service as the cavalry just described. Beyond these an empty space is left a hundred feet broad, parallel to the tents of the tribunes, and stretching along the whole face of the agger on the other side of the market, praetorium and quaestorium and on its furthest side the rest of the equites extraordinarii are encamped facing the market, praetorium and quaestorium. In the middle of this cavalry camp and exactly opposite the praetorium a passage, 50 feet wide, is left leading to the rear side of the camp and running at right angles to the broad passage behind the praetorium. Back to back with these cavalry and fronting the agger and the rearward face of the whole camp are placed the rest of the pedites extraordinarii. Finally the spaces remaining empty to right and left next to the agger on each side of the camp are assigned to foreign troop or to any allies who chance to come in.*

  The whole camp thus form a square, and the way in which the streets are laid out and its general arrangement give it the appearance of a town. The agger is on all sides at a distance of 200 feet from the tents, and this empty space is of important service in several respects. To begin with it provides the proper facilities for marching the troops in and out, seeing that they all march out into this space by their own streets and thus do not come into one street in a mass and throw down or hustle each other. Again it is here that they collect the cattle brought into camp and all the booty taken from the enemy, and keep them safe during the night. But the most important thing of all is that in night attacks neither fire can reach them nor missiles except a very few, which are almost harmless owing to the distance and the space in front of the tents.

32. . . . .

39. . . . As pay the foot-soldier receives two obols a day, a centurion twice as much, and a cavalry-soldier a drachma. The allowance of corn to a foot soldier is about two-thirds of an Attic medimnus a month, a cavalry-soldier receives seven medimni of barley and two of wheat. Of the allies the infantry receive the same, the cavalry one and one-third medimnus of wheat and five of barley, these rations being a free gift to the allies; but in the case of the Romans the quaestor deducts from their pay the price fixed for their corn and clothes and any additional arm they require.

40. . . .

41. When the army on the march is near the place of encampment, one of the tribunes and those centurions who are specially charged with this duty go on in advance, and after surveying the whole ground on which the camp is to be formed, first of all determine from the considerations I mentioned above where the consul's tent should be placed and on which front of the space round this tent the legions should encamp. When they have decided on this, they measure out first the area of the praetorium, next the straight line along which the tents of the tribunes are erected and next the line parallel to this, starting from which the troops form their encampment. In the same way they draw lines on the other side of the praetorium, the arrangement of which I described above in detail and at some length. All this is done in a very short time, as the marking out is a quite easy matter, all the distances being fixed and familiar; and they now plant flags, one on the spot intended for the consul's tent, another on that side of it they have chosen for the camp, a third in the middle of the line on which the tribune's tents will stand, and a fourth on the other parallel line along which the legions will encamp. These latter flags are crimson, but the consul's is white. On the ground on the other side of the praetorium they plant either simple spears or flags of other colours. After this they go on to lay out the streets and plant spears in each street. Consequently it is obvious that when the legions march up and get a good view of the site for the camp, all the parts of it are known at once to everyone, as they have only to reckon from the position of the consul's flag. So that, as everyone knows exactly in which street and in what part of the street his tent will be, since all invariably occupy the same place in the camp, the encampment somewhat resembles the return of an army to its native city."(10.2)

Polybius died circa 124 BC in his eighty second year following a fall from a horse (4).

LIVY

The component parts of the Roman army, from a period earlier than Polybius, were described by Livy. The battle of Vesuvius was fought in 340 BC between the army of Rome and their near neighbours the Latins allied with the peoples of Campania. Livy wrote of it over three hundred years later using records available in his own lifetime.

Livy: History of Rome book 8, chapter 8 [Spillan]
"8. But the battle was very like to a civil war; so very similar was everything among the Romans and Latins, except with respect to courage. The Romans formerly used targets; afterwards, when they began to receive pay, they made shields instead of targets; and what before constituted phalanxes similar to the Macedonian, afterwards became a line drawn up in distinct companies. At length they were divided into several centuries. A century contained sixty soldiers, two centurions, and one standard-bearer.

The spearmen (hastati) formed the first line in fifteen companies, with small intervals between them: a company had twenty light-armed soldiers, the rest wearing shields; those were called light who carried only a spear and short iron javelins. This, which constituted the van in the field of battle, contained the youth in early bloom advancing towards the age of service. Next followed men of more robust age, in the same number of companies, who were called principes, all wearing shields, and distinguished by the completest armour. This band of thirty companies they called antepilani, because there were fifteen others placed behind them with the standards; of which each company consisted of three divisions, and the first division of each they called a pilus. Each company consisted of three ensigns, and contained one hundred and eighty six men. The first ensign was at the head of the Triarii, veteran soldiers of tried bravery; the second, at the head of the Rorarii, men whose ability was less by reason of their age and course of service; the third, at the head of the Accensi, a body in whom very little confidence was reposed. For this reason also they were thrown back to the rear. When the army was marshalled according to this arrangement, the spearmen first commenced the fight. If the spearmen were unable to repulse the enemy, they retreated leisurely, and were received by the principes into the intervals of the ranks. The fight then devolved on the principes; the spearmen followed. The Triarii continued kneeling behind the ensigns, their left leg extended forward, holding their shields resting on their shoulders, and their spears fixed in the ground, with the points erect, so that their line bristled as if enclosed by a rampart. If the principes also did not make sufficient impression in the fight, they retreated slowly from the front to the Triarii. Hence, when a difficulty is felt, 'matters have come to the Triarii,' became a usual proverb. The Triarii rising up, after receiving the principes and spearmen into the intervals between their ranks, immediately closing their files, shut up as it were the openings; and in one compact body fell upon the enemy, no other hope being now left: that was the most formidable circumstance to the enemy, when having pursued them as vanquished, they beheld a new line suddenly starting up, increased also in strength. In general about four legions were raised, each consisting of five thousand infantry and three hundred horse. As many more were added to the Latin levy, who were at that time enemies to the Romans, . . . They came to an engagement not far from the foot of Mount Vesuvius where the road led to the Veseris."(14.6)

17   GERALD OF WALES

Gerald was born in 1145/46 AD at Manorbier castle in Pembrokeshire, Wales. The majority of Wales was not directly subject to the English (i.e. Norman) crown at that time but tribute was paid on occasion: the complete surrender did not take place until 25 April 1283. As a child Gerald was sent to the Benedictine Abbey of Saint Peter at Gloucester and later spent time in Paris. Among his ecclesiastic appointments was included an attachment to the Bishop of Ely who was administering the country during the absence of Richard I at the Crusades.

Gerald of Wales included comments on the people in Ireland in the third part of his *History and Topography of Ireland* completed by 1187 AD following a visit to Ireland. The translation from the Latin by Thomas Forester was published in 1847 by Bohn's Antiquarian Library. The quotations are taken from the edition edited by Thomas Wright dated 1881.

The translation into English published in Bohn's Library of the *Topography of Ireland* and the *Vaticinal History of the Conquest of Ireland* are stated by the editor as *'the first complete translations of these books that have ever appeared.'* The *Itinerary through Wales* and *The Description of Wales* contained therein were translated by Sir Richard Colt-Hoare and had been published in 1806 (2 volumes). The Hoare translation attracts criticism from some quarters as being in error or based upon an inaccurate Latin edition.

The Latin text of Giraldus was published in the Rolls series from 1861 with volumes 1 to 4 edited by Dimmock, volumes 5 and 6 by Brewer and volume 7 by Freeman. The 'Rolls' series is a systematic publication of the wide ranging documents of antiquarian interest held by the Public Record Office.

Gerald died in about 1223. His lifetime spanned Archbishop Thomas a Becket being cut down in Canterbury Cathedral (1170) at the behest of Henry II, the crusades of Richard coeur de lion and the Magna Carta of King John (1215).

IRELAND

Gerald of Wales: Topography of Ireland [Forester]
  Distinction 3 chapters 10 and 11.
"*10. Of the character, customs, and habits of this people.*
. . . For they wear but little woollen, and nearly all they use is black, that being the colour of the sheep in this country. Their clothes are made after a barbarous fashion.

Their custom is to wear small, close-fitting hoods, hanging below the shoulders a cubit's length, and generally made of parti-coloured strips sewn together. Under these, they use woollen rugs instead of cloaks, with breeches and hose of one piece, or hose and breeches joined together, which are usually dyed of some colour.[1] Likewise, in riding, they neither use saddles, nor boots, nor spurs, but only carry a rod in their hand, having a crook at the upper end, with which they both urge forward and guide their horses. They use reins which serve the purpose both of a bridle and a bit, and do not prevent the horses from feeding, as they always live on grass. Moreover, they go to battle without armour, considering it a burden, and esteeming it brave and honourable to fight without it.

But they are armed with three kinds of weapons; namely short spears, and two darts; in which they follow the customs of the Basclenses (Basques); and they also carry heavy battle-axes of iron, exceedingly well wrought and tempered. These they borrowed from the Norwegians and Ostmen, of whom we shall speak hereafter. . . .

[Footnote 1. Seu braecis caligatis, seu caligais braecatis. The account given by Giraldus of the ancient dress of the Irish, in a language which supplied no equivalent terms, is necessarily obscure; but, connecting it with other sources of information, we find that it consisted of the following articles; - 1. What our author calls caputium, was a sort of bonnet and hood, protecting not only the head, but the neck and shoulders from the weather. It was of a conical form, and probably made of the same sort of stuff as the mantle. 2. The cloak or mantle; to describe which Giraldus has framed the Latin word phalingium, from the Irish falach, which signifies a rug or covering of any sort. This cloak has a fringed border sown, or wove down the edges. It was worn almost as low as the ancles, and was usually made of frieze, or some such course material. It was worn by the higher classes of the same fashion, but of better quality, according to their rank and means; and was sometimes made of the finest cloth, with a silken or woollen fringe, and of scarlet or other colours. Many rows of the shag, or fringe, were sown on the upper part of the mantle, partly for ornament and partly to defend the neck from the cold; and along the edges ran a narrow fringe of the same texture as the outer garment. . . .]

The Irish are a rude people, subsisting on the produce of their cattle only, and living themselves like beasts - a people that has not yet departed from the primitive habits of pastoral life. . . . They, therefore, only make patches of tillage; their pastures are short of herbage; cultivation is very rare, and there is scarcely any land sown. . . . They neither employ themselves in the manufacture of flax or wool, or in any kind of trade or mechanical art; . . .

This people, then, is truly barbarous, being not only barbarous in their dress, but suffering their hair and beards (barbis) to grow enormously in an uncouth manner, just like the modern fashion recently introduced; . . . Whatever natural gifts they possess are excellent, in whatever requires industry they are worthless.

11. Of the incomparable skill of the Irish in playing upon musical instruments.

The only thing to which I find that this people apply a commendable industry is playing upon musical instruments; in which they are incomparably more skilful than any other nation I have ever seen. . . . It is astonishing that in so complex and rapid a movement of the fingers, the musical proportions can be preserved, and that throughout the difficult modulations on their various instruments, the harmony is completed with such a sweet velocity, so unequal an equality, so discordant a discord, as if the chords sounded together fourths or fifths. They always begin from B flat, and return to the same, that the whole may be completed under the sweetness of a pleasing sound. . . . The Irish also used strings of brass instead of leather."(24.1)

Gerald of Wales: Topography of Ireland [Forester]
  Distinction 3 chapters 20 and 21.
"20. Of their abominable treachery.

They are given to treachery more than any other nation, and never keep the faith they have pledged, neither shame nor fear withholding them from constantly violating the most solemn obligations, which, when entered into with themselves, they are above all things anxious to have observed. . . .

21. How they always carry an axe in their hands instead of a staff.

From an ancient and wicked custom, they always carry an axe in their hands instead of a staff, that they may be ready promptly to execute whatever iniquity their minds suggest."
(24.2)

Gerald of Wales: Topography of Ireland [Forester]
  Distinction 3 chapter 25.
"25. Of a new and monstrous way of inaugurating their kings.

There are some things which shame would prevent my relating, unless the course of my subject required it. For a filthy story seems to reflect a stain on the author, although it may display his skill. But the severity of history does not allow us either to sacrifice truth or affect modesty; and what is shameful in itself may be related by pure lips in decent words. There is, then, in the northern and most remote part of Ulster, namely, at Kenel Cunil, a nation which practises a most barbarous and abominable rite in creating their king. The whole people of that country being gathered in one place, a white mare is led into the midst of them, and he who is to be inaugurated, not as a prince but as a brute, not as a king but as an outlaw, comes before the people on all fours, confessing himself a beast with no less impudence than imprudence. The mare being immediately killed, and cut in pieces and boiled, a bath is prepared for him from the broth.

Sitting in this, he eats of the flesh which is brought to him, the people standing round and partaking of it also. He is also required to drink of the broth in which he is bathed, not drawing it in any vessel, nor even in his hand, but lapping it with his mouth. These unrighteous rites being duly accomplished, his royal authority and dominion are ratified."(24.3)

A listener might suspect that these events had been especially concocted by a storyteller in one part of Ireland to abuse the reputation of rival folk living in another part. Whether true or not, they were of convenience to Gerald when preparing additional justification for why the pope should invite Henry II of England to expand his French and English empire to include Ireland. The pope's wish was to eradicate unchristian behaviour practised in that island. For his part, Henry could have had no desire to see a foreign monarch fulfil the pope's wish and sit on his back doorstep. Otherwise he may not have been much motivated to subject Ireland to his rule. Perhaps a makeweight in his decision to invade was the relative balance of power between English baronial families. It was known that a group of his noblemen were amassing land in Ireland. The nature of fealty in feudal society was such that Henry may have judged it better they served the same king when on either shore of St George's Channel.

If the bones of this report were true then it is reasoned the act of king making involving bestial intercourse need not have arisen only after the participating tribe arrived in Ireland. Hence, an argument can be developed that the cult had its adherents in other parts of the British Isles and in Continental Europe at some stage of pre-history. The possibility that the white mare can be associated with the goddess Epona of Celtic Europe is briefly examined by H.D.Rankin, Professor of Classics at the University of Southampton (25.1).

The language of the offending twelfth century tribe is assumed to be Celtic though in its origins the ceremony need not have been so. However, the rite is unlikely to predate the introduction of the domesticated horse.

Gerald of Wales: Topography of Ireland [Forester]
  Distinction 3 chapter 26.
"26. How numbers in the island are not baptised, and have never come to the knowledge of the faith.
. . . there are some corners of the land in which many are still unbaptized, and to whom, through the negligence of their pastors, the knowledge of the truth has never penetrated. I heard some sailors relate that, having been once driven by a violent storm, during Lent, to the northern islands and the unexplored expanse of the sea of Connaught, they at last took shelter under a small island. . . . From this land not long afterwards they saw a small boat rowing towards them. It was narrow and oblong, and made of wattled boughs, covered and sewn with the hides of beasts. In it were two men, stark naked, except that they wore broad belts of the skin of some animal fastened round their waists. They had long yellow hair, like the Irish, falling below the shoulders, and covering great part of their bodies. The sailors, finding that these men were from some part of Connaught, and spoke the Irish language, . . . (24.4)

There is a viewpoint that the predominant number of people in the west of Ireland have inhabited the same general area of land since the Bronze Age. They assimilated Iron Age technology by contact with other incoming culturally diverse groups.

That slavery was a fact of life in Ireland up to the time of the Norman invasion is brought out in the report by Giraldus on the outcome of the Synod of Armagh. At the synod it was decreed that all English people who were slaves should be freed. The comment by Gerald on the export of slaves by the Anglo-Saxons to Ireland before the conquest of England in 1066, if not Norman propaganda, suggests this to have been a long standing trade. This transfer of men, women and children due to the slave trade would have been in addition to those taken in looting raids and piracy.

Gerald of Wales: Conquest of Ireland, chapter 18 [Forester]
"The Synod of Armagh.
After these events, a synod of all the clergy of Ireland was convoked at Armagh, in which the arrival of the foreigners in the island was the subject of long debates and much deliberation. At length it was unanimously resolved, that it appeared to the synod that the Divine vengeance had brought upon them this severe judgement for the sins of the people, and especially for this, that they had long been wont to purchase natives of England as well from traders as from robbers and pirates, and reduce them to slavery; and that now they also, by reciprocal justice, were reduced to servitude by that very nation. For it was the common practice of the Anglo-Saxon people, while their kingdom was entire, to sell their children, and they used to send their own sons and kinsmen for sale in Ireland, at a time when they were not suffering from poverty or famine. Hence it might well be believed that by so an enormous a sin the buyers had justly merited to undergo the yoke of servitude, as the sellers had done in former times. It was therefore decreed by the before mentioned synod, and proclaimed publicly by universal accord, that all Englishmen throughout the island who were in a state of bondage should be restored to freedom."(24.5)

The third part of the *Topography of Ireland* contains the 'ancient histories of the Irish' as gleaned by Gerald at the end of the twelfth century from chronicles and hearsay. His account differs in part from modern translations of the Irish annals but remains of interest if only for comparison with information taken at different dates in history. A more fundamental understanding of the nature and development of the cultures and peoples in Ireland is to be obtained from an assessment of the archaeology relevant to the separate regions. The account recorded by Gerald, though not necessarily on the whole believed by him, is reproduced in Appendix 5.

A synopsis of the fables (24.6) is given below. The square brackets contain a summary of the footnotes written by the Victorian editor and translator. The foundation myths were transcribed by Christian men. These men were sufficiently literate to have had a modicum of schooling in the works of Roman and Greek authors. It is understood that the Irish chronicles recorded some of the indigenous data drawn from an oral tradition, though taken unevenly across the several peoples who inhabited Ireland. Carbon-14 dates of the order of 3700 BC have been obtained for Neolithic farming sites in Ireland, see *Archaeology Ireland 22 No.3*.

Summary of Irish Foundation Myths recorded by Gerald of Wales.

Caesara — Granddaughter of Noah arrived at uninhabited
Ireland before the flood with 3 men and 50 women.

Bartholanus — 300 years after the flood with 3 sons Languinus,
Salanus, Ruturugus whose names were conferred on extant localities.
Agriculture.
After 300 years descendants fought the giants and suffered pestilence.
Ruanus survived a vast number of years and was baptised by St. Patrick.

Nemedus — Son of Agnominius from Scythia with 4 sons
Starius, Gerbaueles, Antimus, Fergusius. Fought with pirates.
Descendants peopled whole island for 216 years then left having fought giants.
Uninhabited for 200 years after.
[Irish annals state Formorian pirates drove out the Nemedians.]

Dela's sons — 5 sons of Dela were Gandius, Genandius,
Sagandius, Rutherrargus, Slanius.
They divided the island into 5 parts, each with a portion of Meath.
Descendants of Nemedus.
Slanius united Meath then became the first king of all Ireland.
176 Cantreds in Ireland i.e.5x32 (in 1195?) and 16 in Meath.
[These were the Firbolga of legend, possibly Belgae.]

Milesians — 4 sons of King Milesius came from Spain in 60 ships.
In time Heber (later slain) took the north and Herimon the south (later
the whole - first king of current inhabitants). The Hibernienses derived
from the name Heber or River Hiberus (the Ebro) in Spain.
Also called Gaideli (language Gaidelach) and Scots ‑meritaten (daughter
as descendants of Gaidelus and his wife Scota.— of Akhenaten) &
[These were the Tuatha-de-Danaan who some say Gaythelos
came from North Scotland.]

Basclenses — Basques from Spain settled in Ireland by Gurguntius King of Britons.

Patrick — From King Herimon to the coming of Patrick
131 kings reigned over the same race in Ireland.
Patrick, a native of Britain, arrived in the reign of
Laegerius the son of Nellus the Great.
[Patrick reported in Ireland in 432 AD,
the 4th year of Laeghaire's reign.]

Scotland — When Nellus was King of Ireland, 6 sons of King Muredus of Ulster
sailed for North Britain and expelled from those parts the Picts.
[Muredus or Muireadhach reigned from 451, not in the time of Nial.
In fifth century the Irish tribe of Dalreada in Ulster
began to settle in Cantyre.]

Norsemen — 33 kings from the arrival of Patrick to King Fedlimidius
in whose reign in 838 the Norsemen led by Turgesius
(the English say he was named Gurmund) dominated the whole island.
[If the invader was Thorgils the son of Harold Haarfager then
Gerald's date is wrong.]

The Basque language as spoken today does not have its roots in a Celtic language. Without precluding Basque speaking immigrants to Ireland, there is an alternative scenario whereby the Basclenses represented an admixture of Celt and Iberian, speaking a Celtic dialect, who emigrated from Spain or France. It is apposite the informant of Tacitus believed the Silures of South Wales could have emigrated from Spain. This statement on settlement by Basques arose from the writing of Geoffrey of Monmouth and not from the Irish Annals, according to the translator's note.

There are a good many people living in South Wales, Ireland and Cornwall who look upon themselves as Celtic but who are of modest stature with dark or black hair, a description which is at odds with those of the Celts described by writers of the Roman period whilst in keeping with Iberian ancestors.

People known as the Iberians gave their name to the modern day Iberian peninsula comprising Portugal and Spain. In classical times the name Iberian was used to identify groups living in a wider geography around the shores of the Mediterranean. For example on the coast of Liguria to the north of Italy in the second century BC, see *Plutarch's Life of Aemilius chapter 6*: in the neighbourhood of Sicily about 415 BC, see *Thucydides Peloponnesian War book 6 chapter 88*. It would seem that the Iberians were a group of people having identifiable characteristics of form, aspect or language. They had inhabited the European littoral in the centuries before Rome held sway. Their culture reached back into prehistory. Iberes may be disguised in archaeology under several named type-sites. Pockets of venturesome Iberians in South Wales would prove no surprise at any period following the retreat of the ice sheets.

To accommodate a glimmer of light in the Egyptian origins of Scota the mother of Gaidel (see Appendix 5), it is convenient to recognise from archaeology that a modest component of the peoples in Spain had crossed from North Africa to Spain at a stage of their pre-history. Thus the Irish mythology could incorporate a memory of the mingling of two tribes in Spain.

The activities of the Roman army on the continent prodded motivated groups to decamp to the British Isles in the years following 50 BC. A further movement of fugitives from Rome after the Claudian invasion of Britain in AD 43 is surmised to have impacted on Ireland and entered the folklore prior to the advent of the Celtic Church.

IBERES AND ALBANI, BLACK SEA

Miletus was a Greek city on the Mediterranean coast of modern Turkey. The Milesians had established a number of settlements around the Black Sea. Leading east from the Black Sea a peoples known as the Iberians lived along side the Albani. A group of Amazon women had left a Greek island and settled in the same general area. The island of Delos was held in high regard. It lies between Turkey and Greece.

If literate individuals in Ireland had read the Latin or Greek texts which touched upon Iberians living next to Albanians between the Black Sea and the Caspian at the eastern rim of the Graeco-Roman world, it would not have gone un-noticed that by co-incidence they were 'Hyberians' living along side 'Albion' at the western extremity of the known world. Occident mirrored orient. A progression from such a hypothetical situation is with the re-telling of a history read from books, which must have held a mystique of its own, that some of the detail was transferred and woven into the re-told mythological history of Ireland itself. The era in which individuals first wrote down the history of events in Ireland being divorced from that when the folklore was thus enhanced.

The similarity between data from the *Geography* of Strabo and the early written history of Ireland in the grouping of names and events should be examined from the viewpoint of rising above chance and co-incidence though, equally, then discarded as irrelevant to the Irish setting if so judged.

Alternatively, it can be contemplated the ship full of beautiful women, the Milesians and the sons of Dela had their origin in that end of the Black Sea which also was host to the adventures of Jason and the Argonauts. The Biblical resting place for Noah's Ark, Mount Ararat, is located on the southern approaches to the country of the Iberes. A storyteller could then develop this fact into a notion the Iberes were descended from the people who alighted from the Ark after the flood subsided - thus connecting the Christian people in Ireland with Biblical antecedents whilst avoiding any need to identify with the Jewish nation. In a similar vein, Nemedus may have an equivalence with the Nomades. The Nomades lived in what might be designated Scythia.

Closer to Ireland, a tribe with a similar sounding name and no other obvious link with Nemedus was the Nemetes, living near the Rhine in Pliny's time. The precise text of books available in dark-age Ireland need not have survived to the present day. Nonetheless, to pursue the hypothesis, a set of pertinent quotations from the *Geography* of Strabo are included for consideration. There is no suggestion that kinship ties existed between the peoples of Ireland and the frontiers of Asia in the first century AD. The connection is solely in the affinity of the grouping of names in the written word.

Strabo: Geography book 14, chapter 1.6 [Falconer]
"6. Ephorus relates that Miletus was first founded and fortified by the Cretans on the spot above the sea-coast where at present the ancient Miletus is situated, and that Sarpedon conducted thither settlers from the Miletus in Crete,
[Footnote. According to Pausanias, vii. 2. a friend of Sarpedon, named Miletus, conducted the colony from Crete, founded Miletus, and gave his name to it. Before his arrival the place had the name of Anactoria, and more anciently Lelegis.]
and gave it the same name; that Leleges were the former occupiers of the country, and that afterwards Neleus built the present city.
The present city has four harbours, one of which will admit a fleet of ships. The citizens have achieved many great deeds, but the most important is the number of colonies which they established. The whole Euxine for instance, and the Propentis, and many other places, are peopled with their settlers. . . .
Both the Milesians and the Delians invoke Apollo Ulius, as dispensing health and curing diseases; . . . Apollo is a healer, and Artemis has her name from making persons . . . sound. The sun, also, and moon are associated with these deities,"(15.16)

Murmurings have been made that hyberian and albani were terms used to describe peoples living at the edge of the known world. Such a definition is not to the fore in readily available Latin dictionaries. In early Roman history the name Albani was applied to Sabines or people from Alba, the mother city of Rome built by Ascanius, son of Aeneas (*White's Latin Dictionary*). The word albocracy denotes government by white men or Europeans (*OED*), for example the British Raj in India.

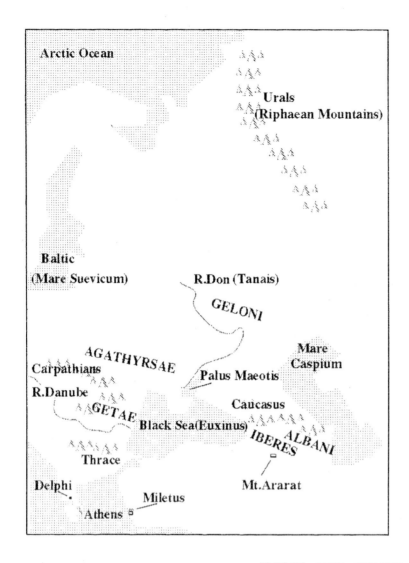

IBERES AND ALBANI

Strabo: Geography book 11, chapter 1.5 [Falconer]
"5. In passing in our geographical description from Europe to Asia, the first part of the country which present themselves are those in the northern division, and we shall therefore begin with these.

Of these parts the first are those about the Tanais, (or Don,) which we have assumed as the boundary of Europe and Asia. These have a kind of peninsula form, for they are surrounded on the west by the river Tanais (or Don) and the Palus Maeotis
[Footnote. Sea of Azov.]
as far as the Cimmerian Bosporus, and that part of the coast of the Euxine which terminates at Colchis; on the north by the Ocean, as far as the mouth of the Caspian Sea;

126

on the east by the same sea, as far as the confines of Albania and Armenia, where the rivers Cyrus and Arxes empty themselves; the latter flowing through Armenia, and the Cyrus through Iberia
[Footnote. Georgia.]
and Albania; on the south is the tract of country extending from the mouth of the Cyrus as far as Colchis, and comprising about 3000 stadia from sea to sea, across the territory of the Albani, and Iberes, so as to represent an isthmus."(15.17)

Strabo: Geography book 11, chapter 2.19 [Falconer]
"19. . . . In their country the winter torrents are said to bring down even gold, which the Barbarians collect in troughs pierced with holes, and lined with fleeces; and hence the fable of the golden fleece. Some say that they are called Iberians (the same name as the western Iberians) from the gold mines found in both countries."(15.18)

Strabo: Geography book 11, chapter 3.1 to 3.6 [Falconer]
"1. The greater part of Iberia is well inhabited, and contains cities and villages where the houses have roofs covered with tiles, and display skill in building; there are market places in them, and various kinds of public edifices. . . .
5. From the Nomades on the north there is a difficult ascent of three days, and then a narrow road by the side of the river Aragus, a journey of four days, which road admits only one person to pass at a time. The termination of the road is guarded by an impregnable wall.
   From Albania the entrance is at first cut through rocks, then passes over a marsh formed by the river, . . .
6. The inhabitants of this country are also divided into four classes; the first and chief is that from which the kings are appointed. The king is the eldest and the nearest of his predecessor's relations. The second administers justice, and is commander of the army.
   The second class consists of priests, whose business it is to settle the respective rights of their own and the bordering people.
   The third is composed of soldiers and husbandmen. The fourth comprehends the common people, who are royal slaves, and perform all the duties of ordinary life."(15.19)

There is no reason to read this structure across as relevant to Ireland aside from supposing that it approximated to many tribal societies.

Strabo: Geography book 11, chapter 4.1 [Falconer]
"1. The Albanians pursue rather a shepherd life, and resemble more the nomadic tribes, except that they are not savages, and hence they are little disposed to war. They inhabit the country between the Iberians and the Caspian Sea, approaching close to the sea on the east, and on the west border upon the Iberians. . . .
5. . . . The Nomades also co-operate with them against foreigners, as they do with the Iberians on similar occasions. When there is no war they frequently attack these people and prevent them from cultivating the ground."(15.20)

Strabo: Geography book 11, chapter 5.1 [Falconer]
"1. The Amazons are said to live among the mountains above Albania."(15.21)

WALES

Giraldus Cambrensis, Gerald of Wales, accompanied the Archbishop of Canterbury on a visit to Wales for the purpose of raising volunteers for the Crusades. The visit ended at Easter 1188. At that time, or shortly thereafter, Gerald wrote *The Itinerary through Wales*, a record of the visit, followed by *The Description of Wales*. The quotations are taken from the translation from the Latin by Sir Richard Colt Hoare first published in 1806 that relied on the texts of Camden (1602) and Wharton (1691). The translation was re-published in the Bohn Library series. Both Camden and Wharton are reported to have drawn upon the Latin text compiled by Powel in 1595. There are extant manuscript copies of Gerald's works.

Gerald of Wales: Description of Wales, book 1 [Colt Hoare]
" Chapter 6. Merionyth and the land of Conan . . . . The natives of that part of Wales excel in the use of long lances, as those of Monmouthshire are distinguished for their management of the bow. It is to be observed, that the British language is more delicate and richer in North Wales, that country being less intermixed with foreigners. Many, however, assert that the language of Cardiganshire, in South Wales, placed as it were in the middle and heart of Cambria, is the most refined.

The people of Cornwall and the Americans speak a language similar to that of the Britons; and from its origin and near resemblance, it is intelligible to the Welsh in many instances, and almost in all; and although less delicate and methodical, yet it approaches, as I judge, more to the ancient British idiom. As in the southern parts of England, and particularly in Devonshire, the English language seems less agreeable, yet it bears more marks of antiquity (the northern parts being much corrupted by the irruptions of the Danes and Norwegians), and adheres more strictly to the original language and ancient mode of speaking; a positive proof of which may be deduced from all the English works of Bede, Rhabanus, and king Alfred, being written according to this idiom."

A Celtic tradition that some of their people were descended from the Trojans was recorded by Ammianus in the fourth century AD. The Welsh folk tale, as told to Gerald, gives this Trojan link as the explanation of how Cambria received its name.

"Chapter 7. Cambria was so called from Camber, son of Brutus; for Brutus, descending from the Trojans, by his grandfather, Ascanius, and father, Silvius, led the remnant of the Trojans, who had long been detained in Greece, into this western isle; and having reigned many years, and given his name to the country and people, at his death divided the kingdom of Wales between his three sons. To the eldest son, Locrinus, he gave that part of the island which lies between the rivers Humber and Severn, and which from him was called Loegria. To his second son, Albanactus, he gave the lands beyond the Humber, which took the name Albania. But to his youngest son, Camber, he bequeathed all that region which lies beyond the Severn and is called after him Cambria; hence the country is properly and truly called Cambria, and its inhabitants Cambrians' or Cambrenses. Some assert that their name was derived from 'Cam' and 'Graeco', that is, distorted Greek, on account of the affinity of their languages, contracted by their long residence in Greece; but this conjecture, though plausible, is not well founded in truth.

The name of Wales was not derived from Wallo, a general, or Wandolena, the queen, as the fabulous history of Geoffrey Arthurius falsely maintains, because neither of these personages are to be found amongst the Welsh; but it arose from a barbarian appellation. The Saxons, when they seized upon Britain, called this nation, as they did all foreigners, Wallenses; and thus the barbarous name remains to the people and their country. . . .

Chapter 8. This people is light and active, hardy rather than strong, and entirely bred up to the use of arms. . . . Almost all the people live upon the produce of their herds, with oats, milk, cheese, and butter; eating flesh in larger proportions than bread. They pay no attention to commerce, shipping or manufacturers, . . . They make use of light arms, which do not impede agility, small coats of mail, bundles of arrows, and long lances, helmets and shields, and more rarely greaves plated with iron. The higher class go to battle mounted on swift and generous steeds, which their country produces; . . . The horsemen, as their situation or occasion requires, willingly serve as infantry, in attacking or retreating; and they either walk barefooted, or make use of high shoes, roughly constructed with untanned leather. . . .

Chapter 9. Not addicted to gluttony or drunkenness, this people who incur no expense in food or dress, and whose minds are always bent upon the defence of their country, and on the means of plunder, are wholly employed in the care of their horses and furniture. . . .

Chapter 10. No one of this nation ever begs, for the houses of all are common to all; and they consider liberality and hospitality amongst the first virtues. So much does hospitality here rejoice in communication, that it is neither offered nor requested by travellers, who, on entering a house, only deliver up their arms. When water is offered to them, if they suffer their feet to be washed, they are received as guests; for the offer of water to wash the feet is with this nation an hospitable invitation. But if they refuse the proffered service, they only wish for morning refreshment, not lodging. The young men move about in troops and families under the direction of a chosen leader. . . .

Those who arrive in the morning are entertained till evening with the conversation of young women, and the music of the harp; . . . and in each family the art of playing on the harp is held preferable to any other learning. . . . The house is not furnished with tables, . . . the guests being seated in threes, instead of couples as elsewhere, they place the dishes before them all at once upon rushes and fresh grass, in large platters or trenchers. They also make use of a thin and broad cake of bread, baked every day, . . . A bed made of rushes, and covered with a course kind of cloth manufactured in the country, called brychan, is then placed along the side of the room, and they all in common lie down to sleep; nor is their dress at night different from that of the day, for at all seasons they defend themselves from the cold only by a thin cloak and tunic. . . .

Chapter 11. The men and the women cut their hair close round to the ears and eyes. The women, after the manner of the Parthians, cover their heads with a large white veil, folded together in the form of a crown.

Both sexes exceed any other nation in attention to their teeth, which they render like ivory, by constantly rubbing them with green hazel and wiping with a woollen cloth. . . . The men shave all their beard except the moustaches. . . . so that this nation more than any other shaves off all pilosity. . . .

Chapter 13. In their musical concerts they do not sing in unison like the inhabitants of other countries, but in many different parts; so that in a company of singers, which one very frequently meets with in Wales, you will hear as many different parts and voices as there are performers, who all at length unite, with organic melody, in one consonance and the soft sweetness of B flat.

In the northern district of Britain, beyond the Humber, and on the borders of Yorkshire, the inhabitants make use of the same kind of symphonious harmony, but with less variety; singing only in two parts, one murmuring in the base, the other warbling in the acute or treble. . . . As the English in general do not adopt this mode of singing, but only those of the northern countries, I believe that it was from the Danes and Norwegians, by whom these parts of the island were more frequently invaded, and held longer under their dominion, that the natives contracted their mode of singing as well as speaking.

Chapter 14. The heads of different families, in order to excite the laughter of their guests, and gain credit by their sayings, make use of great facetiousness in their conversation; at one time uttering their jokes in a light, easy manner, at another time, under the disguise of equivocation, passing the severest censures. . . .

Chapter 15. Nature hath given not only to the highest, but also to the inferior, classes of the people of this nation, a boldness and confidence in speaking and answering, even in the presence of their princes and chieftains. The Romans and Franks had the same faculty; but neither the English, nor the Saxons and Germans, from whom they are descended, had it. . . . the English . . . still retain the exterior fairness of complexion and inward coldness of disposition, . . . The Britons, . . . still retain their brown complexion and that natural warmth of temper from which their confidence is derived. . . .

Chapter 16. There are certain persons in Cambria, whom you will find nowhere else, called Awenddyon, or people inspired; when consulted about any doubtful event, they roar out violently, are rendered beside themselves, and become, as it were, possessed by a spirit. They do not deliver the answer to what is required in a connected manner; but the person who skilfully observes them, will find, after many preambles, and many nugatory and incoherent, though ornamental speeches, the desired explanation in some turn of word; they are then roused from their ecstasy, as from a deep sleep, . . . These prophets are only found among the Britons descended from the Trojans. . . .

Chapter 17. . . . Being particularly attached to family descent, they revenge with vehemence the injuries which may tend to the disgrace of their blood; and being naturally of a vindictive and passionate disposition, they are ever ready to avenge not only recent but ancient affronts; . . . but content themselves with small huts made of the boughs of trees twisted together, constructed with little labour and expense, and sufficient to endure throughout the year. They have neither orchards nor gardens, . . . The greater part of their land is laid down to pasturage; little is cultivated, a very small quantity is ornamented with flowers, and a still smaller is sown. They seldom yoke less than four oxen to their ploughs; the driver walks before, but backwards, . . . Instead of small sickles in mowing, they make use of a moderate-sized piece of iron formed like a knife, with two pieces of wood fixed loosely and flexibly to the head, . . . The boats which they employ in fishing or in crossing the rivers are made of twigs, not oblong nor pointed, but almost round, or rather triangular, covered both within and without with raw hides.

[Footnote. Genealogies were preserved as a principle of necessity under the ancient British constitution. A man's pedigree was in reality his title deed, by which he claimed his birthright in the country. Every one was obliged to show his descent through nine generations, in order to be acknowledged a free native, and by this right he claimed his portion of land in the community. He was affected with respect to legal process in his collateral affinities through nine degrees. For instance, every murder committed had a fine levied on the relations of the murderer, divided into nine degrees; his brother paying the greatest, and the ninth in affinity the least.

This fine was distributed in the same way among the relatives of the victim. A person past the ninth descent formed a new family.
Every family was represented by its elder; and these elders from every family were delegates to the national council. - Owen.]"(24.7)

Gerald of Wales: Description of Wales, book 2 [Colt Hoare]
"They pay no respect to oaths, faith, or truth. . . . This nation conceives it right to commit acts of plunder, theft, and robbery, not only against foreigners and hostile nations, but even against their own countrymen. . . . In war this nation is very severe at the first attack, terrible by their clamour and looks, filling the air with horrid shouts and the deep-toned clangour of very long trumpets; swift and rapid in their advances and frequent throwing of darts. Bold in the first onset, they cannot bear a repulse, being easily thrown into confusion as soon as they turn their backs; and they trust to flight for safety, . . . the princes entrust the education of their children to the care of the principal men of their country, . . . Where they find plenty, and can exercise their power, they levy the most unjust exactions. Immoderate in their love of food and intoxicating drink, . . . They do not engage in marriage, until they have tried, by previous cohabitation, the disposition, and particularly the fecundity, of the person with whom they are engaged. An ancient custom also prevails of hiring girls from their parents at a certain price, and a stipulated penalty, in case of relinquishing their connection. . . . Moreover, through their sins, and particularly that detestable and wicked vice of Sodom, as well as by divine vengeance, they lost Britain, . . . So that their abstinence from that vice, which in their prosperity they could not resist, may be attributed more justly to their poverty and state of exile than to their sense of virtue."(24.8)

The comment on homosexuality is not from Gerald's observations in his own time of British Celts but rather taken from histories. For example Geoffrey of Monmouth, where equally it could have been used as a form of scathing abuse, coupled with knowledge of statements and inferences by authors writing in the classical period. By co-incidence Gerald was thus enabled to seize an opportunity to, in parallel, inflict a criticism of the behaviour of Richard, son of King Henry II. Subsequent to the death of an older brother, Richard succeeded Henry to the throne of England.

Gerald concurred that the word Welsh came from the Saxon word 'vealh' meaning foreign and that the Anglo-Saxons called the Britons 'Wealhas'. The Celtic word for Wales is Cambria or Cymru. The transformation from Brythonic to a recognisable form of Welsh occurred in the years 400 AD to 600 AD with the name 'Cymry' gaining currency after 1100 AD (see John Davies, *A History of Wales* - Welsh 1990, in English published by Penguin Books 1994).

At the end of the twelfth century, the language in England of the ruling feudal class and the Church was Norman French and Latin. English in its dialects arising from within its constituent parts which included Saxon, Jute and Angle overlaid in the east with Danish and Norwegian, was spoken by peoples in a state of servitude. All things English were demolished by the conquering Normans. The characteristic English script only then survived in the context of texts written in Celtic lands. The English roots were in a subset of tribes within the confederation known collectively as Germani to the Romans. Celtic in its various forms was spoken by Scots Gaels in the Highlands and Islands of Scotland, interspersed with Norron against a backdrop of Pictish.

There is a theory that northern Old English and the development of Lowland Scots patois were interlinked. Celtic was the language of Wales, Ireland, Strathclyde, the Isle of Man, Brittany, Cornwall and most of Devon, with pockets of Welsh living in Wiltshire. The genetic inheritance of all these areas may prove more cosmopolitan when the data becomes available.

In the years that followed on, the three principates of Wales were conquered. The Normans pressed on with their conquest of the disparate chieftains and septs in Ireland in order to unify Ireland, Wales, England and the possessions in Continental Europe under the English crown. It has been argued since 924 AD whether or not the Kings of Scotland have acknowledged the overlordship of those ruling the kingdom south of their border. But there is little doubt even among the Scots that on the third of June 1291 for a brief moment Edward the first of England was their lord. This was further enforced in 1296 when Edward took the black rood of Saint Margaret and the stone of Scone back to Westminster with him. The stone of Scone was used in the king making ceremony by the Scots who had come from Ireland.

Margaret was a Saxon noblewoman, the granddaughter of King Edmond 'Ironside' (1016 AD). She became a refugee in Scotland after the success of the Norman invasion of England. Margaret married Malcolm Canmore, Malcolm III, the successor to the throne on the death of the Shakespearian Macbeth.

The history of the land known as Scotland is littered with struggles between people whose ethnic origin includes Picts, Scots, Celts, English, Dane, Norwegian and Norman (26). The events in both Wales and Ireland were similar in nature and, hence, not all aspects of culture in those areas can be taken to be Celtic in their entirety.

18   NORSEMEN : HEIMSKRINGLA

Some tribes of the warlike Germani, who in the time of Imperial Rome lived to the north of the Celts on the shores of the North Sea and the Baltic, evolved as the warlike Danes and Norsemen of the early medieval period. Norsemen raided England from 787 onwards and Ireland from about 795, having visited the Hebrides and Ireland in the seventh century (27). Regular contact with England had been ongoing for four hundred years. The Norse kept alive the history and deeds of their folk in Edda. Edda savants assess these sagas as having been produced between the sixth and fourteenth centuries, though not necessarily written down at the time they were compiled.

Opinions are held that recounting origins, battles and ancestors was practised from the onset of speech and memory. In consequence, snippets from the whole background of the Germanic tribes are looked for in Eddas, all the more so from those of a semi mythical nature.

Points of similarity between Edda material and descriptions from the Roman period of the Germani (and Celts) would be common to a wide range of tribes at that state of civilisation. They include:-

Blood sacrifice at festivals.
Sacrificing humans in special circumstances.
The eating of horse meat stew and drinking of the broth in pagan festivals.
Hanging the heads of slain enemies from the horse's stirrup leather.

The information on Norsemen is taken from the *Heimskringla*, a compilation by Snorre Sturlason of Sagas of the Norse Kings which covers the dates approximately 839 AD to 1177 AD. Snorre Sturlason was born in Iceland in 1178, made visits to Norway, and was killed in Iceland in 1240 AD. The translation from the Icelandic (Norron tongue) was made by Dr. Samuel Laing and published in 1844. The translation was later republished in the Everyman's Library and the quotations are taken from the two volumes in this edition published in 1915 and 1930 respectively.

The editor of Everyman, Ernest Rhys, states in his introduction that Dr. Laing was an Orcadian, steeped in the lore and story of the island, who had been an officer on the staff of Sir John Moore on the Spanish expedition and had returned to this country after the battle of Corunna.

Snorre: The Olaf Sagas, Laing's Introduction xxvii [Laing]
"It was because there really was no language obstacle. Roughly speaking, until the year 1000 there was one language understood over all the north of Europe, with differences hardly greater than some of our present dialects in various parts of Britain, or the differences between Danish, Swedish and Norse to-day. The ancient Rimbelga (iii,c.1) records: *"When the Asia men settled in the North the tongue which we call Norron came with them, and it went through Saxland, Denmark, Sweden, Norway, and part of England."* In the Saga of Gunnlaug Ormstunga (c. 7) we are told: *"In 979 King Ethelred son of Edgar ruled over England. The tongue in England as well as in Norway and Denmark was then one - but it changed in England when William the Bastard conquered England."*(28.1)

The Ynglinga Saga is placed in the category of being semi mythical. The justification as to why their predecessors moved from the banks of the River Don across Europe to the North Sea is unexpected from a nation whose sea marauders put the western world in mortal fear.

Snorre: Norse Kings Sagas [Laing]
The Ynglinga Saga
Chapter 1. Of the Situation of the Countries.
" . . . the eastern part is called Asia, and the western is called by some Europa, by some Enea. [In ancient days it was a common belief that the Romans, Franks, British, and other peoples, were descended from Aeneas and the Trojans.] . . . On the south side of the mountains which lie outside of all inhabited lands runs a river through Swithiod, which is properly called by the name of Tanais, [The modern river Don.] but was formerly called Tanaquisl, or Vanaquisl, and which falls into the Black Sea. The country of the people on the Vanaquisl was called Vanaland, or Vanaheim; and the river separates the three parts of the world, of which the easternmost part is called Asia, and the westernmost Europe.

Chapter 2. Of the people of Asia.
" The country east of the Tanaquisl in Asia was called Asaland, or Asaheim, and the chief city in that land was called Asgaard. [The old gods were called Aeser (sing. Aas) and Snorre derives the word from Asia.] In that city was a chief called Odin, and it was a great place for sacrifice. It was the custom there that twelve temple priests should both direct the sacrifices, and also judge the people.

They were called Diar, [Diar is a rare name of the old gods and is supposed to be a term imported from the Irish in the ninth or tenth century.] or Drotner, [Drot (sing.), a lord. In the pagan age the word was not applied to the gods; but in the Christian period it was used of God and Christ.] and all the people served and obeyed them. Odin was a great and very far-travelled warrior,"

Chapter 3. Of Odin's Brothers.
"Odin had two brothers, the one called Ve, the other Vilje, and they . . . . governed the kingdom when he was absunt. . . ."

Chapter 4. Of Odin's war with the people of Vanaland.
"Odin went out with a great army against the Vanaland people; but they were well prepared, and defended their land, so that victory was changeable, and they ravaged the lands of each other, and did great damage. They tired of this at last, and on both sides appointed a meeting for establishing peace, made a truce, and exchanged hostages. The Vanaland people sent their best men, Njord the Rich, and his son Frey. The people of Asaland sent a man called Hone, whom they thought well suited to be a chief, as he was a stout and very handsome man; and with him they sent a man of great understanding called Mime. On the other side, the Vanaland people sent the wisest man in their community, who was called Kvase. Now, when Hone came to Vanaheim he was immediately made a chief, and Mime came to him with good counsel on all occasions. But when Hone stood in the Things or other meetings, if Mime was not near him, and any difficult matter was laid before him, he always answered in one way - 'Now let others give their advice'; so that the Vanaland people got a suspicion that the Asaland people had deceived them in the exchange of men. They took Mime, therefore, and beheaded him, and sent his head to the Asaland people. Odin took the head, smeared it with herbs so that it should not rot, and sang incantations over it. Thereby he gave it the power that it spoke to him, and discovered to him many secrets. Odin placed Njord and Frey as priests of the sacrifices, and they became Diar of the Asaland people. Njord's daughter Freya was priestess of the sacrifice, and first taught the Asaland people the magic art, as it was in use and fashion among the Vanaland people. . . . "

Chapter 5. Odin divides his kingdom: also concerning Gefion.
" . . . He therefore set his brothers Ve and Vilje over Asgaard; and he himself, with all the gods and a great many other people, wandered out, first westward to Gardarike, [Gardarike is Russia.] and then south to Saxland. [Saxland is North Germany]. He had many sons; and after having subdued an extensive kingdom in Saxland, he set his sons to rule the country. He himself went northwards to the sea, and took up his abode on an island which is called Odinso in Fyen. Then he sent Gefion across the sound to the north [north-east] to discover new countries; and she came to King Gylve, who gave her a ploughgate of land. Then she went to Jotunheim, and bore four sons to a giant, and transformed them into a yoke of oxen. She yoked them to a plough, and broke out the land into the ocean right opposite to Odinso. This land was called Sealand, and there she afterwards settled and dwelt. Skjold, a son of Odin, married her and they dwelt at Leidre. [Near Roskilde in Zeeland. Skjold was the progenitor of the Skjold-unger, the Danish kings.]"

The Norsemen arrived at the shores of the North Sea with horses, herds and wagons. If the detail in this passage is true, Odin's people learnt the practice of agriculture after they had arrived in North Western Europe from a group already in place. The expert ship building skills were developed after their arrival.

If surmised that the Norron speakers expanded northwards when a growing population was frustrated from moving south by a proportionately more populous and warlike confederation, then it is deduced that the front edge of the Germanic hordes arrived in Western Europe after the Celts were established.

"Chapter 6. Of Odin's Accomplishments. [Laing]
When Odin of Asaland came to the north, and the Diar with him, they introduced and taught to others the arts which the people long afterwards have practised. Odin was the cleverest of all, and from him all the others learned their arts and accomplishments; and he knew them first, and knew many more than other people. But now, to tell why he is held in such high respect, we must mention various causes that contributed to it. When sitting among his friends his countenance was so beautiful and dignified, that the spirits of all were exhilarated by it; but when he was in war he appeared dreadful to his foes. This arose from his being able to change his skin and form in any way he liked. Another cause was, that he conversed so cleverly and smoothly, that all who heard him believed him. He spoke everything in rhyme, such as now composed, which we call scald-craft. He and his temple priests were called song-smiths, and from them came the art of song into the northern countries. Odin could make his enemies in battle blind, or deaf, or terror-struck, and their weapons so blunt that they could no more cut than a willow wand; on the other hand, his men rushed forwards without armour, were as mad as dogs or wolves, bit their shields, and were strong as bears or wild bulls, and killed people at a blow, but neither fire nor iron told upon themselves. These were called Berserker. [Berserker - bare shirts: that is, bare of any shirt or mail. The Berserker appear to have gone into battle intoxicated with some exciting drug; as the reaction after their berserker-gang was over, and their lassitude and exhaustion, prove the use of some stimulant previously taken to a great excess. This etymology of the word is challenged by Vigfusson and Cleaseby, who prefer Bear-skins - warriors clad in bearskins.]"

The naked warriors standing at the front of the Celtic army as reported by Polybius (10.1) show a similarity to the berserker. The word naked may imply without armour.

"Chapter 7. Of Odin's Feats.
Odin could transform his shape: his body would lie as if dead, or asleep; but then he would be in shape of a fish, or worm, or bird, or beast, and be off in a twinkling to distant lands upon his own or other people's business. With words alone he could quench fire, still the ocean in tempest, and turn the wind to any quarter he pleased. Odin had a ship which he called Skidbladnir, in which he sailed over wide seas, and which he could roll up like a cloth. [This possibly refers to boats covered with skin or leather - the coracle of the Welsh and Irish.] Odin carried with him Mime's head, which told him all the news of other countries. Sometimes even he called the dead out of the earth, or set himself beside the burial-mounds; whence he was called the ghost-sovereign, and lord of the mounds. He had two ravens, [Hugin and Munin.] to whom he had taught the speech of man; and they flew far and wide through the land, and brought him the news.

In all such things he was pre-eminently wise. He taught all these arts in Runes, and songs which are called incantations, and therefore the Asaland people are called incantation-smiths. Odin understood the art in which the greatest power is lodged, and which he himself practised; namely, what is called magic. By means of this he could know beforehand the pre-destined fate [Orlog - the original law fixed from the beginning. It is curious that this idea of a predestination existed in the religion of Odin.] of men, or their not yet completed lot; and also bring on the death, ill luck, or bad health of people, and take the strength of wit from one person and give it to another. But after such witchcraft followed such weakness and anxiety, that it was not thought respectable for men to practice it; and therefore the priestesses were brought up in this art. . . . People sacrificed to Odin and the twelve chiefs from Asaland, and called them their gods, and believed in them long after."

Strabo knew that Cimbri priestesses practiced human sacrifice (15.11). Tacitus was aware that the Germans believed women had a divine spark of knowledge (5.4).

Chapter 8. Of Odin's Lawgiving.
"Odin established the same law in his land that had been in force in Asaland. Thus he established by law that all dead men should be burned, and their belongings laid with them upon the pile, and the ashes be cast into the sea or buried in the earth. Thus, said he, every one will come to Valhalla [Odin's hall (in heaven) where fallen heroes went after death.] with the riches he had with him upon the pile; and would also enjoy whatever he himself had buried in the earth. For men of consequence a mound should be raised to their memory, and for all other warriors who had been distinguished for manhood a standing stone; which custom remained long after Odin's time. On winter's day [Winter's day was in the middle of October (later 14 October) and summer day in mid-April (later 14 April).] there should be blood-sacrifice for a good year, and in the middle of winter for a good crop; and the third sacrifice should be on summer day, for victory in battle. Over all Swithiod the people paid Odin a scat or tax - so much on each head; but he had to defend the country from enemy or disturbance, and pay the expense of the sacrifice feasts for a good year."(27.1)

Chapter 27.
"King Hake had been so grievously wounded that he saw his days could not be long; so he ordered a warship which he had to be loaded with his dead men and their weapons, and to be taken out to the sea; the tiller to be shipped, and the sails hoisted. Then he set fire to some tar-wood, and he ordered a pile to be made over it in the ship. Hake was almost if not quite dead, when he was laid upon this pile of his. The wind was blowing off the land - the ship flew, burning in clear flame, out between the islets, and into the ocean. Great was the fame of this deed in after times."(27.2)

This aspect of Norse burial practice could not have been brought by Odin's people from Asia.

Chapter 29.

"On returned to Upsal when he was sixty years of age. He made a great sacrifice, and in it offered up his son to Odin. On got an answer from Odin, that he should live sixty years longer; and he was afterwards king in Upsal for twenty-five years . . . Then On fled a second time to Gotland; and for twenty-five years . . . On returned to Upsal, and ruled the kingdom for twenty-five years. Then he made a great sacrifice again for long life, in which he sacrificed his second son, and received the answer from Odin, that he should live as long as he gave him one of his sons every tenth year, and also that he should name one of the districts of his country after the number of sons he should offer to Odin. When he had sacrificed the seventh of his sons he continued to live; but he could not walk, but was carried on a chair. Then he sacrificed the eighth son, and lived thereafter lying in his bed. Now he sacrificed his ninth son, and lived ten years more, but so that he drank out of a horn like a weaned infant. He had now only one son remaining, whom he also wanted to sacrifice, and to give to Odin Upsal and the domains thereunto belonging, under the name of the Ten Lands, but the Swedes would not allow it; so there was no sacrifice, and King On died, and was buried in a mound at Upsal."(27.3)

The principal reason for this tale is interpreted as being to explain the naming of certain districts. Also the tale serves to demonstrate a Nordic parallel with the Celtic-Druid concept of appeasing the gods with a life for a life. In passing it provides a window to see the daily routine of babies taking their mashed food through the tip of animal horns.

Chapter 31. Of King Ottar.

"The Danes took his body, carried it to the land, laid it upon a mound of earth, and let the wild beasts and ravens tear it to pieces."(27.4)

This death occurred in a battle at sea. The action of exposing the corpse (of King Ottar of Sweden) in this way must have had a particular significance.

To what degree the Norse social behaviour reflected a general Germanic tradition is a moot point, but songs, drinking, boasting and eating round a fire would slip into a social description of most societies.

Chapter 32. Of King Adil's Marriage.

"The king was not at home, and Adils and his men ran up to the king's house and plundered it, while others drove a herd of cattle down to the strand. The herd was attended by slave-people, churls, and girls, and they took all of them together."

Footnote. The ordinary way, with the vikings, of victualling their ships, was driving cattle down to the strand and killing them, without regard to the property of friends or enemies; and this was so established a practice that it was expressed in a single word, 'Strandhug.' King Harold Fairhair had prohibited the stranding being committed in his own dominions by his own subjects on their viking cruises; and Rolf Gangar, the son of the Earl of More, having, notwithstanding, landed and made a strandhug in the south of Norway, where the king happened to be, was outlawed; and he in consequence set out on an expedition, in which he conquered and settled in Normandy."(27.5)

Chapter 40. The burning of Upsal.
"It was the custom at that time that he who gave an heir-ship feast after kings or earls, and entered upon the heritage, should sit upon the footstool in front of the high seat, until the full-bowl, which was called the Brage-beaker, [This beaker was drained in honour of Brage, the god of poetry. At banquets it was usual to drink first to the gods, just as nowadays the toast of the king always comes first.] was brought in. Then he should stand up, take the Brage-beaker, make solemn vows to be afterwards fulfilled, and thereupon empty the beaker. Then he should ascend the high seat which his father had occupied."(27.6)

Chapter 41. Of Hjorvard's Marriage.
"In the evening, when the full bowls went round, as was the custom of kings when they were at home, or in the feasts they ordered to be made, they sat and drank together, a man and woman with each other in pairs, and the rest of the company sat and drank all together. But it was the law among the vikings that all who were at the entertainment should drink together in one company all round."(27.7)

Halfdan the Black [839-860]
Chapter 7.
"King Halfdan was a wise man, a man of truth and uprightness - who made laws,"
[He was the author of the Eldsiva law code.] (27.8)

Chapter 8.
[Footnote. "The feast of Jolner, one of the names of Thor, was celebrated by the pagan northmen in mid-winter; and the festivity of Yule derives its name from Jolner.]"(27.9)

Harold the Fairhaired [860-933]
Chapter 20. King Harald the supreme sovereign of Norway.
Of the Settlement of Distant Lands.
"In the discontent when King Harold seized on the lands of Norway, [This taking of the land appears to have been an attempt to introduce the feudal tenures and services.] the out countries of Iceland and the Faroe Isles were discovered and peopled. The Northmen had also a great resort to Shetland, and many men left Norway, flying the country on account of King Harold, and went on viking cruises into the West sea. In winter they were in the Orkney Islands and Hebrides; but marauded in summer in Norway, and did great damage."
. . .

"King Harold had many wives and many children. Among them he had one wife, who was called Ragnhild the Mighty, a daughter of King Eric, from Jutland; and by her he had a son, Eric Bloody-axe. He was also married to Swanhild, a daughter of Earl Eystein; and their sons were Olaf Geirstadealf, Bjorn, and Ragnar Rykkel. Lastly, King Harald married Aashild, a daughter of King Dagsson, up in Ringerike; and their children were Dag, Ring, Gudrod, Skirja, and Ingigerd. It is told that King Harald put away nine wives when he married Ragnhild the Mighty."(27.10)

Whatever form marriage took, this is an example of polygamy and divorce among the Norse nobles.

Chapter 21. Of King Harold's Children.
"King Harold's children were all fostered and brought up by their relations on the mother's side. Guttorm the Duke had poured water over King Harold's eldest son, and had given him his own name. He set the child upon his knee, and was his foster father,"(27.11)

The practice of allowing the maternal uncle to rear the children of noble families was probably for reasons of the children's safety. The uncle's influence would increase if the child survived. In the eyes of paternal uncles the children could signify a waning of power. This interpretation is tempered by a perspective that for a man to rear the child of another showed to the world the childminder's subservience to the father. A similar practice drawing upon other nobles rather than family members occurred among the Welsh, see Giraldus (24.8).

Chapter 22. King Harald's Voyage to the West.
" . . they subdued Caithness and Sutherland, as far as Ekkjalsbakke. [The Oykel, a river.] Earl Sigurd killed Melbridge-Tooth, a Scotch earl, and hung his head to his stirrup leather; but the calf of his leg was scratched by the teeth, which were sticking out from the head, and the wound caused inflammation in his leg, of which the earl died."(27.12)

The northern tribes' penchant for hanging the head of an enemy from the neck of the slayer's horse when he departed the battlefield was recorded by Strabo (15.6).
The people of Scotland continue to celebrate aspects of the Nordic Hogmanay with relish. The emphasis on eating horse flesh at celebrations reinforces the validity of a Norse prehistory in the habitat of wild horses at the frontiers of Asia.

Hakon the Good [934-961]
Chapter 15. King Hakon Upholds and Spreads Christianity.
"He made a law that the festival of Yule should begin at the same time as the Christmas of the Church, and that every man, under penalty, should brew a meal of malt into ale, and therewith keep the Yule holy as long as it lasted. Before him, the beginning of Yule, or the slaughter night, [Hoggn nott, or mid-winter night, at which the Yule of Odin worshippers began, is supposed by Olavius to have taken its name from the slaughtering, hogging, or hewing down of cattle on that night for the festival.] was the night of mid-winter, and Yule was kept for three days thereafter."(27.13)

Chapter 16. About Sacrifices.
"Siguard, earl of Lade, was one of the greatest men for sacrifices, and so had Hakon his father been; and Siguard always presided on behalf of the king at all the festivals of sacrifice in the Drontheim country. It was an old custom, that when there was to be sacrifice all the bonder should come to the spot where the temple stood, and bring with them all that they required while the festival of the sacrifice lasted. To this festival all the men brought ale with them; and all kinds of cattle, as well as horses, were slaughtered, and all the blood that came from them was called laut, and the vessels in which it was collected were called laut-vessels. Laut-staves were made, like sprinkling brushes, with which the whole of the alters and the temple walls, both outside and inside, were sprinkled over, and also the people were sprinkled with the blood; but the flesh was boiled into savoury meat for those present.

The fire was in the middle of the floor of the temple, and over it hung the kettles, and the full goblets were handed across the fire; and he who made the feast, and was a chief, blessed the full goblets, and all the meat of the sacrifice. And first Odin's goblet was emptied for victory and power to his king; thereafter, Njord's and Freya's goblets for peace and a good season. Then it was the custom of many to empty the Brage-beaker; [The bragging-cup, over which boastful vows were made.] and then the guests emptied a goblet to the memory of departed friends, called the remembrance-goblet."(27.14)

Chapter 17. The Thing at Frosta.
" We bonder, King Hakon, when we elected thee to be our king, and got back our udal rights at the Thing held in Drontheim, . . . by this extraordinary proposal - that we should abandon the ancient faith which our fathers and forefathers have held from the oldest times, in the times when the dead were burnt, as well as since that they are laid under mounds,"(27.15)

Chapter 18. The Peasants force King Hakon to offer Sacrifices.
"The harvest thereafter, towards the winter season, there was a festival of sacrifice at Lade, and the king came to it. It had always been his custom before, when he was present at a place where there was sacrifice, to take his meals in a little house by himself, or with some few of his men; but the bonder grumbled that he did not seat himself on his throne at these the most joyous of the meetings of the people. The earl said that the king should do so this time. The king accordingly sat upon his throne. Now when the first full goblet was filled, Earl Sigurd spoke some words over it, blessed it in Odin's name, and drank to the king out of the horn; and the king then took it, and made the sign of the cross over it. Then said Kaare of Gryting, 'What does the king mean by doing so? Will he not sacrifice?' Earl Sigurd replies, ' The king is doing what all of you do, who trust to your power and strength. He is blessing the full goblet in the name of Thor, by making the sign of the hammer over it before he drinks it.' On this there was quietness for the evening. The next day, when the people sat down to table, the bonder pressed the king strongly to eat of horse-flesh; and as he would on no account do so, they wanted him to drink of the soup; and as he would not do this, they insisted he should at least taste the gravy; and on his refusal they were going to lay hands on him.

[The eating of horse-flesh at these religious festivals was considered the most direct proof of paganism in the following times, and was punished by death or mutilation in later days. It was a ceremony apparently commemorative of their Asiatic origin and ancestors. In Norway, or in Iceland, where horse-flesh also was eaten at these pagan festivals, the horse is not an animal that could ever have been in common use for food, as in the plains of Asia; because it cannot, as in Asia, be easily reared and kept in condition. This is perhaps the strongest proof of the truth of the saga tradition of Odin having come into Scandinavia from the banks of the Don - the Tanais.]

Earl Sigurd came and made peace among them, by asking the king to hold his mouth over the handle of the kettle, upon which the fat smoke of the boiled horse-flesh had settled itself; and the king first laid a linen cloth over the handle, and then gaped over it, and returned to the throne; but neither party was satisfied with this."(27.16)

A 'Thing' was an assembly or a court or a council.

King Hakon was a Christian, though by his lifetime the faith had not everywhere been adopted in Norway. The relevance of horse flesh has an echo of the king making ceremony in Ireland which attracted the criticism of Giraldus (24.3).

Chapter 19. Feast of the Sacrifice at More.
"The winter thereafter the king prepared a Yule feast in More, . . . the bonder insisted hard with the king that he should offer sacrifice, and threatened him with violence if he refused. Earl Sugurd tried to make peace between them, and brought it so far that the king took some bits of horse-liver, and emptied all the goblets the bonder filled for him; but as soon as the feast was over the king and the earl returned to Lade. The king was very ill-pleased,"(27.17)

Chapter 27. Egil Uldsaerk's Burial Mound.
"Then he ordered that Egil Uldsaerk, and all the men of his army who had fallen, should be laid in the ships, and covered entirely over with earth and stones."(27.18)

Magnus the Good
Chapter 16. Of the Free-Speaking Song and of the Law-Book.
"Thereafter King Magnus had the law-book composed in writing which is still in use in Drontheim district, and is called The Grey Goose.
[The Grey Goose, so called probably from the colour of the parchment on which it was written, is one of the most curious relics of the Middle Ages, and gives us an unexpected view of the social condition of the Northmen in the eleventh century. Law appears to have been so far advanced among them that the forms were not merely established, but the slightest breach of the legal forms of proceeding involved the loss of the case. The Grey Goose embraces subjects not dealt with probably by any other code in Europe at that period. The provision for the poor, the equality of weights and measures, police of markets and of sea havens, provision for illegitimate children of the poor, inns for travellers, wages of servants and support of them in sickness, protection of pregnant women and even of domestic animals from injury, roads, bridges, vagrants, beggars, are subjects treated of in this code - See Nordisk Tidskrift for Oldkyndighed i H. i B. 1832 om Graagaasen ved Schlegel.]"(27.19)

Laplanders are credited below with making sea-going skin boats. An opinion current in archaeological circles is that there are clans now counted among the Finn or Sami peoples who have lived in one part of Scandinavia or another for between two and a half thousand and five thousand years.

The Sons of Harald
Chapter 6. The Murder of Bentein [1138].
"It is said that Sigurd made the Laplanders construct two boats for him during the winter up in the fjord; and they were fastened together with deer sinews, without nails, and with withes of willow instead of knees, and each boat could carry twelve men. . . . . These boats were so light that no ship could overtake them in the water, according to what was sung at the time [1139]

> *Our skin-sewd Fin boats lightly swim,*
> *over the sea like wind they skim,*
> *Our ships are built without a nail;*
> *Few ships like ours can row or sail.*

In Spring Sigurd and Magnus went south along the coast with the boats which the Laplanders had made;"(27.20)

These medieval Laplanders appear to have made currachs for use at sea in coasting trips. The Laplanders were not Celtic and this is evidence to imply the art of building such seagoing craft in Western Europe predated the arrival of the Celts.

The data on Viking ships is an insight into their times. From this passage (27.22), it can be inferred the warships carried three times as many fighting men as they had oars. The array of Norse ships at battle stations would have been an awesome spectacle.

The expedition to the Don is an example of the widespread influence enjoyed by the Vikings at their zenith, reaching back to the land they had once occupied.

Snorre: Norse Kings Sagas [Laing]
Harold the Stern
Chapter 59.
"Footnote. Busse-ship. A buss is a word still used for a fishing vessel. It appears to have been applied to ships of burden of greater breadth than the warships. The buss was a three masted ship."(27.21)

Hakon the Broad-shouldered
Chapter 6. Erling's Speech.
"Supposing we make an attack on them, and row up against this river-current; then one of the three men who are in each half room
[The whole room was apparently the space between two benches of rowers, in which the men lived; and these were divided into half rooms, viz. on the starboard and larboard sides, and the men belonged to the starboard and larboard oars of the bench.]
must be employed in rowing only, and another must be covering with the shield the man who rows; and what have we then to fight with but one third of our men?"(27.22)

Chapter 7. Of Hakon's Fleet.
"They made ready for battle, carried land-ropes to the shore, turned the sterns of their ships outwards, and bound them all together. They laid the large East-country traders without the other vessels, the one above, the other below, and bound them to the longships. In the middle of the fleet lay the king's ship, and next to it Sigurd's; and on the other side of the king's ship lay Nicholas, and next to him Eindride Jonson. All the smaller ships lay farther off, and they were all nearly loaded with weapons and stones.

[Footnote. The importance of stones, and the enormous quantity required in the battles of those ages, form an element in the military movements of great bodies of men in the countries in which stones are scarce, not sufficiently considered by historians.]"(27.23)

Hakon the Broad-shouldered
Chapter 20. Of King Olaf's Miracle in favour of the Vaeringer of Constantinople.
"It happened once in the Greek country, when Kirialax was emperor there, that he made an expedition against Blokkamannaland. When he came to the Petzina plains, [Pazina-vollo = the plains on the river Bezina, the Don.] a heathen king came against him with an innumerable host. He brought with him many horsemen, and many large wagons, in which were large loop-holes for shooting through. When they prepared for their nights quarters they drew up their wagons, one by the side of the other, without their tents, and dug a great ditch without; all which made a defence as strong as a castle."(27.24)

Among the Edda included in the *Northern Antiquities* compiled by Paul Henri Mallet about 1755 and translated into English by Bishop Percy in 1770 was the fable of 'Balder the Good'. The Edda had been written down in Runic and was without doubt a Norse tale. Mistletoe was a central feature of this Edda. That mistletoe, a plant centre stage in the Druid cult, should have had a role in the Nordic array of gods and mythology flowing from Odin is startling. It is difficult to accept there was no correlation between the ranking given to the same plant by nations with a common boundary. An immediate option is for some crossover to have occurred between the cults within the Celtic and German peoples at a stage in their development if not flowing from a common doctrine. A further matter of note is that the Edda implied the power of the Nordic witches did not match that of the Druids.

In this tale the man's horse was burnt on the funeral pyre with him, as was his wife who had died of 'grief' upon his death.

Percy: Translation of Mallet's Northern Antiquities, volume 2
"The Twenty-Eighth Fable: of Balder the Good.
Certainly, says Gangler, this was a very great victory of Thor's. The dream which Balder had one night, replies Har, was something still more remarkable. This God thought that his life was in extreme danger: wherefore, telling his dream to the other Gods, they agreed to conjure away all the dangers with which Balder was threatened. Then Frigga exacted an oath of Fire, Water, Iron and other Metals, as also of Stones, Earth, Trees, Animals, Birds, Diseases, Poison and Worms, that none of them would do any hurt to Balder. This done, the Gods, together with Balder himself, fell to diverting themselves in their grand assembly, and Balder stood as a mark at which they threw, some of their darts and some of their stones, while others struck at him with a sword. But whatever they could do, none of them could hurt him: which was considered as a great honour to Balder. In the meantime, Loke, moved with envy, changed his shape into that of a strange old women, and went to the palace of Frigga. That Goddess seeing her, asked if she knew what the Gods were at present employed about in their assembly. The pretended old women answered, That the Gods were throwing darts and stones at Balder, without being able to hurt him. Yes, said Frigga, and no sort of arms, whether made of metal or wood, can prove mortal to him: for I have exacted an oath from them all. What, said the woman, have all substances then sworn to do the same honours to Balder?

There is only one little shrub, replied Frigga, which grows on the western side of Valhall, and its name is mistiltein, (the Mistletoe;) of this I took no oath, because it appeared to me too young and feeble. As soon as Loke heard this, he vanished, and resuming his natural shape, went to pluck up the shrub by its roots, and then repaired to the assembly of the Gods. There he found Hoder standing apart by himself, without partaking of the sport, because he was blind. Loke came to him, and asked him, Why he did not also throw something at Balder, as well as the rest. Because I am blind, replied the other, and have nothing to throw with. Come then, says Loke, do like the rest, show honour to Balder by tossing this little trifle at him; and I will direct your arm towards the place where he stands. Then Hoder took the Mistletoe, and Loke guiding his hand, he darted it at Balder; who, pierced through and through, fell down devoid of life: and surely never was seen, either among Gods or men, a crime more shocking and atrocious than this. Balder being dead, the Gods were all silent and spiritless: not daring to avenge his death, out of respect to the sacred place in which it happened. They were all therefore plunged in the deepest mourning, and especially Odin, who was more sensible than all the rest of the loss they had suffered. After their sorrow was a little appeased, they carried the body of Balder down towards the sea, where stood the vessel of that God, which passed for the largest in the world. But when the Gods wanted to launch it into the water, in order to make a funeral pile for Balder, they could never make it stir: wherefore they caused to come from the country of the Giants, a certain Sorceress, who was mounted on a wolf, having twisted serpents by way of a bridle. As soon as she alighted, Odin caused four Giants to come, purely to hold her steed fast, and secure it: which appeared to him so dreadful, that he would first see whether they were able to overthrow it to the ground: for, says he, if you are not able to overthrow it to the earth, I shall never be secure that you have the strength to hold it fast. Then the Sorceress bending herself over the prow of the vessel, set it afloat with one single effort; which was so violent, that the fire sparked from the keel as it was dragging to the water, and the earth trembled. Thor, enraged at the sight of this women, took his mace and was going to dash her head to pieces, had not the Gods appeased him by their intercessions. The body of Balder being then put on board the vessel, they set fire to his funeral pile; and Nanna, his wife, who had died of grief, was burnt along with him. There was also at this ceremony, besides all the Gods and Goddesses, a great number of Giants. Odin laid upon the pile, a ring of gold, to which he afterwards gave the property of producing every ninth night, eight rings of equal weight. Balder's horse was also consumed in the same flames with the body of his master."(29.1)

This connection between the Germanic Edda and the Celtic Druids in identifying a special reverence for or power of mistletoe was observed by Bishop Percy. Percy furthermore equated Frigga with the 'Mother of the Gods'. *"Tacitus, who describes her under the title of 'Mother of the Gods' speaks in like manner of the power she had to protect her votaries in the midst of darts thrown by their enemies. Matrem deim venerantur: Insigne superstitionis, formas aporum gestant. Id pro armis omniumque tutela, securum. Deis culterem etiam inter bostes praestat, c.45."*

As a pipedream, if mistletoe is equated with the Celts and the sorceress riding a wolf with the power of Rome whose founders were suckled by a she wolf and whose standards once showed a wolf, then is this Edda about a German tribe suffering a defeat at the hands of the Celts and then holding back from attacking the Roman armies?

Balder was the second son of Odin. Thor was the first son of Odin. The subject of the twelfth saga is Balder. This saga harks back to Vanheim, a country included in the Ynglinga Saga (27.1) as on the banks of the River Don. The Don discharges into the Black Sea.

Percy: Translation of Mallet's Northern Antiquities, volume 2
"The Twelfth Fable: Of the God Balder.
The second son of Odin is named Balder. He is of an excellent natural temper; and hath the universal praise of mankind: so handsome in his person, and of so dazzling a look, that he seems to dart forth rays of light. To make you comprehend the beauty of his hair, you should be informed that the whitest of all vegetables is called, the 'Eye brow of Balder.' This God, so radiant and graceful, is also the most eloquent and benign; yet such is his nature, that the judgement he has pronounced can never be altered. He dwells in the city of Breidablik, before mentioned. This place is in heaven, and nothing impure can have admittance there: this is confirmed by the following verses: 'Balder hath his palaces in Breidablik, and there I know are columns, upon which are engraven verses, capable of recalling the dead to life.'

The third God is he, whom we call Niord. He dwelleth in a place named Noatun. He is ruler of the winds: he checks the fury of the sea, storms and fire. Whoever would succeed in navigation, hunting or fishing, ought to pray to this God. He is so rich, that he can give to his votaries kingdoms and treasures: and upon this account also he deserves to be invoked. Yet Niord is not of the lineage of the Gods. He was reared at Vanheim, that is, in the country of the Vanes; but the Vanes delivered him up an hostage to the Gods, and received in his place Haner. By this means a peace was re-established between the Gods and the Vanes. Niord took to wife Skada, the daughter of the Giant Tbiasse. She prefers dwelling on the spot where her father inhabits, that is, in the land of the mountains; but Niord loves to reside near the sea: yet they came at length to this agreement between themselves, that they should pass together nine nights among the mountains, and three on the shore of the sea. One day Niord, returning from the mountains, composed this song; 'How do I hate the abode of the mountains? I have only passed nine nights there; but how long and tedious did this seem! There one hears nothing but the howling of wolves, instead of the sweet singing swans, who dwell on the sea-shores.' In answer to this, Skada composed the following verses: 'How is it possible for me to enjoy my rest on the couch of the God of the Ocean; whilst birds in flocks returning each morning from the forest, awake me with their screamings?' Then Skada returned to the mountains, where her father dwells; there snatching up her bow, and fastening on her snow-skates, she often employed herself in the chace of savage beasts."

In this instance was swan understood as a Norse ship? If a day in the life of the gods was a lunar month in the eyes of men, the tale makes better sense. Percy observed as there was no mistaking the word swan, since it was the same in Icelandic as English, *'It was remarkable, that the ancient Icelandic bards should have got hold of that fabulous opinion of the swan's being a singing bird which so generally prevailed among the Greek and Roman poets.'* Furthermore, Percy identified Balder with the Celtic deity Belenos.

" [Footnote. It seems to me probable, that Balder is the same God whom the Noricians and Gauls worshipped under the name Belenus. This was a celebrated God among the Celts. Many inscriptions make mention of him. We even find monuments, where he is exhibited according to his attributes. That which hath been long preserved at the castle of Polignac, represents him with a radiated head, and a large open mouth; which exactly agrees with the picture here given of him in the Edda; as a God resplendent and eloquent. We can easily see, that Belen and Balder came from the same origin, that is, from the Phrygian word Bal, or Balen, which signifies King, and which they formerly applied to the sun.]"(29.2)

Whether or not each aspect of Percy's analysis is correct, his choice of Phrygia in Asia Minor, by design or otherwise, is close to the home of Pythagoras at Samos and hence the account of Zalmoxis given by Herodotus (7.1).

An argument was developed by Samuel Laing in the notes to the Olaf Sagas that an historical figure given the name Odin was living at the turn of the fifth century and the offspring of this powerful figure led their people in Scandinavia and into England. His supposition on the *twelve goder* having their origin in an early Christian church is on less firm ground.

Snorre: The Olaf Sagas, Laing's Additional Notes
" Hengist and Horsa are stated in the Saxon chronicle to have been the sons of Wihtgils, who was the son of Witta; and Witta was the son of Wecta, a son of Woden. This genealogy is rejected, because it brings Woden so near to historical times, making Hengist and Horsa the fourth on descent from the god or warrior Woden. Yet if we apply the same measure of seventeen years to each of these descents from the time of Hengist and Horsa (the year 449) upwards, we find a wonderful coincidence with the other Saxon genealogies of Cerdic, Ida, and Ella, and come within eight years of the two latter. One man of 79 years of age might have been the Odin or Woden of the Scandinavian genealogies, and of the Saxon - the ancestor of Hengist, Cerdic, Ella, and of Harold Haarfager, Gorm, Canute, if he had been born about the year 342, and had died about 421. But were the numerous followers of Odin without any religion before the 4th or 5th century? By no means; not more than the followers of Mahomet before his appearance in the 6th century. Odinism is a new patch upon an old garment. There had been evidently a polytheism, - a worship of Thor, Loke, of a good and evil principle; and a more ancient mythology, upon which the incarnation of Odin, the rude idea of the trinity, the twelve goder, and other ideas and forms of belief and observance borrowed from the Christian church in the early ages of Christianity, have been stitched in the 4th or 5th century."(28.2)

Following the Anglo-Saxons and Jutes to England, the Norse held the kingdom of Northumberland and settled in Shetland, Orkney, Faroes, Iceland, Greenland, Hebrides, North Scotland, Isle of Man, the Eastern coast of Ireland and possibly around Limerick in the West, the Lake District and, so it has been argued, in South West Wales. The Norsemen visited mainland America. The Danes occupied the 'Danelaw' of middle and eastern England. At one stage, Denmark, Norway and England were part of the Great Kingdom of the North initiated by Svein and created by Cnut in the period 995 to 1035 and then divided between his sons.

Kings of Norway to the time of Cnut.

Halfdan the Black	860	Black hair, died aged 40, not first king overall.
Harald I, Fairhair	860	Aged 10 years when succeeded father, died c.934.
Eric Bloodyaxe	930	Ousted in favour of brother when father died.
Hakon I, the Good	934	
Harald II, Greyskin	960	
Hakon II, Jarl	965	
Olaf I, Trygvesson	995	
Eric Jarl	1000	
Olaf II, Saint and King	1015	
Canute the Great	1030	King of Denmark and England.

Samuel Laing, the translator of the Norse Sagas, was not impressed by historians who stated the Danish raids on England began in the year 787 AD and who, furthermore, quoted the Anglo-Saxon Chronicle as the source of their information. He asserts there would have been unbroken contact between the people settling in England from 450 AD onwards and their homelands. The date of 787 is promulgated to this day as a watershed. On probing, the aura surrounding the date has no substance. An overriding willingness to interpret the Latin text rather than the original Saxon in part led to the heresy.

Snorre: The Olaf Sagas, Laing's Additional Notes

"If we turn to the Saxon Chronicle, we find no ground at all for the inference drawn by all our historians from this passage under the date 787, viz. that the first invasion or piratical incursion of the Danes was in the year 787. The passage is this:-

'An. DCCLXXXVII. Her nom Beorhtric cyning Offan dohtor Eadburhge. And on his dagum cwomon aerest III scipu Nordmanna of Heredalande. And tha se gerefa thaer to rad, hi wolde dryfan to thaes cyninges tune. thy the he niste hwaet hi waeron. hine mon of-sloh tha. That waeron tha aerestan scipu Deniscra. monna the Angel-cynes lond gesohton.'

'Anno 787. Here took (in marriage) Beorhtric the King Offa's daughter Eadburhga. And in his days came first three ships of Northmen of Heredaland. And then the sheriff rode thereto; he would drive them to this king's town, because he would inquire what they were. This man they slew. These were the first ships of Danish men who sought the English king's land.'

The following is the Latin version of the passage, given by Gibson:-

'An. 787. Hoc anno cepit (in uxorem) Beorhtricus Rex Offae filiam Eadburgam. Ejus autem temporibus venerunt primum tres naves Norwegiorum de Herethorum terra. Tum eo (regis) praepositus equo vectus illos molitus est compellere ad regis villam, propterea quod nesciret unde essent: ibi autem is occisus est. Istae primae fuerunt naves Danorum quae Anglorum nationem peterent.'

Now this passage appears not to allow of the strict interpretation given to it by our historians. It says that in the year 787 Beorhtric married Offa's daughter, and in his days - not specially in the year 787 - came the three ships; but Beorhtric lived to the year 800. The three ships are stated first to be of Northmen or Norwegians of Heredaland. Heredaland is either Hordaland, an ancient district of Norway of great note in the sagas,- so great that, in the poetry, king of Hordaland is frequently used for king of Norway,- and situated where South Bergen province now is; or it may be the country on the south side of the Drontheim fjord, still called Heredland, or the Indhered, comprehending several extensive parishes, and where formerly the main power of the kings of Norway lay; or Heredalande may mean the king's demesne lands to which the men belonged. In either interpretation these Northmen were strangers to the coast; and the king's officer went to inquire what they were. But Danes from Jutland or Sleswick, who had from the year 450 to the year 585 or 600, when the kingdom of Mercia was established, been yearly coming over the sea in colonies from those coasts (for the Anglo-Saxons all came from that coast), could not suddenly have lost the art of navigating vessels so entirely, that in 180 years afterwards they would be a strange people to the Saxon inhabitants of England, whose great- grand-fathers, in some of the latest settled kingdoms of the Heptarchy, must have been born in that very country. But Northmen from Hordaland, who had to cross the North sea at once from Norway to Northumberland, instead of coasting along from the mouth of the Eyder or Elbe to the mouth of the Rhine and the coast of Flanders, from whence a run across to the south-east coast of England is an affair of a couple of days, might very well be an unknown and strange people, before the year 787, to the inhabitants of Northumberland.

It is for the Anglo-Saxon scholar to determine whether there may not be a mistake in transcribing the original manuscripts of the Saxon Chronicle, with respect to the word Deniscra. If it could be omitted, so as to read that these were the first ships of these men,- viz. of Northmen from Heredaland, - who came to England, it would make sense of the passage. As it stands, the specification of three ships of Northmen or Norwegians, from Heredaland or Hordaland, does not agree with the term Danish men; as the Danish kingdom or name did not in those ages, in the 8th or in the 9th century; either as a whole or in parts under tributary kings, extend to the north of the Gotha river in the Scandinavian peninsula. In the cognate language, the old Norse, the difference of a letter or two would change the demonstrative pronoun expressing 'that' kingdom, viz. of Hordaland or Heredaland, into 'Danish' kingdom. If such a reading could be admitted, of which the Anglo-Saxon scholar only can judge, it would both give sense to the passage, and would agree with what must have been the natural course of events,- viz. that at all times after the establishment of the Heptarchy, as well as before, there were piratical expeditions or commercial communications between the mother country of Holstein, Sleswick and Jutland, viz. the Danish kingdom and the colonies from it in England, to the extent at least that Danes could not be an unknown people, and confounded with Northmen from the north of Norway, or from Hordaland."(28.3)

Bede (died 735 AD) had used records available to himself or the persons he consulted when compiling his history. Whatever diverse Saxon chronicles and king lists were forthcoming from emerging kingdoms, supplemented by Roman authors and the works of learned men from continental Europe, by the year 891 AD the newly appointed archbishop Plegmund of Canterbury (died 923 AD) had transcribed the material into a rational whole. If the detail of the work was diligently carried out by a now anonymous scholar, the outcome, it is supposed, was appreciated by the archbishop and Alfred the king of Wessex. The chronicle entries continued until the year 1154.

The Saxons took their new year from mid-winter's day. The term 'Anno Domini' is attributed to Dionysius Exiguus about 526 AD. The concept of BC was introduced by Bede. At any stage, well intentioned editors could have sought to adjust the dates to the changing modes of reckoning and authoritative cant and so, it may be judged, none of the absolute dates from the early period are trustworthy against a modern calendar.

The section of the Anglo Saxon chronicle from the time the Romans abandoned Britain to its own devices until St Columba founded the monastery at Iona is a form of record of how the German tribes moved to Britain and displaced the Celtic occupants and any other indigenous folk. There was a German presence in Eastern England attested by distinctive pottery types dated to the century prior to the Roman withdrawal. A. and A̲. are readings from different manuscripts.

Anglo-Saxon Chronicle [Gurney, Petrie, Editor J.A.Giles]
"A. 409. This year the Goths took the city of Rome by storm, and after this the Romans never ruled in Britain; and this was about eleven hundred and ten years after it had been built. Altogether they ruled in Britain four hundred and seventy years since Caius Julius first sought the land.
A. 410 - 417.
A. 418. This year the Romans collected all the treasures that were in Britain, and some they hid in the earth, so that no one has since been able to find them; and some they carried with them into Gaul.
A. 419 - 422.
A. 423. This year Theodosius the younger succeeded to the empire.
A. 424 - 429.
A. 430. This year Palladius the bishop was sent to the Scots by pope Celestinus, that he might confirm their faith.
   [Footnote. Palladius and Patricus have sometimes confounded together so that it is difficult to assign to each his respective share of merit in the conversion of the Scots of Ireland. - Ingram]
A. 430. This year Patrick was sent by pope Celestine to preach baptism to the Scots."

That the Roman emperor Honorius wrote to the cities of Britain in 410 AD telling them to look to their own devices has entered the folklore: the information is contained in the works of Zosimus who was alive in 500 AD. A.L.F.Rivet and C.Smith acknowledge that the Greek text contained the word for Britain whereas the remainder of the passage was concerned with moving supplies between Italy and Africa. They propose Bruttium in southern Italy was the intended placename and Britain did not feature in this instruction from Honorius (see *The Place Names of Roman Britain*, published by Batsford Books).

The dates in the Chronicle of 409 AD as the last year the Romans ruled in Britain, or 418 AD when the Romans collected all the treasures in Britain, are sufficient to support the use of 410 AD as a rounded value for their departure. The precise year could have differed in accordance with the point in the seasons at which the Saxon new year was taken from and then counting backward or forward in winters. About 1110 years after the foundation of Rome carries with it a value of about 700 BC to arrive at 409/410 AD. The traditional value is 753 BC for the founding of Rome. In a similar manner almost 470 years after Caesar's first invasion of Britain in 55 BC becomes about 415 AD.

The calculation of measuring the years AD from 753 years after the foundation of Rome was made in the sixth century AD by Exiguus. A date equivalent to 415 AD could well have stood in the original source document as the date from which effective Roman rule ceased and it better links to a date of 418 AD by when portable valuables had been removed to Gaul. The Franks entered Gaul in or by 418 AD. The Goths took Rome in the 1164th year after the founding of that city according to Bede whilst he retained the figure of almost 470 years from Caesar's invasion to the end of Roman rule in Britain.

The opinion held and preached by the British monk or priest Pelagius was that the newborn child had no inherent element of evil. Pelagius did not accept the concept of 'original sin' traced back to Adam. Pelagius was well travelled in Europe, had spent time in Rome and in all probability had visited Jerusalem. This position went against the emerging doctrine of the bishops of the Church at Rome and was dubbed 'the Pelagian heresy'. Jerome (later St Jerome) is reported to have referred to Pelagius as *"a fat dog weighed down with Scots porridge"*.

It is imagined a wish to counter the adherence to the teachings of Pelagius was among the reasons Palladius was posted to the Scots (Irish). The need to deal effectively with the Pelagian heresy was an imperative for the visit to England by bishop Germanicus of Auxerre in 429 AD and again about 431 AD.

A further bone of contention between a conservative Celtic Church isolated by Saxon invasions and the Church of Rome arose over the calculation of the date on which Easter fell, a debate that was settled in favour of the Roman Church at the synod of Whitby in 664 AD.

A date of 432 AD for the arrival of Patrick in Ireland to preach Christianity is given elsewhere. A theory exists that he had been captured and taken to Ireland as a slave when a boy. Galloway is physically close to Ulster. The 397 AD mission of St Ninian to Galloway across the Roman Wall in Britain could readily have been the germ for the conversion of a few souls to Christianity across the water in Ulster. These early evangelists must have had a presence to succeed among the hostility of established cult leaders in robust environments.

"A. 431 - 442.
A. 443. This year the Britons sent over sea to Rome, and begged for help against the Picts; but they had none, because they were themselves warring against Attila, king of the Huns. And they sent to the Angles, and entreated the like of the ethelings of the Angles."

Under the year 429 AD and after Easter, Bede would have it that the Britons lead in person by bishop Germanicus had effected a victory over the Saxons or the Picts or a combined force of the two after *"the priests three times cried, Hallelujah"* (Bede *History* chapter 20). The account is judged to have been copied by Bede from Constantius.

A tentative site of the battle is Mold in Flintshire. The whole episode is doubtful (30). Bede, quoting Gildas, then contented himself with a paragraph condemning the Britons for courting defeat and raced on to the coming of Augustine in 596 AD to preach to the English Nation, of which he was a member. *"The Britons, being for a time delivered from foreign invasions, wasted themselves by civil wars, and then gave themselves up to more heinous crimes."* - Bede *History* summary chapter 22 (30).

"A. 444. This year St. Martin died.
A. 445 - 447.
A. 448. This year John the Baptist revealed his head to two monks, who came from the east to offer up their prayers at Jerusalem, on the spot which was formerly Herod's residence.
A. 449. This year Martianus and Valentinus succeeded to the empire, and reigned seven years. And in their days Hengist and Horsa, invited by Vortigern, king of the Britons, landed in Britain on the shore which is called Wippidsfleet; at first in aid of the Britons, but afterwards they fought against them. King Vortigern gave them land in the south-east of this country, on condition that they should fight against the Picts. Then they fought against the Picts, and had the victory wheresoever they came. They then sent to the Angles; desired a larger force to be sent, and caused them to be told the worthlessness of the Britons, and the excellencies of the land. Then they soon sent thither a larger force in aid of the others. At that time there came men from three tribes in Germany; from the Old-Saxons, from the Angles, from the Jutes. From the Jutes came the Kentish-men and the Wightwarians, that is, the tribe which now dwells in Wight, and that race among the West-Saxons which is still called the race of the Jutes. From the Old-Saxons came the men of Essex and Sussex and Wessex. From Anglia, which has ever more since remained waste betwixt the Jutes and Saxons, came the men of East Anglia, Middle Anglia, Mercia, and all North-humbria. Their leaders were two brothers, Hengist and Horsa: they were the sons of Wihtgils; Wihtgils son of Witta, Witta of Wecta, Wecta of Woden: from this Woden sprang all our royal families, and those of the South-humbrians also.
A. 449. And in their days Vortigern invited the Angles thither, and they came to Britain in three ceols, at the place called Wippidsfleet:"

The Scots and Picts had overwhelmed the defences at the wall and run riot through Roman Britain in 367 AD when the Romanised administration was in place. The unity of the administrative districts and provinces loosened, it is envisaged, after the Roman emperor Honorius relinquished the island and left its citizens to look to their own defence in nominally 410 AD. Thus, the citizens were less well placed after 410 than they had been in 367 to meet the threat posed by the Picts.

Archaeology shows the population of Roman Britain to have been widespread and numerous. The land in England has always supported a larger population than Scotland. Yet the Romanised culture was unable to contain or withstand the finite, and estimated as smaller, numerical strength of the Picts. Historians are left to cogitate on the reasons. Collingwood and Myres observed that *"The legal and administrative system of the late empire favoured economic tyranny. . . to the poor, 'The enemy is kinder than the tax collector'; it needed only the occasion of a barbarian inroad to convert the exasperated peasants into Bacaudae and bring into existence wandering bands of broken men, escaped slaves, and despairing debtors."*

Allowing for Vortigern to have influence over the fragmentary province centred on London or St Albans, where was his logic in offering land for settlement to Hengist and Horsa in North Kent when the Picts were flooding out of Scotland? If the Picts were attacking London from ships approaching via the Thames estuary, this move would have made more strategic sense. Perhaps the Pictish confederation had slaughtered and put to flight all those in authority in eastern England down to the reaches of the Humber by that time. The powerbase of Vortigern, if there was only one of that name, is by custom placed in Wales (where he was called Gwrtheyrn - John Davies, *A History of Wales*).

"A. 450 - 454.

A. 455. *This year Hengist and Horsa fought against king Vortigern at the place which is called Aegels-threp, [Aylesford,] and his brother Horsa was there slain, and after that Hengist obtained the kingdom, and Aesc his son.*

A. 456. *This year Hengist and Aesc slew four troops of Britons with the edge of the sword, in the place which is named Creccanford, [Crayford].*

[Footnote. *The positions usually assigned to various places mentioned in the earlier portion of the chronicles, are often very uncertain, depending chiefly on a supposed or real similarity of names. Where these, however, appear sufficiently probable, they are placed between brackets if otherwise a quaere is added.]*

A. 457. *This year Hengist and his son fought at the place which is called Crecganford, [Crayford,] and there slew four thousand men; and the Britons then forsook Kent, and in great terror fled to London.*

A. 458 - 464.

A. 465. *This year Hengist and Aesc fought against the Welsh near Wippidsfleet, [Ebbsfleet?] and there slew twelve Welsh ealdormen, and one of their own thanes was slain there, whose name was Wipped.*"

The use of the word 'Welsh' [foreign] arouses attention. It could have a significance or be the preferred word of one scribe where another would have used the word 'Briton'.

"A. 462 - 472.

A. 473. *This year Hengist and Aesc fought against the Welsh, and took spoils innumerable; and the Welsh fled from the Angles like fire.*

A. 474 - 476.

A. 477. *This year Aella, and his three sons, Cymen, and Wlencing, and Cissa, came to the land of Britain with three ships, at a place which is named Cymenes-ora, and there slew many Welsh, and some they drove in flight into the wood that is named Andreds-lea.*

A. 478 - 481.

A. 482. *This year the blessed abbat Benedict, by the glory of his miracles, shone in this world, as the blessed Gregory relates in his book of Dialogues.*

A. 483. 484.

A. 485. *This year Aella fought against the Welsh near the bank of Mearcraedsburn.*

A. 486. 487.

A. 488. *This year Aesc succeeded to the kingdom, and was king of the Kentish-men twenty-four years.*

A. 489. 490.

A. 491. This year Aella and Cissa besieged Andredscester, and slew all that dwelt therein, so that not a single Briton was there left.

A. 492 - 494.

A. 495. This year two ealdormen came to Britain, Cerdic and Cynric his son, with five ships, at the place which is called Cerdics-ore, and the same day they fought against the Welsh.

[Footnote. Gibson here introduced into the text a long genealogy, which, as Dr Ingram observes: 'is not justified by a single MS.']

A. 496 - 500.

A. 501. This year Port, and his two sons Bieda and Maegla, came to Britain with two ships, at a place which is called Portsmouth, and they soon effected a landing, and they there slew a young British man of high nobility.

A. 502 - 507.

A. 508. This year Cerdic and Cynric slew a British king, whose name was Natan-leod, and five thousand men with him. After that the country was named Natan-lea, as far Cerdicsford, [Charford.]

A. 509. This year St. Benedict the abbat, father of all monks, went to heaven.

[Footnote. Benedict died, according to Mabillon, in 543.]

A. 510 - 513.

A. 514. This year the West-Saxons came to Britain with three ships, at the place which is called Cerdic's-ore, and Stuf and Whitgar fought against the Britons, and put them to flight.

A. 515 - 518.

A. 519. This year Cerdic and Cynric obtained the kingdom of the West-Saxons; and the same year they fought against the Britons where it is now named Cerdicsford. And from that time forth the royal offspring of the West-Saxons reigned.

A. 520 - 526.

A. 527. This year Cerdic and Cynric fought against the Britons at the place which is called Cerdic's-lea.

A. 528 529.

A. 530. This year Cerdic and Cynric conquered the island of Wight, and slew many men at Whit-garas-byrg, [Carisbrooke, in Wight.]

A. 531 - 533.

A. 534. This year Cerdic, the first king of the West Saxons, died, and Cynric his son succeeded to the kingdom, and reigned from that time twenty-six years; and they gave the whole island of Wight to their two nephews, Stuf and Wihtgar.

A. 535 - 537.

A. 538. This year, fourteen days before the Kalends of March, the sun was eclipsed from early morning till nine in the forenoon.

A. 539.

A. 540. This year the sun was eclipsed on the twelfth before the Kalends of July, and the stars showed themselves full-nigh half an hour after nine in the forenoon.

A. 542 - 543.

A. 544. This year Wihtgar died, and they buried him in Wiht-gara-byrg. [Carisbrooke.]

A. 545. 546.

A. 547. This year Ida began to reign, from whom arose the royal race of North-humbria; and he reigned twelve years, and built Bambrough, which was at first enclosed by a hedge, and afterwards by a wall. Ida was the son of Eoppa, Eoppa of Esa, Esa of Ingwi, Ingwi of Angenwit, Angenwit of Aloc, Aloc of Benoc, Benoc of Brond, Brond of Beldeg, Beldeg of Woden, Woden of Frithowald, Frithowald of Finn, Finn of Godwulf, Godwulf of Geat."

This list of ancestors supports the analysis by Samuel Laing in the notes to the Olaf Sagas (Reference 28.2 in chapter 18 above) that an historical figure given the name Odin (Woden) was living at the turn of the fifth century.

"A. 548 - 551.
A. 552. This year Cynric fought against the Britons at the place which is called Searo-byrig [Old Sarum], and he put the Britons to flight. Cerdic was Cynric's father, Cerdic was the son of Elesa, Elesa of Esla, Esla of Gewis, Gewis of Wig, Wig of Freawin, Freawin of Frithogar, Frithogar of Brond, Brond of Beldeg, Beldeg of Woden. And Ethelbert, the son of Ermenric was born; and in the thirtieth year of his reign he received baptism, the first of the kings in Britain.
A. 553 - 555.
A. 556. This year Cynric and Caewlin fought against the Britons at Berin-Byrig, [Banbury?]
A. 557 - 559.
A. 560. This year Caewlin succeeded to the kingdom of the West-Saxons, and Ida being dead, Alla succeeded to the kingdom of North-humbria, each of whom reigned thirty years. Alla was the son of Iff, Iff of Usfrey, Usfrey of Wilgis, Wilgis of Westerfalcon, Westerfalcon of Seafowl, Seafowl of Sebbald, Sebbald of Sigeat, Sigeat of Swadd, Swadd of Sygar, Sygar of Waddy, Waddy of Woden, Woden of Frithuwulf.
A. 561 - 564.
A. 565. This year Ethelbert succeeded to the kingdom of the Kentish-men, and held it fifty-three years.
[Footnote. Bede [ii.5,] says Ethelbert died on February 23, A.D.616, after a reign of fifty six years. This would make it out that he succeeded to the throne in A.D.560.]
In his days the holy pope Gregory sent us baptism, that was in the two and thirtieth year of his reign: and Columba, a mass-priest, came to the Picts, and converted them to the faith of Christ: they are dwellers by the northern mountains. And their king gave him the island which is called Ii [Iona]: therein are five hides of land, as men say. There Columba built a monastery, and he was abbat there thirty-seven years, and there he died when he was seventy-two years old. His successors still have the place. The Southern Picts had been baptised long before: bishop Ninia, who had been instructed at Rome, had preached baptism to them, whose church and his monastery is at Whitherne, consecrated in the name of St. Martin: there he resteth, with many holy men. Now in Ii there must ever be an abbat, and not a bishop; and all the Scottish bishops ought to be subject to him, because Columba was an abbat and not a bishop."

According to Bede, Ninian was sent among Celts in Galloway in c.397 AD. St Martin's death is given under the year 444 AD above.

"A, 565. This year Columba the presbyter came from the Scots among the Britons, to instruct the Picts, and he built a monastery in the island of Hii. "(31.1)

Nowadays, the king of the Northern Picts rarely enjoys any benign publicity for allowing Columba to settle within his domain and feel secure by his implied protection. From this chronicle entry, the Scots were not in ultimate control of the islands in the locality of Iona by 565 AD, wherever their people had settled.

The compilations of the Anglo Saxon chronicle include the following. It would seem the first edition in modern English rather than a mixture of Saxon, Early English and Latin was produced by Miss Gurney about 1812.

Compilations of the Anglo-Saxon Chronicle

Gerard Langbaine	Papers in Bodleian library. Unfinished.
Wheloc	Chronologia Anglo-Saxonica, 1644 AD.
	Used Bennet or Plegmund manuscript
	and one other (now lost?), thus incomplete.
	Professor of Arabic at Cambridge.
Gibson	3 MS in addition to Wheloc,
	published about 1692.
	Sometime Bishop of London.
Gurney (Miss)	Translated into English about 1812
	from Gibsons text. Published privately.
Ingram	Text and English translation, 1823.
	Later President of Trinity College.
Petrie	Chronicles to 1066 prepared for publication.
	Keeper of records at the Tower of London.

An edition edited by J.A.Giles based upon the work of Mr.Petrie and Miss Gurney and occasional notes from Dr. Ingram was published by Bohn's Antiquarian Library in 1847. The above data and quotations were taken from the 1892 edition (31).

The definition of the Picts in Lempriere (4) reads as follows. It is long in the tooth and might be out of keeping with modern opinion.

Lempriere's Classical Dictionary
"Pictae or Picti. A people of Scythia, called also Agathyrsae. They received this name from their painting their bodies with different colours, to appear more terrible in the eyes of their enemies. A colony of these, according to Servius, Virgil's commentator, emigrated to the northern parts of Britain, where they still preserved their name and their savage manners, but they are mentioned only by later writers. Marcell. 27, c. 18 [8?]. - Claudian. de Hon. Cons. v. 54. - Plin. 4, c. 12. - Mela, 2, c. 1."(4)

The Agathyrsae were identified by Pliny, though in book 4 chapter 26, in his *'Account of Countries'* where they occupied a position to the north of the Black Sea. The Tanais is the River Don which flows into the Black Sea. The Riphaean mountains are the Urals.

Pliny: Natural History book 4, chapter 26 [Bostock & Riley]
"Leaving Taphrae, and going along the mainland, we find in the interior the Auchetae, in whose country the Hypanis has its rise, as also the Neuroe, in whose district the Borysthenes has its source, the Geloni, the Thyssagetae, the Budini, the Basilidae, and the Agathyrsi with their azure-coloured hair. Above them are the Nomades, and then a nation of Anthropophagi or cannibals. On leaving Lake Buges, above the Lake Maeotis we come to the Sauromatae and the Essedones. Along the coast, as far as the river Tanais, are the Maeotae, from whom the lake derives its name, and the last of all, in the rear of them, the Arimaspi. We then come to the Riphaean mountains, and the region known by the name of Pterophorus, because of the perpetual fall of snow there, the flakes of which resemble feathers; . . ."

Whether or not the Victorian footnotes carry any weight against the background of modern scholarship, they are reproduced for the sake of interest.

"[Footnotes.
Auchetae. Lomonossov, in his History of Russia, says that these people were the same as the Sclavoni: but that one meaning of the name 'Slavane' being 'a boaster,' the Greeks gave them the corresponding appellation of Auchetae, from the word which signifies 'boasting.'
Geloni. Of the Geloni, called by Virgil 'picti,' or 'painted,' nothing certain seems to be known: they are associated by Herodotus with the Budini, supposed to belong to the Slavic family by Schafarik. In B.iv.c.108, 109, of his History, Herodotus gives a very particular account of the Budini, who had a city built entirely of wood, the name of which was Gelonus. The same author also assigns to the Geloni a Greek origin.
Agathyrsi. The Agathyrsi are placed by Herodotus near the upper course of the river Maris, in the S.E. of Dacia, or the modern Transylvania. Pliny however seems here to assign them a different locality.]"(17.10)

It remains open to question whether these 'Picti' have any correlation with the Calydonians of Scotland. The hair colour and the act of painting themselves are points of similarity. The habit of boasting by their neighbours, the Auchetae, has an echo of the 'Brage-beaker' so much indulged by the Norsemen. If the Odin foundation myths are believed to a degree, then the Germanic tribes moved from the banks of the Tanais and frontiers of Asia into Western Europe. Not all of them need have migrated by the time of Herodotus or Pliny.

The description of characteristics using a Latin vocabulary would account, in part, for the coincidence of tribes with like sounding names having a wide geographical spread. Pliny listed the tribe of the Scotussaei living in Macedonia or Thrace and the Pictones of Aquitaine. Caesar, *Gallic War* 7.75, included the Pictones in the list of continental tribes requested to furnish troops in support of Vercingetorix in 52 BC. Until evidence to the contrary arises, it is assumed that these like sounding names occurred by chance.

Pliny: Natural History book 4, chapter 17 [Bostock & Riley]
" . . . and Dium, the Xylopolitae, the Scotussaei, a free people, Heraclea Sintica, the Tymphaei, and the Toronaei. Upon the coast of the Macedonian Gulf there are . . . "(17.11)

Pliny: Nat. History book 4, chapter 33 - Gallia Aquitanica [Bostock & Riley]
"In Aquitanica are the Ambilatri, the Anagnutes, the Pictones, the Santoni, a free people, . . . Joining up to the Pictones are the Bituriges,"(17.12)

Herodotus writing in the fifth century BC identified tribes of the Agathyrsi and the Budini who lived well to the north of his civilised world. An explanation for the basis of his knowledge is that the information was associated with excursions into the region north of the Black Sea by the army of Darius, King of Persia. Thus it is deemed Herodotus had available good quality reports for his *History*.

Herodotus: book 4, chapters 100 to 119 [Rawlinson]
"100. . . . As for the inland boundaries of Scythia, if we start from the Ister, we find it enclosed by the following tribes, first the Agathyrsi, next the Neuri, then the Androphagi, and last of all, the Melanchlaeni. . . .
102. The Scythians, reflecting on their situation, perceived that they were not strong enough by themselves to contend with the army of Darius in open fight. They, therefore, sent envoys to the neighbouring nations, whose kings had already met, and were in consultation upon the advance of so vast a host. Now they who had come together were the kings of the Tauri, the Agathyrsi, the Neuri, the Androphagi, the Melanchlaeni, the Geloni, the Budini, and the Sauromatae. . . .
104. The Agathyrsi are a race of men very luxurious, and very fond of wearing gold on their persons. They have wives in common, that so they may be all brothers, and, as members of one family, may neither envy nor hate another. In other respects their customs approach nearly to those of the Thracians. . . .
108. The Budini are a large and powerful nation: they have all deep blue eyes, and bright red hair. There is a city in their territory, called Gelonus, which is surrounded with a lofty wall, thirty furlongs each way, built entirely of wood. All the houses in the place and all the temples are of the same material. Here are temples built in honour of the Grecian gods, and adorned after the Greek fashion with images, alters, and shrines, all in wood.

There is even a festival, held every third year in honour of Bacchus, at which the natives fall into the Bacchic fury. For the fact is that the Geloni were anciently Greeks, who, being driven out of the factories along the coast, fled to the Budini and took up their abode with them. They still speak a language half Greek, half Scythian.

109. The Budini, however, do not speak the same language as the Geloni, nor is their mode of life the same. They are the aboriginal people of the country, and are nomads; unlike any of the neighbouring races, they eat lice. The Geloni, on the contrary, are tillers of the soil, eat bread, have gardens, and both in shape and complexion are quite different from the Budini. The Greeks notwithstanding call these latter Geloni; but it is a mistake to give them the same name. . . .

118. . . . From the moment of his entrance into Europe, he has subjugated without exception every nation that lay in his path. All the tribes of the Thracians have been brought under his sway, and among them even our next neighbours, the Getae.'

119. The assembled princes of the nations, after hearing all that the Scythians had to say, deliberated. At the end opinion was divided - the kings of the Geloni, Budoni, and Sauromatae were in accord, and pledged themselves to give assistance to the Scythians; but the Agathyrsian and Neurian princes, together with the sovereigns of the Androphagi, the Melanchlaeni, and the Tauri, replied to their request as follows . . . "(7.4)

Footnotes to the translation identify *"Androphagi. or 'Man-eaters' "* and *"Melanchlaeni. 'Black-cloaks'. This is probably a translation of the native name."* Furthermore, relating to chapter 104, *"This anticipation of the theory of Plato [Rep.v.] is curious. Was Plato indebted to Herodotus?"*

Ammianus Marcellinus noted the Agathyrsae, living on the eastern borders of Europe, tattooed themselves and coloured their hair blue. Thus, not all the Agathyrsae had moved to Scotland by 375 AD if his history used information that was contemporary.

In mythology, the Agathyrsi, a nation of Scythia, received their name from Agathyrsus, a son of Hercules, see Herodotus book 4.10. Agathyrsus, the eldest, Gelonus and Scythes, the youngest, were in turn born to the same mother, but only the youngest was able to draw a bow in the manner of Hercules and, in accordance with instructions left by Hercules, their mother sent the other two away. Thus, the line of Scythian kings came into existence. Herodotus preferred the account that the Scythians were put under pressure by the Massegetae and in their turn displaced other tribes from land that had become known as Scythia by the time of Herodotus.

There was no intrinsic barrier to the Agathyrsae living to the north east of Greece in the middle of the fifth century BC and finding their way to Scotland in time to fight Agricola by the first century AD. The choice of harsh wintered Scotland as the area of settlement with its relatively limited summer growing season might require further explanation to a citizen of lowland Britain. On arrival at the shores of the North Sea, the Picts would have needed to acquire from others, or develop for themselves, significant skills in boat building even allowing that they were first transported to the British Isles by ships of another tribe.

Eumenius stated that the emperor Constantius Chlorus (305 - 306 AD) initiated a punitive campaign against the Caledonians and other Picts in 306 AD. Cassius Dio wrote that in 209 AD troops of the emperor Severus (193 - 211 AD) were sent against the Caledonians who lived beyond the Meatae.

Ammianus Marcellinus, writing about events in his lifetime, recorded that two tribes of the Picts, namely the Dicalydones and the Verturiones, coupled with the Attacoti and Scoti between them ravaged the country of Roman Britain certainly as far south as London and Kent during the co-ordinated uprising of 367 AD. In a parallel timescale the Franks and Saxons plundered Gaul.

The similarity between the name Dicalydones and the inhabitants of Caledonia identified by Tacitus at the end of the first century is sufficient to concede that the Caledonians were Picts and admit the possibility the Picts had a Germanic dimension. A simplistic division is made into three types of people, to wit Celtic, Germanic, not Celtic and not Germanic; though allowing that the principal culture in any one area at a particular time would reflect aspects of other cultures that had been overlaid, enslaved or absorbed. Some authorities conclude that the Picts were Celtic, and others are ambivalent whilst acknowledging the movement into Scotland of tribes and warrior aristocracy described as Celtic. Some authorities entertain an option that the Pictish language did not have its roots in the Indo European family.

Tacitus: Agricola chapter 11 [Murphy]
" The ruddy hair and lusty limbs of the Caledonians indicate a German extraction."(5.6)

The Roman army commanders in Britain had spent more than thirty five years continuously fighting Celts of assorted hues. They can have been expected to recognise whether a tribe was Celtic or not.

The quotations pertaining to the Agathyrsae are supplied not with the conviction that the Pictish connection is valid but rather to follow through meandering lines of investigation arising from the literature on the subject.

In the Greek world, Calydon was a city 100 miles west of Delphi on the north side of the Gulf of Petrai which develops into the Gulf of Corinth and to the east of the island of Cephalonia. Lempriere's Classical Dictionary contains the following definitions.

Lempriere's Classical Dictionary
"Calydon, a city of Aetolia, where Oeneus the father of Maeleager reigned. The Evenus flows through it, and it receives its name from Calydon the son of Aetolus. During the reign of Oeneus, Diana sent a wild boar to ravage the country, on account of the neglect which had been shown to her divinity by the king. All the princes of the age assembled to hunt this boar, which is greatly celebrated by the poets, under the name of the chase of Calydon, or the Calydonian boar. Meleager killed the animal with his own hand, and gave the head to Atalanta, of which he was enamoured. The skin of the boar was preserved, and was still seen in the age of Pausanias, in the temple of Minerva Alea. The tusks were also preserved by the Arcadians in Tegea, and Augustus carried them away to Rome, because the people of Tegea had followed the party of Anthony. These tusks were shown for a long time at Rome. One of them was about half an ell long, and the other was broken. Vid. Meleager and Atalanta, Appollod. 1, c.8 - Paus. 8,c. 45. - Strab.8.- Homer. 9, v. 577. - Hygin. fab. 174. - Ovid. Met. 8, fab. 4, &c.
Calydonius, a surname of Bacchus."(4)

Ovidius Naso, Ovid the Roman poet, was born on 20th March about 40 BC and died in 17 AD.

Ovid's Metamorphosis book 15 has the line *"quam modo Tydidae Calydonia vulneret hasta,"* and refers to wounding with a Calydonian spear. Irrespective of the context, the term Calydonian spear was used in Roman literature and Calydon was a place famous for a boar hunt. Orca was the name of the northern promontory of Britain (Diodorus book 5.21 onwards) north of which are the Orcades (Orkneys). A tentative interpretation of 'Orca' is the land of 'boar folk' (32.1). A root offered in the *Place Names of Roman Britain* is 'Orca' was from the Old Irish 'orc' translated as piglet. In pedantic terms, this would stem from a language spoken in Scotland in the years BC which had an affinity with Old Irish if not from Old Irish itself. As 'orca' is shown as a type of killer whale (actually of the dolphin family) in Latin / English dictionaries, an alternative potential derivation of the name is in a Latin (or Greek) report of the whales or large sea creatures to be seen in the region. The boar was one of the symbols carved on Pictish stone monuments. Furthermore, a boar was incised on a stone at Dunadd in Argyllshire believed to have been used for the king making ceremonies of the Dalriadic Scots after they arrived from Ulster at the expense of the Picts (32.2). Of equal standing must be that the meaning of the name 'Orca' is unknown and from a language which predates the coming of Celtic or Pictish speakers to the region.

The thought arises that Calydonian was a name given to the tribes in mid or north Scotland by the Romans on account of their principal weapon being the spear and their standard being a boar, to echo the well known tale in Roman literature. In the same vein, the Dicaledonians could have been a more precise observation of warriors who carried either an enhanced spear or two spears apiece. A spear was a useful tool which combined the needs of hunting, defence and attack. If metal was an expensive commodity then its use was better spread among spearheads than the less versatile metal consuming swords, without denying the sword to be the more desirable weapon in its element. As late as the battle of Bannockburn in 1314 AD when the men under Robert the Bruce wholly defeated the English army of Edward II, the strength of the clans lay in their spearmen organised in 'schiltron'. At Bannockburn the Scots employed the long Scottish spear.

Calgacus, by Murphy read as Galcarcus, was named by Tacitus as the warleader of the Caledonians against the forces of Agricola. Calgacus need not have been the name of the man in his own language. Calgacus, may have had the meaning 'the swordsman'.

Tacitus: Agricola chapter 29 [Murphy]
"XXIX. In the opening of the campaign, he despatched his fleet, with orders to annoy the coast by frequent descents in different places, and spread a general alarm. He put himself, in the meantime, at the head of his army equipped for expedition, and taking with him a select band of the bravest Britons, of known and approved fidelity, he advanced as far as the Grampian hills, where the enemy was already posted in force. Undismayed by their former defeat, the Barbarians expected no other issue than a total overthrow, or a brave revenge. Experience had taught them that the common cause required a vigorous exertion of their united strength. For this purpose, by treaties of alliance, and by deputations to the several cantons, they had drawn together the strength of their nation. Upwards of thirty thousand men appeared in arms, and their force was increasing every day. The youth of the country poured in from all quarters, and even the men in years, whose vigour was still unbroken, repaired to the army, proud of their past exploits, and the ensigns of honour which they had gained by their martial spirit.

Among the chieftains distinguished by their birth and valour, the most renowned was Galgacus. The multitude gathered round him, eager for action, and burning with uncommon ardour. He harangued them to the following effect:

XXX. "When I consider the motives that have roused us to this war; when I reflect on the necessity that now demands our firmest vigour, I expect everything great and noble from that union of sentiment that pervades us all. From this day I date the freedom of Britain. We are the men, who never crouched in bondage. Beyond this spot there is no land, where liberty can find a refuge. Even the sea is shut against us, while the Roman fleet is hovering on the coast. To draw the sword in the cause of freedom is the true glory of the brave, and, in our condition, cowardice itself would throw away the scabbard. In the battles, which have been hitherto fought with alternate vicissitudes of fortune, our countrymen might well repose some hopes in us; they might consider us as their last resource; they know us to be the noblest sons of Britain, placed in the last recesses of the land, in the very sanctuary of liberty. We have not so much as seen the melancholy regions where slavery has debased mankind. We have lived in freedom, and our eyes have been unpolluted by the sight of ignoble bondage."

"The extremity of the earth is ours: defended by our situation, we have to this day preserved our honour and the rights of men. But we are no longer safe in our obscurity; our retreat is laid open; the enemy rushes on, and, as things unknown are ever magnified, he thinks a mighty conquest lies before him. But this is the end of the habitable world, and rocks and brawling waves fill all the space behind. The Romans are in the heart of our country; no submission can satisfy their pride; no concessions can appease their fury. While the land has anything left, it is the theatre of war; when it can yield no more, they explore the sea for hidden treasure. Are the nations rich, Roman avarice is their enemy. Are they poor, Roman ambition lords it over them. The east and the west have been rifled, and the spoiler is still insatiate. The Romans, by a strange singularity of nature, are the only people who invade, with equal ardour, the wealth and the poverty of nations. To rob, to ravage, and to murder, in their imposing language, are the arts of civil policy. When they have made the world a solitude, they call it peace." "(5.7)

Tacitus put the speech into the mouth of Calgacus as he addressed his own troops followed with another by Agricola to the Roman soldiers. The speech of Tacitus identified Calgacus as a Caledonian. In the flesh, if Calgacus existed as an individual and was not an invention after the manner of the captured Caractacus, who was paraded through the streets of Rome by Claudius, then he need not have been a Caledonian. There were other tribes in Scotland and fugitives from the fighting further south.

This episode of the Roman excursion into Scotland can be discarded as not much more than Tacitus writing a glorious biography of his father-in-law, Agricola. Tacitus would not have used a version of events that differed widely from the official reports sent to the emperor Domitian at Rome, whereas the interpretation of the reasoning behind decisions can be his near fiction.

The expedition was a touch less of a disaster than Caesar's first invasion of Britain. But if Agricola was so successful, why did the Roman Empire not stretch that extra hundred miles to the Pentland Firth and cover the whole of the known world at that compass point? The section of the *Agricola* covering Roman activity in Scotland is reproduced in Appendix 3. The battle of Mons Graupius occurred about 83 AD; some forty years from the Claudian invasion and the country was not subdued in its entirety!

As the incursions into Roman Britain in 367 AD by people from outside the empire are given the credit for creating such havoc at widely spread archaeological sites, the numbers of the invaders must have been large. The invaders must have operated in sufficiently large groups to cast aside the local civic organisation. No doubt the numbers were swollen by army deserters and ruffians in general. The size of the population in Roman Britain has been variously estimated between one and a quarter million and three million people. This leads to speculation that the population size of the confederation of tribes which spilled over Hadrian's Wall was of the order of two hundred thousand at least in order to produce the hordes of fighting men able to run riot through the country.

J.A.MacCulloch writing in 1911, when living at the Rectory on the Isle of Skye, was of the opinion that the Scots name of 'Cruithne' for the Picts was derived via the q-Celtic p-Celtic transformation of words from Pretani, an early name for inhabitants of Britain. *"Irish Goidals called the Picts who came to Ireland Cruithne = Qritani = Pretani"* (33.1). He noted Eumenius in 306 AD described the northern tribes as *"Caledonii and Picts"* and added that St Columba required an interpreter when preaching to the Picts (reported in Adamnan's life of St Columba). As Columba was a Scot from Northern Ireland then, if the report was true, the Pictish speech of sixth century Western Scotland differed significantly from the Q-Celtic dialect of the Scots.

Bede, who completed his *History* by 731 AD, recorded that the language of the English, Britons, Scots, and Picts together with Latin were in his time spoken in Britain.

In 731 AD the Pictish nation retained its identity. Its language was sufficiently different to be registered as separate to the Celtic Scots, the Celtic British and the dialect of Norron spoken by the English. A conclusion that can be made from this evidence is that if the Picts were of a Germanic origin then they came from an earlier wave than the forebears of the English, Danes and Norsemen. An alternative conclusion is that they had adopted a language modification after settling in Scotland. This points to the arrival of warriors rather than family groups or settlement alongside a more dominant society.

Bede lived at Jarrow on the River Tyne in North East England in what is now County Durham, a place geographically not far south of Pictland. It can be expected that it was commonplace for the people living on the Tyne to have made contact by sea with the Picts. In consequence he must be trusted as a source of what they themselves said on the tradition surrounding their arrival in Scotland. Nonetheless, this folk history may have been a thousand years old when recounted to Bede.

The quotations are taken from the translation from the Latin by John Stevens in 1723 as edited by J.A.Giles in 1840 and republished in 1892. The Latin text is taken from the edition produced by Charles Plummer in 1896.

Bede book 1 chapter 1 [Stevens]
"This Island at present, following the number of the books in which the Divine law was written, contains five nations, the English, Britons, Scots, Picts, and Latins, each in its own particular dialect cultivating the sublime study of Divine truth. The Latin tongue is, by the study of the Scriptures, become common to all the rest. At first this island had no other inhabitants but the Britons, from whom it derived its name, and who, coming over into Britain, as is reported, from Armorica, possessed themselves of the southern parts thereof. When they, beginning at the south, had made themselves masters of the greatest part of the island, it happened that the nation of the Picts, from Scythia, as is reported, putting to sea, in a few long ships, were driven by the winds beyond the shores of Britain, and arrived on the northern coasts of Ireland, where, finding the nation of the Scots, they begged to be allowed to settle among them, but could not succeed in obtaining their request. . . . "(30.1).

The Latin of the above section, from which it is seen the possibility exists that Bede meant five languages rather than five nations, reads as follows.

Venerabilis Baedae [Plummer]
"Haec in praesenti, iuxta numerum librorum, quibus lex diuina scripta est, quinque gentium linguis, unam eandemque summae ueritatis et uerae sublimitatis scientiam scrutatur, et confitetur, Anglorum uidelicet, Brettonum, Scottorum, Pictorum et Latinorum, quae meditatione scripturarum ceteris omnibus est facta communis.
In primis autem haec insula Brettones solum, a quibus nomen accepit, incolas habuit; qui de tractu Armoricano, ut fertur, Brittaniam aduecti, australes sibi partes illius uindicarunt.
Et cum plurimam insulae partem, incipientes ab Austro, possedissent, contigit gentem Pictorum de Scythia, et perhibent longis nauibus non multis Oceanum ingressam, circumagente flatu uentorum, extra fines omnes Brittaniae Hiberniam peruenisse, eiusque septentrionales oras intrasse, atque inuenta ibi gente Scottorum, sibi quoque in partibus illius sedes petisse, nec inpetrare potuisse."(34.1)

The text continues:-

" . . . The Picts, accordingly, sailing over to Britain, began to inhabit the northern parts thereof, for the Britons were possessed of the southern. Now the Picts had no wives, and asked them of the Scots; who would not consent to grant them upon any other terms, than that when any difficulty should arise, they should choose a king from the female royal race rather than from the male: which custom, as is well known, has been observed among the Picts to this day."(30.1)

The Scythia of classical writers was the broad sweep of land across Northern Europe and into Asia, beyond the border of the known world. In this context convention allows that Scythia is in Scandinavia, in view of the settlement pattern of the Picts, more readily than situated to the north of the Black Sea. From Norway, Orkney beckons.

In the mists of time, the men in the folk tale need only have come directly from Shetland, Orkney, or even Scotland, if the local population was expanding beyond the capability of the land to sustain it.

Having taken Scots wives, the next generation would have been reared as Scots-speaking albeit with a few other dialect words to boot. The situation invites a parallel to be drawn with those Norsemen who settled in France and became the Normans, speaking in their Norman French. Moreover, it is not certain where the diverse peoples of Ireland set off from before entering Ireland. In Irish fables one ancestral group is said to have come from Scythia.

Alternatively, the Picts may have originated in the peoples of the Mesolithic, Neolithic or Bronze Age cultures within Scotland and these equally could have colonised the region from the south. If ultimately science traces such home grown roots, then the folk tale containing their history served no other purpose than to explain away their habit of allowing descent in the female line when appropriate.

The selection of male leaders from the female line can indicate that a very old structure of society has remained intact. It is self evident that it had always been more easy to identify the mother than the father of a child. Tacitus mentioned the Sitones as being ruled by a woman, though they were living at the edge of the known world and hence in an area from where the reports were subject to distortion.

Tacitus: Germania chapter 45 [Murphy]
"Beyond the Suiones, we next find the nation of Sitones, differing in nothing from the former, except the tameness with which they suffer a woman to reign over them. Of this people, it is not enough to say, that they have degenerated from civil liberty; they are sunk below slavery itself. At this place ends the territory of the Suevians."(5.8)

According to the account written by Tacitus, the Suiones lived on the coast of Northern Europe, not the British Isles, and built boats that were pointed at both ends.

In Northern Britain the confederation of the Brigantes was ruled by Queen Cartimandua during the years following the Roman invasion of 43 AD. Coupled with the position of Boudicca, this shows it was not unusual for situations to exist whereby highborn women could exercise power beyond the strength of their sword arm among the societies in Albion and Northern Europe.

The evidence of Pictish place names to a large degree relies upon the word 'pit' as meaning a piece of land. Such place names cover North Eastern Scotland encompassing Fife, Angus, Atholl, Buchan and Moray. This survival of place names is somewhat misleading because it is known the Picts were in control of Western Scotland prior to the time of the invasion and settlement by the Dalriadic Scots from Ulster dated to about 450 AD onwards. Dal Riata is translated as Riata's portion and was the name of a Scots kingdom in County Antrim (32.3).

The area of Scotland associated with the Pictish place names has a blood group distribution of approximately 35% to 40% group A, which indicates a Scandinavian or Germanic origin, and 50% to 55% group O. The group O blood could indicate a 'not Germanic' underlying population which by implication predates the arrival of the Germanic peoples. The context of these arguments is Britain and not the world stage. As an alternative scenario, the incoming population may have contained the observed variation in blood types. Blood group O is common throughout Britain.

If these conclusions are valid then this is an additional piece of evidence that the Picts had a Germanic component in their origin. It rests on a proposition that their numbers were too large to have been overwhelmed by the Norse and the English finding favour.

An accepted derivation of the word 'Pict' is that it came from the Latin for painted or tattooed, thus describing the observed habit of the population. Furthermore, 'Picti' had a sound similar to the name 'Pretani' by which some inhabitants of Britain were known in a previous era and the two became confused. Over time the 'Picts' adopted the name 'Picts' if, indeed, they had not always called themselves 'Pechts', 'Pihtas' or 'Pehtas'. The tribes to the north of the Brigantes and those occupying Scotland as recorded in the second century AD by Ptolemy in his lists or in other authors includes:- Orci, Cornovi, Lugi, Smertae, Caereni, Decantae, Carnonacae, Epidii [opposite Ulster], Creones, Caledonii, Dicaledonians, Meatae, Verturiones, Taezali, Vacomagi, Venicones, Damnonii, Novantae, Votadini, Selgovae, Carvetii. Allowing that a few were a Roman appellation rather than the name known to the tribe and others were recorded in error, a proportion of these named tribes can be promoted as having evolved into the Pictish nation, if ever thus united.

An accessible document listing co-ordinates of locations in Scotland, England, and Wales identified in the *Geography* of Claudius Ptolemaeus is *The Place Names of Roman Britain* written by A.L.F.Rivet and Colin Smith published by B.T.Batsford Ltd. in 1979. Ptolemy compiled his *Geography* in eight books between 140 AD and 150 AD. It has survived via the world of Arabic scholarship and is known under the title of the *Almagest*. It is reported the information on Britain is in book 2.

Christianity was introduced to Scotland by, among others, St Ninian in 397 AD when he set up a missionary church and monastery at Whitehern in Galloway, thus leaving in the Glasgow region the Christian adherents in the 'St. Kentigern's country'. St Columba, who was either of the royal line of Ulster or a leading Druid family, settled in Iona by 563 AD and proceeded to convert the Picts as far north as Inverness. The position of missionary cells are to be found in place names containing the word 'kil' (26).

After the Roman province was left to its own devices in nominally 410 AD, the Picts raided the south. It is to be pondered whether any substantial part of their population moved south to be later absorbed into English kingdoms.

Bede recorded that, in 449 AD, Vortigern offered land for settlement to the Angles on condition they repulsed the Picts, which initially they did. However, in the fullness of time, the Angles made common cause with the Picts.

By 603 AD, the English Aethelfrith held his kingdom between the River Humber and River Forth. A son of Aethelfrith married a Pictish princess and was in consequence the father of a Pictish king. Edwin, king of the Northern English, had his capital at Edinburgh. The Picts, who had been kept at bay by the Northern English, defeated an army of Northern English which had crossed the Forth in 685 AD. The Picts then became the dominant regional force until 761, Angus MacFergus being their leader from 731 AD to 761 AD. Kenneth MacAlpine of Kintyre (844 to 860), a Dalriada Scot on his father's side with a Pictish mother, defeated or tricked the Picts and henceforth the Picts became integrated into the peoples of Scotland in Northern Albion and melted away as a separate entity (26).

The Picts are known by their characteristic standing stones with incised decoration. Three Pictish warriors on a stone from Birsay in Orkney and a stone from Hilton of Caboll, Ross-shire showing two men and a woman on horses are currently identified as the only examples of standing stones on which figures of Picts are present (32.4). Further Pictish fine art is to be seen in their stunning silverwork and jewellery as exemplified by the hoard from St. Ninian's Isle, Shetland (35).

A theory has been advanced that both the stonework and metalwork were the output of a restricted number of craftsmen. If so, they, nevertheless, reflect a Pictish school of art rather than imported design and artifacts.

Archaeological finds to date offer no hint that the Picts had a script of their own but they used Ogham, when influenced by the Irish, and Runic, when influenced by Scandinavians. To date, a cogent translation of Pictish Ogham has eluded those in the field. The introduction of Christianity through the tradition of both the Celtic and English Church was accompanied by the Latin alphabet if, indeed, it had not been known to Picts from contact with the Roman Empire during the four hundred year occupation of Britain south of the wall.

THE 'ROLLS SERIES': CHRONICLES OF SCOTLAND

In 1857 the Master of the Rolls initiated the publication of a range of documents relevant to the history of the British Isles from the Invasion of the Romans to Henry VIII. These documents are known colloquially as the 'Rolls Series'.

The *Buik of the Chroniclis of Scotland* published in 1858 was '*A metrical version of The History of Hector Boece*' written in Scots by William Stewart and edited for the Rolls series by William B.Turnball. The history written by Hector Boece is believed to have been first published in 1526-27 in Paris and produced in Latin. Using William Turnball's preface as a source of data, Margaret the sister of Henry VIII of England and mother of James V of Scotland commissioned Stewart to make a translation of Boece's History into verse and John Bellenden to translate the same Boece History into prose. Bellenden's prose version was published in 1540 with a second edition to follow, it was reprinted in 1821. Stewart is identified as William Stewart and he began his work in 1531 and may have completed it by the end of 1533; its first general publication was in the Rolls series. In the first instance, Boece, who died about 1534, ended his history of Scotland at the death of James I in 1436. A posthumous edition of the History in 1574 contained additional work by Boece and a completion to the end of the reign of James III by Ferrerius. The manuscript used for the Rolls series was held by the Public Library at Cambridge (K.k.ii.16.).

The Pechtis feature widely in the text. A superficial examination has produced no additional data on the nature and origin of the Picts. The record of the early period set down by Boece is reckoned as fable, or an admixture of fable and imaginative invention, from a well read classical scholar versed in the Irish annals for the period the Scoti lived in Ireland. On balance Boece should be given credit for recording the wealth of colour and history handed down the generations in an oral tradition, a format where romance, heroism and betrayal hold the listener's ear above the precision of dates and analysis.

Conventional wisdom holds that the Greeks adopted the Phoenician alphabet about the time of the first Olympiad, which is nominally set at 776 BC. There were a number of scripts that had evolved around the Mediterranean and the Middle East. These include cuniform, the hieroglyphs of Egypt and the Linear A and Linear B of Crete. Crete reached its zenith between 1600 BC and 1400 BC. Celtic Ogham and Germanic Runic at their roots reflect an affinity with the Greek alphabet, or its source. There is no impetus to look beyond Greece towards the orient or to a more remote epoch.

Following the tried and tested procedure of the Romans, children of the Celtic ruling classes were educated in the Roman manner. Latin quickly spread as the written language of the subjugated Celts.

Both Ogham and Runic developed over the centuries as they ran in parallel with the Roman alphabet. In the modern era extant examples of literature written in an Iberian script, Ogham and Runic are to be found on the 'Internet'. As ever, some information and opinion there offered may be weighed as more valid than others.

Certainly in antiquity Runic characters and possibly Ogham were employed when casting lots to predetermine the outcome of events. At the present day they have attracted their portion of clotted nonsense and dross that would seem to have little continuity with the distant past.

OGHAM. This alphabet comprises about twenty characters, each of which has up to five lines scratched above, on, or below a long (usually horizontal) line. It is often stated that Ogham was restricted to the British Isles with the greatest evidence for its use coming from Ireland and Wales. An alternative viewpoint is that these areas reflect a survival pattern rather than the zones of Europe in which at sometime it has been used. It was a script found among Celtic peoples.

The Ogham letters look sterile until each character is given a Celtic name to parallel the alphabet in English. When this is done they are brought to life in a manner not unlike the dots on a musical stave. Celtic legend credits Ogma with inventing Ogham. The Roman poet Lucan made mention of a god of the Gauls who was associated with language. The Irish legend would have it that Phaenius, king of the Scythians and grand ancestor of the Milesian race, invented Ogham (see Appendix 5 chapter 7). Ogma is at once more acceptable than Phaenius when spelling out the name in Ogham. The Celtic name Ogmius has been equated with the hero Hercules (4).

The Book of Ballymote, which dates from the end of the fourteenth century, supplies information on different types of Ogham. One subgroup of Ogham did not contain the vowels and comprised 16 letters.

A set of Ogham letter names coupled to Old Irish and another to the "Tree Alphabet" are to be found in relevant literature and on the 'Internet'. Who knows what sense they would have made to Boudicca? The "Tree Alphabet" whereby many letters are coupled with tree names is known from around 1000 AD.

Some scholars postulate that Ogham had its origins as a secret script of the Druids. Caesar informs us that the Celts used Greek characters in their public and private transactions and that the Druids did not commit any of their own matters to writing but rather committed them to memory, *Gallic War* book 6.14 (1.6).

The format of the Ogham script intimates that it was a code rather than a stand alone set of characters which evolved to represent speech. It would have proved equally attractive for encoding the Greek alphabet, or its precursors, as progressing to the Roman. The script is better suited than Greek or Latin to the everyday materials of its time as it is readily amenable to being whittled out on a piece of wood with a knife or dagger.

IBERIAN SCRIPT. Strabo wrote in his *Geography* that the Turdetani and the Turduli were the most intelligent of the Iberians and that they possessed an alphabet and a set of ancient writings and laws, Strabo book 3.1.6 (15.1). There is a theory this Iberian script was derived from a Punic or Phoenician script and arose through contact with Phoenician trading settlements on the coast of Spain.

RUNIC. The Runic alphabet is referred to as the 'futhark' from the sequence of its opening letters, somewhat as 'alphabet' is composed from the first two letters of the Greek. Runic was widespread and was used in the written word, on monuments and on coins among peoples of a Germanic origin up until the medieval period.

Some authorities consider Runic to have come about after the Roman Empire had expanded to the boundary of the Germanic peoples in the early centuries AD. The mainstream of opinion concludes from the shape of the characters that at first it was copied from the Greek and then later modified by contact with the Roman alphabet. Any thoughts that Phoenician traders had an influence over the introduction of the script would gain momentum if research ever points to the early centres of Runic being in coastal areas.

Pliny the Elder ensured that Phoenicians are given credit for introducing the original sixteen letter script to the Greeks. The standard Greek alphabet then developed over time. The Athenian alphabet of the sixth century BC had twenty four letters.

In Nordic accounts, the introduction of Runic was attributed to Odin. It has been proposed that the Odin in question was an historic person of the same name as the mythological figurehead.

The following table contains data extracted from *Mallet's Northern Antiquities*, edited by J.A.Blackwell and published in the Bohn Classical Library series in 1847 (36.1). The characters differ in detail from those found in other publications. Specialist advice from a more recent publication ought to be consulted should it be desired to examine the topic in more accurate detail. There are differing sets of Runic characters associated with geographic areas and periods of history. Among these variants are German Runes and Gothic characters.

RUNIC CHARACTERS - EXAMPLES

An interpretation of the Runic characters given in the edition of *Mallet's Northern Antiquities* edited by J.A.Blackwell is shown below. The characters and names differ in detail from those found in other publications. Blackwell noted that *The Runic, like the ancient Greek alphabet, originally contained only sixteen letters.*

	ORIGINAL 16 RUNIC CHARACTERS			SCANDINAVIAN RUNES	ANGLO-SAXON RUNES
Name	Signification	Figure	Power		
fe	money	ᚡ	F	ᚡ	ᚡ
ur	a pre-ox	ᚢ	U	ᚢ	ᚢ
thurs	a giant	ᚦ	D or TH	D ᚦ / TH ᚦ	ᛗ ᚦ
os	an estuary	ᚨ	O	ᚨᛒᛡ	ᚥ
reid	a ride	ᚱ	R	ᚱ	ᚱ
Kon	an ulcer	ᚲ	K	ᚲ	ᚻᛦ
hagi	hail	✳	H	✳	ᚻ
naud	need	ᚾ	N	ᛀᚾ	ᚾ
is	ice	ᛁ	I	ᛁ	ᛁ
air	year	ᚨ	A	ᚨᛂ	ᛆ
sol	the sun	ᛋ	S	ᛋ	ᛋ
Tyr	the God Tyr	↑	T	ᛘ	↑
bjork	a birch tree	ᛒ	B	ᛒ	ᛒ
logr	a lake	ᛚ	L	ᛚ	ᛚ
maer	a man	ᛩ	M	ᛩ	ᛗ
yr	a bow	ᛨ	Y	ᛨ	ᚼ
			E	✝	ᛗ
			AE		ᚬ
			OE		ᚩ
			J		φ
			W		ᚹ
			P	ᛒ	ᛕᚻ

169

Name Signification	Power	SCANDINAVIAN RUNES	ANGLO-SAXON RUNES
[In the relevant literature there is	V	ᚹ	
no shortage of names allocated	G		ᚷ
to the later Anglo-Saxon and	G	ᚱ	ᚷ
Scandinavian runes. Solid facts are	Q		ᚣᚾ
less easily come upon than opinion.]	C		ᚻ
	CH		
	TS		
	X		ᚣ
	ing		ᚩ

22   BRITISH COINS

Coinage struck by the Celtic tribes is the subject of a wide range of studies and relevant publications. Of significance was a Greek coin struck about the year 350 BC for Philip II of Macedonia - the father of Alexander the Great. The obverse shows a head of Apollo and the reverse a two horse chariot driven by a charioteer with the word Philip below. The coin had an appeal among the Celts and it was progressively copied and re-copied across Europe. In 200 BC a Helvetii copy included a rendering of the word Philip. A stylised version of the design was struck by the Bellovaci of Northern France by 100 BC. This same design, translated into a horse with a single wheel below, circulated among tribes in Britain approaching 400 years after the demise of Philip II.

As the Belgae were in all probability of Germanic extraction, the term Celtic coinage is a misnomer when applied to the output of the Belgic dynasties.

Restricting attention to the British Isles, the coins produced by a number of Continental tribes are found in Britain. These include those of the Ambiani, Suessiones, Bellovaci, Morini, the Amorican tribes and the Continental Atrebates.

In the British Isles the tribes to which the striking of coins is attributed (to date) are limited to what is now England, with the activity decreasing from the south and the south-east.

The state of the coinage reflects the state of the nation. The production and circulation of coinage within an area can give an indication of the degree and level of local economic activity and trade. As a boundary condition it can reflect the egoism of a ruler on the periphery of an area where coinage was used as a medium of exchange. Examples are given below of tribes living in the British Isles that produced coins together with the individuals and places whose names are derived from the inscriptions where they occur. Coins of this period were produced using both striking and moulding techniques.

Phillip II of Macedonia (382 - 336 BC): gold stater.

Obverse: laureate head of Apollo to right. Reverse: two horse chariot.

Bellovaci, a Belgic people: gold stater, second or first century BC.
Either a British derivative or a Gaulish original (38).
The stylised design has its origin in the stater of Phillip II of Macedonia.

Obverse: head to left, hair emphasised. Reverse: horse to left, wheel under.

The above coins are at approximately 200% scale. They were taken from *A Literary and Historic Atlas of Europe* compiled by J.G.Bartholomew and published in the Everyman's Library Series by J.M.Dent & Sons from the edition reprinted in 1915.

EXAMPLES OF TRIBES IN BRITAIN THAT PRODUCED COINS
PRIOR TO THE ROMAN CONQUEST

Personal Names	Approximate dates		Evidence from inscription
DUROTRIGES			
Un-inscribed	60 BC	- 50 AD	
CRAB			CRAB in angles
BRITISH REMI			
Un-inscribed	45 BC	- 25 BC	
ATREBATES (and REGNI)			
COMMIUS	35 BC	- 20 BC	COMMIOS
TINCOMMIUS	20 BC	- 5 AD	TINCOMMIVS
EPPILLUS	5 AD	- 10 AD	EPPILLV
			COMM
CALLEVA - Silchester			CALLEV
VERICA	10 AD	- 40 AD	VERICA REX
EPATICCUS	25 AD	- 35 AD	EPATICCV
CANTII			
Un-inscribed	65 BC	- 20 BC	
DUBNOVELLAUNUS	15 BC	- 1 BC	DVBNOVELLAVNOS
VOSENOS	c.5 AD		VOSII
EPPILLUS	10 AD	- 25 AD	EPPILLVS
also Atrebates			
AMMINUS	15 AD		A
TRINOVANTES			
ADDEDOMAROS	15 BC	- 1 BC	
DIRAS	c.1 AD		DIRAS
DUBNOVELLAUNUS	1 AD	- 10 AD	
also Cantii			
CATUVELLAUNI			
TASCIOVANUS	20 BC	- 10 AD	TASCIOV
VERULAMIUM - St Albans			VERLAMIO
CAMULODUNUM-Colchester			CAMVL
ANDOCO	5 AD	- 15 AD	ANDOCO
CUNOBELIN	10 AD	- 40 AD	CYNOBELINVS
CAMULODUNUM-Colchester			CAMVL
EPATICCUS	25 AD	- 35 AD	
Also Atrebates. The inclusion			
under Catuvellauni may be in error.			

DOBUNNI (also DOBUNI)

Un-inscribed	40 BC	-	10 AD	
ANTED				ANTEDRIG
Also given as ANTEDRIGUS				
EISU				EISVRIG
INAM (or INARA)				INAM or INARA
CATTI				CATTI
COMUX				COMVX
CORIO				CORIO
BODVOC				BODVOC

ICENI

Un-inscribed	30 BC	-	10 AD	
DURO				CAN
				DVRO
ANTED				ANTED
ECEN				
ED				
ECE				
SAENU				
AESU				
PRASUTAGUS	60 AD			SUB RII PRASTO R
				ESICO FECIT

CORITANI

IAT ISO			IAT ISO
ALE SCA			ALE SCA
AUN COST			AVN COST
ESUP ASU			IISVP ASV
VEP CORF	*		VEP CORF
VEP			VEP
DUMNO TIGIR SENO	*		DVMN(OC?)
TIGIR SENO			
VOLISIOS DUMNOCVEROS	*		VOLI
			SIOS
			DVMNOCOVEROS
VOLISIOS DUMNOVELLAUNOS	*		VOLI
			SIOS
			DVMNOVELAVNOS
VOLISIOS CARTIVEL	*		VOLI
			SIOS
			CARTIVEL

BRIGANTES

*The coins included above as Coritani are listed under the tribal confederation of the Brigantes by some authorities. 'Cartivel' is tentatively attributed to Queen Cartimandua of the Brigantes by some authors.

The inscriptions are examples of the Celtic written word. The populations of the coin producing tribes need not all have been of Celtic stock but the practice spread through the influence of Belgic and Celtic people. The Roman alphabet was used for the inscriptions in preference to Greek or Ogham, if Ogham was available. The body of knowledge on Celtic coin types grows by the year.

The evidence from archaeology shows there were people in Ireland who were masters of intricate metal work. It is concluded the societies of which they were members had no need of coinage at a time when contemporary aristocrats in Europe were striking their own denominations. The first coinage produced in Ireland was for 'Sihtric' at Dublin and dated to 995 ±3 years, the prototype English 'Crux' penny having been struck in 991 to 992 AD (37). This coinage was a product of the Viking settlement at Dublin, the mint for the Hiberno-Norse coinage continued to operate for approximately 150 years.

Howel Dda who died c.948 was the earliest ruler in Wales known to have struck coins and to the present time stands in singular isolation among Welsh princes prior to the annexation of Wales by the Norman kings of England.

The first indigenous coins struck in Scotland were for King David I (1124 to 1153).

Following the Roman withdrawal, coins began to be minted in England between 575 to 600 AD based upon Merovingian models from France. (See also References 37 to 40).

The use of 'VER' for Verulam or Verulamium (St Albans), 'CAMVL' for Camulodunum (Colchester) and 'CALLEV' for Calleva (Silchester) in a pre Roman context adds weight to the opinion that pre-Roman place names were retained in the Romanized name of some local and tribal administrative centres. For example, Calleva Atrebates as the name of Roman Silchester.

The wider topic was approached from a different direction by Nicholas Higham (Staff tutor in History) and Barri Jones (Professor of Archaeology) of the University of Manchester who postulated the name of 'Carvetii' as a sept of the Brigantes living in the region of Carlisle. The name Carvetii was derived from a Roman inscription from Old Penrith referring to a senator in either a cohort or canton of the Carvetii coupled with a Roman milestone from Brougham inscribed R.P.C.Car. The letters R.P.C. are by custom read as Res Publica Civitatis and Car was reasonably interpreted as Carvetiorum (41).

The drive for literacy among leaders of tribes who had brushed against the written word must have been immense. A need to have a person able to read and write within the household would have been imperative. The act of recording yesterday's thoughts and agreements for tomorrow or sending messages over a distance was a tool in a new dimension that cut through time itself. To record and read the sounds of your own tongue in the received alphabet was a welcome innovation.

23   SOME CALENDAR SYSTEMS

The following information on calendar systems should be taken as indicative only.

When dipping into a translation it is not in all cases plain to which calendar system the information is referred. For example whether dates have been adjusted to the Gregorian calendar or remain as in the text from which they were translated. A further trap when counting backwards is that there was no year zero, the twelve months of year 1 AD were preceded by the twelve months of year 1 BC. Thus, there were approximately three years between New Year's day 2 BC and New Year's day 2 AD. Calendars that were based upon counting days were prone to error and the solstice and equinox themselves move westwards with time.

The first use of the term 'Anno Domini' is attributed to Dionysius Exiguus from about 516 AD (4) or 526 AD by other authorities. Dionysius erroneously calculated that Christ was born 753 years after the founding of Rome (4). However, Dionysius should be given credit for perhaps observing that it would have proved unduly complicated to have moved further back than the last modifications to the leap year made by Augustus in what is now 4 AD. The counting of years BC is said to have been introduced by Bede in about 748 AD (4) though by 735 AD according to other authorities since Bede 'went to the Lord' in 735 AD.

An explanation tinged with caution of the interpretation of the term year was given by Pliny. It is considered that some of the lengths of time mentioned in the Old Testament were measured in moon years (i.e.months) originally and then, at a later date, were by mistake taken as solar years.

Pliny: Natural History book 7, chapter 49 [Bostock & Riley]
Chapter 49. (48.) - The Greatest Length of Life.
"All these statements, however, have originated in a want of acquaintance with the accurate measurement of time. For some nations reckon the summer as one year, and the winter as another; others again, consider each of the four seasons a year; the Arcadians, for instance, whose years were of three months each. Others, such as the Egyptians, calculate by the moon, and hence it is that some individuals among them are said to have lived as many as one thousand years."(17.13)

Pliny: Natural History book 2, chapter 79 [Bostock & Riley]
"The days have been computed by different people in different ways. The Babylonians reckoned from one sunrise to the next; the Athenians from one sunset to the next; the Umbrians from noon to noon; the multitude universally from light to darkness; the Roman priests and those who presided over the civil day, also the Egyptians and Hipparchus, from midnight to midnight."(17.14)

The manner of segregating the day and night into identifiable segments differed among states and cultures. As an example, 'Vigiliae' was a Roman military term connected with night duty.

1st	vigilia	6 pm to 9 pm using the modern 2 x 12 hour day
2nd		9 pm to midnight
3rd		12 midnight to 3 am
4th		3 am to 6 am.

THE GREEKS counted from the first 'recorded' Olympiad in 776 BC. The Games on the slopes of Mount Olympus were held every four years.

Herodotus set down his perception of a conversation between Solon of Athens and Croesus. This Croesus gave rise to the saying 'as rich as'. The footnote explains that Herodotus had got the wrong end of the stick in his arithmetic for calendar years.

Herodotus: book 1, chapters 32 [Rawlinson]
"32. When Solon had thus assigned these youths the second place, Croesus broke in angrily, "What, stranger of Athens, is my happiness, then, so utterly set at nought by thee, that thou dost not even put me on a level with private men?"

"Oh ! Croesus," replied the other, "thou askedst [sic] a question concerning the condition of man, of one who knows that the power above us is full of jealousy, and fond of troubling our lot. A long life gives one to witness much, and experience much oneself, that one would not choose. Seventy years I regard as the limit of the life of man.
[Footnote. "The days of our years are threescore years and ten" (Ps. xc. 10)]
In these seventy years are contained, without reckoning intercalary months, twenty-five thousand and two hundred days. Add an intercalary month to every other year, that the seasons may come round at the right time, and there will be, besides the seventy years, thirty five such months, making an addition of one thousand and fifty days. The whole number of the days contained in the seventy years will thus be twenty-six thousand two hundred and fifty, whereof not one but will produce events like the rest. Hence man is wholly accident. For thyself, oh ! Croesus, I see that thou art wonderfully rich, and art the lord of many nations;"
[Footnote. No commentator on Herodotus has succeeded in explaining the curious mistake whereby the solar year is made to average 375 days. That Herodotus knew the true solar year was not 375, but more nearly 365 days, is clear from book ii. ch. 4. Two inaccuracies produce the error in Herodotus. In the first place he makes Solon count his months at 30 days each, whereas it is notorious that the Greek months, after the system of intercalation was introduced, were alternatively of 29 and 30 days. By this error his first number is raised from 24,780 to 25,200; and also his second number from 1033 to 1050. Secondly, he omits to mention that from time to time (every 4th τριετηριο probably) the intercalary month was omitted altogether.] (7.5)

The above passage in Herodotus *per se* contains false information. If not from the hand of Herodotus then the whole calculation would have needs be inserted by a later well meaning copyist. It cannot result from one or two errors in transcription.

Rawlinson supplied the information "*Croesus most probably reigned from B.C. 568 to B.C. 554. Solon certainly outlived the first usurpation of the government of Athens by Pisistratus, which was B.C. 560.*"

The quotation from Book 2.4 identified by Rawlinson in his note is as follows.

Herodotus: book 2, chapters 3 to 4 [Rawlinson]
". . . I got much other information also from a conversation with these priests while I was at Memphis, and I even went to Heliopolis and to Thebes, expressly to try whether the priests of those places would agree in their accounts with the priests of Memphis. The Heliopolitans have the reputation of being the best skilled in history of all the Egyptians.
. . .

4. Now with regard to mere human matters, the account which they gave, and in which all agreed, were the following. The Egyptians, they said, were the first to discover the solar year, and to portion out its course into twelve parts. They obtained this knowledge from the stars. (To my mind they contrive their year much more cleverly than the Greeks, for these last every other year intercalate a whole month, but the Egyptians, dividing the year into twelve months of thirty days each, add every year a space of five days besides, whereby the circuit of the seasons is made to return with uniformity.)

[Footnote. This at once proves they intercalated the quarter day, making their year to consist of 365 ¼ days, without which the seasons could not return to the same periods. The fact of Herodotus not understanding their method of intercalation does not argue that the Egyptians were ignorant of it.]

The Egyptians, they went on to affirm, first brought into use the names of the twelve gods, which the Greeks adopted from them;"(7.6)

Greek City States lacked commonality on year end and calendar detail. It is supposed they each juggled moon months and the turning points of the solar year to obtain a degree of convergence with nature in the medium term.

Dating events in the works of classical Greek authors relies upon their text showing the first, second, third or fourth year of the nth Olympiad and the first re-instituted Olympiad by custom being attributed a date of 776 BC. *"The Olympic games were observed every fifth year, or, so to speak with greater exactness, after a revolution of four years, and in the first month of the fifth year, and they continued for five successive days. . . . The games were exhibited at the time of the full moon, next after the summer solstice; therefore the Olympiads were of unequal length, because the time of the full moon differs 11 days every year, and for that reason they sometimes began the next day after the solstice, and at other times four weeks after."(4).*

The summer solstice was a secure anchor point. Its use prevented calendar drift, albeit there was a variation of a few days between cycles and the first day of the cycle.

THE ROMANS counted from the foundation of Rome in 753 BC. Thus, as an example, 4 BC is equivalent to 749 years after the founding of Rome (AUC) and the 4th year of the 193rd Olympiad.

Numa was among the earliest leaders in Rome. Plutarch's own understanding of the calendar used by the early Roman state was recorded within his 'life' of Numa.

Plutarch's Lives: Numa [Stewart and Long]
"18. He also dealt with astronomical matters, not with perfect accuracy, and yet not altogether without knowledge. During the reign of Romulus the months had been in a state of great disorder, some not containing twenty days, some five and thirty, and some even more because the Romans could not reconcile the discrepancies which arise from reckoning by the sun and the moon, and only insisted upon one thing, that the year should consist of three hundred and sixty days.

Numa reckoned the variation to consist of eleven days as the lunar year contains three hundred and fifty four days, and the solar year three hundred and sixty-five. He doubled these eleven days and introduced them every other year, after February, as an intercalary month, twenty two days in duration, which was called by the Romans Mercedinus. This was a remedy for the irregularities of the calendar which itself required more extensive remedies.

He also altered the order of the months, putting March, which used to be the first month, third, and making January the first, and February the second, which then had been the twelfth. There are many writers who say that these months, January and February, were added to the calendar by Numa, and that originally there had only been ten months in the year, just as some barbarians have three, and in Greece the Arcadians have four, and the Acarnanians six. The Egyptians originally had but one month in their year, and are afterwards said to have divided it into four months; wherefore, though they live in the newest of all countries, they appear to be the most ancient of all nations, and in their genealogies reckon an incredible number of years, because they count their months as years."(42.1)

JULIAN CALENDAR. It had become obvious that the Roman calendar was out of keeping with the seasons. In 46 BC, after consulting with the Egyptians (e.g. Sosigenes) among others, Julius Caesar authorised a revision of the Roman calendar. To put matters back on the correct footing, the year 46 BC was decreed to have 445 days and is often referred to as the 'Year of Confusion'.

After 46 BC each year had 365 days with an additional leap year day to be included every four years. The year opened on the first of January and comprised twelve months, each of 30 days or 31 days except for February. The names of 'fifth' to 'tenth' month (December) were retained though they took their name from an archaic period when March was the first month of their year. February had 29 days for three years and 30 days in a leap year. The 'fifth month' of the Roman year was renamed after Julius Caesar - July in modern terminology. At a later stage, Augustus had a mind to re-name a month in his own honour and chose the 'sixth month' which is now named August. As Augustus (emperor 27 BC to 14 AD) considered that he was no less a man than Caesar, he also required 31 days in his month and so February was reduced by one day to 28 (and 29) days to compensate.

The driving requirement for the revised calendar was to put Roman festivals firmly back into their correct slot with regard to season or solar event. It is mooted that the first day of January in 45 BC was selected to coincide with a new moon. Otherwise, it is to be mused why they chose not to initiate their new calendar about seven days earlier at the winter solstice. An alternate explanation is that the first day of January was determined by a desire that the spring equinox should occur on the twenty fifth of March, as had been the case in antiquity. The Vernal Equinox is the changeover to when the hours of daylight become greater than the hours of darkness, which on our present calendar was on 21st March in 2007, 20th March in 2008 and 2009 (GMT).

Augustus had further corrected the Calendar in 11 BC by ordering that the 12 ensuing years were to be without intercalation (no leap years) and another correction to the leap year was made in 4 AD as the former period had been 3 years (4).

A number of books express a viewpoint that after Caesar's intervention, the year comprised twelve months alternating between 31 days and 30 days except for the last month: other authorities do not concur. Furthermore some say that we arrived at our

Jan = 31 28(29) 31 30 31 30 31 31 30 31 30 31 = Dec

day sequence following Augustus naming the then sixth month after himself and his successors dabbling over the next century. A case is made that in a leap year Caesar counted the sixth day before the Calends of March, i.e. February 24th, twice.

If when using translations from Latin a need arises to deal with the number of days between events, then it is best that the assumptions on month length are defined in the exercise. Be wary of translations that offer, with the best intentions, the dates in modern format.

GREGORIAN CALENDAR. Over centuries, differences built up between the Julian Calendar and the solar tropical year. In 1582 Pope Gregory XIII ordered that the 4th of October was to be followed by the 15th of October and from then on only every fourth century should be a leap year to give a finer tuning. The countries of Italy, Spain, France and Portugal made the change in 1582. Other countries followed in due course. The British Empire made the changeover in 1752 when 2nd September was followed by 14th September and henceforth New Year's Day was taken as 1st January. Prior to 1752, in England New Year's day had been 25th March which was the date of the Vernal Equinox when the Julian Calendar had been adopted (43).

On a day to day basis after 1752 the 25th March slipped to 5th April, a date that was retained in the United Kingdom as the beginning of the Financial Year. The 6th April replaced 5th April when the year 1800 was not a leap year under the Gregorian calendar though it would have been under the Julian. The financial year was left unchanged in 1900.

THE COPTIC ERA began 29th August, 284 AD.

284 was the year when Diocletian became emperor of Rome. Diocletian carried out a severe persecution of Christians throughout the Empire. The Coptic Church reckons years from this date in commemoration of the martyrdom of so many Christians.

THE JEWISH ERA began about 3760 BC. The year comprises twelve months of alternately 30 and 29 days giving a year of 354 days. A 30 day month is inserted as last but one in the third, sixth, eighth, eleventh, fourteenth, seventeenth and nineteenth years of a nineteen year cycle, giving a year of 384 days in those cases. To allow that certain religious days fall or do not fall on particular days of the week, the length of a year may be altered by a day; thus, a year may contain 353, 354, 355, 383, 384 or 385 days (43). Clearly this calendar was compiled with a knowledge of the 19 year Meton cycle. The numbers in the example above may not coincide exactly with those used in the Bible.

The day begins at sunset which is taken to be 6 p.m. It is noted that two consecutive lunar months take 59 days. The first month of the Jewish year always includes the spring equinox.

The Jewish Calendar continues in use to the present day. It is not a model that has been developed to work with piecemeal data from classical literature; it exists. This calendar illustrates the complexity that can accompany the use of months selected to approximate to the length of observed lunar periods and then accommodate that calendar to stay in contact with the solar year and return to a common starting point over a cycle of years.

EGYPTIAN YEAR. The third century BC Egyptian Manetho, who wrote in Greek, is reported to have stated that Saites the Hyksos king of Egypt increased the length of the month by 12 hours to 30 days and increased the length of the year by 6 days to a total of 365 days. The translator of Manetho, W.G.Waddell, Professor of Classics in Fuad el Awal University Cairo, noted 5 days were added to the 360 day year at least by the pyramid age and that a reconciliation between the lunar and solar year had been made in approximately 4236 BC (45). Leap years are dealt with in the relevant literature.

In keeping with other cultures worldwide, both the Mayas of South America and the ancient Egyptians used a 360 day calculation with 5 days sitting outside the main unit to complete the solar year, though there is no evidence to connect the two.

METON CYCLE. In 19 tropical solar years there are 6939.6 days and in 235 lunar months there are 6939.7 days, approximately. The establishment of this cycle is credited to the Greek astronomer Meton in about 430 BC. Hence, nineteen years is a convenient time frame within which to rationalise calendars based upon either system. There is evidence for the use of this nineteen year cycle before the lifetime of Meton.

In the year 2006 the moon was setting and rising at its most extremes on the horizon of the earth. The variation in the lunar monthly orbit about the earth has an 18.6 year cycle, or thereabouts. On average the moon rises approximately fifty minutes later each day. This value reduces to the order of thirty minutes near to the time of the autumn equinox, being less than thirty minutes when the observer moves north [from London]. This data is found in an article by Paul Simons in the London Times of 7th October, 2006.

The plane containing the moon's motion around the earth makes an angle of about 5 degrees with that of the earth around the sun, this angle is the lunar inclination. The relative alignment of the moon, earth and sun repeats itself in approximately 223 synodic moon months. This 223 month cycle goes under the name of the Saros cycle. The Saros cycle has a value close to 18 years, 11 days and 8 hours. It is pertinent to the prediction of an eclipse of the moon by the earth, whether penumbral, partial or full (44). The Saros cycle is not the same as the lunar precessional period of about 18.6 years; thus, events in the night sky rarely repeat themselves with precision.

ANGLO-SAXON CALENDAR. It is understood that the Anglo-Saxon new year was taken from the winter solstice (though it is awkward to determine) and that their months were lunar months. It is possible they used the eight year cycle having thirteen months in years three, six and eight and twelve in the others and then removed two days and one day from alternate total cycles, see Kenneth Harrison, *The primitive Anglo-Saxon calendar, Antiquity Vol. XLVII No.188 December 1973*. If in doubt they could always reset their calculations at the winter solstice. It is open to doubt as to whether many of them were much fussed by such need for accuracy in any case. The Anglo-Saxons may have had a knowledge of the Meton cycle.

It is readily observed that, counting the first and last moon in the total, in general the start of the new sequence of eight years is associated with the ninety ninth moon; the first new moon of the new eight year sequence being the hundredth of the old. In each cycle the old moon would encroach a further 0.0527 lunar months into the new eight year cycle. Thus, approximately every nineteenth of the eight year solar cycles would be ushered in by the ninety eighth moon and not the ninety ninth.

At the eastern end of our landmass, the Chinese once employed a sixty year cycle comprising five sets of twelve years as a principal unit of time. The Chinese count a new moon from the dark night between a waning and a waxing moon. In general, their traditional new year begins with the second new moon after the winter solstice, but when a complication arises with the phases of the moon in the eleventh moon month of the old year against a backdrop of the Chinese star signs prevailing at the time of the winter solstice, then the third new moon ushers in the new year. Thus, their variable 'lunar year' remains in contact with their solar year.

Tacitus stated that the Germans counted elapsed time by nights.

Tacitus: Germania chapter 11 [Murphy]
"11. . The general assembly, if no sudden alarm calls the people together, has its fixed and stated periods, either at the new or full moon. This is thought the season most propitious to public affairs. Their account of time differs from that of the Romans; instead of days they reckon the number of nights. Their public ordinances are so dated; and their proclamations run in the same style. The night, according to them, leads the day. Their meetings are, except in case of chance emergencies, on fixed days, either at new moon or full moon: such seasons they believe to be the most auspicious for beginning business."(5.4)

SCANDINAVIAN YEAR. The year began at the winter solstice and the months ran from one new moon to the next (36). In the ninth month there was a festival lasting nine days' in which nine (or eight) sacrifices were offered each day. In Sweden there was also a particular festival every eight (some say nine e.g. Adam of Bremen) years. Three important festivals of the year were as follows.

Winter solstice.	'Jul' in honour of Frey for a good and fruitful year. The mother night, which produces all the others.
1st Qtr. 2nd moon of year.	Goddess Goa. Honour earth, fruitfulness, victory.
Beginning of Spring.	Odin god of battle. Happy success in expeditions.

The onset of winter on 'Winter's Day' in mid October and the arrival of summer on 'Summer's Day' in mid April played their role in the celebrations.
"The saga reckoning of years is so many winters;"(28).

CELTIC YEAR. There were four main festivals in the Celtic year of which Beltain and Samain were the most important (*New Larousse Encyclopedia of Mythology*, Hamlyn).

Samain	1st November	All gods, union of gods and mother goddesses.
Imbolc	1st February	Goddess Brigit at a later date, renewal. [Also 2nd Feb.]
Beltain	1st May	God Belenos.
Lughnasa	1st August	God Lugos, Lugh, Lleu.

As our modern calendar was rationalised by Julius Caesar, slightly altered by Augustus and adjusted for drift by Gregory, it is difficult to appreciate why the Celtic festivals remain so conveniently positioned at the first of each of four months.

The Celtic festivals can be expected to predate Caesar. Moreover, the Celts in Ireland and the Druid tradition within that Celtic framework were never subject to Roman occupation.

No simple argument presents itself as to why these Celtic festivals have any connection with the sun and hence the solstice and equinox, although Caesar stated that the Celts celebrated the new year and the first of the month. This statement by Caesar came from the time before he re-arranged the calendar.

A less fraught solution is to accept the statement by Pliny that the Celts took the first day of the month as the day after the fifth night of the moon.

Pliny: Natural History book 16, chapter 95 [Bostock & Riley]
"This is done more particularly on the fifth day of the moon, the day which is the beginning of their months and years, as also of their ages, which, with them, are but thirty years. This day they select because the moon, though not yet in the middle of her course, has already considerable power and influence; and they call her by a name which signifies, in their language, the all-healing."(17.2)

No doubt it was actually the fifth night which was recognised as the Celts counted by nights (Caesar's *Gallic Wars*, 6.18). The thirty years is taken to represent a Celtic large unit of time in a similar manner to the modern use of a century. It would have been sensible to arrange meetings and festivals five days after the new moon was seen rather than guess that it was about to be seen.

The number of days on the modern calendar between the first of May, August, November, February and May is 92, 92, 92, 89 (90). These principal dates in the Celtic calendar do conveniently divide the solar year into four approximately equal parts.

Statements in *Early Astronomy* by W.M.O'Neal, on the time between the solar events are as follows.

"Though the sun moves eastward amongst the fixed stars by an average of almost 1° per day, it advances at a slightly variable rate. Today the Sun spends 92.72 days between the spring equinox and the summer solstice, 93.66 days between the summer solstice and the autumn equinox, 89.84 days between the autumn equinox and the winter solstice, and 88.98 days between the winter solstice and the Spring equinox." (44.1. Note. The preface was written in January 1986.)

"Kallippos, c.370 BC, . . . Beginning with the spring equinox, . . . Modern calculation indicates that in Kallippos's times the values were 94.1, 92.3, 88.6, 90.4 days."(44.2).

At their origin, the Celtic festivals could well have coincided with, or have been a fixed number of days, or lunar sub sequence after, the spring equinox, the summer solstice, the autumn equinox and the winter solstice. The festivals stayed locked to their calendar dates and the equinox and solstice moved relentlessly on. 'Imbolc', for example, can claim to be a festival to witness the passing of the mid point between the winter solstice and the spring equinox in the northern hemisphere.

A value of approximately forty days after the solar events of solstice and equinox promotes itself when positioning Celtic festivals against the backdrop of modern calendar dates. A value closer to 36 days would pertain to 45 BC.

COLIGNY CALENDAR

Fragments of a bronze tablet approximately 1.5 metres wide by 1 metre in height were found at Coligny, near to Lyon in France in 1897. The words of its inscription were written with Latin letters in the Celtic language. The tablet is set out in sixteen columns and covers a total of 62 lunar months, which approximates to five solar years. The months were divided into the first fifteen days and the second set of fourteen or fifteen days on alternate months. The calendar is dated at circa AD 200.

The language shows some affinity with q-Celtic and is not exclusively of a p-Celtic format. Coligny lies at the upper reaches of the River Solnan, a tributary of the River Saone in France. In Caesar's time, the Saone ran through the lands of the Aedui and the Sequani. The calendar is kept at a museum in Lyons. The two halves of each month are interpreted as the waxing and waning of the moon, a position that is at odds with the account given by Pliny that months began on the 5th day (night) of the moon. The year on the calendar began with or in the month of Samon.

A set of twelve moon cycles falls about eleven days short of the solar year. The approximation at five solar years would have shown obvious inaccuracies. A better solution is a thirty solar year cycle equating to 371 moon cycles e.g. 5 x5 years of a total of 62 moons plus 5 years of 61 moons suitably positioned within the 25 cycles of 62 moons. Even so a further moon cycle would need to be added after about every six of these thirty-year cycles to stay in contact with the solar year. Pliny stated that the Celts used thirty years as their unit of measurement.

H.D.Rankin, Professor of Classics at the University of Southampton, observed that traces of q-Celtic wording were included in the inscription on the Coligny Calendar. *"Traces of q-Celtic are discernible in Gaul, in tribal names such as 'Sequani' and Quariates'. The Coligny Calendar, the oldest Celtic written work of significance that survives, has q-Celtic forms such as 'equos' instead of Brythonic or Gaulish 'epos' which we might expect. If we supposed that this was evidence of sacral archaism in the language of the Calendar (MacWhite 1957:16), we should only be agreeing to the priority of q-Celtic in a particular region. Its general seniority would not be established."*(25.2) He gave further examples as 'quimon' and 'qut' from the Calendar. 'Eqvos' was the name of a month listed on the Calendar.

At face value this Coligny Calendar is a good example of the type of calendar used by Celts, but maybe not all Celts. Academic discussion continues on whether or not its use was restricted to the local district or it found acceptance over a wider area of Gaul. Did it represent an amendment of an earlier reckoning process to take account of the Julian Calendar that by then had held sway in occupied Gaul for two hundred years? How many true Celts lived in the British Isles and what was their influence?

NINETEEN YEAR CYCLE IN BRITAIN

A calendar system linked to a nineteen-year cycle was reported by Diodorus as that used by some Hyperborians. In this passage he does not name Britain as the relevant island. Other passages in his *History* show that he was familiar with its name and broad locality. In this instance perhaps Diodorus closely followed his source documents.

Diodorus: Histories book 2, chapter 3 [Booth]
"Now, since we have thus far spoken of the northern parts of Asia, it is convenient to observe something relating to the antiquity of the Hyperboreans.

Amongst them that have written old stories much like fables, Hecateus and some others say, that there is an island in the ocean over against Gaul, (as big as Sicily) under the arctic pole, where the Hyperboreans inhabit; so called, because they lie beyond the breezes of the north wind. That the soil here is very rich, and very fruitful; and the climate temperate, insomuch as there are two crops in the year.

They say that Latona was born here, and therefore, that they worship Apollo above all other gods; and because they are daily singing songs in praise of this god, and ascribing to him the highest honours, they say that the inhabitants demean themselves, as if they were Apollo's priests, who has there a stately grove and renowned temple, of round form, beautified with many rich gifts. That there is a city likewise consecrated to this god, whose citizens are most of them harpers, who, playing on the harp, chant sacred hymns to Apollo in the temple, setting forth his glorious acts. The Hyperboreans use their own natural language; but of long and antient [sic] time have had a special kindness for the Grecians, and more especially for the Athenians and them of Delos. And that some of the Grecians passed over to the Hyperboreans, and left behind them divers presents, inscribed with Greek characters; and that Abaris formerly travelled thence into Greece, and renewed the antient league of friendship with the Delians.

They say, moreover, that the moon in this island seems as if it were near to the earth, and represents in the face of it excrescences like the spots in the earth. And that Apollo once in nineteen years comes into the island; in which space of time the stars perform their courses, and return to the same point; and therefore the Greeks call the revolution of nineteen years the Great Year. At this time of his appearance (they say) that he plays upon the harp, and sings and dances all the night, from the vernal equinox to the rising of the Pleiades, solacing himself with the praises of his own successful adventures. The sovereignty of this city, and the care of the temple (they say) belongs to the Boreades, the posterity of Boreas, who hold the principality by descent in a direct line from that ancestor."(11.5)*

In Roman mythology, Latona was the mother of Apollo and Diana. In Greek mythology Lato (or Leto) was a daughter of the Titan Coeus and Phoebe, her father was Saturn according to Homer. Zeus was the father of Lato's twins Apollo and Artemis. The Greek Artemis and Zeus equate with the Roman Diana and Jupiter (4).

Hecateus of Miletus, an historian, was born about 549 BC. He arises in Herodotus, *Histories* 2.143 (4). He died about 476 BC. In this case Hecateus of Abdera, a contemporary of Alexander the Great, was the historian whose works had been perused by Diodorus (46). The 'among others' is by common acceptance taken to include Pytheas of Marseilles who visited Britain between about 350 BC and 300 BC.

Diana had many attributes, one of which was goddess of the moon. Apollo was held distinct from Helios by Homer but in later times took the sun under his mantle.

The nub of the data is that a temple existed where the priesthood assiduously kept note of the elapsed lunar months and solar years. A nineteen year period had been determined after which the relationships between the cycles of the moon and sun repeated themselves. The source data used by Diodorus in the first century BC had been written down by Hecataeus between about 315 and 250 BC. The nineteen-year cycle would repeat itself every nineteen years from a set point anywhere within the cycle. The point selected in the cycle of events by the priests concerned was the vernal equinox in the initiating solar year of the nineteen.

It could not have gone un-noticed that after every nine or ten cycles of nineteen years or so there would need to be an accommodation of the fact that the moon had proceeded one day further in its orbit at the time of the equinox. Thus, any coincidence of a set lunar event with the equinox would slip away. Surely the solar solstice and equinox must have held precedence in resetting a lunar calendar or else a lunar calendar would loose lock with the seasons. An ability to predict an eclipse hovered in the background.

Though driving an additional nail into an altar once every vernal equinox would keep account of years passing, a medium to pass on the detail of thoughts and observations to succeeding generations was desirable. A need to refine algorithms and appropriate calculations must have arisen from time to time. Failure to address these needs may have put both the priesthood and calendar into at least disrepute if not jeopardy.

The historical sequence of relative motion between the earth's orbit, the moon, the sun and the seasonal pattern of stars in the night sky are better examined with a computer program and access to knowledgeable advice.

The pleiades are a group of 6 (once 7) stars visible to the naked eye on the shoulder of the constellation of Taurus (*Chamber's Dictionary*). The vernal equinox is when the hours of daylight equal the hours of darkness and daylight hours are on the increase i.e. the beginning of Spring. The constellation of Taurus, or parts of it, would have been the first constellation rising in the night sky at the time of the vernal equinox between, in round terms, 2350 BC and 250 BC. The hyperborean sky watchers could well have designed a different pattern of figures to describe the night sky to those used in the 'zodiac' of which Taurus is a part.

Either Britain or Ireland was in all reason the *island in the ocean over against Gaul, (as big as Sicily) under the arctic pole.* The temple, by common consent, was a henge. A henge on the mainland being the preferred option. Avebury, Stonehenge or Arbor Low are presented for consideration, though any major henge then existing could have been the site visited or reported upon.

The implications for use of a calendar based upon these time cycles in Britain and hence eventually by Druids is seductive. Conventional wisdom in archaeology dissociates a Druid priesthood from henge monuments in their hey-day or at any time thereafter.

Ammianus, Book 15.9.4, implied that Druidism may have predated the incursion of Celts into Western Europe. *"The Druids affirm that a portion of the people was really indigenous to the soil, but that other inhabitants poured in from the islands on the coast, and from the districts across the Rhine, having been driven from their former abodes by frequent wars, and sometimes by inroads of the tempestuous sea."(22.1)*

Caesar, GW 6.13, sourced the institution in Britain. *"Over all these Druids . . . This institution is supposed to have been devised in Britain, and to have been brought over from it into Gaul; and now those who desire to gain a more accurate knowledge of that system generally proceed thither for the purpose of studying it."(1.6)*

Smith's Dictionary (46) contains the following entry on the real meaning of Leto.

Leto (Λητω) . . . We shall pass over the various speculations of modern writers respecting the origin and nature of this divinity, and shall mention only the most probable, according to which Leto is "the obscure" or "concealed," not as a physical power, but as a divinity yet quiescent and invisible, from whom is issued the visible divinity with all his splendour and brilliancy. This view is supported by the account of her genealogy given by Hesiod; and her whole legend seems to indicate nothing else but the issuing from darkness to light, and a return from the latter to the former."

There is no hint that Leto in an abstruse way conveys the name the occupants of Britain used for their island.

Whilst the Hyperboreans who lived, according to Diodorus, in *"an island in the ocean over against Gaul, (as big as Sicily) under the arctic pole,"* could well have been Britons; Hyperborei was a generic term for people who lived 'beyond the north wind'. They occupied the northern parts of Europe to the edge of Asia, well beyond the tribes in contact with the Mediterranean world. For convenience, several passages relevant to Hyperborei in classical texts are reproduced in Appendix 7. It well may be that they were the root stock to which Celtic culture was grafted after the Celts entered Europe in about 850 BC. An option that the term should be reserved for people living at the megalithic north-western fringe of Europe may find merit with some minds.

PRECESSION OF THE EQUINOXES. It is in the nature of things with respect to the orbit of the earth about the sun that the equinoxes and the solstices slip to the west over the centuries. Thus, the set of (apparently fixed) stars which are first seen in the night sky at the time of the spring equinox gradually moves from one constellation to another, from one sign of the Zodiac to another if the stars have been so designated. Such a move occurred around 2350 BC from Gemini to Taurus, by 250 BC into Aries and by 1950 AD into Pisces (44.3). The complete cycle has a period of about 25,730 years to return to the same point. Hence, one degree, of the three hundred and sixty, slips in a tad more than seventy-one years.

Platonic year is the name given to this 25,730 year cycle. The time variation between one cycle and another attracts the attention of people with the equipment to take and ponder fine measurements.

A society where the astronomers employed differing constellations to mark out the night sky, or celebrated the opening of their year by another event, would observe the change as appropriate to their system. The precursors of a group with knowledge of such happenings would of needs have acquired a means of recording the observed data for use by future generations. It cannot be wholly coincidence that there was a bull cult among the Mediterranean cultures e.g. Apis in Egypt and subsequently 'the golden calf' of the bible entered upon the scene.

24 DISCUSSION

New and emerging tools set to capture the essence of biology will in their turn prove a fairy godmother to history. Work flowing from the Carbon–14 revolution and ingenious observations of isotopic elements are with us. The 'haplotype' (short for haploid genotype, the genetic constitution of an individual chromosome) and variations thereof have entered the vocabulary of archaeology.

As examples of progress, attention is drawn to two papers concerned with milk. The papers were both submitted at *The Second International Symposium on Biomolecular Archaeology* held at Stockholm University, Sweden, 7 – 9 September 2006.

Detecting milk in the palaeodiet with calcium isotopes – Nan-chin Chu, Gideon Henderson, Robert Hedges of the University of Oxford. The paper seeks to differentiate between the level of milk consumption of individuals by using an analysis of their bones and hence determine whether dairy products were important to a given group of people.

In another paper given at the 2006 Swedish Symposium its author observes a plausible case can be made for a homogenous core connecting members of the European Nation States. *"Lactase persistence is common in people of European descent but, with the exception of some Middle Eastern and African pastoralist groups, is rare or absent in other global populations. . . . We find that under plausible conditions of limited gene flow between dairying and non-dairying cultures, a disproportionately high component of European ancestry will trace back to Europe's earliest lactase persistent pastoralists."* See *Diffusing culture, migrating genes: Milking the origins of Europeans* – Mark Thomas, Department of Biology, University College, London.

Milk is widely used but not much known for its survival value in archaeological digs.

A simplistic approach to the distinction made at the onset of the age of Aries to identify Celts to authors in the classical world was that they were unified by a common language and likewise the German tribes.

Gerald of Wales: Description of Wales, book 1 [Colt Hoare]
"Chapter 15. Nature hath given not only to the highest, but also to the inferior, classes of the people of this nation, a boldness and confidence in speaking and answering, even in the presence of their princes and chieftains. The Romans and Franks had the same faculty; but neither the English, nor the Saxons and Germans, from whom they are descended, had it."(24.7)

After allowing for the twelfth century observation of Gerald, there remains the relative percentage of blood group mix and the analysis of archaeological DNA as distinguishing factors. At the dawn of the age of Pisces, the gene pool soup has a larger number of contributing factors whilst the tribal marking of language is inappropriate.

The dynamics of Celtic culture spreading across Western Europe, whether using Iron Age A, B, C, Hallstatt, La Tene, Arras, and Aylesford, overlaying, absorption or displacement, is found in books describing the archaeology of a region. Caesar was more explicit for Gaul in 58 BC.

Caesar: Gallic War book 1, chapters 1 [Mcdevitte]
"1. All Gaul is divided into three parts, One of which the Belgae inhabit, the Aquitani another, those who in their own language are called Celts, in ours Gauls, the third. All these differ from each other in language, customs and laws. The river Garonne separates the Gauls from the Aquitani; the Marne and the Seine separate them from the Belgae. . . the Germans who dwell beyond the Rhine . . ."(1.1)

Caesar's enquiries established that the Belgae had their origin in Germanic tribes who had crossed the Rhine into Gaul. He was less precise as to whether they spoke a Celtic or German dialect.

Professor Rankin subscribed to the opinion of Chadwick (1966) and Tierney (1960) that the similarity between Strabo, Diodorus and Caesar on the subject of the Druids points to Poseidonius as being the source common to all three. Furthermore, both Diodorus and Ammianus Marcellinus identified the first century BC ex captive Timagenes as an authority on Celtic matters (25.3). From this situation arises an unease with regard to how many independent observations were available as the basis for the descriptions of Celts written down by the earlier authors. As a counterbalance, if Divitiacus was indeed an Arch-Druid, then his links with Julius Caesar can only have added accuracy to Caesar's account of the Druids' position in Celtic society.

Pliny, who died in 79 AD, had visited Germany around 50 AD. Tacitus (55 to 120 AD) was well placed to receive the best information from his military connections through his father-in-law Agricola and access to the books and notes of Pliny the Elder. Archaeologists are in general of the opinion German tribes arrived on the coast of the North Sea after the Celts had established themselves in Western Europe.

Pliny: Natural History book 4, chapter 28. Germany [Bostock & Riley]
"The whole of the shores of this sea as far as the Scaldis [Scheldt], a river of Germany, is inhabited by nations, the dimensions of whose respective territories it is quite impossible to state, so immensely do the authors differ who have touched upon this subject. . . .There are five German races; the Vandili, parts of whom are the Burgundiones, the Varini, the Carini, and the Gutones: the Ingaevones, forming a second race, a portion of whom are the Cimbri, the Teutoni, and the tribes of the Chauci. The Istaevones, who join up to the Rhine, are the third race; while the Hermiones, forming a fourth, dwell in the interior, and include the Suevi, the Hermunuri, the Chatti, and the Cherusci: the fifth race is that of the Basternae, adjoining the Daci previously mentioned."(17.1)

Tacitus: Germania chapter 1 [Murphy]
"1. The whole vast country of Germany is separated from Gaul, from Rhaetia, and Pannonia, by the Rhine and the Danube; from Dacia and Sarmatia, by a chain of mountains, and, where the mountains subside, mutual dread forms a sufficient barrier. The rest is bounded by the ocean, embracing in its depth of water several spacious bays, and islands of prodigious extent, whose kings and peoples are now, in some measure, known to us, the progress of our arms having made recent discoveries."(5.3)

The diversion into the nature of Julius Caesar shows the man differed from the giant stature of his honed public image. The Celts and Germans came close to defeating the Roman armies. But for the Roman habit of raising conscripts among recently subdued nations to fight against those still free, the men from Italy would not have secured an empire.

An appreciation of routes by which succeeding cultures spread across Europe is enhanced by an examination of an Atlas showing physical geography. The relative position of mountains and rivers awakes an echo of why cities evolved and the imperative behind sites of historic land battles.

The major rivers, for example the Don, the Danube, the Rhine, the Rhone were significant obstructions in themselves to the movement of nomadic peoples with their possessions. The 22 miles of the English Channel remains a barrier a thousand miles wide separating the culture of London from that of the Parisi.

Ireland is readily visible from Snowdonia in Wales but the fifteen miles of the North Channel between Galloway or Kintyre and Ulster provides a shorter sea trip than across St George's Channel from St David's Head to Wexford.

The solution to carrying across cattle is to take a bull calf rather than a full grown five year old bull. A judgement could be made on the size of the craft and the level of risk posed by an animal against a loss of provisions in the medium term. War elephants were carried across the English Channel in army transports to support the Claudian invasion of England in 54 AD. The logistics of sea travel by whole clan groups was awkward and complicated by any hostile intent of the indigenous population.

Over a few generations the wagon living, semi nomadic tribes out of Asia emerged from a chrysalis awakening as the roving Norsemen having the salt sea coursing through their veins. Both Celt and German adapted to the routine of mixed farming and, hemmed in by others, to settlement in a general clan area, though the MacGregors, in their hearts, never subdued their partiality for rustling cattle.

The chronicles do not re-kindle the smell of wood, thatch, muck and animals that pervade the scene they portray. The killing, agony, death, apprehension and other hardships of everyday living in the Celtic and German social patterns require but a modest imagination to recognise from the texts.

Otherwise, with the exception of demonstrably harder teeth and more widespread parasite infestation, the people of the Iron Age were very much the same as we are now. It is to be hoped that our society does not regress.

The Celtic and German tribes continued their westward migration and were dominant in colonizing North America in the second millennium of the Christian era. It now only remains to pass across into northern Asia to complete the circle of the globe at temperate latitudes and approach the River Don from the east.

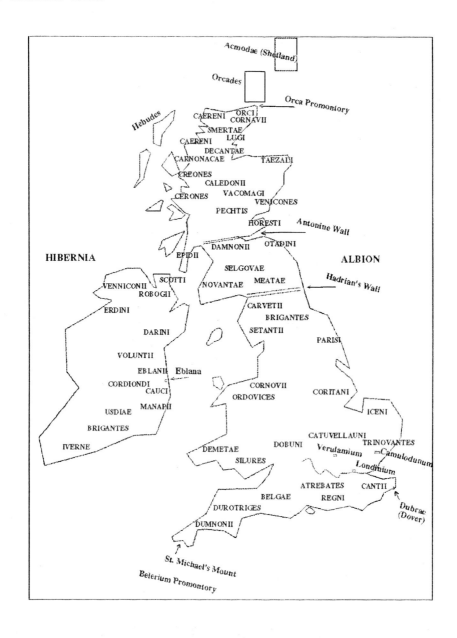

APPENDICES

EVENTS in ROMAN CONQUEST of BRITAIN

71 BC circa	Divitiacus the Aeduan held sway in part of Britain until c. 71 BC.	G.W. 2.4
57 BC	Nobles of Bellovaci, a Belgic people, move to Britain from Gaul.	G.W. 2.14
55 BC	Caesar sends Commius, king of the Continental Belgic Atribates, to Britain. Julius Caesar's 1st expedition. 2 legions.	G.W. 4.21 G.W. 4.22
54 BC	Julius Caesar's 2nd expedition. 5 legions and 2,000 cavalry. Cassivellaunus of the Catuvellauni elected British war leader.	G.W. 5.8
43 AD	Bericus, British tribal leader, fled to Romans. Claudian Invasion. Claudius visits Colchester. Vespasian, a future emperor, among the generals. Togodumnus (killed in battle) and Caractacus, both sons of Cynobellinus, led Britons. Silures stubborn resistance. Ordovices, Caractacus lost a decisive battle in their territory.	Cas.Dio 60.19 Tacitus Annals 12.39
52 AD circa	Caractacus given up in chains to Romans by Cartimandua, queen of the Brigantes. Caractacus exhibited in Rome then pardoned by Claudius.	Tacitus Annals 12.36
61 AD	Boudicca led uprising. Colchester, London and St Albans all sacked.	
78 AD	Ordovices routed Roman cavalry. Agricola takes up post in Britain.	Tacitus Agricola 18
82 AD	Irish deposed kinglet finds Agricola's protection. Agricola entered Caledonia.	
83 AD circa	Battle at Mount Graupius against Caledonians. Calgacus, a distinguished leader of Britons or Caledonians.	
122 AD circa	Hadrian's wall initiated, Tyne to Solway. Emperor visited area.	
140 to 190 AD	Antonine wall (turf and earth) established in 140 to 145 AD from Forth to Clyde by Rom. Gov. Lollius Urbicus. Various occupations, by 190 AD withdrawal south to Hadrian's wall.	

APPENDIX 1 - CLAUDIAN INVASION OF BRITAIN
contained in the Roman History of Cassius Dio

Cassius Dio (c.163 AD to 235 AD) was the author of *The Roman History*. The quotations are taken from the translation from the Greek by Herbert Baldwin Foster published in 1905 by Pafraets Book Company, Troy, New York. (21)

43 AD Claudian Invasion of Britain.

Cassius Dio: Roman History, book 60, chapters 19 to 23 [Herbert Baldwin Foster]
"(19). At the same time that these events were happening in the City Aulus Plautius, a senator of great renown, made a campaign against Britain. The cause was that a certain Bericus, who had been ejected from the island during a revolution, had persuaded Claudius to send a body of troops there. This Plautius after he was made general had difficulty in leading his army beyond Gaul. The soldiers objected, on the grounds that their operations were to take place outside the limits of the known world, and would not yield him obedience until the arrival of Narcissus, sent by Claudius, who mounted the tribunal of Plautius and tried to address them. This made them more irritated than ever and they would not allow the newcomer to say a word, but all suddenly shouted together the well known phrase: "Ho! Ho! the Saturnalia!" (For at the festival of Saturn slaves celebrate the occasion by donning their masters' dress.) After this they at once followed Plautius voluntarily, but their delay had brought the expedition late in the season. Three divisions were made in order that they might not be hindered in advancing (as might happen to a single force), and some of them in their voyage across became discouraged because they were buffeted into a backward course, whereas others acquired confidence from the fact that a flash of light starting from the east shot across to the west, the direction in which they were sailing. So they came to anchor on the shore of the island and found no one to oppose them. The Britons as a result of their enquiries had not expected that they would come and had therefore not assembled beforehand. Nor even at this time would they come into closer conflict with the invaders, but took refuge in the swamps and in the forests, hoping to exhaust their opponents in some other way, so that the latter as in the days of Julius Caesar would sail back empty-handed.

(20) Plautius accordingly had considerable trouble in searching for them. – They were not free and independent but were parcel[l]ed out among various kings. – When at last he did find them, he conquered first Caratacus and next Togodumnus, children of Cynobelinus, who was dead. After the flight of those kings he attached by treaty a portion of the Bodunni, ruled by a nation of the Catuellani [Catuvellauni - Compiler]. Leaving a garrison there he advanced farther. On reaching a certain river, which the barbarians thought the Romans would not be able to cross without a bridge, - a conviction which led them to encamp in rather careless fashion on the opposite bank, - he sent ahead Celtae [Other translators give Germans. - Compiler] who were accustomed to swim easily in full armo[u]r across the most turbulent streams. These fell unexpectedly upon the enemy, but instead of shooting at any of the men confined themselves to wounding the horses that drew their chariots and consequently in the confusion not even the mounted warriors could save themselves. Plautius sent across also Flavius Vespasian, who afterwards obtained the imperial office, and his brother Sabinus, a lieutenant of his. So they likewise got over the river in some way and killed a number of the foe, who were not aware of their approach. The survivors, however, did not take to flight, and on the next day joined issue with them again. The two forces were rather evenly matched until Gnaeus Hosidius Geta, at the risk of being captured, managed to conquer the barbarians in such a way that he received triumphal hono[u]rs without having ever been consul.

Thence the Britons retired to the river Thames at a point near where it empties into the ocean and the latter's flood-tide forms a lake. This they crossed easily because they knew where the firm ground in this locality and the easy passages were; but the Romans in following them up came to grief at this spot. However, when the Celtae swam across again and some others had traversed a bridge a little way up stream, they assailed the barbarians from many sides at once and cut down large numbers of them. In pursuing the remainder incautiously they got into swamps from which it was not easy to make one's way out, and in this way lost many men.

(21) Shortly after Togodumnus perished, but the Britons so far from yielding stood together all the more closely to avenge his death. Because of this fact and his previous mishap Plautius became alarmed, and instead of advancing farther proceeded to guard what he had already gained and sent for Claudius. He had been notified to do this in case he met with any particularly stubborn resistance, and a large reinforcement for the army, consisting partly of elephants, had been assembled in advance.

When the message reached him, Claudius entrusted domestic affairs (including the management of the soldiers) to his colleague Vitellius, whom he had caused to become consul like himself for the entire six months' period, and started himself on the expedition. He sailed down the river to Ostia, and from there followed the coast to Massilia. Thence advancing partly by land and partly along the water courses he came to the ocean and crossed over to Britain, where he joined the legions that were waiting for him near the Thames. Taking charge of these he crossed the stream, and encountering the barbarians, who had gathered at his approach, he defeated them in a pitched battle and captured Camulodunum, the capital of Cynobelinus. Next he extended his authority over numerous tribes, in some cases by treaty, in others by force, and was frequently, contrary to precedent, saluted as imperator. The usual practice is that no single person may receive this title more than once from one and the same war. He deprived those he conquered of their arms and assigned them to the attention of Plautius, bidding him to subjugate the regions that were left. Claudius himself now hastened back to Rome, sending ahead the news of the victory by his sons-in-law, Magnus and Silanus.

(22) The senate on learning of his achievement gave him the title of Britannicus and allowed him to celebrate a triumph.

They voted also that there should be an animal festival commemorating the event and that an arch bearing a trophy should be erected in the City and a second in Gaul, because it was from that district that he had set sail in crossing over to Britain. They bestowed on his son the same honorific title as upon him, so that Claudius was known in a way as Britannicus Proper. Messalina was granted the same privilege of front seats as Livia had enjoyed and also the use of the carpentum. These were the hono[u]rs bestowed upon the imperial family.

The memory of Gaius disgusted the senators so much that they resolved that all the bronze coinage which had his image stamped upon it should be melted down. Though this was done, yet the bronze was converted to no better use, for Messalina made statues of Mnester the dancer out of it. Inasmuch as the latter had once been on intimate terms with Gaius, she made this offering as a mark of gratitude for his consenting to a liaison with her. She had been madly enamo[u]red of him, and when she found herself unable in any way either by promises or by frightening him to persuade him to have intercourse with her, she had a talk with her husband and asked him that the man might be forced to obey her, pretending that she wanted his help for some different purpose. Claudius accordingly told him to do whatsoever he should be ordered by Messalina. On these terms he agreed to enjoy her, alleging that he had been commanded to do so by her husband. Messalina adopted this same method with numerous other men, and committed adultery feigning that Claudius knew what was taking place and countenanced her unchastity.

(23) Portions of Britain, then, were captured at this time in the manner described. After this, during the second consulship of Gaius Crispus and the first of Titus Statilius, Claudius came to Rome at the end of a six months' absence from the city (of which time he had spent only sixteen days in Britain) and celebrated his triumph. In this he followed the well-established precedents, even to the extent of ascending the steps of the capitol on his knees, with his sons-in-law supporting him on either side. He granted to the senators taking part with him in the procession triumphal hono[u]rs, this not merely to the ex-consuls . . . for he was accustomed to do that most lavishly on other occasions and with the slightest excuse. Upon Rufrius Pollio . . . "(21.4)

APPENDIX 2 - BRITAIN IN THE ANNALS OF TACITUS

The *Annals of Tacitus* as translated by Alfred John Church and William Jackson Brodribb was first published in 1869. The quotations are taken from the reprint in 1888 published by Macmillan and Company, London.(6) The compiler's observations on the translation are given in cursive brackets.

Tacitus: Annals, Introduction by Church and Brodribb [Church & Brodribb]
"Tacitus's Annals begin with the accession of Tiberius and, as originally written, ended with Nero's death. They thus embraced a period of 54 years, from A.D.14 to 68. The history of the reign of Caius Caesar (Caligula), and of the first six years of that of Claudius - in all a period of 10 years, from A.D. 37 to 47 - is lost. So also is his narrative of the last three years of Nero's reign, A.D. 66 - 68. . . ."(6)

Tacitus: Annals book 2, chapters 22 to 24. [A.D. 16 to 19] [Church & Brodribb]
"22. . . . The Army of Tiberius Caesar, after thoroughly conquering the tribes between the Rhine and the Elbe, . . .
23. When the summer was at its height, some of the legions were sent back overland into winter-quarters, but most of them Caesar put on board the fleet and brought down the river Amisia to the ocean. At first the calm waters merely sounded with the oars of a thousand vessels or were ruffled by the sailing ships. Soon a hailstorm bursting . . .
24. . . . many were wrecked on distant islands, and the soldiers . . . Germanicus's trireme alone reached the country of the Chausi. . . . The Agrivarii, who had lately been admitted to our alliance, restored to us several whom they had ransomed from the inland tribes. Some had been carried to Britain and were sent back by the petty chiefs."(6.3)

Tacitus: Annals book 12, chapters 31 to 40. [A.D. 48 - 54] [Church & Brodribb]
"31. Meanwhile, in Britain, Publius Ostorius, the propraetor, found himself confronted by disturbance. The enemy had burst into the territories of our allies with all the more fury, as they imagined that a new general would not march against them with winter beginning and with an army of which he knew nothing. Ostorius, well aware that first events are those which produce alarm or confidence, by a rapid movement of his light cohorts, cut down all who opposed him, pursued those who fled, and lest they should rally, and so an unquiet and treacherous peace might allow no rest to the general and his troops, he prepared to disarm all whom he suspected, and to occupy with encampments the whole country to the Avon and Severn."

{The River 'Sabrina' was the River Seven but there is some debate as to whether the 'Antona' was the River Avon. There is a possibility that the Antona was the River Nene and the Iceni, who were causing the uprising, therefore lived beyond that river. - Compiler}

"The Iceni, a powerful tribe, which war had not weakened, as they had voluntarily joined our alliance, were the first to resist. At their instigation the surrounding nations chose as a battle-field a spot walled in by a rude barrier, with a narrow approach, impenetrable to cavalry. Through these defences the Roman general, though he had with him only the allied troops, without the strength of the legions, attempted to break, and having assigned their positions to his cohorts, he equipped even his cavalry for the work of infantry. Then at a given signal they forced the barrier, routing the enemy who were entangled in their own defences. The rebels, conscious of their guilt, and finding escape barred, performed many noble feats. In this battle, Marius Ostorius, the general's son, won the reward for saving a citizen's life.
32. The defeat of the Iceni quieted those who were hesitating between war and peace. Then the army was marched against the Cangi; their territory was ravaged, spoil taken everywhere without the enemy venturing on an engagement, or if they attempted to harass our march by stealthy attacks, their cunning was always punished. And now Ostorius had advanced within a little distance of the sea, facing the island of Hibernia, when feuds broke out among the Brigantes and compelled the general's return, for it was his fixed purpose not to undertake any fresh enterprise till he had consolidated his previous successes. The Brigantes indeed, when a few who were beginning hostilities had been slain and the rest pardoned, settled down quietly; but on the Silures neither terror nor mercy had the least effect; they persisted in war and could be quelled only by legions encamped in their country. That this might be the more promptly effected, a colony of a strong body of veterans was established at Camulodunum on the conquered lands, as a defence against the rebels, and as a means of imbuing the allies with respect for our laws."

Appendix 2: Britain in the Annals of Tacitus

{The objective of settling veterans at Colchester in Essex was to release troops to go to the Silures in Wales. - Compiler. Some translations prefer Marcus to Marius Ostorius.}

"33. The army then marched against the Silures, a naturally fierce people and now full of confidence in the might of Caractacus, who by many an indecisive and many a successful battle had raised himself far above all other generals of the Britons. Inferior in military strength, but deriving an advantage from the deceptiveness of the country, he at once shifted the war by a stratagem into the territory of the Ordovices, where, joined by all who dreaded peace with us, he resolved on a final struggle. He selected a position for the engagement in which advance and retreat alike would be difficult for our men and comparatively easy for his own, and then on some lofty hills, wherever their sides could be approached by a gentle slope, he piled up stones to serve as a rampart. A river too of varying depth was in his front, and his armed bands were drawn up before his defences.

34. Then too the chieftains of the several tribes went from rank to rank encouraging and confirming the spirit of their men by making light of their fears, kindling their hopes, and by every other warlike incitement. As for Caractacus, he flew hither and thither, protesting that that day and that battle would be the beginning of the recovery of their freedom, or of everlasting bondage. He appealed, by name, to their forefathers who had driven back the dictator Caesar, by whose valour they were free from the Roman axe and tribute, and still preserved inviolate the persons of their wives and of their children. While he was thus speaking, the host shouted applause; every warrior bound himself by his national oath not to shrink from weapons or wounds.

35. Such enthusiasm confounded the Roman general. The river too in his face, the rampart they had added to it, the frowning hilltops, the stern resistance and masses of fighting men everywhere apparent, daunted him. But his soldiers insisted on battle, exclaiming that valour could overcome all things; and the prefects and tribunes, with similar language, stimulated the ardour of the troops. Ostorius having ascertained by a survey the inaccessible and the assailable points of the position, led on his furious men, and crossed the river without difficulty. When he reached the barrier, as long as it was a fight with missiles, the wounds and the slaughter fell chiefly on our soldiers; but when we had formed the military testudo, and the rude, ill-compacted fence of stones was torn down, and it was an equal hand-to-hand engagement, the barbarians retired to the heights. Yet even there, both light and heavy-armed soldiers rushed to the attack; the first harassed the foe with missiles, while the latter closed with them, and the opposing ranks of the Britons were broken, destitute as they were of the defence of breast-plates or helmets. When they faced the auxiliaries, they were felled by the swords and javelins of our legionaries; if they wheeled round, they were again met by the sabres and spears of the auxiliaries. It was a glorious victory; the wife and daughter of Caractacus were captured, and his brothers too were admitted to surrender.

36. There is seldom safety for the unfortunate, and Caractacus, seeking the protection of Cartismandua, queen of the Brigantes, was put in chains and delivered up to the conquerors, nine years after the beginning of the war in Britain. His fame had spread thence, and reached to the neighbouring islands and provinces, and was actually celebrated in Italy. All were eager to see the great man, who for so many years had defied our power. Even at Rome the name of Caractacus was no obscure one; and the emperor, while he exalted his own glory, enhanced the renown of the vanquished. The people were summoned as to a grand spectacle; the praetorian cohorts were drawn up under arms in the plain in front of their camp; then came a procession of the royal vassals, and the ornaments and neck-chains, and the spoils which the king had won in wars with other tribes, were displayed. Next were to be seen his brothers, his wife and daughter; last of all, Caractacus himself. All the rest stooped in their fear to abject supplication; not so the king, who neither by humble look nor speech sought compassion.

37. When he was set before the emperor's tribunal, he spoke as follows: "Had my moderation in prosperity been equal to my noble birth and fortune, I should have entered this city as your friend rather than as your captive; and you would not have disdained to receive, under a treaty of peace, a king descended from illustrious ancestors and ruling many nations. My present lot is as glorious to you as it is degrading to myself. I had men and horses, arms and wealth. What wonder if I parted with them reluctantly? If you Romans choose to lord it over the world, does it follow that the world is to accept slavery? Were I to have been at once delivered up as a prisoner, neither my fall nor your triumph would have become famous. My punishment would be followed by oblivion, whereas, if you save my life, I shall be an everlasting memorial of your clemency.'

Upon this the emperor granted pardon to Caractacus, to his wife and to his brothers. Released from their bonds, they did homage also to Agrippina who sat near, conspicuous on another throne, in the same language of praise and gratitude. It was indeed a novelty, quite alien to ancient manners, for a woman to sit in front of Roman standards. In fact, Agrippina boasted that she was herself a partner in the empire which her ancestors had won."

{The emperor was Claudius. Although it was the custom for authors to put words into the mouths of historic personages, these events in Rome were within living memory and may have had a good basis in truth.- Compiler}

"38. The Senate was then assembled, and speeches were delivered full of pompous eulogy on the capture of Caractacus. It was as glorious, they said, as the display of Syphax by Scipio, or of Perses by Lucius Paulus, or indeed of any captive prince by any of the generals to the people of Rome. Triumphal distinctions were voted to Ostorius, who thus far had been successful, but soon afterwards met with reverses; either because, when Caractacus was out of the way, our discipline was relaxed under an impression that the war was ended, or because the enemy, out of compassion for so great a king, was more ardent in his thirst for vengeance. Instantly they rushed from all parts on the camp-prefect, and legionary cohorts left to establish fortified positions among the Silures, and had not speedy succour arrived from towns and fortresses in the neighbourhood, our forces would then have been totally destroyed. Even as it was, the camp-prefect, with eight centurions, and the bravest of the soldiers, were slain; and shortly afterwards, a foraging party of our men, with some cavalry squadrons sent to their support, was utterly routed.

39. Ostorius then deployed his light cohorts, but even thus he did not stop the flight, till our legions sustained the brunt of the battle. The strength equalised the conflict, which after a while was in our favour. The enemy fled with trifling loss, as the day was on the decline. Now began a series of skirmishes, for the most part like raids, in woods and morasses, with encounters due to chance or to courage, to mere heedlessness or to calculation, to fury or to lust of plunder, under directions from the officers, or sometimes even without their knowledge. Conspicuous above all in stubborn resistance were the Silures, whose rage was fired by words rumoured to have been spoken by the Roman general, to the effect, that as the Sugambri had been formerly destroyed or transplanted into Gaul, so the name of the Silures ought to be blotted out. Accordingly they cut off two of our auxiliary cohorts, the rapacity of whose officers let them make incautious forays; and by liberal gifts of spoil and prisoners to the other tribes, they were luring them into revolt, when Ostorius, worn out by the burden of his anxieties, died, to the joy of the enemy, who thought that a campaign at least, though not a single battle, had proved fatal to a general whom none could despise.

40. The emperor on hearing of the death of his representative appointed Aulus Didius in his place, that the province might not be left without a governor. Didius, though he quickly arrived, found matters far from prosperous, for the legion under the command of Manlius Valens had meanwhile been defeated, and the disaster had been exaggerated by the enemy to alarm the new general, while he again magnified it, that he might win the more glory by quelling the movement or have a fairer excuse if it lasted. This loss too had been inflicted on us by the Silures, and they were scouring the country far and wide, till Didius hurried up and dispersed them. After the capture of Caractacus, Venutius of the Brigantes, as I have already mentioned, was pre-eminent in military skill; he had long been loyal to Rome and had been defended by our arms while he was united in marriage to the queen Cartismandua. Subsequently a quarrel broke out between them, followed instantly by war, and he then assumed a hostile attitude towards us. At first, however, they simply fought against each other, and Cartismandua by cunning stratagems captured the brothers and kinsfolk of Venutius. This enraged the enemy, who were stung with shame at the prospect of falling under the dominion of a woman. The flower of their youth, picked out for war, invaded her kingdom. This we had foreseen; some cohorts were sent to her aid and a sharp contest followed, which was at first doubtful but had a satisfactory determination. The Legion under the command of Caesius Nasica fought with a similar result. For Didius, burdened with years and covered with honours, was content with acting through his officers and merely holding back the enemy. These transactions, though occurring under two propraetors, and occupying several years, I have closely connected, lest, if related separately, they might be less easily remembered. I now return to the chronological order."(6.4)

{Cartismandua is today spelt Cartimandua. There must always be a suspicion that the general Ostorius was killed and, as was their custom, Roman historians did not record such adverse events but needed some explanation in the text. This was in the spirit of walls falling down through the ravages of time and not because of some action by the enemy. - Compiler}

Tacitus: Annals book 14, chapters 29 to 39. [A.D. 61] [Church & Brodribb]

"29. In the consulship of Caesonius Paetus and Petronius Turpilianus, a serious disaster was sustained in Britain, where Aulus Didius, the emperor's legate, had merely retained our existing possessions, and his successor Veranius, after having ravaged the Silures in some trifling raids, was prevented by death from extending the war. While he lived, he had a great name for manly independence, though, in his will's final words, he betrayed a flatterer's weakness; for, after heaping adulation on Nero, he added that he should have conquered the province for him, had he lived for the next two years.

Appendix 2: Britain in the Annals of Tacitus

Now, however, Britain was in the hands of Suetonius Paulinus, who in military knowledge and in popular favour, which allows no one to be without a rival, vied with Corbulo, and aspired to equal the recovery of Armenia by the subjugation of Rome's enemies. He therefore prepared to attack the island of Mona which had a powerful population and was a refuge for fugitives. He built flat-bottomed vessels to cope with the shallows, and uncertain depths of the sea. Thus the infantry crossed, while the cavalry followed by fording, or, where the water was deep, swam by the side of their horses.

30. On the shore stood the opposing army with its dense array of armed warriors, while between the ranks dashed women, in black attire like the Furies, with hair dishevelled, waving brands. All around, the Druids, lifting up their hands to heaven, and pouring forth dreadful imprecations, scared our soldiers by the unfamiliar sight, so that, as if their limbs were paralysed, they stood motionless, and exposed to wounds. Then urged by their general's appeals and mutual encouragements, not to quail before a troop of frenzied women, they bore the standards onwards, smote down all resistance, and wrapped the foe in the flames of his own brands. A force was next set over the conquered, and their groves, devoted to inhuman superstitions, were destroyed. They deemed it indeed a duty to cover their alters with the blood of captives and to consult their deities through human entrails.

31. Suetonius while thus occupied received tidings of the sudden revolt of the province. Prasutagus, king of the Iceni, famed for his long prosperity, had made the emperor his heir along with his two daughters, under the impression that this token of submission would put his kingdom and his house out of the reach of wrong. But the reverse was the result, so much so that his kingdom was plundered by centurions, his house by slaves, as if they were the spoils of war. First, his wife Boadicea was scourged, and his daughters outraged. All the chief men of the Iceni, as if Rome had received the whole country as a gift, were stripped of their ancestral possessions, and the king's relatives were made slaves. Roused by these insults and the dread of worse, reduced as they now were into the condition of a province, they flew to arms and stirred to revolt the Trinobantes and others who, not yet cowed by slavery, had agreed in secret conspiracy to reclaim their freedom. It was against the veterans that their hatred was most intense. For these new settlers in the colony of Camulodunum drove people out of their houses, ejected them from their farms, called them captives and slaves, and the lawlessness of the veterans, was encouraged by the soldiers, who lived a similar life and hoped for similar licence. A temple also erected to the Divine Claudius was ever before their eyes, a citadel, as it seemed, of perpetual tyranny. Men chosen as priests had to squander their whole fortunes under the pretence of religious ceremonial. It appeared too no difficult matter to destroy the colony, undefended as it was by fortifications, a precaution neglected by our generals, while they thought more of what was agreeable than of what was expedient.

32. Meanwhile, without any evident cause, the statue of victory at Camulodunum fell prostrate and turned its back to the enemy, as though it fled before them. Women exited to frenzy prophesied impending destruction; ravings in a strange tongue, it was said, were heard in their Senate-house; their theatre resounded with wailings, and in the estuary of their Tamesa had been seen the appearance of an overthrown town; even the ocean had worn the aspect of blood, and, when the tide ebbed, there had been left the likenesses of human forms, marvels interpreted by the Britons, as hopeful, by the veterans as alarming. But as Suetonius was far away, they implored aid from the procurator, Catus Decianus. All he did was to send two hundred men, and no more, without regular arms, and there was but in the place a small military force. Trusting to the protection of the temple, hindered too by secret accomplices in the revolt, who embarrassed their plans, they had constructed neither fosse nor rampart; nor had they removed their old men and women, leaving their youth alone to face the foe. Surprised, as it were, in the midst of peace, they were surrounded by an immense host of barbarians. All else was plundered or fired in the onslaught; the temple where the soldiers had assembled, was stormed after two days siege. The victorious enemy met Petilius Cerialis, commander of the ninth legion, as he was coming to the rescue, routed his troops, and destroyed all his infantry. Cerialis escaped with some cavalry into the camp, and was saved by its fortifications. Alarmed by this disaster and by the fury of the province which he had goaded into war by his rapacity, the procurator Catus crossed over into Gaul."

> {Trinobantes are now referred to as Trinovantes. At the present day there are people in religious sects who talk in tongues. There is a hypothesis the Druids used a separate and by implication older language in which they learned their verses and protected their oral tradition. - Compiler}

"33. Suetonius, however, with wonderful resolution, marched amid a hostile population to Londinium, which though undistinguished by the name of a colony, was much frequented by a number of merchants and trading vessels. Uncertain whether he should choose it as a seat of war, as he looked round at his scanty force of soldiers, and remembered with what a serious warning the rashness of Petilius had been punished, he resolved to save the province at the cost of a single town. Nor did the tears and weeping of the people, as they implored his aid, deter him from giving the signal of departure and receiving into his army all who would go with him.

Those who were chained to the spot by the weakness of their sex, or the infirmity of age, or the attractions of the place, were cut off by the enemy. Like ruin fell on the town of Verulamium, for the barbarians, who delighted in plunder and were indifferent to all else, passed by the fortresses with military garrisons, and attacked whatever offered most wealth to the spoiler, and was unsafe for defence. About seventy thousand citizens and allies, it appeared, fell in the places which I have mentioned. For it was not on making prisoners and selling them, or on any of the barter of war, that the enemy was bent, but on slaughter, on the gibbet, the fire and the cross, like men soon about to pay the penalty, and meanwhile snatching at instant vengeance.

34. Suetonius had the fourteenth legion with the veterans of the twentieth, and auxiliaries from the neighbourhood, to the number of about ten thousand armed men, when he prepared to break off delay and fight a battle. He chose a position approached by a narrow defile, closed in at the rear by a forest, having first ascertained that there was not a soldier of the enemy except at the front, where an open plain extended without any danger from ambucades. His legions were in close array; round them, the light-armed troops, and the cavalry in dense array on the wings. On the other side, the army of the Britons, with its masses of infantry and cavalry, was confidently exulting, a vaster host than ever had assembled, and so fierce in spirit that they actually brought with them, to witness the victory, their wives riding in wagons, which they had placed on the extreme border of the plain.

35. Boadicea, with her daughters before her in a chariot, went up to tribe after tribe, protesting that it was indeed usual for Britons to fight under the leadership of women. 'But now,' she said, ' it is not as a woman descended from noble ancestry, but as one of the people that I am avenging lost freedom, my scourged body, the outraged chastity of my daughters. Roman lust has gone so far that not our very persons, nor even age or virginity, are left unpolluted. But heaven is on the side of a righteous vengeance; a legion which dared to fight has perished; the rest are hiding themselves in their camp, or are thinking anxiously of flight. They will not sustain even the din and the shout of so many thousands, much less our charge and our blows. If you weigh well the strength of the armies, and the causes of the war, you will see that in this battle you must conquer or die. This is a woman's resolve; as for men, they may live and be slaves.'

36. Nor was Suetonius silent at such a crisis. Though he confided in the valour of his men, he yet mingled encouragements and entreaties to disdain the clamours and empty threats of the barbarians. 'There,' he said, 'you see more women than warriors. Unwarlike, unarmed, they will give way the moment they have recognised that sword and that courage of their conquerors, which have so often routed them. Even among many legions, it is a few who really decide the battle, and it will enhance their glory that a small force should earn the renown of an entire army. Only close up the ranks, and having discharged your javelins, then with shields and swords continue the work of bloodshed and destruction, without a thought of plunder. When once the victory has been won, everything will be in your power.'

  Such was the enthusiasm which followed the general's address, and so promptly did the veteran soldiery, with their long experience of battles, prepare for the hurling of the javelins, that it was with confidence in the result that Suetonius gave the signal of battle.

37. At first, the legion kept its position, clinging to the narrow defile as a defence; when they had exhausted their missiles, which they discharged with unerring aim on the closely approaching foe, they rushed out in a wedge-like column. Similar was the onset of the auxiliaries, while the cavalry with extended lances broke through all who offered a strong resistance. The rest turned their back in flight, and flight proved difficult, because the surrounding wagons had blocked their retreat. Our soldiers spared not to slay even the women, while the very beasts of burden, transfixed by the missiles, swelled the piles of bodies. Great glory, equal to that of our old victories, was won on that day. Some indeed say that there fell little less than eighty thousand of the Britons, with a loss to our soldiers of about four hundred, and only as many wounded. Boadicea put an end to her life by poison. Poenius Postumus too, camp-prefect of the second legion, when he knew of the success of the men of the fourteenth and twentieth, feeling that he had cheated his legion out of like glory, and had contrary to all military usage disregarded the general's orders, threw himself on his sword.

38. The whole army was then brought together and kept under canvas to finish the remainder of the war. The emperor strengthened the forces by sending from Germany two thousand legionaries, eight cohorts of auxiliaries, and a thousand cavalry. On their arrival the men of the ninth had their number made up with legionary soldiers. The allied infantry and cavalry were placed in new winter quarters, and whatever tribes still wavered or were hostile were ravaged with fire and sword. Nothing however distressed the enemy so much as famine, for they had been careless about sowing corn, people of every age having gone to war, while they reckoned on our supplies as their own. Nations, too, so high-spirited inclined the more slowly to peace, because Julius Classicanus, who had been sent as a successor to Catus and was at variance with Suetonius, let private animosities interfere with the public interest, and had spread an idea that they ought to wait for a new governor who, having neither the anger of an enemy nor the pride of a conqueror, would deal mercifully with those who had surrendered.

At the same time he stated in a despatch to Rome that no cessation of fighting must be expected, unless Suetonius were superseded, attributing that general's disasters to perverseness and his successes to good luck.

39. Accordingly, one of the imperial freedmen, Polyclitus, was sent to survey the state of Britain, Nero having great hopes that his influence would be able not only to establish a good understanding between the governor and the procurator, but also to pacify the rebellious spirit of the barbarians. And Polyclitus, who with his enormous suite had been a burden to Italy and Gaul failed not, as soon as he had crossed the ocean, to make his progresses a terror even to our soldiers. But to the enemy he was a laughing stock, for they still retained some of the fire of liberty, knowing nothing yet of the power of freedmen, and so they marvelled to see a general and an army who had finished such a war cringing to slaves. Everything, however, was soften down for the emperor's ears, and Suetonius was retained in the government; but as he subsequently lost a few vessels on the shore with the crews, he was ordered, as though the war continued, to hand over his army to Petronius Turpilianus, who had just resigned his consulship. Petronius neither challenged the enemy nor was himself molested, and veiled this tame inaction under the honourable name of peace."(6.5)

APPENDIX 3 - THE AGRICOLA OF TACITUS

The text of the *Agricola* is taken from the translation by Arthur Murphy (1727-1805) first published in 1793 and published in the Everyman's Library series from 1908. The quotation is from the edition reprinted in 1917.

The *Agricola* is believed to have been first written down after Tacitus served as consul in 97 AD. The activities of the Roman commander Agricola in Scotland are reported from chapter 22 onwards and the battle of Mons Graupius from chapter 29. The compiler's observations on the translation are given in cursive brackets.

"THE LIFE OF
CNAEUS JULIUS AGRICOLA

I. To transmit to posterity the lives and characters of illustrious men, was an office frequently performed in ancient times. Even in the present age, incurious as it is about its own concerns, the same good custom has prevailed, whenever a great and splendid virtue has been able to surmount those two pernicious vices, which not only infest small communities, but are likewise the bane of large and flourishing cities; I mean the vices of insensibility to merit, on the one hand, and envy, on the other. With regard to the usage of antiquity, it is further observable, that, in those early seasons of virtue, men were led by the impulse of a generous spirit to a course of action worthy of being recorded; and, in like manner, the writer of genius undertook to perpetuate the memory of honourable deeds, without any motives of flattery, and without views of private ambition, influenced only by the conscious pleasure of doing justice to departed merit. Many have been their own historians, persuaded that in speaking of themselves they should display an honest confidence in their morals, not a spirit of arrogance or vainglory. Rutilius and Scaurus left an account of their own lives, and the integrity of the narrative has never been called in question; so true it is, that the age which is most fertile in bright examples, is the best qualified to make a fair estimate of them. For the present undertaking, which professes to review the life of a great man now no more, I judged it necessary to premise an apology, led as I am, by the nature of my subject, to encounter an evil period, in which every virtue struggled with adversity and oppression.

II. We have it upon record, that Arulenus Rusticus, for the panegyric of Paetus Thrasea, and Herennius Senecio, for that of Helvidius Priscus, were both capitally convicted. Nor was it enough that those excellent authors fell a sacrifice to the tyrant's power; persecution raged against their books, and, by an order to the triumvirs, in the forum and the place of popular convention, the monuments of genius perished in the flames. The policy of the times, no doubt, intended that in the same fire the voice of the Roman people should be stifled, the freedom of the senate destroyed, and the sentiments of the human heart suppressed for ever. To complete the work, all sound philosophy was proscribed, every liberal art was driven into banishment, and nothing fair and honourable was suffered to remain. Of our passive temper we gave ample proof; and as former times had tasted of liberty even to a degree of licentiousness, so we exhausted the bitter cup of slavery to the very dregs. Restrained by the terrors of a merciless inquisition from the commerce of hearing and speaking, and, by consequence, deprived of all exchange of sentiment, we should have resigned our memory with our other faculties, if to forget had been as easy as to submit in silence.

III. At length, indeed, we begin to revive from our lethargy; but we revive by slow degrees, though the emperor Nerva, in the beginning of this glorious era, found means to reconcile two things, till then deemed incompatible; namely, civil liberty and the prerogative of the prince; though his successor Trajan continues to heal our wounds, and by a just and wise administration to diffuse the blessings of peace and good order through every part of the empire; and though it is apparent, that hopes of the constitution are now conceived by all orders of men, and not only conceived, but rising every hour into confidence and public security. And yet, such is the infirmity of the human mind, that, even in this juncture, the remedy operates more slowly than the disease. For as the body natural is tardy in its growth, and rapid in decay, so the powers of genius are more easily extinguished than promoted to their full maturity. There is a charm in indolence that works by imperceptible degrees; and that listless inactivity, which at first is irksome, grows delightful in the end.

Need I mention that in the course of fifteen years, a large portion of human life! many fell by unavoidable accidents, and the most illustrious men in Rome were cut off by the insatiate cruelty of the prince? A few of us, it is true, have survived the slaughter of our fellow-citizens; I had almost said, we have survived ourselves: for in that chasm, which slavery made in our existence, we cannot be said to have lived, but rather to have crawled in silence, the young towards the decrepitude of age, and the old to dishonourable graves.

And yet I shall not regret the time I have spent in reviewing those days of despotism; on the contrary, it is my intention, even in such weak colouring as mine, to give a memorial of our slavery, that it may stand in contrast to the felicity of the present period.

In the meantime, the following tract is dedicated to the memory of Agricola, my father-in-law. The design, as it springs from filial piety, may merit a degree of approbation; it will, at least, be received with candour.

IV. Cnaeus Julius Agricola was born at the ancient and respectable colony of Forojulium. His grandfather, by the maternal as well as the paternal line, served the office of imperial procurator; a trust of importance, which always confers the equestrian dignity. His father, Julius Graecinus, was a member of the senate, distinguished by his eloquence and philosophy. His merit gave umbrage to Caligula. Being commanded by that emperor to undertake the prosecution of Marcus Silanus, he refused to comply, and was put to death. Julia Procilla, Agricola's mother, was respected for the purity of her manners. Under her care, and as it were in her bosom, the tender mind of the son was trained to science and every liberal accomplishment. His own ingenuous disposition guarded him against the seductions of pleasure. To that happy temperament was added the advantage of pursuing his studies at Marseilles, that seat of learning, where the refinements of Greece were happily blended with the sober manners of provincial economy.

He has often declared in my hearing, that in the first career of youth he felt himself addicted to philosophical speculations with more ardour than consisted with the duties of a Roman and a senator; but his taste was soon reformed by the admonitions of his mother. In fact, it cannot be matter of wonder, that a sublime and warm imagination, struck with the forms of moral beauty and the love of science, should aspire to reach the glory of the philosophic character. As he grew up to manhood, his riper judgment weaned him from vain pursuits, and during the rest of his life he preserved, what is difficult to attain, that temperate judgment, which knows where to fix the bounds even of wisdom itself.

V. His first rudiments of military knowledge were acquired in Britain, under the conduct of Suetonius Paulinus, that experienced officer; active, vigilant, yet mild in command. Agricola was soon distinguished by his general, and selected to live with him at headquarters. Honoured in this manner, he did not, as is usual with young men, mix riot and dissipation with actual service; nor did he avail himself of his rank of military tribune to obtain leave of absence, in order to pass his time in idle pleasures and ignorance of his duty. To know the province, and make himself known to the army; to learn from men of experience, and emulate the best examples; to seek no enterprise with a forward spirit, and to decline none with timid caution, were the rules he laid down to himself; prudent with valour, and brave without ostentation.

A more active campaign had never been known, nor was Britain at any time so fiercely disputed. Our veteran forces were put to the sword; our colonies smoked on the ground; and the legions were intercepted on their march. The struggle was then for life; we fought afterwards for fame and victory. In a juncture so big with danger, though the conduct of the war was in other hands, and the glory of recovering the province was justly ascribed to the commander-in-chief, yet so fair an opportunity did not fail to improve a young officer, and plant in his mind the early seeds of military ambition. The love of fame took possession of him, that principle of noble minds, but out of season in an evil period when virtue suffered by sinister constructions, and from an illustrious name the danger was as great as from the most pernicious character.

VI. He returned from Britain to enter on the gradations of the civil magistracy, and married Domitia Decidiana, a lady of high rank and splendid descent. By that alliance he gained an accession of strength and credit, that served to forward him in the road to public honours. The conjugal state proved a source of domestic happiness. They lived in perfect harmony, endeared by the tenderest affection, and each ascribing to the other the felicity which they enjoyed. But the merit of Decidiana could not be too much acknowledged. The praise of a valuable wife should always rise in proportion to the weight of censure, that falls on such as violate the nuptial union.

Agricola obtained the office of quaestor; and the province of Asia, of which Salvius Titianus was proconsul, fell to his lot. Neither the place nor the governor could warp his integrity. The wealth of the inhabitants invited the hand of rapacity; and Titianus, by the bias of his nature prone to acts of avarice, was ready, on terms of mutual connivance, to cooperate in any scheme of guilt and plunder; but Agricola maintained his honour and his principles. During his stay in Asia his family was increased by the birth of a daughter, who proved soon after, when he lost his infant son, a source of consolation. The intermediate space between the expiration of his quaestorship and his advancement to the post of tribune of the people, he had the prudence to pass in calm tranquillity. Even during the year of his tribuneship he acted with the same reserve, aware of those disastrous times, when, under the tyranny of Nero's reign, the want of exertion was the truest wisdom. He discharged the office of praetor with the same moderation and silent dignity, having no occasion, as his good fortune would have it, to sit in judicature. That branch of the magistrate's business did not fall to his share. The pageantry of public spectacles, which belonged to his department, he conducted with economy and magnificence, short of profusion, yet with due regard to popularity.

In the following reign, being appointed by Galba one of the commissioners to inspect the state of oblations to the several temples, he managed the inquiry with so much skill and well-tempered judgment, that no species of sacrilegious rapine, except the plunder committed by Nero, was suffered to pass without redress.

VII. In the course of the following year a dreadful misfortune happened in his family, and proved to him a severe stroke of affliction. A descent from Otho's fleet, which roved about in quest of depredations, was made on the coast of Liguria. The freebooters plundered the city of Intemelium, and in their fury murdered Agricola's mother, then residing upon her own estate. They laid waste her lands, and went off with a considerable booty. Agricola set out immediately to pay the last tribute of filial piety, and being informed on his way that Vespasian aspired to the imperial dignity, he declared at once in favour of that party.

In the beginning of the new reign, the government of Rome, and the whole administration, centred in Mucianus, Domitian being at that time too young for business, and from the elevation of his father claiming no other privilege than that of being debauched and profligate without control. Agricola was despatched to raise new levies. He executed that commission with so much zeal and credit to himself, that Mucianus advanced him to the command of the twentieth legion, then quartered in Britain, and for some time unwilling to swear fidelity to Vespasian. The officer who had the command of that corps was suspected of seditious practices, and the men had carried their insolence to such a pitch, that they were even formidable to the consular generals. Their commander was of praetorian rank; but either on account of his own disaffection, or the turbulent spirit of the soldiers, his authority was too feeble. Agricola succeeded to the command of the legion, and to the task of punishing the guilty. He acquitted himself with consummate address, and singular moderation, wishing that the men should have the merit of voluntary compliance, and not seem to have yielded, with sullen submission, to the authority of their general.

{At this time three Roman legions were in Britain. The twentieth legion, called Valens Victrix, possibly was stationed at Chester. – Compiler.}

VIII. The government of Britain was at that time committed to Vettius Bolanus, a man of milder disposition than consisted with the genius of those ferocious islanders. Agricola, that he might not seem to eclipse his superior officer, restrained his martial ardour, submitting with deference to his commander-in-chief, and, in every part of his conduct, uniting to his love of glory a due regard for the service. Bolanus was soon recalled, and Petilius Cerealis, an officer of consular rank, succeeded to the command. The field of warlike enterprise was laid open to Agricola. Under the new commander, he was, at first, no more than a common sharer in the dangers of the campaign; but in a short time his talents had their free career. The general, to make his experiment, sent him at the head of detached parties, and afterwards, encouraged by the event, employed him in more important operations. Agricola never betrayed a symptom of vain-glory. From the issue of his expeditions, however successful, he assumed no merit. It was the general that planned the measure, and he himself was no more than the hand that executed. By this conduct, vigorous in action, but modest in the report of his exploits, he gained a brilliant reputation, secure from the envy that attends it.

IX. On his return to Rome, Vespasian advanced him to the patrician rank, and soon after to the government of the province of Aquitania; an appointment of the first importance, leading directly to the honours of the consulship, to which he then aspired with the concurrence of the prince. The military mind, trained up in the school of war, is generally supposed to want the power of nice discrimination. The jurisdiction of the camp is little solicitous about forms and subtle reasoning; military law is blunt and summary, and where the sword resolves all difficulties, the refined discussions of the forum are never practised [sic]. Agricola, however, indebted to nature for a certain rectitude of understanding, was not out of his sphere even among men versed in questions of jurisprudence. His hours of business and relaxation had their stated periods. In the council of the province, or on the tribunal of justice, he discharged the duties of his station with awful gravity, intent to inquire, often severe, but more inclined to soften the rigour of the law. The functions of the magistrate being despatched, he divested himself of his public character; the man in authority was no longer seen. In his actions no tincture of arrogance, no spleen, no avarice was ever seen. Uncommon as it may appear, the sweetness of his manners took nothing from his authority, nor was the impression made by his amiable qualities lessened by the inflexibility of the judge.

To say of a character truly great, that integrity and a spirit above corruption made a part of it, were mere tautology, as injurious to his virtues, as it is unnecessary. Even the love of fame, that fine incentive of generous minds, could neither betray him into an ostentatious display of virtue, nor induce him to practise [sic] those specious arts that court applause, and often supply the place of merit. The little ambition of rising above his colleagues was foreign to his heart. He avoided all contention with the procurators of the prince. In struggles of that nature he knew that victory may be obtained without glory, and a defeat is certain disgrace. In less than three years he was recalled from his province, to take upon him the consular dignity.

Appendix 3: The Agricola of Tacitus

The voice of fame marked him out, at the same time, for the government of Britain: the report was current, but neither contrived, nor cultivated, by himself. He was mentioned, because he was worthy. Common fame does not always err: it often takes the lead, and determines the choice. During his consulship, though I was then very young, he agreed to a marriage between me and his daughter, who certainly might have looked for a prouder connection. The nuptial ceremony was not performed till the term of his consulship expired. In a short time after he was appointed governor of Britain, with the additional honour of a seat in the pontifical college.

X. If I here presume to offer a description of Britain and the manners of the people, it is not my intention to dispute with the number of authors, who have gone before me, either the fame of genius, or diligence in the research. The fact is, Britain was subdued under the conduct of Agricola, and that circumstance may justify the present attempt. Antecedent writers adorned conjecture with all the graces of language: what I have to offer will have nothing but the plain truth to recommend it.

Britain, of all the islands known to the Romans, is the largest. On the east, it extends towards Germany; on the west towards Spain; and on the south, it lies opposite to the coast of Gaul. The northern extremity is lashed by the billows of a prodigious sea, and no land is known beyond it. The form of the island has been compared by two eloquent writers (Livy among the ancients, and Fabius Rusticus among the moderns) to an oblong shield, or a two-edged axe. The comparison, if we except Caledonia, may be allowed to be just, and hence the shape of a part has been, by vulgar error, ascribed to the whole. Caledonia stretches a vast length of way towards the north. The promontories, that jut out into the sea, render the form of the country broken and irregular, but it sharpens to a point at the extremity, and terminates in the shape of a wedge.

By Agricola's order the Roman fleet sailed round the northern point, and made the first certain discovery that Britain is an island. The cluster of isles called the Orcades, till then wholly unknown, was in this expedition added to the Roman empire. Thule, which had lain concealed in the gloom of winter and a depth of eternal snows, was also seen by our navigators. The sea in those parts is said to be a sluggish mass of stagnated water, hardly yielding to the stroke of the oar, and never agitated by winds and tempests. The natural cause may be, that high lands and mountains, which occasion commotions in the air, are deficient in those regions; not to mention that such a prodigious body of water, in a vast and boundless ocean, is heaved and impelled with difficulty. But a philosophical account of the ocean and its periodical motions is not the design of this essay; the subject has employed the pen of others. To what they have said, I shall only add, that there is not in any other part of the world an expanse of water that rages with such uncontrollable dominion, now receiving the discharge of various rivers, and, at times, driving their currents back to their source. Nor is it on the coast only that the flux and reflux of the tide are perceived: the swell of the sea forces its way into the recesses of the land, forming bays and islands in the heart of the country, and foaming amidst hills and mountains, as in its natural channel.

XI. Whether the first inhabitants of Britain were natives of the island, or adventitious settlers, is a question lost in the mists of antiquity. The Britons, like other barbarous nations, have no monuments of their history. They differ in the make and habit of their bodies, and hence various inferences concerning their origin. The ruddy hair and lusty limbs of the Caledonians indicate a German extraction. That the Silures were at first a colony of Iberians is concluded, not without probability, from the olive tincture of the skin, the natural curl of the hair, and the situation of the country, so convenient to the coast of Spain. On the side opposite to Gaul the inhabitants resemble their neighbours on the continent; but whether that resemblance is the effect of one common origin, or of the climate in contiguous nations operating on the make and temperament of the human body, is a point not easy to be decided. All circumstances considered, it is rather probable that a colony from Gaul took possession of a country so inviting by its proximity. You will find in both nations the same religious rites, and the same superstition. The two languages differ but little. In provoking danger they discover the same ferocity, and in the encounter, the same timidity. The Britons, however, not yet enfeebled by a long peace, are possessed of superior courage. The Gauls, we learn from history, were formerly a warlike people; but sloth, the consequence of inactive times, has debased their genius, and virtue died with expiring liberty. Among such of the Britons, as have been for some time subdued, the same degeneracy is observable. The free and unconquered part of the nation retains at this hour the ferocity of the ancient Gauls.

XII. The strength of their armies consists in infantry, though some of their warriors take the field in chariots. The person of highest distinction guides the reins, while his martial followers, mounted in the same vehicle, annoy the enemy. The Britons were formerly governed by a race of kings: at present they are divided into factions under various chieftains; and this disunion, which prevents their acting in concert for a public interest, is a circumstance highly favourable to the Roman arms against a warlike people, independent, fierce, and obstinate. A confederation of two or more states to repel the common danger is seldom known: they fight in parties, and the nation is subdued.

The climate is unfavourable; always damp with rains, and overcast with clouds. Intense cold is never felt. The days are longer than in our southern regions; the nights remarkably bright, and, towards the extremity of the island, so very short, that between the last gleam of day and the returning dawn the interval is scarce perceptible. In a serene sky, when no clouds intervene to obstruct the sight, the sun, we are told, appears all night long, neither setting in the west, nor rising in the east, but always moving above the horizon. The cause of this phenomenon may be, that the surface of the earth, towards the northern extremities, being flat and level, the shade never rises to any considerable height, and, the sky still retaining the rays of the sun, the heavenly bodies continue visible.

The soil does not afford either the vine, the olive, or the fruits of warmer climates; but it is otherwise fertile, and yields corn in great plenty. Vegetation is quick in shooting up, and slow in coming to maturity. Both effects are reducible to the same cause, the constant moisture of the atmosphere and the dampness of the soil. Britain contains, to reward the conqueror, mines of gold and silver, and other metals. The sea produces pearls, but of a dark and livid colour. This defect is ascribed by some to want of skill in this kind of fishery: the people employed in gathering, content themselves in gleaning what happens to be thrown upon the shore, whereas in the Red Sea the shell-fish are found clinging to the rocks, and taken alive. For my part, I am inclined to think that the British pearl is of an inferior quality. I cannot impute to avarice a neglect of its interest.

XIII. The Britons are willing to supply our armies with new levies; they pay their tribute without a murmur; and they perform all the services of government with alacrity, provided they have no reason to complain of oppression. When injured, their resentment is quick, sudden, and impatient; they are conquered, not broken-hearted; reduced to obedience, not subdued to slavery. Even Julius Caesar, the first of the Romans who set his foot in Britain at the head of an army, can only be said by a prosperous battle to have struck the natives with terror, and to have made himself master of the sea-shore. The discoverer, not the conqueror of the island, he did no more than show it to posterity. Rome could not boast of a conquest. The civil wars broke out soon after, and, in that scene of distraction, when the swords of the leading men were drawn against their country, it was natural to lose sight of Britain. During the peace that followed, the same neglect continued: Augustus called it the wisdom of his counsels, and Tiberius made it a rule of state policy.

That Caligula meditated an invasion of Britain is a fact well known; but the expedition, like his mighty preparations against Germany, was rendered abortive by the capricious temper of the man, resolving always without consideration and repenting without experiment. The grand enterprise was reserved for the emperor Claudius, who transported into Britain an army composed of regular legions, besides a large body of auxiliaries. With the officers appointed to conduct the war he joined Vespasian, who there laid the foundation of that success which afterwards attended him. Several states were conquered, kings were led in captivity, and the Fates beheld Vespasian giving an earnest of his future glory.

XIV. The first officer of consular rank, that commanded in Britain, was Aulus Plautius. To him succeeded Ostorius Scapula; both eminent for their military character. Under their auspices the southern part of Britain took the form of a province, and received a colony of veterans. Certain districts were assigned to Cogidunus, a king who reigned over part of the country. He lived within our own memory, preserving always his faith unviolated, and exhibiting a striking proof of that refined policy, with which it has ever been the practice of Rome to make even kings accomplices in the servitude of mankind.

{Aulus Plautius was commander at the time of the Claudian invasion of Britain in 43 AD.
Caractacus was made prisoner and sent to Rome by Ostorius Scapula,
see also Tacitus *Annals* book 12, 31 to 40.}

The next governor was Didius Gallus. He preserved the acquisitions made by his predecessors, without aiming at an extension of territory, and without any advantage, except a few forts, which he built on the remote borders of the province, in hopes of gaining some pretension to the fame of having enlarged the frontier. Veranius succeeded to the command, but died within the year. Suetonius Paulinus was the next in succession. That officer pushed on the war in one continued series of prosperity for two years together. In that time he subdued several states, and secured his conquest by a chain of posts and garrisons. Confiding in the strength which he had thus established, he formed the plan of reducing the isle of Mona, the grand resource from which the malcontents drew their supplies. But having, in that expedition, turned his back on the conquered provinces, he gave an opportunity for a general revolt.

XV. The Britons, relieved from their fears by the absence of the commander-in-chief, began to descant on the horrors of slavery. They stated their grievances, and, to inflame resentment, painted everything in the most glaring colours.

"What was now the consequence of their passive spirit? The hand of oppression falls on the tame and abject with greater weight. Each state was formerly subject to a single king, but now two masters rule with an iron rod. The general gluts himself with the blood of the vanquished, and the imperial procurator devours our property. Those haughty tyrants may act in concert, or they may be at variance; but in either case the lot of the Britons is the same. The centurions of the general, and the followers of the tax-gatherer, add pride and insolence to injustice and rapacity. Nothing, is safe from avarice, nothing by lust unviolated. In the field of battle, the booty is for the brave and warlike: at present, cowards and abject wretches seize the possessions of the natives; to them the Britons tamely yield up their children; for them they make new levies, and, in short, the good of his country is the only cause in which a Briton has forgot to die. Compute the number of men born in freedom, who inhabit the island, and the Roman invaders are but a handful. It was thus the Germans argued, and they shook off the yoke. No ocean rolled between them and the invader: they were separated by a river only. The Britons have every motive to excite their valour. They have their country to defend, and they have their liberty to assert; they have wives and children to urge them on; and they have parents, who sue to them for protection. On the part of the Romans, if we except luxury and avarice, what incentives are there to draw them to the field? Let British valour emulate the virtue of ancient times, and the invaders, like their own deified Caesar, will abandon the island. The loss of a single battle, and even a second, cannot decide the fate of a whole people. Many advantages list on the side of misery. To attack with fury and persevere with constancy, belongs to men who groan under oppression. The gods, at length, behold the Britons with an eye of compassion: they have removed the Roman general from his station; they detain him and his army in another island. The oppressed have gained an advantage, too often difficult to obtain; they can now deliberate: they are met in council. In designs like these, the whole danger lies in being detected: act like men, and success will be the issue of the war."

XVI. Inflamed by these and such like topics, the spirit of revolt was diffused through the country. With one consent they took up arms, under the conduct of Boadicea, a queen descended from a race of royal ancestors. In Britain there is no rule of distinction to exclude the female line from the throne, or the command of armies. The insurgents rushed to the attack with headlong fury; they found the Romans dispersed in their garrisons; they put all to the sword; they stormed the forts; they attacked the capital of the colony, which they considered as the seat of oppression, and with fire and sword laid it level with the ground. Whatever revenge could prompt, or victory inspire, was executed with unrelenting cruelty; and if Suetonius, on the first intelligence, had not hastened back by rapid marches, Britain had been lost. By the event of a single battle the province was recovered, though the embers of rebellion were not quite extinguished. Numbers of the malcontents, conscious of their share in the revolt, and dreading the vengeance of Suetonius, still continued under arms.

The truth is, notwithstanding the excellent qualities that distinguished the Roman general, it was the blemish of his character, that be proceeded always against the vanquished, even after they surrendered, with excessive rigour. Justice, under his administration, had frequently the air of revenge for a personal injury. In his public proceedings he mingled too much of his own passions, and was therefore recalled, to make way for Petronius Turpilianus, a man of less asperity, new to the Britons, and, having no resentments, likely to be satisfied on moderate terms. He restored the tranquillity of the island, and, without attempting anything further, resigned the province to Trebellius Maximus, an officer of no experience, by nature indolent and inactive, but possessed of certain popular arts that reconciled the minds of men to his administration. The Barbarians, at this time, had acquired a taste for elegant and alluring vices. The civil wars, which soon afterwards convulsed the empire, were a fair apology for the pacific temper of the general. His army, however, was not free from intestine discord. The soldiers, formerly inured to discipline, grew wanton in idleness, and broke out into open sedition. To avoid the fury of his men, Trebellius was obliged to save himself by flight. Having lain for some time in a place of concealment, he returned with an awkward air to take upon him the command. His dignity was impaired, and his spirit humbled. From that time his authority was feeble and precarious. It seemed to be a compromise between the parties; the general remained unmolested, the soldiers uncontrolled, and on these terms the mutiny ended without bloodshed. Vettius Bolanus was the next commander; but the distractions of the civil war still continuing, he did not think it advisable to introduce a plan of regular discipline. The same inactive disposition on the part of the general, and the same mutinous spirit among the soldiers, still prevailed. The only difference was, that the character of Bolanus was without a blemish. If he did not establish his authority, he lived on good terms with all; beloved, though not respected.

XVII. When Britain, with the rest of the Roman world, fell to the lot of Vespasian, the ablest officers were sent to reduce the island; powerful armies were set in motion, and the spirit of the natives began to droop. In order to spread a general terror, Petilius Cerealis fell with sudden fury on the Brigantes, in point of numbers the most considerable state in the whole province. Various battles were fought, with alternate success, and great effusion of blood. At length the greatest part of that extensive country was either subdued, or involved in all the calamities of war.

The fame of Cerealis grew to a size that might discourage the ablest successor; and yet under that disadvantage Julius Frontinus undertook the command. His talents did not suffer by the comparison. He-was a man truly great, and sure to signalise himself, whenever a fair opportunity called forth his abilities. He reduced to subjection the powerful and warlike state of the Silures, and, though in that expedition he had to cope not only with a fierce and obstinate enemy, but with the difficulties of a country almost impracticable, it was his glory that he surmounted every obstacle.

{78AD}

XVIII. Such was the state of Britain, and such the events of war, when Agricola arrived about the middle of summer, to take upon him the command. He found an army lulled in indolence and security, as if the campaign was at an end, while the enemy was on the watch to seize the first opportunity. The Ordovicians, not long before his arrival, had fallen upon a party of horse, that happened to be quartered in their district, and put them almost all to the sword. By this blow the courage of the Britons was once more revived: the bold and resolute declared for open war, while others, less sanguine, were against unsheathing the sword, till the character and genius of the new governor should be better known.

Many things conspired to embarrass Agricola: the summer was far advanced; the troops were stationed at different quarters, expecting a cessation of arms during the remainder of the year: and to act on the defensive, content with strengthening the weakest stations, was in the opinion of the best officers the most prudent measure. These were circumstances unfavourable to a spirit of enterprise; but the general resolved to put his army in motion, and face the danger without delay. For this purpose, he drew together various detachments from the legions, and, with the addition of a body of auxiliaries, marched against the enemy. The Ordovicians continuing to decline an engagement on the open plain, he determined to seek them on their heights, and, to animate his men by his own example, he advanced at the head of the line. A battle ensued, and the issue was the destruction of the Ordovician state. Knowing of what moment it is to follow the first impressions of fame, and little doubting but that everything would fall before an army flushed with victory, Agricola formed a plan for the reduction of the isle of Mona, from which Paulinus had been recalled by the general insurrection of the province, as already mentioned.

For the execution of an enterprise so sudden and important, no measures had been concerted, and, by consequence, no vessels were ready to transport the troops. The genius and resolution of the general supplied all deficiencies. He drafted from the auxiliaries a chosen band, well acquainted with the fordable places, and inured, to the national practice of swimming across lakes and rivers with such dexterity, that they could manage their arms and guide their horses at the same time. This select corps, free from the encumbrance of their baggage, dashed into the water, and made their way with vigour toward the island. This mode of attack astonished the enemy, who expected nothing less than a fleet of transports, and a regular embarkation. Struck with consternation, they thought nothing impregnable to men who waged so unusual a war. In despair they sued for peace, and surrendered the island. The event added new lustre to the name of Agricola, who had thus set out with a spirit of enterprise, and crowded so much glory into that part of the year, which is usually trifled away in vain parade and the homage of flatteries. The moderation with which he enjoyed his victory was remarkable. He had reduced the vanquished to obedience, and the act, he said, did not deserve the name of victory, nor even of an expedition. In his dispatches to Rome he assumed no merit, nor were his letters, according to custom, decorated with sprigs of laurel: but this self-denial served only to enhance his fame. From the modesty of a commander who could undervalue such important services, men inferred that projects of vast extent were even then in his contemplation.

XIX. Agricola was well acquainted with the manners and national character of the Britons: he knew by the experience of past events, that conquest, while it loads the vanquished with injury and oppression, can never be secure and permanent. He determined, therefore, to suppress the seeds of future hostility. He began a reform in his own household; a necessary work, but attended often with no less difficulty than the administration of a province. He removed his slaves and freedmen from every department of public business. Promotions in the army no longer went by favour, or the partiality of the centurions; merit decided, and the man of worth, Agricola knew, would be the most faithful soldier. To know everything, and yet overlook a great deal; to forgive slight offences, and treat matters of importance with due severity, was the rule of his conduct; never vindictive, and in many instances disarmed by penitence. The prevention of crimes was what he wished, and to that end, in the disposal of offices, he made choice of men, whose conduct promised to supersede the necessity of punishment.

The exigencies of the army called for large contributions of corn and other supplies, and yet he lightened the burden by just and equal assessments, providing at the same time against the extortion of the tax-gatherer, more odious and intolerable than even the tax itself.

It had been the settled practice of the collectors to engross all the corn, and then, adding mockery to injustice, to make the injured Briton wait at the door of the public granary, humbly supplicating that he might be permitted to re-purchase his own grain, which he was afterwards obliged to sell at an inferior price. A further grievance was, that instead of delivering the requisite quantity of corn at the nearest and most convenient magazines, the Britons were forced to make tedious journeys through difficult cross-country roads, in order to supply camps and stations at a remote distance; and thus the business, which might have been conducted with convenience to all, was converted into a job to gratify the avarice of a few.

XX. In the first year of Agricola's administration these abuses were all suppressed. The consequence was, that peace, which, through the neglect or connivance of former governors, was no less terrible than war itself, began to diffuse its blessings, and to be relished by all. As soon as the summer opened, he assembled his army, and marched in quest of the enemy. Ever present at the head of the lines, he encouraged the strenuous by commendation; he rebuked the sluggard who fell from his rank; he went in person to mark out the station for encampments; he sounded the estuaries, and explored the woods and forests. The Britons, in the meantime, were by sudden incursions kept in a constant alarm. Having spread a general terror through the country, he then suspended his operations, that, in the interval of repose, the Barbarians might taste the sweets of peace. In consequence of these measures, several states, which till then had breathed a spirit of independence, were induced to lay aside their hostile intentions, and to give hostages for their pacific behaviour. Along the frontier of the several districts which had submitted, a chain of posts was established with so much care and judgment, that no part of the country, even where the Roman arms had never penetrated, could think itself secure from the vigour of the conqueror.

{79AD}

XXI. To introduce a system of new and wise regulations was the business of the following winter. A fierce and savage people, running wild in woods, would be ever addicted to a life of warfare. To wean them from those habits, Agricola held forth the baits of pleasure, encouraging the natives, as well by public assistance as by warm exhortations, to build temples, courts of justice, and commodious dwelling-houses. He bestowed encomiums on such as cheerfully obeyed; the slow and uncomplying were branded with reproach; and thus a spirit of emulation diffused itself, operating like a sense of duty. To establish a plan of education, and give the sons of the leading chiefs a tincture of letters, was part of his policy. By way of encouragement, he praised their talents, and already saw them, by the force of their natural genius, rising superior to the attainments of the Gauls. The consequence was, that they who had always disdained the Roman language, began to cultivate its beauties. The Roman apparel was seen without prejudice, and the toga became a fashionable part of dress. By degrees the charms of vice gained admission to their hearts: baths, and porticos, and elegant banquets, grew into vogue; and the new manners, which, in fact, served only to sweeten slavery, were by the unsuspecting Britons called the arts of polished humanity.

XXII. In the course of the third year the progress of the Roman arms discovered new nations, whose territories were laid waste as far as the estuary called the firth of Tay. The legions had to struggle with all the difficulties of a tempestuous season; and yet the Barbarians, struck with a general panic, never dared to hazard an engagement. The country, as far as the Romans advanced, was secured by forts and garrisons. Men of skill and military science observed that no officer knew better than Agricola, how to seize, on a sudden view, the most advantageous situation, and, accordingly, not one of the stations, fortified by his direction, was taken by storm; not one was reduced to capitulate; not one was surrendered or abandoned to the enemy. At every post, to enable the garrison to stand a siege, a year's provision was provided, and each place having strength sufficient, frequent sallies were made; the besiegers were repulsed; and the Romans passed the winter secure from danger. The consequence of these precautions was, that the enemy, who had been accustomed to retrieve in the winter what they lost in the antecedent summer, saw no difference of seasons: they were defeated everywhere, and reduced to the last despair. Avarice of fame was no part of Agricola's character; nor was he ever known to arrogate to himself the praises due to other officers. From the commander of a legion to the lowest centurion, all found in their general a willing witness of their conduct. In his manner of expressing his disapprobation, he was thought to mix a degree of asperity. The truth is, his antipathy to bad men was equalled by nothing but his politeness to the deserving. His anger soon passed away, and left no trace behind. From his silence you had nothing to fear. Scorning to disguise his sentiments, he acted always with a generous warmth, at the hazard of making enemies. To harbour secret resentment was not in his nature.

XXIII. The business of the fourth campaign was to secure the country, which had been overrun, not conquered, in the preceding summer; and if the spirit of the troops and the glory of the Roman name had been capable of suffering any limits, there was in Britain itself a convenient spot, where the boundary of the empire might have been fixed.

The place for that purpose was, where the waters of the Glota and Bodotria, driven up the country by the influx of, two opposite seas, are hindered from joining by a narrow neck of land, which was then guarded by a chain of forts. On the south side of the isthmus, the whole country was bridled by the Romans, and evacuated by the enemy, who was driven, as it were, into another island.

{The Glota or Clota is the River Clyde, the Bodotria is the River Forth.

Ireland was featured briefly by Tacitus among the activities attributed to the year AD 82,

the fifth year of Agricola's time as governor.}

XXIV. In the fifth summer, Agricola made an expedition by sea. He embarked in the first Roman vessel that ever crossed the estuary; and having penetrated into regions till then unknown, he defeated the inhabitants in several engagements, and lined the coast, which lies opposite to Ireland, with a body of troops; not so much from an apprehension of danger, as with a view to future projects. He saw that Ireland, lying between Britain and Spain, and at the same time convenient to the ports of Gaul, might prove a valuable acquisition, capable of giving an easy communication, and, of course, strength and union, to provinces disjoined by nature.

Ireland is less than Britain, but exceeds in magnitude all the islands of the Mediterranean. The soil, the climate, the manners and genius of the inhabitants, differ little from those of Britain. By the means of merchants resorting thither for the sake of commerce, the harbours and approaches to the coast are well known. One of their petty kings, who had been forced to fly from the fury of a domestic faction, was received by the Roman general, and, under a show of friendship, detained to be of use on some future occasions. I have often heard Agricola declare that a single legion, with a moderate band of auxiliaries, would be sufficient to complete the conquest of Ireland. Such an event, he said, would contribute greatly to bridle the stubborn spirit of the Britons, who, in that case, would see, with dismay, the Roman arms triumphant, and every spark of liberty extinguished round their coast.

XXV. In the campaign which began in the sixth summer, having reason to apprehend a general confederacy of the nations beyond the firth of Bodotria, and fearing, in a country not yet explored, the danger of a surprise, Agricola ordered his ships to sail across the gulf; and gain some knowledge of those new regions. The fleet, now acting for the first time in concert with the land-forces, proceeded in sight of the army, forming a magnificent spectacle, and adding terror to the war. It frequently happened that in the same camp were seen the infantry and cavalry intermixed with the marines, all indulging their joy, full of their adventures, and magnifying the history of their exploits; the soldier describing, in the usual style of military ostentation, the forests which he had passed, the mountains which he climbed, and the Barbarians whom he put to the rout; while the sailor, no less important, had his storms and tempests, the wonders of the deep, and the spirit with which he conquered winds and waves.

At the sight of the Roman fleet, the Britons, according to intelligence gained from the prisoners, were struck with consternation, convinced that every resource was cut off, since the sea, which had always been their shelter, was now laid open to the invader. In this distress, the Caledonians resolved to try the issue of a battle. Warlike preparations were instantly begun with a degree of exertion, great in reality, but, as is always the case in matters obscure and distant, magnified by the voice of fame. Without waiting for the commencement of hostilities, they stormed the Roman forts and castles, and by provoking danger, made such an impression, that several officers in Agricola's army, disguising their fear under the specious appearance of prudent counsels, recommended a sudden retreat, to avoid the disgrace of being driven back to the other side of the firth. Meanwhile Agricola received intelligence that the enemy meditated an attack in various quarters at once, and thereupon, lest superior numbers, in a country where he was a stranger to the defiles and passes, should be able to surround him, he divided his army, and marched forward in three columns.

XXVI. The Caledonians, informed of this arrangement, changed their plan, and, in the dead of night, fell with their united force upon the ninth legion, then the weakest of the Roman army. They surprised the advanced guard, and having, in the confusion of sleep and terror, put the sentinels to the sword, they forced their way through the entrenchments. The conflict was in the very camp, when Agricola, who had been informed that the Barbarians were on their march, and instantly pursued their steps, came up to the relief of the legion. He ordered the swiftest of the horse and light infantry to advance with expedition, and charge the enemy in the rear, while his whole army set up a general shout. At break of day the Roman banners glittered in view of the Barbarians, who found themselves hemmed in by two armies, and began to relax their vigour. The spirit of the legion revived. The men perceived that the moment of distress was over, and the struggle was now for glory. Acting no longer on the defensive, they rushed on to the attack. In the very gates of the camp a fierce and obstinate engagement followed. The besieged legion, and the forces that came to their relief, fought with a spirit of emulation; the latter contending for the honour of succouring the distressed, and the former to prove that they stood in no need of assistance. The Caledonians were put to the rout; and if the woods and marshes had not favoured their escape, that single action had put an end to the war.

XXVII. By this victory, so complete and glorious, the Roman army was inspired with confidence to such a degree, that they now pronounced themselves invincible. Nothing could stand before them: they desired to be led into the recesses of the country, and, by following their blow, to penetrate to the extremity of the island. Even the prudent of the day before changed their tone with the event, and talked of nothing but victory and conquest. Such is the tax, which the commanders of armies must always pay; the merit of success is claimed by all; calamity is imputed to the general only.

The Caledonians, notwithstanding their defeat, abated nothing from their ferocity. Their want of success, they said, was not to be ascribed to superior courage; it was the chance of war, or, perhaps, the skill of the Roman general. In this persuasion they resolved to keep the field. They listed the young men of their nation; they sent their wives and children to a place of safety; they held public conventions of the several states, and with solemn rites and sacrifices formed a league in the cause of liberty. The campaign ended in this manner, and the two armies, inflamed with mutual animosity, retired into winter quarters.

XXVIII. In the course of the same summer, a cohort of the Usipians which had been raised in Germany, and thence transported to serve in Britain, performed an exploit so daring and extraordinary, that in this place it may be allowed to merit attention. Having murdered the centurion who was left in the command, and also the soldiers, who, for the purpose of introducing military discipline, had been incorporated with the several companies, they seized three light galleys, and forcing the masters on board, determined to sail from the island. One of the pilots made his escape, and suspicion falling on the other two, they were both killed on the spot. Before their design transpired, the deserters put to sea, to the astonishment of all who beheld their vessels under way.

They had not sailed far, when they became the sport of winds and waves. They made frequent descents on the coast in quest of plunder, and had various conflicts with the natives, victorious in some places, and in others beat back to their ships. Reduced at length to the extremity of famine, they fed on their companions, at first devouring the weakest, and afterwards deciding among themselves by lot. In this distress they sailed round the extremity of the island, and, through want of skill in navigation, were wrecked on the continent, where they were treated as pirates, first by the Suevians, and afterwards by the Frisians. Being sold to slavery, and in the way of commerce turned over to different masters, some of them reached the Roman settlements on the banks of the Rhine, and there grew famous for their sufferings, and the bold singularity of their voyage.

In the beginning of the following summer Agricola met with a stroke of affliction by the loss of a son, about a year old. He did not upon this occasion affect, like many others, the character of a man superior to the feelings of nature; nor yet did he suffer his grief to sink him down into unbecoming weakness. He felt the impression; but regret was lost in the avocations of war.

{Scotland, Mount Graupius.}

XXIX. In the opening of the campaign, he despatched his fleet, with orders to annoy the coast by frequent descents in different places, and spread a general alarm. He put himself, in the meantime, at the head of his army equipped for expedition, and taking with him a select band of the bravest Britons, of known and approved fidelity, he advanced as far as the Grampian hills, where the enemy was already posted in force. Undismayed by their former defeat, the Barbarians expected no other issue than a total overthrow, or a brave revenge. Experience had taught them that the common cause required a vigorous exertion of their united strength. For this purpose, by treaties of alliance, and by deputations to the several cantons, they had drawn together the strength of their nation. Upwards of thirty thousand men appeared in arms, and their force was increasing every day. The youth of the country poured in from all quarters, and even the men in years, whose vigour was still unbroken, repaired to the army, proud of their past exploits, and the ensigns of honour which they had gained by their martial spirit. Among the chieftains distinguished by their birth and valour, the most renowned was Galgacus. The multitude gathered round him, eager for action, and burning with uncommon ardour. He harangued them to the following effect:

{Here Galgacus, elsewhere Calgacus, may have the meaning the swordsman. - Compiler.}

XXX. " When I consider the motives that have roused us to this war; when I reflect on the necessity that now demands our firmest vigour, I expect everything great and noble from that union of sentiment that pervades us all. From this day I date the freedom of Britain. We are the men, who never crouched in bondage. Beyond this spot there is no land, where liberty can find a refuge. Even the sea is shut against us, while the Roman fleet is hovering on the coast. To draw the sword in the cause of freedom is the true glory of the brave, and, in our condition, cowardice itself would throw away the scabbard.

In the battles, which have been hitherto fought with alternate vicissitudes of fortune, our countrymen might well repose some hopes in us; they might consider us as their last resource; they know us to be the noblest sons of Britain, placed in the last recesses of the land, in the very sanctuary of liberty. We have not so much as seen the melancholy regions where slavery has debased mankind. We have lived in freedom, and our eyes have been unpolluted by the sight of ignoble bondage."

"The extremity of the earth is ours: defended by our situation, we have to this day preserved our honour and the rights of men. But we are no longer safe in our obscurity; our retreat is laid open; the enemy rushes on, and, as things unknown are ever magnified, he thinks a mighty conquest lies before him. But this is the end of the habitable world, and rocks and brawling waves fill all the space behind. The Romans are in the heart of our country; no submission can satisfy their pride; no concessions can appease their fury. While the land has anything left, it is the theatre of war; when it can yield no more, they explore the sea for hidden treasure. Are the nations rich, Roman avarice is their enemy. Are they poor, Roman ambition lords it over them. The east and the west have been rifled, and the spoiler is still insatiate. The Romans, by a strange singularity of nature, are the only people who invade, with equal ardour, the wealth and the poverty of nations. To rob, to ravage, and to murder, in their imposing language, are the arts of civil policy. When they have made the world a solitude, they call it peace."

XXXI. "Our children and relatives are dear to us all. It is an affection planted in our breast by the hand of nature. And yet those tender pledges are ravished from us to serve in distant lands. Are our wives, our sisters, and our daughters, safe from brutal lust and open violation? The insidious conqueror, under the mask of hospitality and friendship, brands them with dishonour. Our money is conveyed into their treasury, and our corn into their granaries. Our limbs and bodies are worn out in clearing woods, and draining marshes: and what have been our wages? Stripes and insult. The lot of the meanest slave, born in servitude, is preferable to ours: he is sold but once, and his master maintains him; but Britain every day invites new tyrants, and every day pampers their pride. In a private family the slave who is last bought in, provokes the mirth and ridicule of the whole domestic crew; and in this general servitude, to which Rome has reduced the world, the case is the same: we are treated at first as objects of derision, and then marked out for destruction."

"What better lot can we expect? We have no arable lands to cultivate for a master; no mines to dig for his avarice; no harbours to improve for his commerce. To what end should the conqueror spare us? Our virtue and undaunted spirit are crimes in the eyes of the conqueror, and will render us more obnoxious. Our remote situation, hitherto the retreat of freedom, and on that account the more suspected, will only serve to inflame the jealousy of our enemies. We must expect no mercy. Let us therefore dare like men. We all are summoned by the great call of nature; not only those who know the value of liberty, but even such as think life on any terms the dearest blessing. The Trinobantes, who had only a woman to lead them on, were able to carry fire and sword through a whole colony. They stormed the camps of the enemy, and, if success had not intoxicated them, they had been, beyond all doubt, the deliverers of their country. And shall not we, unconquered, and undebased by slavery, a nation ever free, and struggling now, not to recover, but to ensure our liberties, shall we not go forth the champions of our country? Shall we not, by one generous effort, show the Romans, that we are the men whom Caledonia has reserved to be assertors of the public weal? [sic]"

XXXII. "We know the manners of the Romans: and are we to imagine that their valour in the field is equal to their arrogance in time of peace? By our dissensions their glory rises; the vices of their enemies are the negative virtues of the Roman army; if that may be called an army, which is no better than a motley crew of various nations, held together by success, and ready to crumble away in the first reverse of fortune. That this will be their fate, no one can doubt, unless we suppose that the Gaul, the German, and (with shame I add) the Britons, a mercenary band, who hire their blood in a foreign service, will adhere from principle to a new master, whom they have lately served, and long detested. They are now enlisted by awe and terror: break their fetters, and the man who forgets to fear, will seek revenge."

"All that can inspire the human heart, every motive that can excite us to deeds of valour, is on our side. The Romans have no wives in the field to animate their drooping spirit; no parents to reproach their want of courage. They are not listed in the cause of their country: their country, if any they have, lies at a distance. They are a band of mercenaries, a wretched handful of devoted men, who tremble and look aghast as they roll their eyes around, and see on every side objects unknown before. The sky over their heads, the sea, the woods, all things conspire to fill them with doubt and terror. They come like victims delivered into our hands by the gods, to fall this day a sacrifice to freedom."

"In the ensuing battle be not deceived by false appearances; the glitter of gold and silver may dazzle the eye; but to us it is harmless, to the Romans no protection. In their own ranks we shall find a number of generous warriors ready to assist our cause. The Britons know that for our common liberties we draw the avenging sword. The Gauls will remember that they once were a free people; and the Germans, as the Usipians lately did, will desert their colours.

The Romans have left nothing in their rear to oppose us in the pursuit, their forts are ungarrisoned; the veterans in their colonies droop with age; in their municipal towns, nothing but anarchy, despotic government, and disaffected subjects. In me behold your general; behold an army of freeborn men. Your enemy is before you, and, in his train, heavy tributes, drudgery in the mines, and all the horrors of slavery. Are those calamities to be entailed upon us? Or shall this day relieve us by a brave revenge? There is the field of battle, and let that determine. Let us seek the enemy, and, as we rush upon him, remember the glory delivered down to us by our ancestors; and let each man think that upon his sword depends the fate of all posterity."

XXXIII. This speech was received, according to the custom of Barbarians, with war songs, with savage howlings, and a wild uproar of military applause. Their battalions began to form a line of battle; the brave and warlike rushed forward to the front, and the field glittered with the blaze of arms. The Romans on their side burned with equal ardour. Agricola saw the impatient spirit of his men, but did not think proper to begin the engagement, till he confirmed their courage by the following speech: " It is now, my fellow-soldiers, the eighth year of our service in Britain. During that time, the genius and good auspices of the Roman empire, with your assistance and unwearied labour, have made the island our own. In all our expeditions, in every battle, the enemy has felt your valour, and by your toil and perseverance the very nature of the country has been conquered. I have been proud of my soldiers, and you have had no reason to blush for your general. We have carried the terror of our arms beyond the limits of any other soldiers, or any former general; we have penetrated to the extremity of the land. This was formerly the boast of vain-glory, the mere report of fame; it is now historical truth. We have gained possession sword in hand; we are encamped on the utmost limits of the island. Britain is discovered, and by the discovery conquered."

"In our long and laborious marches, when you were obliged to traverse moors, and fens, and rivers, and to climb steep and craggy mountains, it was still the cry of the bravest amongst you, When shall we be led to battle? When shall we see the enemy? Behold them now before you. They are hunted out of their dens and caverns; your wish is granted, and the field of glory lies open to your swords. One victory more makes this new world our own; but remember that a defeat involves us all in the last distress. If we consider the progress of our arms to look back is glorious; the tract of country that lies behind us, the forests which you have explored, and the estuaries which you have passed, are monuments of eternal fame. But our fame can only last, while we press forward on the enemy. If we give ground, if we think of a retreat, we have the same difficulties to surmount again. The success, which is now our pride, will in that case be our worst misfortune. We are not sufficiently acquainted with the course of the country; the enemy knows the defiles and marshes, and will be supplied with provisions in abundance. We have not those advantages, but we have hands that can grasp the sword, and we have valour, that gives us everything. With me it has long been a settled principle, that the back of a general or his army is never safe. Which of you would not rather die with honour, than live in infamy? But life and honour are this day inseparable; they are fixed to one spot. Should fortune declare against us, we die on the utmost limits of the world; and to die where nature ends, cannot be deemed inglorious."

XXXIV. "If our present struggle were with nations wholly unknown; if we had to do with an enemy new to our swords, I should call to mind the example of other armies. At present what can I propose so bright and animating as your own exploits? I appeal to your own eyes: behold the men drawn up against you: are they not the same, who last year, under covert of the night, assaulted the ninth legion, and, upon the first shout of our army, fled before you? A band of dastards! who have subsisted hitherto, because of all the Britons they are the most expeditious runaways."

"In woods and forests the fierce and noble animals attack the huntsmen, and rush on certain destruction; but the timorous herd is soon dispersed, scared by the sound and clamour of the chase. In like manner, the brave and warlike Britons have long since perished by the sword. The refuse of the nation still remains. They have not stayed to make head against you; they are hunted down; they are caught in the toils. Benumbed with fear, they stand motionless on yonder spot, which you will render for ever memorable by a glorious victory. Here you may end your labours, and close a scene of fifty years by one great one glorious day. Let your country see, and let the commonwealth bear witness, if the conquest of Britain has been a lingering work, if the seeds of rebellion have not been crushed, that we at least have done our duty."

XXXV. During this harangue, whilst Agricola was still addressing the men, a more than common ardour glowed on every countenance. As soon as the general ended, the field rung with shouts of applause. Impatient for the onset, the soldiers grasped their arms. Agricola restrained their violence, till he formed his order of battle. The auxiliary infantry, in number about eight thousand, occupied the centre; the wings consisted of three thousand horse. The legions were stationed in the rear, at the head of the entrenchments, as a body of reserve to support the ranks, if necessary, but otherwise to remain inactive, that a victory, obtained without the effusion of Roman blood, might be of higher value.

The Caledonians kept possession of the rising grounds, extending their ranks as wide as possible, to present a formidable show of battle. Their first line was ranged on the plain, the rest in a gradual ascent on the acclivity of the hill. The intermediate space between both armies was filled with the charioteers and cavalry of the Britons, rushing to and fro in wild career, and traversing the plain with noise and tumult. The enemy being greatly superior in number, there was reason to apprehend that the Romans might be attacked both in front and flank at the same time. To prevent that mischief, Agricola ordered his ranks to form a wider range. Some of the officers saw that the lines were weakened into length, and therefore advised that the legions should be brought forward into the field of action. But the general was not of a temper to be easily dissuaded from his purpose. Flushed with hope, and firm in the hour of danger, he immediately dismounted, and, dismissing his horse, took his stand at the head of the colours.

XXXVI. The battle began, and at first was maintained at a distance. The Britons neither wanted skill nor resolution. With their long swords, and targets of small dimension, they had the address to elude the missive weapons of the Romans, and at the same time to discharge a thick volley of their own. To bring the conflict to a speedy decision, Agricola ordered three Batavian and two Tungrian cohorts to charge the enemy sword in hand. To this mode of attack those troops had been long accustomed, but to the Britons it was every way disadvantageous. Their small targets afforded no protection, and their unwieldy swords, not sharpened to a point, could do but little execution in a close engagement. The Batavians rushed to the attack with impetuous fury; they redoubled their blows, and with the bosses of their shields bruised the enemy in the face, and having overpowered all resistance on the plain, began to force their way up the ascent of the hill in regular order of battle. Incited by their example, the other cohorts advanced with a spirit of emulation, and cut their way with terrible slaughter. Eager in pursuit of victory, they pressed forward with determined fury, leaving behind them numbers wounded, but not slain, and others not so much as hurt.

{A target was a shield, a buckler was a small round shield.
The term claymore is reported as not being a precisely accurate equivalent to the term 'long sword',
although it is used in translations to indicate a weapon of that class. - Compiler.}

The Roman cavalry, in the meantime, was forced to give ground. The Caledonians, in their armed chariots rushed at full speed into the thick of the battle, where the infantry were engaged. Their first impression struck a general terror, but their career was soon checked by the inequalities of the ground, and the close-embodied ranks of the Romans. Nothing could less resemble an engagement of the cavalry. Pent up in narrow places, the Barbarians crowded upon each other, and were driven or dragged along by their own horses. A scene of confusion followed. Chariots without a guide, and horses without a rider, broke from the ranks in wild disorder, and flying every way, as fear and consternation urged, they overwhelmed their own files, and trampled down all who came in their way.

XXXVII. Meanwhile, the Britons who had hitherto kept their post on the hills, looking down with contempt on the scanty numbers of the Roman army, began to quit their station. Descending slowly, they hoped, by wheeling round the field of battle, to attack the victors in the rear. To counteract their design, Agricola ordered four squadrons of horse, which he had kept as a body of reserve, to advance to the charge. The Britons poured down with impetuosity, and retired with equal precipitation. At the same time, the cavalry, by the directions of the general, wheeled round from the wings, and fell with great slaughter on the rear of the enemy, who now perceived that their own stratagem was turned against themselves.

The field presented a dreadful spectacle of carnage and destruction. The Britons fled; the Romans pursued; they wounded, gashed, and mangled the runaways; they seized their prisoners, and, to be ready for others, butchered them on the spot. Despair and horror appeared in various shapes: in one part of the field the Caledonians, sword in hand, fled in crowds from a handful of Romans; in other places, without a weapon left, they faced every danger and rushed on certain death. Swords and bucklers, mangled limbs and dead bodies, covered the plain. The field was red with blood. The vanquished Britons had their moments of returning courage, and gave proofs of virtue and of brave despair. They fled to the woods, and, rallying their scattered numbers, surrounded such of the Romans as pursued with too much eagerness.

Agricola was everywhere present. He saw the danger, and, if he had not in the instant taken due precaution, the victorious army would have had reason to repent of too much confidence in success. The light-armed cohorts had orders to invest the woods. Where the thickets were too close for the horse to enter, the men dismounted to explore the passes, and where the woods gave an opening, the rest of the cavalry rushed in and scoured the country. The Britons, seeing that the pursuit was conducted in compact and regular order, dispersed a second time, not in collected bodies, but in consternation, flying in different ways to remote lurking places, solicitous only for their personal safety, and no longer willing to wait for their fellow-soldiers.

Night coming on, the Romans, weary of slaughter, desisted from the pursuit. Ten thousand of the Caledonians fell in this engagement: on the part of the Romans, the number of slain did not exceed three hundred and forty, among whom was Aulus Atticus, the prefect of a cohort. His own youthful ardour, and the spirit of a high-mettled horse, carried him with too much impetuosity into the thickest of the enemy's ranks.

{The Roman casualty figures are not believable unless they only included Roman citizens and did not include the auxiliary troops. – Compiler.}

XXXVIII. The Roman army, elated with success, and enriched with plunder, passed the night in exultation. The Britons, on the other hand, wandered about, uncertain which way to turn, helpless and disconsolate. The mingled cries of men and women filled the air with lamentations. Some assisted to carry off the wounded; others called for the assistance of such as escaped unhurt; numbers abandoned their habitations, or, in their frenzy, set them on fire. They fled to obscure retreats, and, in the moment of choice, deserted them; they held consultations, and having inflamed their hopes, changed their minds in despair; they beheld the pledges of tender affection, and burst into tears; they viewed them again, and grew fierce with resentment. It is a fact well authenticated, that some laid violent hands upon their wives and children, determined with savage compassion to end their misery.

The following day displayed to view the nature and importance of the victory. A deep and melancholy silence all around; the hills deserted; houses at a distance involved in smoke and fire, and not a mortal discovered by the scouts; the whole a vast and dreary solitude. Agricola was at length informed by those who were sent out to explore the country, that no trace of the enemy was anywhere to be seen, and no attempt made in any quarter to muster their forces. Upon this intelligence, as the summer was far advanced, and to continue the war, or extend its operations in that season of the year; was impracticable, he resolved to close the campaign, and march his army into the country of the Horestians. That people submitted to the conqueror, and delivered hostages for their fidelity. Orders were now issued to the commander of the fleet to make a coasting voyage round the island. For this expedition a sufficient equipment was made, and the terror of the Roman name had already gone before them. Agricola, in the meantime, led his army into winter quarters, proceeding at the head of the cavalry and infantry by slow marches, with intent that, by seeming to linger in the enemy's country, he might impress with terror a people who had but lately submitted to his arms. The fleet, after a prosperous voyage, arrived at the Trutulensian harbour, and sailing thence along the eastern coast; returned with glory to its former station.

XXXIX. The account of these transactions, sent to Rome by Agricola, was plain and simple, without any decoration of language to heighten the narrative. Domitian received it in the true spirit of his character; with a smile on his countenance, and malignity at his heart. The mock-parade of his own German triumph, in which the slaves, whom he had purchased, walked with dishevelled hair, in the dress and manner of captives taken in war, came fresh into his mind. He felt the reproach and ridicule which that frolic occasioned, and the transition was painful to a real victory, attended with a total overthrow of the enemy, and the applause of all ranks of men. He now began to fear that the name of a private citizen might overshadow the imperial title. That reflection planted thorns in his breast. The eloquence of the forum was in vain suppressed; in vain the talents of men and every liberal art were put under an absolute prohibition, if a subject was to rob the prince of all military glory. Superior excellence in every other kind might be endured; but renown in arms belonged to the emperor, as a branch of his prerogative.

By these and such like reflections that restless spirit was distracted. He retired to brood in private over his discontent. His solitude was known to be dangerous. To be alone and innocent was no part of his character. Weary of his retreat and his own wounded spirit, he at last resolved to nourish resentment in sullen silence, till the tide of popularity, which attended the general, should ebb away, and the affection of the army had time to cool. Agricola was still in Britain, and had the command of the army and the province.

XL. Domitian, in the meantime, caused a decree to pass the senate, by which triumphal ornaments, the honour of a statue crowned with laurel, and all other marks of distinction, usually substituted in the place of a real triumph, were granted to Agricola. The language of compliment was freely lavished on this occasion. The emperor had also the art to circulate a report, that the province of Syria, at that time vacant by the death of Atilius Rufus, an officer of consular rank, was intended for Agricola, in order to do him honour by an appointment always given to men of the highest eminence. It is added as a fact, at that time currently believed, that a commission was actually made out, and sent by a favourite freedman, who was much in the emperor's confidence, to be delivered to Agricola, in case the messenger found him still possessed of his authority in Britain. But the freedman, we are told, met him on his passage in the narrow straits, and without so much as an interview returned to Rome. For the truth of this anecdote I do not pretend to vouch: it was imagined perhaps as a stroke of character, that marked the genius of Domitian. However that may be, Agricola resigned the command, and delivered to his successors a quiet and well-ordered government.

Lest his arrival at Rome should draw together too great a concourse, he concealed his approach from his friends, and entered the city privately in the dead of night. With the same secrecy, and in the night also, he went as commanded to present himself to the emperor. Domitian received him with a cold salute, and, without uttering a word, left the conqueror of Britain to mix with the servile creatures of the court.

The fame of a great military character is always sure to give umbrage to the lazy and inactive. But to soften prejudices, Agricola resolved to shade the lustre of his name in the mild retreat of humble virtues. With this view, he resigned himself to the calm enjoyments of a domestic life. Plain in his apparel, easy of access, and never attended by more than one or two friends, he was remarkable for nothing but the simplicity of his appearance; insomuch that they, who knew no criterion of merit but external show and grandeur, as often as they saw Agricola, were still to seek for the great and illustrious character. His modesty was art, which a few only could understand.

XLI. After his recall from Britain, he was frequently accused before Domitian, and as often acquitted, unheard, and without his knowledge. The ground of those clandestine proceedings was neither a crime against the state, nor even an injury done to any individual. His danger rose from a different source; from the heart of a prince who felt an inward antipathy to every virtue; from the real glory of the man, and from the praises bestowed upon him by those worst of enemies, the dealers in panegyric.

The fact was, in the distress of public affairs, which soon after followed, the name of Agricola could not be suffered to remain in obscurity. By the rashness or inactivity of the commanders-in-chief, the armies of the empire were lost in Maesia, Dacia, Germany, and Pannonia. Every day brought an account of some new misfortune; forts besieged and taken; garrisons stormed, and whole cohorts with their commanding officers made prisoners of war. Amidst these disasters the struggle was not to secure the banks of a river, nor to defend the frontier: the very possession of the provinces, and the winter quarters of the legions, were fiercely disputed. In times like those, when calamity followed calamity, and every successive year was marked by the defeat and slaughter of armies, the voice of the people called aloud for Agricola to be employed in the public service. The vigour of his conduct, his firmness in danger, and his known experience, were the general topics, in opposition to the cowardice and insufficiency of other commanders. By remonstrances of the same tendency, it is certain that the ears of Domitian were often wounded. Amongst his freedmen, those who had the interest of their master at heart made a fair representation, while others urged the same arguments, not with honest motives, but with an insidious design to exasperate the mind of a tyrant fatally bent on mischief. In this manner Agricola, by his own talents, and the treacherous arts of pernicious men, was every day in danger of rising to the precipice of glory.

XLII. The year was now at hand, in which Agricola was to have by lot the proconsulship of Asia or of Africa; but the death of Civica, who had been lately murdered in his government, gave at once a warning to Agricola, and a precedent to Domitian. At this point of time, the spies of the court thought proper to pay their visits to Agricola. The design of those pretended friends was to discover, whether the government of a province would be acceptable. They contented themselves, in their first approaches, with suggesting to him the value of tranquillity in a private station, and then obligingly undertook, by their interest at court, to obtain permission for him to decline the office. At length the mask fell off: by adding menaces to their insidious advice, they gained their point, and hurried him away to the presence of the emperor. Domitian knew the part he had to act; with a concerted countenance, and an air of distant pride, he heard Agricola's apology, and complied with his request, conscious of his own treachery, yet receiving thanks for it without a blush. The proconsular salary, which had been usually granted in like cases, was withheld upon this occasion; perhaps, in resentment because it was not solicited, or the better reason might be, that the prince might not seem to gain by compromise, what he had a right to command.

To hate whom we have injured is a propensity of the human mind: in Domitian it was a rooted principle. Prone by nature to sudden acts of rage, if at any time he had the policy to disguise his anger, it was only smothered, to break out with fiercer rage. And yet that implacable temper was disarmed by the moderation and wisdom of Agricola, who was not in that class of patriots who conceive that by a contumacious spirit they show their zeal for liberty, and think they gain immortal glory, when by rashness they have provoked their fate. By his example the man of heroic fortitude may be informed, that even in the worst of times, and under the most despotic prince, it is possible to be great and good with moderation. He may further learn, that a well-managed submission, supported by talents and industry, may rise as high in the public esteem, as many of those who have courted danger, and, without any real advantage to their country, died the victims of pride and vain ambition.

XLIII. The death of Agricola was felt by his family with the deepest sorrow, by his friends with tender concern, and even by foreigners, and such as had no knowledge of his person, with universal regret. During his illness, the common people, and that class of men who care little about public events, were constantly at his door, with anxiety making their inquiries. In the forum, and all circular meetings, he was the subject of conversation. When he breathed his last, no man was so hardened as to rejoice at the news.

He died lamented, and not soon forgotten. What added to the public affliction was a report that so valuable a life was ended by a dose of poison. No proof of the fact appearing, I leave the story to shift for itself. Thus much is certain; during his illness, instead of formal messages, according to the usual practice of courts, the freedmen most in favour, and the principal physicians of the emperor, were assiduous in their visits. Was this the solicitude of friendship, or were these men the spies of state?

On the day that closed his life, while he was yet in the agony of death, the quickest intelligence of every symptom was conveyed to Domitian by messengers in waiting for the purpose. That so much industry was exerted to hasten news, which the emperor did not wish to hear, no man believed. As soon as the event was known, Domitian put on an air of sorrow, and even affected to be touched with real regret. The object of his hatred was now no more, and joy was a passion which he could more easily disguise than the fears that distracted him. The will of the deceased gave him entire satisfaction; he was named joint heir with Agricola's excellent wife, and his most dutiful daughter, and this the tyrant considered as a voluntary mark of the testator's love and esteem. A mind like his, debauched and blinded by continued flattery, could not perceive, that by a good father none but an evil prince is ever called to a share in the succession.

XLIV. Agricola was born on the ides of June, in the third consulship of Caligula; he died on the tenth before the calends of September, during the consulship of Collega and Priscus, in the fifty-sixth year of his age. As to his person, about which in future times there may be some curiosity, he was of that make and stature which may be said to be graceful, not majestic. His countenance had not that commanding air which strikes with awe: a sweetness of expression was the prevailing character. You would have been easily convinced that he was a good man, and you would have been willing to believe him a great one.

Though he was snatched away in the vigour of life, yet if we consider the space his glory filled in the eyes of mankind, he may be said to have died full of years. Possessing all the best enjoyments, that spring from virtue, and from virtue only; adorned with every dignity, which either the consular rank or triumphal honours could bestow; what further advantage could he derive from fortune? Immoderate riches he never desired, content with an honourable independence. His wife and daughter left in a state of security, his honours blooming round him, his fame unblemished, his relations flourishing, and every tie of friendship preserved to the last, he may be considered as supremely happy, that he did not live to see the tempestuous times that soon after followed. It is indeed true, that to have reached the present auspicious era, and to have seen Trajan in possession of the imperial dignity, would have been the happy consummation of his wishes. To that effect we have often heard him, with a kind of prophetic spirit, express his sentiments; but to counterbalance his untimely end, it is at least some consolation, that he escaped that black and horrible period, in which Domitian no longer broke out in sudden fits and starts of cruelty, but, throwing off all restraint, proceeded in one continued course of unrelenting fury, as if determined to crush the commonwealth at a blow.

XLV. Agricola did not live to see the senate-house invested by an armed force; the members of that august assembly surrounded by the praetorian bands; men of consular rank destroyed in one promiscuous carnage, and a number of illustrious women condemned to exile, or obliged to fly their country. Carus Metius, that detested informer, had as yet gained but a single victory. The sanguinary voice of Messalinus was heard in the Albanian citadel only; and even Massa Bebius was at that time labouring under a prosecution. In a short time after, with our own hands we dragged Helvidius to a dungeon; our eyes beheld the distress and melancholy separation of Mauricus and Rusticus; we were stained with the innocent blood of Senecio. Even Nero had the grace to turn away his eyes from the horrors of his reign. He commanded deeds of cruelty but never was a spectator of the scene. Under Domitian, it was our wretched lot to behold the tyrant, and to be seen by him; while he kept a register of our sighs and groans. With that fiery visage, of a dye so red, that the blush of guilt could never colour his cheek, he marked the pale languid countenance of the unhappy victims, who shuddered at his frown.

With you, Agricola, we may now congratulate: you are blessed, not only because your life was a career of glory, but because you were released, when it was happiness to die. From those who attended your last moments, it is well known that you met your fate with calm serenity; willing, as far as it depended on the last act of your life, that the prince should appear to be innocent. To your daughter and myself you left a load of affliction. We have lost a parent, and, in our distress, it is now an addition to our heartfelt sorrows, that we had it not in our power to watch the bed of sickness, to soothe the languor of declining nature, to gaze upon you with earnest affection, to see the expiring glance, and receive your last embrace. Your dying words would have been ever dear to us; your commands we should have treasured up, and graved them on our hearts. This sad comfort we have lost, and the wound, for that reason, pierces deeper. Divided from you by a long absence, we had lost you four years before. Every tender office, we are well convinced, thou best of parents, was duly performed by a most affectionate wife; but fewer tears bedewed your cold remains, and, in the parting moment, your eyes looked up for other objects, but they looked in vain, and closed for ever.

XLVI. If in another world there is a pious mansion for the blessed; if, as the wisest men have thought, the soul is not extinguished with the body; may you enjoy a state of eternal felicity! From that station behold your disconsolate family; exalt our minds from fond regret and unavailing grief to the contemplation of your virtues. Those we must not lament; it were impiety to sully them with a tear. To cherish their memory, to embalm them with our praises, and, if our frail condition will permit, to emulate your bright example, will be the truest mark of our respect, the best tribute your family can offer. Your wife will thus preserve the memory of the best of husbands, and thus your daughter will prove her filial piety. By dwelling constantly on your words and actions, they will have an illustrious character before their eyes, and, not content with the bare image of your mortal frame, they will have, what is more valuable, the form and features of your mind. I do not mean by this to censure the custom of preserving in brass or marble the shape and stature of eminent men; but busts and statues, like their originals, are frail and perishable. The soul is formed of finer elements, and its inward form is not to be expressed by the hand of an artist with unconscious matter: our manners and our morals may in some degree trace the resemblance. All of Agricola, that gained our love, and raised our admiration, still subsists, and will ever subsist, preserved in the minds of men, the register of ages, and the records of fame. Others, who figured on the stage of life, and were the worthies of a former day, will sink, for want of a faithful historian, into the common lot of oblivion, inglorious and unremembered; whereas Agricola, delineated with truth, and fairly consigned to posterity, will survive himself, and triumph over the injuries of time."(5)

Oppidum at Wheathampstead, Hertfordshire; approximately 90 acres. [O.S. TL 184135]

East side looking South.   'The Slad' ploughed out boundary ditch butting against a bank on the right hand side of this photograph.

West side looking South.   'Devil's Dyke' boundary ditch.

APPENDIX 4 - JULIUS CAESAR IN BRITAIN

CONTENTS   A4.1   BACKGROUND
                       A4.2   55 BC: FIRST INVASION
                       A4.3   54 BC: SECOND INVASION
                       A4.4   CICERO'S LETTERS REFERRING TO BRITAIN

A4.1 BACKGROUND

Julius Caesar invaded Britain in 55 BC with two legions (the seventh and the tenth) of the Roman army. The legions were cut to pieces on the beach and were taken off again within weeks. It would have been sooner if they had not lost in raids by the Britons most of the transport ships that were with them. During this period of between two and four weeks there were few occasions when cohorts moved from the beach. An interpretation to this effect of the record made by Caesar in his *Gallic War* is given below.

A full strength infantry legion comprised between 4,200 and 5,000 men. To take eight thousand men to a beach and then remove them within so short a time was an achievement, albeit the numbers returning could have been significantly below those that had so recently set sail from Gaul.

The Roman expeditionary force left Boulogne about midnight and put ashore on the British coast in the late afternoon of the day following, some fifteen hours later. According to his own account, Caesar arrived in Britain four or five days before the full moon immediately preceding the autumn equinox. He arrived back at Boulogne before the autumn equinox. In 55 BC, Caesar came, did not stray far from the beach and was fortunate to escape with his life.

Caesar's invasion stratagem is envisaged as including being in Britain during late summer when the local corn would be ready for harvesting and was, therefore, ready to be looted by his soldiers for their sustenance. His objective to see for himself the nature of the peoples and the topography came to nothing.

If the tribes offering tribute to Caesar were advancing beyond contemporary diplomatic politeness then conventional opinion is the ambassadors were from those tribes that were about to be annexed (before Caesar came) by Cassivellaunus. They thought it a last hope to offer a small part of their possessions to Rome rather than lose everything to the Catuvellauni.

Strabo, who was a boy at the time of the events, was not overawed by the achievements of Caesar.

Strabo: Geography book 4, chapter 5.3 [Hamilton]
"3. Divus Caesar twice passed over to the island, but quickly returned, having effected nothing of consequence, nor proceeded far into the country, as well on account of some commotions in Keltica, both among his own soldiers and among the barbarians, as because of the loss of many of his ships at the time of the full moon, when both the ebb and flow of the tides were greatly increased. Nevertheless he gained two or three victories over the Britons, although he had transported thither only two legions of his army, and brought away hostages and slaves and much other booty."(15.22)

The second invasion was in 54 BC. It was mounted with five legions and 2,000 cavalry carried in an armada of ships. This was an enormous resource for an expeditionary force and it is difficult to equate the cost/reward ratio with anything except failure. In military terms, this failure was less catastrophic than that of the first invasion. Again, the Britons would seem to have caused havoc in damaging his ships, though Caesar records the cause as bad weather, should it be preferred to believe him.

Caesar's legions had successes. They took at some price a fort of a local chieftain about twelve miles from the coast of Kent. But overall, Cassivellaunus, using a mixture of guile and bravery was arguably shown to be the better tyrant of the two. Cassivellaunus saw off the legions before the Autumn equinox. It possibly had been an initial intention of Caesar to overwinter a group of men in Britain.

Having marched through Kent and forded the Thames in the vicinity of Brentford, it is inferred from the text that the Roman legions proceeded towards the capital of the Trinovantes. This capital would have been sited in the west of Hertfordshire or in southern Essex; it need not at that point in history have settled at the oppidum near by Colchester in Essex.

It would seem apparent the Roman army had no intelligence that they were passing to the south of the home base of Cassivellaunus. At least not until they were informed by tribes submitting voluntarily to Rome. This could be accepted as evidence that the Romans failed to capture the British warriors alive. Furthermore, that they did not find members of the general population north of the Thames who could give them any directions as to the whereabouts of the headquarters. It is credible that this headquarters was defended by the local population who, being significantly outnumbered when approached by the legions, melted into the woods. A prime choice is the site at Wheathampstead on the River Lea in Hertfordshire or certainly an oppidum in that area. No hint of traces of a relevant Roman marching camp has been found in the environs of Wheathampstead to date.

Cassivellaunus was leading a military group drawn from several confederations. He was unlikely to have been based upon any one oppidum, but his men needed food and support in the field.

If Caesar was at his naval camp then the events north of the Thames were not from his own eyewitness account. The report that Caesar was at the naval camp which suffered an attack at that time, around the 5th of August, comes from Cicero and was not mentioned by Caesar.

Commius was unlikely to have been wildly popular in Britain once the realisation dawned that Julius Caesar would not return with a larger force. At a later date Commius joined an unsuccessful uprising on the continent against Rome and subsequently moved to Southern Britain. In this move to Britain, he is assumed to have been accompanied by a good number of the continental Atrebates, a Belgic tribe.

The quotations are taken from the translation by W.A.McDevitte published in the Bohn's Library series. The compiler's observations on Caesar's narrative are in cursive brackets.

A4.2 55 BC: JULIUS CAESAR'S FIRST INVASION OF BRITAIN

Caesar: Gallic War book 4.20 to 4.38 [Mcdevitte]

"20.- During the short part of the summer which remained, Caesar, although in these countries, as all Gaul lies towards the north, the winters are early, nevertheless resolved to proceed into Britain, because he discovered that in almost all the wars with the Gauls succours had been furnished to our enemy from that country; and even if the time of year should be insufficient for carrying on the war, yet he thought it would be of great service to him if he only entered the island, and saw into the character of the people, and got knowledge of their localities, harbours, and landing places, all which were for the most part unknown to the Gauls.

{Possibly true. It shows he took all the right minded actions. – Compiler.}

For neither does any one except merchants generally go thither, nor even to them was any portion of it known, except the sea-coast and those parts which are opposite Gaul. Therefore, after having called up to him the merchants from all parts, he could learn neither what was the size of the island, nor what or how numerous were the nations which inhabited it, nor what system of war they followed, nor what customs they used, nor what harbours were convenient for a great number of large ships.

{This section is not in keeping with ambassadors from several states promising to submit to Rome. It has the flavour of having been written after the event to show that he had sought intelligence but it was not available. – Compiler.}

21.- He sends before him Caius Volusenus with a ship of war, to acquire a knowledge of these particulars before he in person should make a descent upon the island, as he was convinced that this was a judicious measure. He commissioned him to thoroughly examine into all matters, and then return to him as soon as possible.

{Thus, Caesar's account showed it was not his fault they had a disastrous landing. – Compiler.}

He himself proceeds to the Morini with all his forces. He orders ships from all parts of the neighbouring countries, and the fleet which the preceding summer he had built for the war with the Veneti, to assemble in this place. In the meantime, his purpose having been discovered, and reported to the Britons by merchants, ambassadors come to him from several states of the island, to promise that they will give hostages and submit to the government of the Roman people.

{It was the fault of the merchants that the opposing forces were waiting for him when he landed. This gave him some justification for having right on his side. He was going to the support of tribes friendly to Rome who may well have been harassed by the Catuvellauni. - Compiler.}

Having given them an audience, he after promising liberally, and exhorting them to continue in that purpose, sends them back to their own country, and with them Commius, whom upon subduing the Atrebates, he had created king there, a man whose courage and conduct he esteemed, and who he thought would be faithful to him, and whose influence ranked highly in those countries. He orders him to visit as many states as he could, and persuade them to embrace the protection of the Roman people, and apprize them that he would shortly come thither. Volusenus, having viewed the localities as far as means could be afforded one who dared not to leave his ship and trust himself to barbarians, returns to Caesar on the fifth day, and reports what he had there observed.

22.- While Caesar remains in these parts for the purpose of procuring ships, ambassadors come to him from a great portion of the Morini, to plead their excuse respecting their conduct on the late occasion; alleging that it was as men uncivilised, and as those who were unacquainted with our custom, that they had made war upon the Roman people, and promising to perform what he should command. Caesar, thinking that this had happened fortunately enough for him, because he neither wished to leave an enemy behind him, nor had an opportunity for carrying on the war, by reason of the time of year, nor considered that employment in such

Appendix 4: Julius Caesar in Britain

trifling matters was to be preferred to his enterprise on Britain, imposes a large number of hostages; and when these were brought, he received them to his protection. Having collected together and provided about eighty transport ships, as many as he thought necessary for conveying over two legions, he assigned such of war as he had besides to the quaestor, his lieutenants, and officers of cavalry. There were in addition to these eighteen ships of burden which were prevented, eight miles from that place, by winds, from being able to reach the same port. These he distributed amongst the horse; the rest of the army he delivered to Q.Titurius Sabinus and L.Aurunculeius Cotta, his lieutenants, to lead into the territories of the Manapii and those cantons of the Morini from which ambassadors had not come to him. He ordered P. Sulpicius Rufus, his lieutenant, to hold possession of the harbour, with such a garrison as he thought sufficient.

23.- These matters being arranged, finding the weather favourable for his voyage, he set sail about the third watch, and ordered the horse to march forward to the farther port, and there embark and follow him.

As this was performed rather tardily by them, he himself reached Britain with the first squadron of ships, about the fourth hour of the day, and there saw the forces of the enemy drawn up in arms on all the hills.

The nature of the place was this: the sea was confined by mountains so close to it that a dart could be thrown from their summit upon the shore. Considering this by no means a fit place for disembarking, he remained at anchor till the ninth hour, for the other ships to arrive there. Having in the meantime assembled the lieutenants and military tribunes, he told them both what he had learnt from Volusenus, and what he wished to be done; and enjoined them (as the principle of military matters, and especially as maritime affairs, which have a precipitate and uncertain action, require) that all things should be performed by them at a nod and at the instant.

Having dismissed them, meeting both with wind and tide favourable at the same time, the signal being given and the anchor weighed, he advanced about seven miles from that place, and stationed his fleet over against an open and level shore.

24.- But the barbarians, upon perceiving the design of the Romans, sent forward their cavalry and charioteers, a class of warriors of whom it is their practice to make great use in their battles, and following with the rest of their forces endeavoured to prevent our men landing. In this was the greatest difficulty, for the following reasons, namely, because our ships on account of their great size, could be stationed only in deep water; and our soldiers, in places unknown to them, with their hands embarrassed, oppressed with a large and heavy weight of armour, had at the same time to leap from the ships, stand amidst the waves, and encounter the enemy; whereas they, either on dry ground, or advancing a little way into the water, free in all their limbs, in places thoroughly known to them, could confidently throw their weapons and spur on their horses, which were accustomed to this kind of service. Dismayed by these circumstances and altogether untrained in this mode of battle, our men did not all exert the same vigour and eagerness which they had been wont to exert in engagements on dry ground.

{The third watch of the night was about midnight. The first hour of the Roman day approximated to 6 a.m.– Compiler.}

{He arrived at between about nine o'clock and ten o'clock in the morning. He had no cavalry with him on his arrival. – Compiler.}

{The ships had arrived in front of the cliffs at Folkestone or Dover which was a stupid thing to have done. It showed a lack of planning - hence Caesar's identifying Volusenus as responsible for the information upon which the planning was based. Dover was probably a port for merchants where the channel crossing was made without losing sight of land. – Compiler.}

{He had missed the tide. The ninth hour was about three o'clock in the afternoon, alternatively 6:00 pm when allowing for 15 hours daylight split into 12 equal parts.

By mid afternoon the situation had become difficult and the possibility loomed of returning to France in darkness. Wind and tide may also have delayed him in massing his forces. – Compiler.}

{His troops were seasick and dispirited and were cut to pieces or drowned as they waded ashore. – Compiler.}

25.- When Caesar observed this, he ordered the ships of war, the appearance of which was somewhat strange to the barbarians and the motion more ready for service, to be withdrawn a little from the transport vessels, and to be propelled by their oars, and be stationed towards the open flank of the enemy, and the enemy to be beaten off and driven away with slings, arrows, and engines: which plan was of great service to our men; for the barbarians being startled by the form of our ships and the motions of our oars and the nature of our engines, which was strange to them, stopped, and shortly after retreated a little.

And while our men were hesitating, chiefly on account of the depth of the sea, he who carried the eagle of the tenth legion, after supplicating the gods that the matter might turn out favourably to the legion, exclaimed, 'Leap, fellow soldiers, unless you wish to betray your eagle to the enemy. I, for my part, will perform my duty to the commonwealth and my general.' When he had said this with a loud voice, he leaped from the ship and proceeded to bear the eagle toward the enemy. Then our men, exhorting one another that so great a disgrace should not be incurred, all leaped from the ship. When those in the nearest vessels saw them, they speedily followed and approached the enemy.

26.- The battle was maintained vigorously on both sides.

Our men, however, as they could neither keep their ranks, nor get firm footing, nor follow their standards, and as one from one ship and another from another assembled around whatever standards they met, were thrown into great confusion.

But the enemy, who were acquainted with all the shallows, when from the shore they saw any coming from a ship one by one, spurred on their horses, and attacked them while embarrassed; many surrounded a few, others threw their weapons upon our collected forces on their exposed flank. When Caesar observed this, he ordered the boats of the ships of war and the spy sloops to be filled with soldiers, and sent them up to the succour of those whom he had observed in distress. Our men, as soon as they made good their footing on dry ground, and all their comrades had joined them, made an attack upon the enemy, and put them to flight, but could not pursue them very far, because the horse had not been able to maintain their course at sea and reach the island. This alone was wanting to Caesar's accustomed success.

27.- The enemy being thus vanquished in battle, as soon as they recovered after their flight, instantly sent ambassadors to Caesar to negotiate about peace. They promised to give hostages and perform what he should command. Together with these ambassadors came Commius the Atrebatian, who, as I have above said, had been sent by Caesar into Britain. Him they had seized upon when leaving his ship, although in the character of ambassador he bore the general's commission to them, and thrown into chains: then after the battle was fought, they sent him back, and in suing for peace cast the blame of that act upon the common people, and entreated that it might be pardoned on account of their indiscretion.

Caesar, complaining that after they had sued for peace, and had voluntarily sent ambassadors into the continent for that purpose, they had made war without a reason, said that he would pardon their indiscretion, and imposed hostages, a part of whom they gave immediately; the rest they said they would give in a few days, since they were sent for from remote places.

{The tide was about to turn and his transports would have had to withdraw to stay afloat. He sacrificed the warships and had them beached so as to form some barrier to the horseman and charioteers who controlled the beach. In this manner he hoped to get some troops landed and established ashore. – Compiler.}

{Chaos ensued for the Roman army. - Compiler.}

{There must have been blood and bodies everywhere, in the water and on the beach. - Compiler.}

{It is speculated the military text books laid down that when the enemy had been put to flight they should be pursued and killed or captured. Having claimed a victory, since he would not admit of defeat, Caesar had to give a plausible reason for not pursuing the enemy. – Compiler.}

{Commius had not delivered the hoped for bending of the knee from his noble relations who held sway on the south coast of Britain or the Romans did not make a landing in territory under their domain. At a later stage, Commius rebelled against Rome and is reported to have moved to southern Britain with a number of Belgae in a small migration of people as well as nobles. – Compiler.}

Appendix 4: Julius Caesar in Britain

In the meantime they ordered their people to return to the country parts, and the chiefs assembled from all quarters, and proceeded to surrender themselves and their states to Caesar.

28.- A peace being established by these proceedings four days after we had come into Britain, the eighteen ships, to which reference has been made above, and which conveyed the cavalry, set sail from the upper port with a gentle gale; when, however, they were approaching Britain and were seen from the camp, so great a storm suddenly arose that none of them could maintain their course at sea; and some were taken back to the port from which they had started; -others, to their great danger, were driven to the lower part of the island, nearer to the west; which, however, after having cast anchor, as they were getting filled with water, put out to sea through necessity in a stormy night, and made for the continent.

{By the 4th or 5th day Caesar had already recognised he had a disaster on his hands and needed empty ships for his troops, therefore, he sent back the cavalry and awaited the return of the empty ships. - Compiler.}

29.- It happened that night to be full moon, which usually occasions very high tides in that ocean; and that circumstance was unknown to our men. Thus, at the same time, the tide began to fill the ships of war which Caesar had provided to convey over his army, and which he had drawn up on the strand; and the storm began to dash the ships of burden which were riding at anchor against each other; nor was any means afforded our men of either managing them or of rendering any service.

{The Roman troops were hemmed in their camp and could not defend their boats spread over a wider area and themselves. The Britons smashed the ships on the shore and cast adrift the ships at anchor. – Compiler.}

A great many ships having been wrecked, inasmuch as the rest, having lost their cables, anchors, and other tackling, were unfit for sailing, a great confusion, as would necessarily happen, arose throughout the army; for there were no other ships in which they could be conveyed back, and all things which are of service in repairing vessels were wanting, and corn for the winter had not been provided in those places, because it was understood by all that they would certainly winter in Gaul.

{The Romans had lost a large proportion of their supplies. - Compiler.}

30.- On discovering these things the chiefs of Britain, who had come up after the battle was fought to perform those conditions which Caesar had imposed, held a conference, when they perceived that the cavalry, and ships, and corn were wanting to the Romans, and discovered the small number of our soldiers from the small extent of the camp (which, too, was on this account more limited than ordinary because Caesar had conveyed over his legions without baggage), and thought that the best plan was to renew the war, and cut off our men from corn and provisions and protract the affair till winter; because they felt confident that if they were vanquished or cut off from a return, no one would afterwards pass over into Britain for the purpose of making war.

{The Roman army produced camps of a standard size by the book. It was apparent to friend and foe that this camp was not a two legion camp. The Romans had sustained a heavy loss of life and presumably had great difficulty in setting up camp on the beach when under attack. - Compiler.}

Therefore, again entering into a conspiracy, they began to depart from the camp by degrees and secretly bring up their people from the country parts.

31.- But Caesar, although he had not as yet discovered their measures, yet, both from what had occurred to his ships, and from the circumstances that they had neglected to give the promised hostages, suspected that the thing would come to pass which really did happen. He therefore provided remedies against all contingencies; for he daily conveyed corn from the country parts into the camp, used the timber and brass of such ships as were most seriously damaged for repairing the rest, and ordered whatever things besides were necessary for this object to be brought to him from the continent. And thus, since that business was executed by the soldiers with the greatest energy, he effected that, after the loss of twelve ships, a voyage could be made well enough in the rest.

{The Romans had eighty ships of burden when they left port, to lose only twelve does not justify the space allocated to the explanation by Caesar of the damage. – Compiler.}

32.- While these things are being transacted, one legion had been sent to forage, according to custom, and no suspicion of war had arisen as yet, and some of the people remained in the country parts, others went backwards and forwards to the camp, they who were on duty at the gates of the camp reported to Caesar that a greater dust than was usual was seen in that direction in which the legion had marched.

{One legion, half the force, when so many were busy repairing the ships. This appears to be a high percentage of his manpower unless that legion was significantly depleted in numbers. – Compiler.}

Caesar, suspecting that which was, - that some new enterprise was undertaken by the barbarians, ordered the two cohorts that were on duty to march into that quarter with him, and two other cohorts to relieve them on duty; the rest to be armed and follow him immediately. When he had advanced some little way from the camp, he saw that his men were overpowered by the enemy and scarcely able to stand their ground, and that, the legion being crowded together, weapons were being cast on them from all sides.

{The Britons harvested or burnt all the crops around the Roman camp and the Romans were forced to forage further afield or starve. The Britons caught the Romans in a trap. – Compiler.}

For as all the corn was reaped in every part with the exception of one, the enemy, suspecting that our men would repair to that, had concealed themselves in the woods during the night. Then attacking them suddenly, scattered as they were, and when they had laid aside their arms, and were engaged in reaping, they killed a small number, threw the rest into confusion, and surrounded them with their cavalry and chariots.

{The Romans lost a lot of men in an avoidable situation.- Compiler}

33.- Their mode of fighting with their chariots is this: firstly, they drive about in all directions and throw their weapons and generally break the ranks of the enemy with the very dread of their horses and the noise of their wheels; and when they have worked themselves in between the troops of horse, leap from their chariots and engage on foot. The charioteers in the meantime withdraw some little distance from the battle, and so place themselves with the chariots that, if their masters are overpowered by the number of the enemy, they may have a ready retreat to their own troops. Thus they display in battle the speed of a horse, the firmness of infantry; and by daily practice and exercise attain to such expertness that they are accustomed, even on a declining and steep place, to check their horses at full speed, and manage and turn them in an instant and run along the pole, and stand on the yoke, and thence betake themselves with the greatest celerity to their chariots again.

34.- Under these circumstances, our men being dismayed by the novelty of this mode of battle, Caesar most seasonably brought assistance; for upon his arrival the enemy paused, and our men recovered from their fear; upon which, thinking the time unfavourable for provoking the enemy and coming to an action, he kept himself to his own quarter, and a short time having intervened, drew back the legions into the camp.

{The Romans retreated to their camp. – Compiler.}

While these things were going on, and all our men engaged, the rest of the Britons, who were in the fields, departed. Storms then set in for several successive days, which both confined our men to camp and hindered the enemy from attacking us.

{The Romans were hemmed in their camp on the sea shore repairing their ships and awaiting transports from Gaul. – Compiler.}

In the meantime the barbarians despatched messengers to all parts and reported to their people the small number of our soldiers, and how good an opportunity was given for obtaining spoil and for liberating themselves for ever, if they should only drive the Romans from their camp. Having by these means speedily got together a large force of infantry and of cavalry, they came up to the camp.

35.- Although Caesar anticipated that the same thing which had happened on former occasions would then occur - that, if the enemy were routed, they would escape from danger by their speed; still, having got about thirty horse, which Commius the Atribatian, of whom mention has been made, had brought over with him, he drew up the legions in order of battle before the camp. When the action commenced, the enemy were unable to sustain the attack of our men long, and turned their backs; our men pursued them as far as their speed and strength permitted, and slew a great number of them; then, having destroyed and burnt everything far and wide, they retreated to their camp.

36. - The same day, ambassadors sent by the enemy came to Caesar to negotiate a peace. Caesar doubled the number of hostages which he had before demanded; and ordered that they should be brought over to the continent, because, since the time of the equinox was near, he did not consider that, with his ships out of repair, the voyage ought to be deferred till winter. Having met with favourable weather he set sail a little after midnight, and all his fleet arrived safe at the continent, except two ships of burden which could not make the same port which the other ships did, and were carried a little lower down.

37.- When our soldiers, about 300 in number, had been drawn out of these two ships, and were marching to the camp, the Morini, whom Caesar, when setting forth for Britain, had left in a state of peace, excited by the hope of spoil, at first surrounded them with a small number of men, and ordered them to lay down their arms, if they did not wish to be slain; afterwards, however, when they, forming a circle, stood on their defence, a shout was raised and about 6000 of the enemy soon assembled; which being reported, Caesar sent all the cavalry in the camp as a relief to his men.

In the meantime our soldiers sustained the attack of the enemy, and fought most valiantly for more than four hours, and, receiving but few wounds themselves, slew several of them. But after our cavalry came in sight, the enemy, throwing away their arms, turned their backs, and a great number of them were killed.

38.- The day following Caesar sent Labienus, his lieutenant with those legions which he had brought back from Britain, against the Morini, who had revolted; who, as they had no place to which they might retreat, on account of the drying up of their marshes (which they had availed themselves of as a place of refuge the preceding year), almost all fell into the power of Labienus. In the meantime Caesar's lieutenants, Q.Titurius and L. Cotta, who had led the legions into the territories of the Menapii, having laid waste all their lands, cut down their corn and burnt their houses, returned to Caesar because the Menapii had concealed themselves in their thickest woods. Caesar fixed the winter quarters of all the legions amongst the Belgae. Thither only two British states sent hostages; the rest omitted to do so. For these successes, a thanksgiving of twenty days was decreed by the senate upon receiving Caesar's letter."(1.14)

{Possibly by now the 'cavalry' ships had returned empty. Caesar's men were drawn up in order ready to embark and were harried all the time. They boarded their ships under cover of night. – Compiler.}

{The rearguard comprising some 300 men had died in Britain. – Compiler.}

{A force of 6000 was sufficiently large to explain away, on paper, the loss of the rearguard. - Compiler.}

{Some historians are of the opinion these hostages were from the same tribes who sent ambassadors before Caesar left Gaul for Britain.
This must have ranked as among the worst weeks of Caesar's military career. The remnants of two legions returned to Gaul after spending between two and four weeks fighting for their lives on the shore of Britain. - Compiler.}

A4.3 54 BC: JULIUS CAESAR'S SECOND INVASION OF BRITAIN

Caesar: Gallic War book 5, chapters 1 to 24 [McDevitte]

"1.- Lucius Domitius and Appius Claudius being consuls, Caesar when departing from his winter quarters in Italy, as he had been accustomed to do yearly, commands the lieutenants whom he appointed over the legions to take care that during the winter as many ships as possible should be built, and the old repaired. He plans the size and shape of them. For despatch of lading, and for drawing them on shore, he makes them a little lower than those which we have been accustomed to use in our sea; and that so much the more, because he knew that, on account of the frequent changes of tide, less swells occurred there; for the purpose of transporting burdens and a great number of horses, a little broader than those which we use in other seas. All these he orders to be constructed for lightness and expedition, to which object their lowness contributes greatly. He orders those things which are necessary for equipping ships to be brought thither from Spain. . . .

2.-These things being finished, and the assizes being concluded, he returns into Hither Gaul, and proceeds thence to the army. When he had arrived there, having made a survey of the winter quarter, he finds that, by the extra-ordinary ardour of the soldiers, amidst the utmost scarcity of all materials, about six hundred ships of that kind which we have described above, and twenty-eight ships of war, had been built, and were not far from that state that they might be launched in a few days. Having commended the soldiers and those who had presided over the work, he informs them what he wishes to be done, and orders all the ships to assemble at port Itius, from which port he had learned that the passage into Britain was shortest, about thirty miles from the continent. He left what seemed a sufficient number of soldiers for that design; . . .

. . .

5.-These matters being settled, Caesar went to port Itius with the legions. There he discovers that forty ships which had been built in the country of the Meldi [Footnote. *In Meldis.* Some copies have *in Belgis;*], having been driven back by a storm, had been unable to maintain their course, and had returned to the same port from which they had set out; he finds the rest ready for sailing, and furnished with everything. In the same place, the cavalry of the whole of Gaul, in number 4,000, assembles, and the chief persons of all the states; . . .

. . .

8.-When these things were done Labienus, left on the continent with three legions and 2,000 horse, to defend the harbours and provide corn, and discover what was going on in Gaul, and take measures according to the occasion and according to the circumstances; he himself, with five legions and a number of horse, equal to that which he was leaving on the continent, set sail at sunset and borne forward by a gentle south-west wind, he did not maintain his course, in consequence of the wind dying away about midnight, and being carried on too far by the tide, when the sun rose, espied Britain passed on his left. Then, again, following the change of tide, he urged on with the oars that he might make that part of the island in which he had discovered the preceding summer that there was the best landing-place, and in this affair the spirit of our soldiers was very much to be extolled; for they with the transports and heavy ships, the labour of rowing, not being discontinued, equalled the speed of the ships of war."

{Caesar set out with between 20,000 and 25,000 infantry and 2,000 cavalry. But for rowing continuously, his ships would have been swept into the North Sea. – Compiler.}

"All the ships reached Britain nearly at mid-day; nor was there seen a (single) enemy in that place, but, as Caesar afterwards found from some prisoners, though large bodies of troops had assembled there, yet being alarmed by the great number of our ships, more than eight hundred of which, including the ships of the preceding year, and those private vessels which each had built for his own convenience, had appeared at one time, they had quitted the coast and concealed themselves among the higher points."

{As Caesar did not know, in the event, where his troops would reach land how could his opponents. – Compiler.}

"9.- Caesar, having disembarked his army and chosen a convenient place for the camp, when he discovered from the prisoners in what part the forces of the enemy had lodged themselves, having left ten cohorts and 300 horse at the sea, to be a guard to the ships, hastens to the enemy, at the third watch, fearing the less for the ships for this reason, because he was leaving them fastened at anchor upon an even and open shore; and he placed Q.Atrius over the guard of the ships. He himself, having advanced by night about twelve miles, espied the forces of the enemy.

Appendix 4: Julius Caesar in Britain

They, advancing to the river with their cavalry and chariots from the higher ground, began to annoy our men and give battle. Being repulsed by our cavalry, they concealed themselves in woods, as they had secured a place admirably fortified by nature and by art, which, as it seemed, they had before prepared on account of a civil war; for all the entrances to it were shut up by a great number of felled trees. They themselves rushed out of the woods to fight here and there, and prevented our men from entering their fortifications. But the soldiers of the seventh legion, having formed a testudo and thrown up a rampart against the fortification, took the place and drove them out of the woods, receiving only a few wounds. But Caesar forbade his men to pursue them in their flight any great distance; both because he was ignorant of the nature of the ground, and because, as a great part of the day was spent, he wished time to be left for the fortification of the camp.

10.- The next day, early in the morning, he sent both foot-soldiers and horse in three divisions on an expedition to pursue those who had fled. These having advanced a little way, when already the rear was in sight, some horse came to Caesar from Quintus Atrius, to report that the preceding night, a very great storm having arisen, almost all the ships were dashed to pieces and cast upon the shore, because neither the anchors and cables could resist, nor could the sailors and pilots sustain the violence of the storm; and thus great damage was received by that collision of the ships."

{The Britons had successfully attacked the ships and damaged them. - Compiler.}

"11.- These things being known, Caesar orders the legions and cavalry to be recalled and to cease from their march; he himself returns to the ships: he sees clearly before him almost the same things which he had heard of from the messengers and by letter, about forty ships being lost, the remainder seemed capable of being repaired with much labour. Therefore he selects workmen from the legions, and orders others to be sent for from the continent; he writes to Labienus to build as many ships as he could with those legions which were with him. He himself, though the matter was one of great difficulty and labour, yet thought it to be most expedient for all the ships to be brought up on shore and joined with the camp by one fortification. In these matters he employed about ten days, the labour of the soldiers being unremitting even during the hours of night."

{The Roman army was stranded in Britain. – Compiler.}

"The ships having been brought up on shore and the camp strongly fortified, he left the same forces which he did before as a guard for the ships; he sets out in person for the same place he had returned from. When he had come thither, greater forces of the Britons had already assembled at that place, the chief command and management of the war having been entrusted to Cassivellaunus, whose territories a river, which is called the Thames, separates from the maritime states at about eighty miles from the sea. At an earlier period perpetual wars had taken place between him and the other states; but greatly alarmed by our arrival, the Britons had placed him over the whole war and the conduct of it.

. . .

15.- The horse and charioteers of the enemy contended vigorously in a skirmish with our cavalry on the march; yet so that our men were conquerors in all parts, and drove them to their woods and hills; but, having slain a great many, they pursued too eagerly, and lost some of their men. But the enemy, after some time had elapsed, when our men were off their guard, and occupied in the fortification of the camp, rushed out of the woods, and making an attack upon those who were placed on duty before the camp, fought in a determined manner; and two cohorts being sent by Caesar to their relief, and these severally the first of two legions, when these had taken up their position at a very small distance from each other, as our men were disconcerted by the unusual mode of battle, the enemy broke through the middle of them most courageously, and retreated thence in safety. That day, Q. Laberius Durus, a tribune of the soldiers was slain. The enemy, since more cohorts were sent against them, were repulsed."

{The Britons won that engagement and caused the Roman army considerable difficulty. - Compiler}

"16.- In the whole of this method of fighting since the engagement took place under the eyes of all and before the camp, it was perceived that our men, on account of the weight of their arms, inasmuch as they could neither pursue retreating, nor quit their standards, were little suited to this kind of enemy; that the horse also fought with great danger, because they generally retreated even designedly, and, when they had drawn off our men a short distance from the legions, leaped from their chariots and fought on foot in unequal battle. But the system of cavalry engagement is wont to produce equal danger, and indeed the same, both to those who retreat and those who pursue. To this was added, that they never fought in close order, but in small parties and at great distances, and had detachments placed, and then the one relieved the other, and the vigorous and fresh succeeded the wearied.

17.- The following day the enemy halted on the hills, a distance from our camp, and presented themselves in small parties, and began to challenge our horse to battle with less spirit than the day before. But at noon, when Caesar had sent three legions, and all the cavalry with C. Trebonius, the lieutenant, for the purpose of foraging, they flew upon the foragers suddenly from all quarters, so that they did not keep off from the standards and the legions. Our men making an attack on them vigorously, repulsed them; nor did they cease to pursue them until the horse, relying on relief, as they saw the legions behind them, drove the enemy precipitately before them, and, slaying a great number of them, did not give them either the opportunity of rallying or halting, or leaping from their chariots. Immediately after this retreat, the auxiliaries who had assembled from all sides, departed; nor after that time did the enemy ever engage with us in very large numbers.

18.- Caesar, discovering their design, leads his army into the territories of Cassivellaunus to the river Thames; which river can be forded in one place only, and that with difficulty. When he had arrived there, he perceives that numerous forces of the enemy were marshalled on the other bank of the river; the bank also was defended by sharp stakes fixed in front, and stakes of the same kind fixed under the water were covered by the river. These things being discovered from prisoners and deserters, Caesar, sending forward the cavalry, ordered the legions to follow them immediately. But the soldiers advanced with such speed and such ardour, though they stood above the water by their heads only, that the enemy could not sustain the attack of the legions and of the horse, and quitted the banks, and committed themselves to flight.

19.- Cassivellaunus, as we have stated above, all hope of battle being laid aside, the greater part of his forces being dismissed, and about 4,000 charioteers only being left, used to observe our marches and retire a little from the road, and conceal himself in intricate and woody places, and in those neighbourhoods in which he had discovered we were about to march, he used to drive the cattle and the inhabitants from the fields into the woods; and, when our cavalry, for the sake of plundering and ravaging the more freely, scattered themselves among the fields, he used to send out charioteers from the woods by all the well known roads and paths, and, to the great danger of our horse, engage with them; and this source of fear hindered them from straggling very extensively. The result was that Caesar did not allow excursions to be made to a great distance from the main body of the legions, and ordered that damage should be done to the enemy in ravaging their lands and kindling fires only so far as the legionary soldiers could, by their own exertion and marching accomplish it."

> {Caesar did not know the strength of the forces of Cassivellaunus. 4,000 charioteers was deemed a sufficiently large number to reasonably explain the level of achievement of the Roman army to Caesar's peers in the Senate at Rome and other army commanders. It would appear that the Britons tracked the legions and picked off any group they could isolate and hence bring larger numbers to bear against.- Compiler}

"20.- In the meantime, the Trinobantes, almost the most powerful state of those parts, from which the young man Mandubratius embracing the protection of Caesar had come to the continent of Gaul to him (whose father, Imanuentius, had possessed the sovereignty in that state, and had been killed by Cassivellaunus; he himself had escaped death by flight), send ambassadors to Caesar, and promise that they will surrender themselves to him and perform his commands; they entreat him to protect Mandubratius from the violence of Cassivellaunus, and send to their state some one to preside over it, and possess the government. Caesar demands forty hostages from them, and corn for his army, and sends Mandubratius to them. They speedily performed the things demanded, and sent hostages to the number appointed and the corn.

21.- The Trinobantes being protected and secured from any violence of the soldiers, the Cenimagni, the Segontiaci, the Ancalites, the Bibroci, and the Cassi, sending embassies, surrendered themselves to Caesar. From them he learns that the capital town of Cassivellaunus was not far from that place, and was defended by woods and morasses, and a very large number of men and of cattle had been collected in it. (Now the Britons, when they have fortified the intricate woods, in which they are wont to assemble for the purpose of avoiding the incursion of an enemy, with an entrenchment and a rampart, call them a town.) Thither he proceeds with his legions: he finds the place admirably fortified by nature and art; he, however, undertakes to attack it in two directions. The enemy, having remained only a short time, did not sustain the attack of our soldiers, and hurried away on the other side of the town. A great amount of cattle were found there, and many of the enemy were taken and slain in their flight.

Appendix 4: Julius Caesar in Britain

22.- While these things are going forward in those places, Cassivellaunus sends messengers into Kent, which we have observed above, is on the sea, over which districts four several kings reigned, Cingetorix, Carvilius, Taximagulus, and Segonax, and commands them to collect all their forces, and unexpectedly assail and storm the naval camp."

{The Britons attacked the ships again, possibly after some had been repaired. It is stated in Collingwood and Myres in *Roman Britain and English Settlements* page 50, 2nd edition that from the writings of Cicero, it is thought that Caesar was actually at the Naval Camp at the time of the attack, this is placed about the 5th August by Collingwood and Myers.

Among the 'fragments' published in Reference 1 along side the translation of Caesar's *Gallic War* is an extract from a letter written by Cicero to his brother Quintus which is taken to date from the time of the second invasion of Britain.

"Cicero: Letter to his brother Quintus, 3, 1.
From Britain Caesar wrote to me on the kalends of September, and I received his letter the fourth day before the kalends of October, it contained satisfactory information concerning Britain; in which letter he informed me that you were not with him when he went down to the sea, to prevent my being surprised at receiving no letter from you, &c." (1.17)

Caesar had sailed from Britain by the autumn equinox.

If this is the correspondence referred to in Collingwood and Myers then some adjustment was made to the dates under translation to account for the period before the introduction of the Julian Calendar and the naming of the month of August in honour of his successor Augustus. - Compiler}

"When they had come to the camp, our men, after making a sally, slaying many of their men, and also capturing a distinguished leader named Lugotorix, brought back their own men in safety. Cassivellaunus, when this battle was reported to him, as so many losses had been sustained, and his territories laid waste, being alarmed most of all by the desertion of the states, sends ambassadors to Caesar about a surrender through the mediation of Commius the Atrebatian. Caesar, since he had determined to pass the winter on the continent, on account of the sudden revolts of Gaul, and as much of the summer did not remain, and he perceived that even that could be easily protracted, demands hostages, and prescribes what tribute Britain should pay each year to the Roman people; he forbids and commands Cassivellaunus that he wage not war against Mandubratius or the Trinobantes."

{Therefore, it may be supposed, when Caesar had set out with five legions and 2,000 cavalry, he had previously let it be known that part of the army would overwinter in Britain. Commius belonged to the Belgic aristocracy who ruled the tribe of the Atribates which occupied both sides of the Channel. It is doubtful that Cassivellaunus, or the Druids through whose offices he must have received his overall generalship, held Commius in much regard as Commius was a client king of Rome. Commius later took part in a revolt on the Continent and subsequently moved to Britain. - Compiler}

Appendix 4: Julius Caesar in Britain

{Whatever was the nature of Commius, at some time after the British expedition Roman officers crudely abused the well established customs of parley when they tried to kill him at a conference.

Caesar: Gallic War book 8 chapter 23 [McDevitte]
"Ambassadors flock in from the other states, which were waiting for the issue of the [war with the] Bellovaci: they gave hostages, and receive his orders; all except Commius, whose fears restrained him from entrusting his safety to any person's honour. For the year before, while Caesar was holding the assizes in Hither Gaul, Titus Labienus, having discovered that Commius was tampering with the states, and raising a conspiracy against Caesar, thought he might punish his infidelity without perfidy: but judging that he would not come to his camp at his invitation, and unwilling to put him on his guard by the attempt, he sent Caius Volusenus Quadratus, with orders to have him put to death under pretence of a conference. To effect his purpose, he sent with him some chosen centurions. When they came to the conference, and Volusenus, as had been agreed on, had taken hold of Commius by the hand, and one of the centurions, as if surprised at so uncommon an incident, attempted to kill him, he was prevented by the friends of Commius, but wounded him severely in the head by the first blow. Swords were drawn on both sides, not so much with a design to fight as to effect an escape, our men believing that Commius had received a mortal stroke: and the Gauls, from the treachery which they had seen, dreading that a deeper design lay concealed. Upon this transaction, it was said that Commius made a resolution never to come within sight of any Roman."(1.18)

In a later encounter, Commius on horseback pierced Volusenus in the thigh with a lance.
Caesar *Gallic War* 8.48. - Compiler}

"23.- When he had received the hostages, he leads back the army to the sea, and finds the ships repaired. After launching these, because he had a large number of prisoners, and some of the ships had been lost in the storm, he determines to convey back his army at two embarkations. And it so happened, that out of so large a number of ships, in so many voyages, neither in this nor the previous year was any ship missing which conveyed soldiers; but very few out of those which were sent back to him from the continent empty, as the soldiers of the former convoy had been disembarked, and out of those (sixty in number) which Labienus had taken care to have built, reached their destination; almost all the rest were driven back, and when Caesar had waited for them for some time in vain, lest he should be debarred from a voyage by the season of the year, inasmuch as the equinox was at hand, he of necessity stowed his soldiers the more closely, and a very great calm coming on, after he had weighed anchor at the beginning of the second watch, he reached land at break of day and brought all the ships in safety."

{Eighty transports had been judged sufficient for two infantry legions on the outward voyage in 55 BC. Evidently the Romans had lost most of their boats and the sixty new boats sent across by Labienus were all that were available to take the remaining legions off the beaches. Caesar would have expected to be attacked as his available forces diminished at embarkation and he took advantage of a period of no hostilities to get them all off together. - Compiler}

"24.- The ships having been drawn up and a general assembly of the Gauls held at Samarobriva, because the corn that year had not prospered in Gaul by reason of the drought, . . ." (1.16)

{The drought in Gaul occurred at a time when there were storms across the channel in Britain, according to Caesar. - Compiler}

A4.4 CICERO'S LETTERS REFERRING TO BRITAIN
A4.4.1 Background

The surviving letters written by Cicero are dated from 68 BC onwards up to his death in December 43 BC. Caesar had made an expedition to Britain in 55 BC and by 54 BC Quintus, the brother of Cicero, was serving as legatus under Caesar and accompanied Caesar to Britain in the expedition of 54 BC. Trebatius, a friend of Cicero, served under Caesar in Gaul. Atticus (Titus Pomponius) was a good friend of Cicero and they were further linked by the marriage of Quintus to the sister of Atticus - until their divorce in 44 BC. The dates given to the letters and the identifying reference system differ between translators, as does the use of months such as July and August and a judgement as to how to translate dates occurring before the adoption of the Julian calendar into their modern equivalent.

The numbering system of E.S.Shuckburgh, e.g. CXXXIX, in general follows the arrangement of letters produced by Tyrrell and Purser given in round brackets (e.g. FVII,8). Evelyn Shirley Shuckburgh, 1843 – 1906, a son of Robert Shuckburgh rector of Aldborough in Norfolk, stated in his preface to *The Letters of Cicero* that the work was the first complete translation into English of the extant correspondence of Cicero; the quotations are taken from the 1908 edition published in the Bohn's Library series. William Melmoth made his translation before 1804. Some examples of translations of the same letter by both Melmoth and Shuckburgh are shown for completeness.

A4.4.2
Cicero: Letter to Trebatius (A.U.699) - letter 9, book 2 [Melmoth]
"I never write to Caesar or Balbus, without taking occasion to mention you in the advantageous terms you deserve: . . . But more of this another time: in the mean while, let me advise you, who know so well how to manage securities for others, to secure yourself from the British charioteers. . . ." (2.3)

A4.4.3
Cicero: Letter to Trebatius (A.U.699) - letter 10, book 2 [Melmoth]
" . . . I am informed there is neither gold nor silver in all Britain. If that should be the case, I would advise you to seize one of the enemy's military cars, and drive back to us with all expedition. But if you think you shall be able to make your fortune without the assistance of British spoils, by all means establish yourself in Caesar's friendship. To be serious; . . . "(2.4)

A4.4.4
Cicero: Letter to C.Trebatius Testa (In Gaul). Rome, [Shuckburgh]
June (54 BC) - letter CXXXIX (F VII,8)
" . . . I am waiting for a letter from you dated 'Britain.' "(47.1)

In the event Trebatius did not venture to Britain.

Cicero: Letter to Trebatius (A.U.699) - letter 11, book 2 [Melmoth]
" . . . I expect a letter upon your arrival in Britain. Farewel."(2.7)

A4.4.5
Cicero: Letter to his brother Quintus (In Gaul). Rome.
[Shuckburgh] 3rd June (54 BC) - letter CXL (Q FR II, 13)
" . . . Only let me have Britain to paint in colours supplied by yourself, but with my own brush."(47.2)

Quintus, the brother of Cicero, was Caesar's lieutenant on the second expedition to Britain.

A4.4.6
Cicero: Letter to Atticus [Shuckburgh]
(in Epirus or on his journey to Asia). Rome,
24th? June (54 BC) - letter CXLII (A.IV,16 and part of 17)
" . . . From my brother's letter I gather surprising indications of Caesar's affection for me, and they have been confirmed by a very cordial letter from Caesar himself. The result of the British war is a source of anxiety. For it is ascertained that the approaches to the island are protected by astonishing masses of cliff. Moreover, it is now known that there isn't a pennyweight of silver in that island, nor any hope of booty except from slaves, among whom I don't suppose you can expect any instructed in literature or music."(47.3)

A4.4.7
Cicero: Letter to Atticus (in Epirus). Rome. [Shuckburgh]
27th July (54 BC) - letter CXLIII (A.IV,15)
" . . . Judging from my brother Quintus's letter, I suspect that by this time he is in Britain. I await news of him with anxiety."(47.4)

A4.4.8
Cicero: Letter to his brother Quintus (In Britain). [Shuckburgh]
Rome, September (54 BC) - letter CXLVI (Q FR II, 15)
" . . . I don't like your 'Sophoclean Banqueters' at all, though I see that you played your part with a good grace."
[Footnote. In the 'Banqueters' of Sophocles, Achilles is excluded from a banquet in Tenedos. Some social mishap seems to have occurred to Quintus in camp.]
"I come now to a subject which, perhaps, ought to have been my first. How glad I was to get your letter from Britain ! I was afraid of the ocean, afraid of the coast of the island. The other parts of the enterprise I do not underrate; but yet they inspire more hope than fear, and it is the suspense rather than any positive alarm that renders me uneasy. You, however, I can see, have a splendid subject for description, topography, natural features of things and places, manners, races, battles, your commander himself - what themes for your pen!"(47.5)

A4.4.9
Cicero: Letter to his brother Quintus (In Britain). [Shuckburgh]
Arpinum and Rome, 28th September (54 BC) - letter CXLVII (Q FR III, 1)
" . . . I now come to your letters which I received in several packets when I was at Arpinum. For I received three from you in one day, and, indeed, as it seemed, despatched by you at the same time - one of considerable length, in which your first point was that my letter to you was dated earlier than that to Caesar. . . . As for the British expedition, I conclude from your letter that we have no occasion either for fear or exultation. As to public affairs, about which you wish Tito to write to you, I have written to you hitherto somewhat more carelessly than usual, because I knew that all events, small or great, were reported to Caesar. . . . Your fourth letter reached me on the 13th of September, dated the 10th of August from Britain. . . . Just as I was folding up this epistle letter-carriers arrived from you and Caesar (20th September) after a journey of twenty days. How anxious I was ! How painfully I was affected by Caesar's most kind letter !"
[Footnote. Apparently referring to the death of his daughter Iulia.]
" . . . From Britain I have received a letter of Caesar's dated the 1st of September, which reached me on the 27th, satisfactory enough as far as the British expedition is concerned, in which, to prevent my wondering at not getting one from you, he tells me that you were not with him when he reached the coast. To that letter I made no reply, not even a formal congratulation, on account of his mourning."(47.6)

This letter as translated by W.A.McDevitte (1.16) is quoted briefly in Appendix A4.3.

Appendix 4: Julius Caesar in Britain

A4.4.10
  Cicero: Letter to Atticus (in Asia). Rome, [Shuckburgh]
  October (54 BC) - letter CLIII (A.IV,18)
  " . . . I received a letter on the 24th of October from my brother and from Caesar, dated from the nearest coasts of Britain on the 26th of September. Britain done with - - hostages taken - - no booty - - a tribute, however, imposed; they were on the point of bringing back the army."(47.7)

A4.4.11
  Cicero: Letter to Trebatius (A.U.699) - letter 12, book 2 [Melmoth]
  "I am glad , for my sake, as well as yours, that you did not attend Caesar into Britain: as it has not only saved you the fatigue of a very disagreeable expedition, but me likewise that of being the perpetual auditor of your wonderful exploits. . . . "(2.1)

A4.4.12
  Cicero: Letter to C.Trebatius Testa (In Gaul). Rome, [Shuckburgh]
  November (54 BC) - letter CLVI (F VII,16)
  "In the 'Trojan Horse' just at the end, you remember the words, 'Too late they learn wisdom.' You, however, old man, were wise in time. Those first snappy letters of yours were foolish enough, and then - ! I don't at all blame you for not being over-curious in regard to Britain. For the present, however, you seem to be in winter quarters somewhat short of warm clothing, and therefore not caring to stir out:
  'Not here and there, but everywhere,
  Be wise and ware:
  No sharper steel can warriors bear.' "
  [Footnote. 'Trojan Horse' by Livius Andronicus or Naevius.](47.8)

  Cicero: Letter to Trebatius (A.U.699) - letter 16, book 2 [Melmoth]
  "You remember the character given of the Phrygians in the play;"
  [Footnote. A tragedy called the Trojan Horse, which seems, by Cicero's frequent quotations from it, to have been in great esteem.]
  " 'that their wisdom ever came too late.' but you are resolved, my dear cautious old gentleman, that no imputation of this kind shall be fixed upon you. Thank heaven, indeed, you wisely subdued the romantic spirit of your first letters, as you were not so obstinately bent upon new adventures, as to hazard a voyage for that purpose into Britain, and who, in truth, can blame you. I imagine, that has immoveably fixed you in your winter quarters, . . . that you are the most profound sage in the law, throughout the whole city of Samarobriva. Farewel."
  [Footnote. A principal town in Gaul, now called Amiens, and where Trebatius seems to have had his winter-quarters.](2.8)

A4.4.13
  Cicero: Letter to C.Trebatius Testa (In Gaul). Rome, [Shuckburgh]
  November (54 BC) - letter CLX (F VII,10)
  "I have read your letter which informs me that our Caesar considers you a great lawyer. You must be glad to have found a country where you have the credit of knowing something. But if you had gone to Britain also, I feel sure that there would not have been in all that great island anyone more learned in law than you. . . .. However, I am told that you are having a sufficiently warm time of it where you are - news which makes me much alarmed for you."
  [Footnote. He seems to refer to the rising of the Nervii against the Roman winter quarters (Caes.B.G.v.39 seq.). Elsewhere the translator notes the Nervii destroyed a Roman legion in the winter uprising of 54 BC and put Quintus Cicero in great danger.]
  "However, in military matters you are much more cautious than at the bar, seeing that you wouldn't take a swim in the ocean, fond of swimming as you are, and wouldn't take a look at the British charioteers, ... By heavens, our conversation, whether serious or jesting, will be worth more not only than the enemy, but even than our 'brothers' the Aedui."
  [Footnote. A title granted to the Aedui by the Senate (Caes.B.G.i,33; Tac.Ann.xi,25.)](47.9)

Cicero: Letter to Trebatius (A.U.699) - letter 15, book 2 [Melmoth]
"I perceive, by your letter, that my friend Caesar looks upon you as a most wonderful lawyer; and are you not happy in being thus placed in a country where you make so considerable a figure upon so small a stock. But with how much greater advantage would your noble talents have appeared, had you gone into Britain? Undoubtedly there would not have been so profound a sage in the law throughout all that extensive island. . . . We hear, however, there has been hot work in your part of the world, which somewhat alarmed me for your safety; but I comforted myself with considering that you are not altogether so desperate a soldier, as you are a lawyer. It is a wonderful consolation, indeed, to your friends, to be assured that your passions are not an over-match for your prudence. Thus, as much as I know you love the water, you would not venture, I find, to cross it with Caesar; and tho' nothing keep you from the combats in Rome,"
   [Footnote. Alluding to his fondness of the gladiatorial games.]
"you were much too wise, I perceive, to attend them in Britain. . . . The truth is, one hour's gay, or serious conversation together, is of more importance to us, than all the foes and all the friends that the whole nation of Gaul can produce."(2.9)

A4.4.14
   Cicero: Letter to C.Trebatius Testa (In Gaul). Rome, [Shuckburgh]
         March? (53 BC) - letter CLXXI (F VII,14)
   " . . . But if you have forgotten how to write, all the fewer clients will lose their causes by having you as their advocate ! If you have forgotten me, I will take the trouble of paying you a visit where you are, before I have quite faded out of your mind. If it is a terror of the summer camp that is disheartening you, think of some excuse to get off, as you did in the case of Britain."(47.10)

Cicero: Letter to Trebatius (A.U.700) - letter 15, book 3 [Melmoth]
"If it were not for the compliments you sent me by Chrysippus, the freedman of Cyrus the architect, I should have imagined I no longer possessed a place in your thoughts. . . . Perhaps, however, you may have forgotten the use of your pen, and so much the better, let me tell you, for your clients; as they will lose no more causes by its blunders. But if it is myself only that has escaped your remembrance, I must endeavour to refresh it by a visit, before I am worn out of your mind beyond all power of recollection. After all, is it not the apprehensions of the next summer's campaign, that has rendered your hand too unsteady to perform its office? If so, you must e'en play over again the same gallant stratagem you practised last year in relation to your British expedition, and frame some heroic excuse for your absence. . . . "(2.2)

A4.4.15

For the sake of completeness, the quotation containing a reference to Divitiacus the Aeduan, see chapter 2 main text, is as follows.

Cicero: De Divinatione Book 1.41 [W.A.Falconer, Loeb Classical Library 1923.]
"Nor is the practice of divination disregarded even among uncivilized tribes, if indeed there are Druids in Gaul - and there are, for I knew one of them myself, Divitiacus, the Aeduan, your guest and eulogist. He claimed to have that knowledge of nature which the Greeks call 'physiologia,' and he used to make predictions, sometimes by means of augury and sometimes by means of conjecture."

APPENDIX 5 - RECORDS OF IRELAND from GIRALDUS

The quotation is taken from the third section of *The Topography of Ireland* as written down by Giraldus Cambrensis following his visit to Ireland in circa 1185 AD. The translation from the Latin was by Thomas Forester (24). The information is not necessarily the same as would be found in a modern translation of the Irish Annals. This extract from the 'Topography' is a report made from sight of chronicles and hearsay by an interested party at the close of the twelfth century but with footnotes as provided by the editor and translator coming from the Victorian era. There may be some basis of fact intertwined with the mythological history.

Gerald of Wales: Topography of Ireland, Distinction 3 chapter 1. [Forester]
"Of the first arrival of Caesara, the granddaughter of Noah, before the flood.
According to the most ancient histories of the Irish, Caesara, a granddaughter of Noah, "
 [Footnote According to some of the Irish legends, long before the arrival of Caesara, Ireland had received a colony, consisting chiefly of beautiful women, led by three daughters of Cain and their husbands.]
"hearing that the flood was near to hand, resolved to escape by sailing with her companions to the farthest islands of the west, as yet uninhabited by any human being, hoping that, where sin had never been committed, the flood, its avenger, would not come. The ships in company with her having been lost by shipwreck, that in which she herself sailed, with three men and fifty women, was saved, and thrown by chance on the coast of Ireland in the year before the flood. But although, with ingenuity laudable to a woman, she had planned to escape the destined visitation, it was not in her power by any means to avoid the common and almost universal fate. The shore where the ship first came to land was called the bay of small ships, and the mound of earth in which she was buried is called the tomb of Caesara to this day. But it appears to be matter of doubt how, if nearly all perished in the flood, the memory of these events and their arrival could have been preserved. However, those who first committed to writing these accounts must be answerable for them. For myself, I compile history: it is not my business to impugn it. Perhaps some record of these events was found, inscribed on a stone or a tile, as we read was the case with the art of music before the flood.
Chapter 2
How Bartholanus was the second immigrant, three hundred years after the flood.
In the three hundredth year after the flood, Bartholanus, "
 [Footnote. He is called in the Irish annals Partholan, and is said to have been the ninth in descent from Noah. Some MSS of Giraldus read Serah, instead of Terah, as the name of his father. According to the Irish legend, he was driven from Greece on account of his wickedness, and passing by Sicily, and along the coasts of Spain, reached Ireland, and landed at Inber-Sceine, on the coast of Kerry, on a Wednesday, the 14th day of May. This event is said to have taken place three hundred years after the deluge.]
"the son of Terah, a descendant from Japhet, the son of Noah, with his three sons and their wives, is reported to have landed on the coast of Ireland, either by chance or design; having either erred in their course, or, as the better opinion is, mistaken the country. He had three sons, Languinus, "
 [Footnote Another reading of the MSS. is Langurius.]
"Salanus, and Ruturugus, whose names having been conferred on localities where they are still extant, their memories have been perpetuated, so that they seem still to live among us. Lake Lagini "
 [Footnote. Lagurini, according to another reading.]
"derived its name from the eldest son; and a very high mountain, towering over the sea which flows between Britain and Ireland, is named after the second son. St. Dominic having many ages afterwards built a noble monastery at the foot of this mountain, it is now better known by the name of Mount Dominic. Ruturugus, who succeeded his two brothers, gave his name to Lake Ruturugus.
 We find few remarkable occurrences in the time of Bartholanus; indeed not any, except that four "
 [Footnote According to the Irish legends, seven lakes burst forth on the arrival of Partholan.]
"vast lakes burst suddenly out of the bowels of the earth, and four woods were felled and grubbed up, as agriculture made progress, and having been cleared with great toil, were turned into open country. For at that period the whole country, except some of the mountains, and generally even these, was overspread by immense forests and dense thickets, so that an open plain suitable for tillage, could scarcely be found. Even to the present day such spots are very rare in comparison with the woods.

However, Bartholanus and his sons and grandsons were no less fortunate in their affairs than in having a numerous posterity; for in three hundred years after their arrival, his descendants are said to have already increased to the number of nine thousand men. At length, having gained the victory in a great battle he fought with the Giants, since human prosperity is never durable, and

'Et quoniam faciles dare summa deos, eademque tueri	'Although the gods their bounties freely send,
Difficiles, et quia summis hunc numina rebus	Slow are their aids such favours to defend,
Crescendi posuere modum;	And highest fortunes find the speediest end.
In se magna, summisque negatum	Thus great things soonest fail, the noblest die,
Stare diu, nimiumque graves sub pondere lapsus.'	The loftiest totter, and in ruins lie.'

Bartholanus, with nearly all his people, was carried off by a sudden pestilence, which probably was produced by the air being corrupted by the putrefying carcasses of the slain giants. Ruanus alone is said to have escaped the mortality, and to have lived, as ancient chronicles inform us, for a vast number of years (more indeed than it is easy to believe), surviving till the time of St. Patrick, by whom he was baptized."

[Footnote. A different account of the long existence of Ruanus, who is elsewhere called Tuan, is given in the Ogygia, p.4:- 'In varias brutorum formas per multa saecula transmutatus tandem circa AD.527, e salmone, filius Carelli regis Ultoniae evasit.' (After having been for many ages transmitted into the shape of various animals, at last, about the year of our Lord 527, he came out from that of a salmon, as the son of Carell, king of Ulster.) It appears that the earliest Irish races held the eastern doctrine of the transmigration of souls; and fabulous accounts of the transmutation of the human species into animals received credit in Ireland even as late as the time of Giraldus. See before, Distinct. ii. c.19.]

"It is reported that he gave a faithful account of the history of Ireland, having related to St. Patrick all the national events, the memory of which had faded, from their great antiquity. For there is nothing so firmly fixed in the mind that it is not lost by neglect and the lapse of time. Notwithstanding Ruanus had extorted from death a long truce, he could not succeed in making a permanent peace with him; for, although he had warded off his attacks for a term far exceeding the common and usual bounds of this mortal life, he could not escape the fate which awaits all miserable flesh. As far as can be collected from Irish annals, Ruanus is stated to have had his life prolonged for many years beyond the utmost longevity of the ancient patriarchs, although this account may appear very incredible and open to objection.

Chapter 3

How, thirdly, Nemedus came from the country of Scythia, with his four sons.

Bartolanus and all his descendants having thus perished under the stroke of a prolonged and severe pestilence, the land remained for some time uncolonized, until Nemedus, "

[Footnote. Nemedus, according to the legends, was the eleventh in descent from Noah, and came from the shores of the Euxine Sea, with his four sons.]

"son of Agnominius, a Scythian, was with his four sons conveyed over to the shores of the desolated country. The names of his sons were Starius, Gerbaueles, Antimus, and Fergusius. In the time of Nemedus, four lakes suddenly burst their bounds, and the inundations swept off many thickets and woods, and cleared the ground, so that it was converted into open fields. He fought four battles with the pirates "

[Footnote. These were the Fomorians, powerful sea-rovers from Africa, who are celebrated in the old Irish poetry.]

"who were continually making devastations in Ireland, and was always victorious. He died in an island on the south of Ireland, to which he bequeathed his name, which it still bears. Nemedus's sons, grandsons, and great-grandsons, with their posterity, increased so fast and in such numbers, that they soon peopled the whole island, and every corner of it, to an extent never before known. But since

'Plus gravitatis habent res quae cum tempore crescunt, et	Things that are slow of growth, the longest last;
Rara solet subitis rebus inesse fides;'	What springs up suddenly, decays as fast;'

as their numbers had suddenly increased, so they sunk under sudden and unexpected calamities, and their fall was quicker than their rise. The greater part soon perished in the war with the Giants, "

[Footnote. The Nemedians, according to the Irish annals, were driven from Ireland not by the giants, but by the invasion of the Pirate Fomorians.]

"who were then numerous in the island, and by various sufferings and misfortunes. The rest, determining to take refuge in flight from the number-less evils with which they were threatened at that time, embarked in ships, and part of them sailed to Scythia, the rest to Greece. The descendants of Nemedus held possession of Ireland during two hundred and sixteen years; and for two hundred years afterwards it was uninhabited.

Chapter 4

Of the fourth immigration by the five brothers and sons of Dela.

These events having occurred in the order related, at length five chiefs, all brothers, who were the sons of Dela, and among the descendants of Nemedus, who had taken refuge in Greece, arrived in Ireland, and, finding it uninhabited, divided the country into five equal parts, of which each took one.

[Footnote. The colony brought by Dela were those known in Irish legend by the name of the Firbolgs. They are said to have arrived in Ireland in the year 1024 after the Deluge. Some antiquarians have identified them with the Belgae, and pretend that they went from Britain to Ireland.]

Their bounds meet at a stone standing near the castle of Kyllari, in Meath, which stone is called the navel of Ireland, because it stands in the middle of the country."

[Footnote. This spot was called Usneach, now Usny Hill, in the parish of Killare, Westmeath. It was a celebrated place of pagan worship.]

"Hence that part of Ireland is called Meath (Media), because it lies in the middle of the island; but it formed neither of the five famous provinces whose names I have before mentioned. For when the aforesaid five brothers, Gandius, Genandius, Sagandius, Rutherrargus, and Slanius, had divided the island into five parts, each of those parts had a small portion of Meath, abutting on the stone just mentioned; inasmuch as that territory had from the earliest times been the richest part of the country, having a level plain, and being very fertile and productive of corn. Hence none of the five brothers wished to be shut out from it.

Chapter 5

Of Slanius, the first sole king of Ireland.

In process of time, as fortune changed, and according to wont caused many disasters, Slanius alone obtained the monarchy of the whole of Ireland. Hence he is called the first king of Ireland. He first reunited the five portions of Meath, and forming them into one province, appropriated the whole of Meath to the royal table. Hence Meath continues to this day a separate province, since the time that Slanius, as already stated, detached it from the other five; nor does it contain as much land as one of the other five, but only one-half. For as even in the time of Slanius each of those provinces contained thirty-two cantreds, Meath was content with sixteen only. The number of all the cantreds in Ireland is one hundred and seventy-six. Cantred is a word common to both languages, British and Irish, and signifies a quantity of land usually containing one hundred vills. Including these brothers and their successors, nine kings succeeded each other; but their reigns were short, and altogether lasted only thirty years. Slanius was buried on a hill in Meath,"

[Footnote. Slieve Slange, now called Slieve Donard, in the county Down.]

"which takes its name from him.

Chapter 6

Of the fifth immigration, when the sons of king Milesius came over from Spain; and how Herimon and Heber divided the land between them.

The nation being much enfeebled, and almost exterminated, by various hostilities among themselves, and still more by the war they waged, with great loss, against another branch of the posterity of Nemedus, "

[Footnote. These were the Tuatha-de-Danaan, who, according to the Irish antiquaries, came from the north of Scotland to the north of Ireland. They were, according to tradition, far more civilised than any of the colonies who preceded them.]

"which had also come over from Scythia; at last, four nobles, sons of king Milesius, "

[Footnote. The Milesians are the most celebrated of all the legendary colonies of Ireland, and those from whom the modern Irish claim descent.]

"arrived from Spain with a fleet of sixty ships, and quickly reduced the whole island under their dominion, no one opposing them. In process of time, the two most distinguished of these nobles, namely, Heber and Herimon, divided the kingdom between them in two equal portions, the southern part falling to Herimon, and the northern to Heber.

Appendix 5: Records of Ireland from Giraldus

Chapter 7

How the brothers quarrelled, and Heber having been slain, Herimon was the first sole king of the Irish people.

After reigning jointly for some time prosperously and happily enough, as no faith can be put in a kingly consort, and power is always impatient of being shared, reckless ambition, the mother of mischief, tore asunder by degrees the ties of brotherly concord, soon broke every bond of peace, and the prosperous state of affairs was alloyed by discord, which perverts and disturbs everything. After several engagements between the brothers, with the doubtful issues common to war, victory at last declared in favour of Herimon; and his brother Heber being slain in a battle, "

[Footnote. This battle is said to have taken place near Glashill, in Offaly.]

"Herimon obtained the sole possession of the entire kingdom of Ireland, and, became the first monarch of the Irish race who inhabit the island to the present day. According to some statements, the Irish (Hibernienses) derived their name from the aforesaid Heber; or rather, according to others, they were so named from the Hiberus (the Ebro), a river in Spain. They are likewise called Gaidelus, and also Scots. Ancient histories relate that one Gaidelus, a grandson of Phaenius, "

[Footnote. Phaenius, king of the Scythians, was the grand ancestor of the Milesian race, and the first purifier of the Irish tongue, which, according to the legend, was the general language of the human race before the confusion of tongues at Babel. He also invented the Ogham characters. Nial, Phaenius's younger son, went to Egypt, married the princess Scota, and had a son, Gaidel, from whom came the name Gael. From Scota the Irish of the Milesian race were called Scoti, or Scots, and to them this name belonged, until it, as well as that of Gael, was carried to the Irish colonies into Scotland. Their leaders were Heber (Eiber) and Herimon, or Heremon (Eireamon).]

"after the confusion of tongues at the tower of Nimrod, was deeply skilled in various languages. On account of this skill, Pharaoh, king of Egypt, gave him his daughter Scota for wife. Since, therefore, the Irish, as they say, derive their original lineage from these two, Gaidelus and Scota, as they were born, so are they called Gaideli and Scots. This Gaidelus, they assert, formed the Irish tongue, which is therefore called Gaidelach, as if it were collected from all languages. The northern part of the British island is also called Scotia, because a tribe which sprung from them is understood to inhabit that country. This is proved by the affinity of the two nations in language and habits, in arms as well as in customs, even to the present day.

Chapter 8

Of Gurguntius, king of the Britons, who brought over the Basclenses to Ireland, and settled them in the country.

According to the British history, "

[Footnote. This chapter is taken from Geoffrey of Monmouth, lib. iii. c. 12. The Basclenses are evidently the Basques, but this colony does not appear to be admitted by the Irish writers.]

"Gurguntius, king of the Britons, the noble son of Belinus, and grandson of the famous Brennus, as he was returning from Denmark, which his father had formerly subdued, and, on its rebelling, he had again subjugated, met with a fleet in the Orkney islands, on board which the Barsclenses had sailed thither from Spain. Their chieftains having presented themselves to the king, and told him whence they came, and the object of their expedition, namely, to settle in some country in the western parts, earnestly entreated him to give them land to dwell in. At length the king, by the advice of his counsellors, granted them the island, now called Ireland, which was then almost deserted, or thinly peopled, that they might settle there. He also gave them pilots from his own fleet to steer them to the island. Hence it appears that the kings of Britain have claims to Ireland by some right, although it be ancient. We read also that Arthur, the famous king of the Britons, had the kings of Ireland tributary to him, and that some of them came to his court at the great city of Caerleon.

Chapter 9

Of the triple, and new, claim.

The city of Bayonne stands on the frontier of Gascony, and is under the same government. It is also the capital of Basclonia (Biscay), from whence the Irish came. At the present day, Gascony and the whole of Aquitaine are under the same rule as Britain."

[Footnote. Henry II., by his marriage with Eleanor of Guienne, acquired the duchy of Aquitaine and the county of Poitou, embracing, with their dependencies, the whole of the south-west of France, as far as the Pyrenees.]

"The kings of Britain besides this claim, have also new claims of two sorts in this respect. One is the voluntary cession and spontaneous offer of fealty by the princes of Ireland (for every one is free to renounce his own rights); the other is the confirmation of the title by the Pope."

[Footnote. Giraldus has preserved the bulls of Popes Adrian and Alexander.]

"For Jove thundering on the western confines of the ocean, and Henry II., king of England, directing an expedition into those parts, the petty kings of the West, alarmed at his thunderings, warded off the bolt by means of a treaty of peace. But we shall treat of this more fully in the proper place.

. . .

Chapter 16

How many kings reigned from Herimon to the coming of Patrick, by whom the island was converted to the faith.
From the first arrival, then, of this king, namely, Herimon, to the coming of Patrick, one hundred and thirty-one kings of the same race reigned in Ireland. Patrick, a native of Britain, and a man eminent for the sanctity of his life, came over to the island during the reign of Laegerius, the son of Nellus the great; "

[Footnote. Laeghaire, the son of Nial; the latter, popularly called Nial of the Nine Hostages, was one of the most powerful monarchs of the Milesian race. Laeghaire is said to have ascended the throne in the year 428, and St. Patrick is reported to have come to Ireland in the fourth year of this reign, that is in AD 432.]

". . . It seems proper to remark in this place, that when the before mentioned Nellus became sole king of Ireland, the six sons of Muredus, king of Ulster, sailed with a numerous fleet and took possession of the northern parts of Britain; "

[Footnote. This was the celebrated Dalreadic colony, but Giraldus has made some confusion of dates and circumstances. It was in the course of the fifth century that the Irish tribe of Dalreada in Ulster began to settle on the promontory of Cantyre, whence they gradually spread themselves over the surrounding districts. There was no Muredus, or Muireadhach, king of Ulster, in the time of Nial, but a king of that name began to reign in 451.]

"and their posterity, known by the special name of Scots, inhabit that corner of Britain to the present day.

What caused them to migrate there, and how and with what treachery, rather than force, they expelled from those parts the nation of the Picts, long so powerful, and vastly excelling them in arms and valour, it will be my business to relate, when I come to treat of the remarkable topography of that part of Britain."

[Footnote. Giraldus speaks elsewhere of his intention to write a Topography of Scotland, but nothing is known of it. See the present book, Distinc. i. c. 21.]

. . .

Chapter 36

How many kings reigned from the time of St. Patrick to the coming of Turgesius.

Thirty three kings of this race reigned in Ireland, from the arrival of St. Patrick to the time of king Fedlimidius, "

[Footnote. In the text of the printed edition this king is called Felmidius, but the various readings of other manuscripts is adopted here, as being more correct. He was, in fact, Feidlim-mac-Criomthan, king of Munster, one of the celebrated monarchs of Irish history. According to the Irish annalists, his eagerness in following up domestic feuds gave an advantage to the northern invaders.]

"during a period of four hundred years; during whose days the Christian faith diffused here remained unshaken.

Chapter 37

How in the time of king Fedlimidius, the Norwegians, under their chief Turgesius, subjugated Ireland.

In the time of this king Fedlimidius, in the year 838, the Norwegians landed on the coast of Ireland from a very large fleet, and taking possession of the country with a strong hand . . . . "

[Footnote. Turgesius is a corruption of the Scandinavian name Thorgils, a son of Harald Haarfager, who succeeded Halfdan the Black about the year 861, and was king of all Norway from about . . . . The date assigned by Giraldus to the invasion of Thorgil is therefore incorrect.]

". . .

Chapter 38

How the English say that it was Gurmund, the Irish that it was Turgesius, who conquered the island.

It appears, however, to me very extraordinary that our English people proclaim that Gurmund conquered the island, and built the castles and sunk the ditches I have just referred to, making no mention whatever of Turgesius; while the Irish and their written annals attribute these to Turgesius, and are altogether silent respecting Gurmund."(24.6)

APPENDIX 6 - THE GERMANIA OF TACITUS

The text of the *Germania* is taken from the translation by Arthur Murphy (1727-1805) first published in 1793 and published in the Everyman's Library series from 1908, the quotation is from the edition reprinted in 1917.

The *Germania* is believed to have been first written down during the second consulship of Trajan, referred to in chapter 37 of the work and dated to 98 AD. The first twenty-seven chapters deal with Germany in general, specific tribes are reported thereafter, beginning with the northern tribes and then continuing from chapter 43 onwards with those found near to or along the banks of the River Danube.

"A TREATISE ON THE SITUATION, MANNERS, & PEOPLE OF GERMANY

I. The whole vast country of Germany is separated from Gaul, from Rhaetia, and Pannonia, by the Rhine and the Danube; from Dacia and Sarmatia, by a chain of mountains, and, where the mountains subside, mutual dread forms a sufficient barrier. The rest is bounded by the ocean, embracing in its depth of water several spacious bays, and islands of prodigious extent, whose kings and peoples are now, in some measure, known to us, the progress of our arms having made recent discoveries. The Rhine has its source on the steep and lofty summit of the Rhaetian Alps, from which it precipitates, and, after winding towards the west, directs its course through a long tract of country, and falls into the Northern Ocean. The Danube, gushing down the soft and gentle declivity of the mountain Abnoba, visits several nations in its progress, and at last, through six channels. (the seventh is absorbed in fens and marshes), discharges itself into the Pontic Sea.

II. The Germans, there is reason to think, are an indigenous race, the original natives of the country, without any intermixture of adventitious settlers from other nations. In the early ages of the world, the adventurers who issued forth in quest of new habitations, did not traverse extensive tracts of land; the first migrations were made by sea. Even at this day the Northern Ocean, vast and boundless, and, as I may say, always at enmity with mariners, is seldom navigated by ships from our quarter of the world. Putting the dangers of a turbulent and unknown sea out of the case, who would leave the softer climes of Asia, Africa, or Italy, to fix his abode in Germany? where nature offers nothing but scenes of deformity: where the inclemency of the seasons never relents; where the land presents a dreary region, without form or culture, and, if we except the affection of a native for his mother-country, without an allurement to make life supportable. In all songs and ballads, the only memorials of antiquity amongst them, the god Tuisto, who was born of the Earth, and Mannus, his son, are celebrated as the founders of the German race. Mannus, it is said, had three sons, from whom the Ingaevones, who bordered on the sea-coast; the Hermiones, who inhabit the midland country; and the Istaevones, who occupy the remaining track, have all respectively derived their names. Some indeed, taking advantage of the obscurity that hangs over remote and fabulous ages, ascribe to the god Tuisto a more numerous issue, and thence trace the names of various tribes, such as the Marsians, the Gambrivians, the Suevians, and the Vandals. The ancient date and authenticity of those names are, as they contend, clearly ascertained. The word Germany is held to be of modern addition. In support of this hypothesis, they tell us that the people who first passed the Rhine, and took possession of a canton in Gaul, though known at present by the name of Tungrians, were, in that expedition, called Germans, and thence the title assumed by a band of emigrants, in order to spread a general terror in their progress, extended itself by degrees, and became, in time, the appellation of a whole people. They have a current tradition that Hercules visited those parts. When rushing to battle, they sing, in preference to all other heroes, the praises of that ancient worthy.

III. The Germans abound with rude strains of verse, the reciters of which, in the language of the country, are called Bards. With this barbarous poetry they inflame their minds with ardour in the day of action, and prognosticate the event from the impression which it happens to make on the minds of the soldiers, who grow terrible to the enemy, or despair of success, as the war-song produces an animated or a feeble sound. Nor can their manner of chanting this savage prelude be called the tone of human organs: it is rather a furious uproar; a wild chorus of military virtue. The vociferation used upon these occasions is uncouth and harsh, at intervals interrupted by the application of their bucklers to their mouths, and by the repercussion bursting out with redoubled force. An opinion prevails among them, that Ulysses, in the course of those wanderings which are so famous in poetic story, was driven into the Northern Ocean, and that, having penetrated into the country, he built, on the banks of the Rhine, the city of Asciburgium, which is inhabited at this day, and still retains the name given originally by the founder.

It is further added, that an altar dedicated to Ulysses, with the name of Laertes, his father, engraved upon it, was formerly discovered at Usciburgium. Mention is likewise made of certain monuments and tombstones, still to be seen on the confines of Germany and Rhaetia, with epitaphs or inscriptions in Greek characters. But these assertions it is not my intention either to establish or to refute; the reader will yield or withhold his assent, according to his judgment [sic] or his fancy.

IV. I have already acceded to the opinion of those, who think that the Germans have hitherto subsisted without intermarrying with other nations, a pure; unmixed, and independent race, unlike any other people, all bearing the marks of a distinct national character. Hence, what is very remarkable in such prodigious numbers, a family likeness throughout the nation; the same form and feature, stern blue eyes, ruddy hair, their bodies large and robust, but powerful only in sudden efforts. They are impatient of toil and labour; thirst and heat overcome them; but, from the nature of their soil and climate, they are proof against cold and hunger.

V. The face of the country, though in some parts varied, presents a cheerless scene, covered with the gloom of forests, or deformed with wide-extended marshes; towards the boundaries of Gaul, moist and swampy; on the side of Noricum and Pannonia, more exposed to the fury of the winds. Vegetation thrives with sufficient vigour. The soil produces grain, but is unkind to fruit-trees; well stocked with cattle, but of an under-size, and deprived by nature of the usual growth and ornament of the head. The pride of a German consists in the number of his flocks and herds: they are his only riches, and in these he places his chief delight. Gold and silver are withheld from them; is it by the favour or the wrath of Heaven? I do not, however, mean to assert that in Germany there are no veins of precious ore; for who has been a miner in those regions? Certain it is, they do not enjoy the possession and use of those metals with our sensibility. There are, indeed, silver vessels to be seen amongst them, but they were presents to their chiefs or ambassadors; the Germans regard them in no better light than common earthenware. It is, however, observable, that near the borders of the empire, the inhabitants set a value upon gold and silver, finding them subservient to the purposes of commerce. The Roman coin is known in those parts, and some of our specie is not only current, but in request. In places more remote, the simplicity of ancient manners still prevails: commutation of property is their only traffic. Where money passes in the way of barter, our old coin is the most acceptable, particularly that which is indented at the edge, or stamped with the impression of a chariot and two horses, called the SERRATI and BIGATI. Silver is preferred to gold, not from caprice or fancy, but because the inferior metal is of more expeditious use in the purchase of low-priced commodities.

VI. Iron does not abound in Germany, if we may judge from the weapons in general use. Swords and large lances are seldom seen. The soldier grasps his javelin, or, as it is called in their language, his Fram; an instrument tipped with a short and narrow piece or iron, sharply pointed, and so commodious, that, as occasion requires, he can manage it in close engagement, or in distant combat. With this, and a shield, the cavalry is completely armed. The infantry have an addition of missive weapons. Each man carries a considerable number, and, being naked, or, at least, not encumbered by his light mantle, he throws his weapon to a distance almost incredible. A German has no attention to the ornament of his person: his shield is the object of his care, and this he decorates with the liveliest colours. Breastplates are uncommon. In the whole army you will not see more than one or two helmets. Their horses have neither swiftness nor elegance of shape, nor are they trained to the various evolutions of the Roman cavalry. To advance in a direct line, or wheel suddenly to the right, is the whole of their skill, and this they perform in so compact a body, that not one is thrown out of his rank. According to the best estimate, the infantry form the national strength, and, for that reason, always fight intermixed with the cavalry. The flower of their youth, able by their vigour and activity to keep pace with the movements of the horse, are selected for this purpose, and placed in the front lines. The number of these is fixed and certain: each canton sends a hundred, from these circumstances called Hundreders by the army. The name was at first numerical only: it is now a title of honour. Their order of battle presents the form of a wedge. To give ground in the heat of action, provided you return to the charge, is military skill, not fear or cowardice. In the most fierce and obstinate engagement, even when the fortune of the day is doubtful, they make it a point to carry off their slain. To abandon their shield is a flagitious [sic] crime. The person guilty of it is interdicted from religious rites, and excluded from the assembly of the state. Many, who survived their honour on the day of battle, have closed a life of ignominy by a halter.

VII. The kings in Germany owe their election to the nobility of their birth; the generals are chosen for their valour. The power of the former is not arbitrary or unlimited; the latter command more by warlike example than by their authority. To be of prompt and daring spirit in battle, and to attack in the front of the lines, is the popular character of the chieftain: when admired for his bravery, he is sure to be obeyed. Jurisdiction is vested in the priests. It is theirs to sit in judgment [sic] upon all offences. By them, delinquents are put in irons, and chastised with stripes. The power of punishing is in no other hands. When exerted by the priests, it has neither the air of vindictive justice, nor of military execution; it is rather a religious sentence, inflicted with the sanction of the god, who, according to the German creed, attends their armies on the day of battle. To impress on their minds the idea of a tutelar deity, they carry with them to the field certain images and banners, taken from their usual depository, the religious groves.

A circumstance which greatly tends to inflame them with heroic ardour, is the manner in which their battalions are formed. They are neither mustered nor embodied by chance. They fight in clans, united by consanguinity, a family of warriors. Their tenderest pledges are near them in the field. In the heat of the engagement, the soldier hears the shrieks of his wife, and the cries of his children. These are the darling witnesses of his conduct, the applauders of his valour, at once beloved and valued. The wounded seek their mothers and their wives: undismayed at the sight, the women count each honourable scar, and suck the gushing blood. They are even hardy enough to mix with the combatants, administering refreshment, and exhorting them to deeds of valour.

VIII. From tradition, they have a variety of instances of armies put to rout, and by the interposition of their wives and daughters again incited to renew the charge. Their women saw the ranks give way, and rushing forward in the instant, by the vehemence of their cries and supplications, by opposing their breasts to danger, and by representing the horrors of slavery, restored the order of the battle. To a German mind the idea of a woman led into captivity is insupportable. In consequence of this prevailing sentiment, the states which deliver as hostages the daughters of illustrious families, are bound by the most effectual obligation. There is, in their opinion, something sacred in the female sex, and even the power of foreseeing future events. Their advice is, therefore, always heard; they are frequently consulted, and their responses are deemed oracular. We have seen, in the reign of Vespasian, the famous Veleda revered as a divinity by her countrymen. Before her time, Aurinia and others were held in equal veneration; but a veneration founded on sentiment and superstition, free from that servile adulation which pretends to people heaven with human deities.

IX. Mercury is the god chiefly adored in Germany. On stated days they think it lawful to offer to him human victims. They sacrifice to Hercules and Mars such animals as are usually slain in honour of the gods. In some parts of the country of the Suevians, the worship of Isis is established. To trace the introduction of ceremonies, which had their growth in another part of the world, were an investigation for which I have no materials: suffice it to say, that the figure of a ship (the symbolic representation of the goddess) clearly shows that the religion was imported into the country. Their deities are not immured in temples, nor represented under any kind of resemblance to the human form. To do either, were, in their opinion, to derogate from the majesty of superior beings. Woods and groves are the sacred depositories; and the spot being consecrated to those pious uses, they give to that sacred recess the name of the divinity that fills the place, which is never profaned by the steps of man. The gloom fills every mind with awe; revered at a distance, and never seen but with the eye of contemplation.

X. Their attention to auguries, and the practice of divining by lots, is conducted with a degree of superstition not exceeded by any other nation. Their mode of proceeding by lots is wonderfully simple. The branch of a fruit-tree is cut into small pieces, which, being all distinctly marked, are thrown at random on a white garment. If the question of public interest be depending, the priest of the canton performs the ceremony; if it be nothing more than a private concern, the master of the family officiates. With fervent prayers offered up to the gods, his eyes devoutly raised to heaven, he holds up three times each segment of the twig, and as the marks rise in succession, interprets the decrees of fate. If appearances prove unfavourable, there ends all consultation for that day: if, on the other hand, the chances are propitious, they require, for greater certainty, the sanction of auspices. The well-known superstition, which in other countries consults the flight and notes of birds, is also established in Germany; but to receive intimation of future events from horses is a peculiar credulity of the country. For this purpose a number of milk-white steeds, unprofaned by mortal labour, are constantly maintained at the public expense, and placed to pasture in the religious groves. When occasion requires, they are harnessed to a sacred chariot, and the priest, accompanied by the king, or chief of the state, attends to watch the motions and the neighing of the horses. No other mode of augury is received with such implicit faith by the people, the nobility, and the priesthood. The horses, upon these solemn occasions, are supposed to be the organs of the gods, and the priests their favoured interpreters. They have still another way of prying into futurity, to which they have recourse, when anxious to know the issue of an important war. They seize, by any means in their power, a captive from the adverse nation, and commit him in single combat with a champion selected from their own army. Each is provided with weapons after the manner of his country, and the victory, wherever it falls, is deemed a sure prognostic of the event.

XI. In matters of inferior moment the chiefs decide; important questions are reserved for the whole community. Yet even in those cases where all have a voice, the business is discussed and prepared by the chiefs. The general assembly, if no sudden alarm calls the people together, has its fixed and stated periods, either at the new or full moon. This is thought the season most propitious to public affairs. Their account of time differs from that of the Romans; instead of days they reckon the number of nights. Their public ordinances are so dated; and their proclamations run in the same style. The night, according to them, leads the day. Their passion for liberty is attended with this ill consequence: when a public meeting is announced, they never assemble at the stated time. Regularity would look like obedience: to mark their independent spirit, they do not convene at once, but two or three days are lost in delay.

When they think themselves sufficiently numerous, the business begins. Each man takes his seat, completely armed. Silence is proclaimed by the priests, who still retain this coercive authority. The king, or chief of the community, opens the debate: the rest are heard in their turn, according to age, nobility of descent, renown in war, or fame for eloquence. No man dictates to the assembly: he may persuade, but cannot command. When anything is advanced not agreeable to the people, they reject it with a general murmur. If the proposition pleases, they brandish their javelins. This is their highest and most honourable mark of applause; they assent in a military manner, and praise by the sound of their arms.

XII. In this council of state, accusations are exhibited, and capital offences prosecuted. Pains and penalties are proportioned to the nature of the crime. For treason and desertion, the sentence is to be hanged on a tree: the coward and such as are guilty of unnatural practices, are plunged under a hurdle into bogs and fens. In these different punishments, the point and spirit of the law is, that crimes which affect the state may be exposed to public notoriety: infamous vice cannot be too soon buried in oblivion. He who is convicted of transgressions of an inferior nature, pays a mulct of horses, or of cattle. Part of that fine goes to the king or the community, and part to the person injured or to his family. It is in these assemblies that princes are chosen and chiefs elected to act as magistrates in the several cantons of the state. To each of these judicial officers, assistants are appointed from the body of the people, to the number of a hundred, who attend to give their advice, and strengthen the hands of justice.

XIII. A German transacts no business, public or private, without being completely armed. The right of carrying arms is assumed by no person whatever, till the state has declared him duly qualified. The young candidate is introduced before the assembly, where one of the chiefs, or his father, or some near relation, provides him with a shield and javelin. This, with them, is the manly gown: the youth from that moment ranks as a citizen; till then he was considered as part of the household; he is now a member of the commonwealth. In honour of illustrious birth, and to mark the sense men entertain of the father's merit, the son, though yet of tender years, is called to the dignity of a prince or chief. Such as are grown up to manhood, and have signalised themselves by a spirit of enterprise, have always a number of retainers in their train. Where merit is conspicuous, no man blushes to be seen in the list of followers, or companions. A clanship is formed in this manner, with degrees of rank and subordination. The chief judges the pretensions of all, and assigns to each man his proper station. A spirit of emulation prevails among his whole train, all struggling to be the first in favour, while the chief places all his glory in the number and intrepidity of his Companions. In that consists his dignity; to be surrounded by a band of young men is the source of his power; in peace, his brightest ornament; in war, his strongest bulwark. Nor is his fame confined to his own country; it extends to foreign nations, and is then of the first importance, if he surpasses his rivals in the number and courage of his followers. He receives presents from all parts; ambassadors are sent to him; and his name alone is often sufficient to decide the issue of a war.

XIV. In the field of action, it is disgraceful to the prince to be surpassed in valour by his Companions; and not to vie with him in martial deeds, is equally a reproach to his followers. If he dies in the field, he who survives him survives to live in infamy. All are bound to defend their leader, to succour him in the heat of action, and to make even their own actions subservient to his renown. This is the bond of union, the most sacred obligation. The chief fights for victory; the followers for their chief. If, in the course of a long peace, the people relax into sloth and indolence, it often happens that the young nobles seek a more active life in the service of other states engaged in war. The German mind cannot brook repose. The field of danger is the field of glory. Without violence and rapine, a train of dependants cannot be maintained. The chief must show his liberality, and the followers expect it. He demands, at one time this warlike horse, at another, that victorious lance imbrued with the blood of the enemy. The prince's table, however inelegant, must always be plentiful: it is the only pay of his followers. War and depredation are the ways and means of the chieftain. To cultivate the earth, and wait the regular produce of the seasons, is not the maxim of a German: you will more easily persuade him to attack the enemy, and provoke honourable wounds in the field of battle. In a word, to earn by the sweat of your brow, what you might gain by the price of your blood, is, in the opinion of a German, a sluggish principle, unworthy of a soldier.

XV. When the state has no war to manage, the German mind is sunk in sloth. The chase does not afford sufficient employment. The time is passed in sleep and gluttony. The intrepid warrior, who in the field braved every danger, becomes in time of peace a listless sluggard. The management of his house and lands he leaves to the women, to the old men, and the infirm part of his family. He himself lounges in stupid repose, by a wonderful diversity of nature exhibiting in the same man the most inert aversion to labour, and the fiercest principle of action. It is a custom established in the several states, to present a contribution of corn and cattle to their chieftains. Individuals follow the example, and this bounty proves at once an honour to the prince, and his best support. Presents are also sent from the adjacent states, as well by private persons, as in the name of the community. Nothing is so flattering to the pride of the chiefs as those foreign favours, consisting of the best horses, magnificent armour, splendid harness, and beautiful collars. The Romans have lately taught them to receive presents of money.

XVI. The Germans, it is well known, have no regular cities; nor do they allow a continuity of houses. They dwell in separate habitations, dispersed up and down, as a grove, a meadow, or a fountain, happens to invite. They have villages, but not in our fashion, with a series of connected buildings. Every tenement stands detached, with a vacant piece of ground round it, either to prevent accidents by fire, or for want of skill in the art of building. They neither know the use of mortar nor of tiles. They build with rude materials, regardless of beauty, order, and proportion. Particular parts are covered over with a kind of earth so smooth and shining that the natural veins have some resemblance to the lights and shades of painting. Besides these habitations, they have a number of subterraneous caves, dug by their own labour, and carefully covered over with dung; in winter their retreat from cold, and the repository of their corn. In those recesses they not only find a shelter from the rigour of the season, but in times of foreign invasion, their effects are safely concealed. The enemy lays waste the open country, but the hidden treasure escapes the general ravage; safe in its obscurity, or because the search would be attended with too much trouble.

XVII. The clothing in use is a loose mantle, made fast with a clasp, or when that cannot be had, with a thorn. Naked in other respects, they loiter away whole days by the fireside. The rich wear a garment, not, indeed, displayed and flowing, like the Parthians, or the people of Sarmatia, but drawn so tight that the form of the limbs is palpably expressed. The skins of wild animals are also much in use. Near the frontier, on the borders of the Rhine, the inhabitants wear them, but with an air of neglect, that shows them altogether indifferent about the choice. The people who live more remote, near the northern seas, and have not acquired by commerce a taste for new-fashioned apparel, are more curious in the selection. They choose particular beasts, and, having stripped off the furs, clothe themselves with the spoil, decorated with parti-coloured spots, or fragments taken from the skins of fish that swim the ocean as yet unexplored by the Romans. In point of dress there is no distinction between the sexes, except that the garment of the women is frequently made of linen, adorned with purple stains, but without sleeves, leaving the arms and part of the bosom uncovered.

XVIII. Marriage is considered as a strict and sacred institution. In the national character there is nothing so truly commendable. To be contented with one wife, is peculiar to the Germans. They differ, in this respect, from all other savage nations. There are, indeed, a few instances of polygamy; not, however, the effect of loose desire, but occasioned by the ambition of various families, who court the alliance of the chief distinguished by the nobility of his rank and character. The bride brings no portion; she receives a dowry from her husband. In the presence of her parents and relations, he makes a tender of part of his wealth; if accepted, the match is approved. In the choice of the presents, female vanity is not consulted. There are no frivolous trinkets to adorn the future bride. The whole fortune consists of oxen, a caparisoned horse, a shield, a spear, and a sword. She in return delivers a present of arms, and, by this exchange of gifts, the marriage is concluded. This is the nuptial ceremony, this the bond of union, these their hymeneal gods. Lest the wife should think her sex an exemption from the rigours of the severest virtue, and the toils of war, she is informed of her duty by the marriage ceremony, and thence she learns that she is received by her husband to be his partner in toil and danger, to dare with him in war, and suffer with him in peace. The oxen yoked, the horse accoutred, and the arms given on the occasion, inculcate this lesson; and thus she is prepared to live, and thus to die. These are the terms of their union: she receives her armour as a sacred treasure, to be preserved inviolate, and transmitted with honour to her sons, a portion for their wives, and from them descendible to her grandchildren.

XIX. In consequence of these manners, the married state is a life of affection and female constancy. The virtue of the woman is guarded from seduction; no public spectacles to seduce her; no banquets to inflame her passions; no baits of pleasure to disarm her virtue. The art of intriguing by clandestine letters is unknown to both sexes. Populous as the country is, adultery is rarely heard of: when detected, the punishment is instant, and inflicted by the husband. He cuts off the hair of his guilty wife, and, having assembled her relations, expels her naked from his house, pursuing her with stripes through the village. To public loss of honour no favour is shown. She may possess beauty, youth, and riches; but a husband she can never obtain. Vice is not treated by the Germans as a subject of raillery, nor is the profligacy of corrupting and being corrupted called the fashion of the age. By the practice of some states, female virtue is advanced to still higher perfection: with them none but virgins marry. When a bride has fixed her choice, her hopes of matrimony are closed for life. With one husband, as with one life, one mind, one body, every woman is satisfied; in him her happiness is centred; her desires extend no further; and the principle is not only an affection for her husband's person, but a reverence for the married state. To set limits to population, by rearing up only a certain number of children, and destroying the rest, is accounted a flagitious crime. Among the savages of Germany, virtuous manners operate more than good laws in other countries.

XX. In every family the children are reared up in filth. They run about naked, and in time grow up to that strength and size of limb which we behold with wonder. The infant is nourished at the mother's breast, not turned over to nurses and to servants. No distinction is made between the future chieftain and the infant son of a common slave.

On the same ground, and mixed with the same cattle, they pass their days, till the age of manhood draws the line of separation, and early valour shows the person of ingenuous birth. It is generally late before their young men enjoy the pleasures of love; by consequence, they are not enfeebled in their prime. Nor are the virgins married too soon. Both parties wait to attain their full growth. In the warm season of mutual vigour the match is made, and the children of the marriage have the constitution of their parents. The uncle by the mother's side regards his nephews with an affection nothing inferior to that of their father. With some, the relation of the sister's children to their maternal uncle is held to be the strongest tie of consanguinity, insomuch that in demanding hostages, that line of kindred is preferred, as the most endearing objects of the family, and, consequently, the most tender pledges. The son is always heir to his father. Last wills and testaments are not in use. In case of failure of issue, the brothers of the deceased are next in succession, or else the paternal or maternal uncles. A numerous train of relations is the comfort and the honour of old age. To live without raising heirs to yourself is no advantage in Germany.

XXI. To adopt the quarrels as well as the friendships of your parents and relations is held to be an indispensable duty. In their resentments, however, they are not implacable. Injuries are adjusted by a settled measure of compensation. Atonement is made for homicide by a certain number of cattle, and by that satisfaction the whole family is appeased: a happy regulation, than which nothing can be more conducive to the public interest, since it serves to curb that spirit of revenge which is the natural result of liberty in the excess. Hospitality and convivial pleasures are nowhere so liberally enjoyed. To refuse admittance to a guest were an outrage against humanity. The master of the house welcomes every stranger, and regales him to the best of his ability. If his stock falls short, he becomes a visitor to his neighbour, and conducts his new acquaintance to a more plentiful table. They do not wait to be invited, nor is it of any consequence, since a cordial reception is always certain. Between an intimate and an entire stranger no distinction is made. The law of hospitality is the same. The departing guest receives as a present whatever he desires, and the host retaliates by asking with the same freedom. A German delights in the gifts which he receives; yet by bestowing he imputes nothing to you as a favour, and for what he receives he acknowledges no obligation.

XXII. In this manner the Germans pride themselves upon their frankness and generosity. Their hours of rest are protracted to broad daylight. As soon as they rise, the first thing they do is to bathe, and generally, on account of the intense severity of the climate, in warm water. They then betake themselves to their meal, each on a separate seat, and at his own table. Having finished their repast, they proceed completely armed to the despatch of business, and frequently to a convivial meeting. To devote both day and night to deep drinking is a disgrace to no man. Disputes, as will be the case with people in liquor, frequently arise, and are seldom confined to opprobrious language. The quarrel generally ends in a scene of blood. Important subjects, such as the reconciliation of enemies, the forming of family alliances, the election of chiefs, and even peace and war, are generally canvassed in their carousing festivals. The convivial moment, according to their notion, is the true season for business, when the mind opens itself in plain simplicity, or grows warm with bold and noble ideas. Strangers to artifice, and knowing no refinement, they tell their sentiments without disguise. The pleasure of the table expands their hearts, and call forth every secret. On the following day the subject of the debate is again taken into consideration, and thus two different periods of time have their distinct uses; when warm, they debate; when cool, they decide.

XXIII. Their beverage is a liquor drawn from barley or from wheat, and, like the juice of the grape, fermented to a spirit. The settlers on the banks of the Rhine provide themselves with wine. Their food is of the simplest kind; wild apples, the flesh of an animal recently killed, or coagulated milk. Without skill in cookery, or without seasoning to stimulate the palate, they eat to satisfy nature. But they do not drink merely to quench their thirst. Indulge their love of liquor to the excess which they require, and you need not employ the terror of your arms; their own vices will subdue them.

XXIV. Their public spectacles boast of no variety. They have but one sort, and that they repeat at all their meetings. A band of young men make it their pastime to dance entirely naked amidst pointed swords and javelins. By constant exercise, this kind of exhibition has become an art, and art has taught them to perform with grace and elegance. Their talents, however, are not let out for hire. Though some danger attends the practice, the pleasure of the spectator is their only recompense. In the character of a German there is nothing so remarkable as his passion for play. Without the excuse of liquor (strange as it may seems!), in their cool and sober moments they have recourse to dice, as to a serious and regular business, with the most desperate spirit committing their whole substance to chance, and when they have lost their all, putting their liberty and even their persons upon the last hazard of the die. The loser yields himself to slavery. Young, robust, and valiant, he submits to be chained, and even exposed to sale. Such is the effect of a ruinous and inveterate habit. They are victims to folly, and they call themselves men of honour. The winner is always in a hurry to barter away the slaves acquired by success at play; he is ashamed of his victory, and therefore puts away the remembrance of it as soon as possible.

XXV. The slaves in general are not arranged at their several employments in the household affairs, as is the practice at Rome. Each has his separate habitation, and his own establishment to manage. The master considers him as an agrarian dependant, who is obliged to furnish a certain quantity of grain, of cattle, or of wearing apparel. The slave obeys, and the state of servitude extends no further. All domestic affairs are managed by the master's wife and children. To punish a slave with stripes, to load him with chains, or condemn him to hard labour, is unusual. It is true, that slaves are sometimes put to death, not under colour of justice, or of any authority vested in the master; but in a transport of passion, in a fit of rage, as is often the case in a sudden affray; but it also true, that this species of homicide passes with impunity. The freedmen are not of much higher consideration than the actual slaves; they obtain no rank in the master's family, and, if we accept the parts of Germany where monarchy is established, they never figure on the stage of public business. In despotic governments they rise above the men of ingenuous birth, and even eclipse the whole body of the nobles. In other states the subordination of the freedmen is a proof of public liberty.

XXVI. The practice of placing money at interest, and reaping the profits of usury, is unknown in Germany; and that happy ignorance is a better prevention of the evil than a code of prohibitory laws. In cultivating the soil, they do not settle on one spot, but shift from place to place. The state or community takes possession of a certain tract proportioned to its number of hands; allotments are afterwards made to individuals according to their rank and dignity. In so extensive a country, where there is no want of land, the partition is easily made. The ground tilled in one year, lies fallow the next, and a sufficient quantity always remains, the labour of the people being by no means adequate to the extent or goodness of the soil. Nor have they the skill to make orchard plantations, to enclose the meadow grounds, or to lay out and water gardens. From the earth they demand nothing but corn. Hence their year is not, as with the Romans, divided into four seasons. They have distinct ideas of winter, spring, and summer, and their language has terms for each; but they neither know the blessings nor the name of autumn.

XXVII. Their funerals have neither pomp nor vain ambition. When the bodies of illustrious men are to be burned, they choose a particular kind of wood for the purpose, and have no other attention. The funeral pile is neither strewed with garments nor enriched with fragrant spices. The arms of the deceased are committed to the flames, and sometimes his horse. A mound of turf is raised to his memory, and this, in their opinion, is a better sepulchre than those structures of laboured grandeur, which display the weakness of human vanity, and are, at best, a burden to the dead. Tears and lamentations are soon at an end, but their regret does not so easily wear away. To grieve for the departed is comely in the softer sex. The women weep for their friends; the men remember them.

XXVIII. This is the sum of what I have been able to collect touching the origin of the Germans, and the general manners of the people. I now shall enter into a more minute description of the several states, their peculiar rites, and the distinctive character of each; observing at the same time, which were the nations that first passed the Rhine, and transplanted themselves into Gaul. That the Gauls, in ancient times, were superior to the Germans, we have the authority of Julius Caesar, that illustrious historian of his own affairs. From what is stated by that eminent writer, it is highly probable that colonies from Gaul passed over into Germany: for, in fact, how could a river check the migrations of either nation, when it increased in strength, and multiplied its numbers? So weak an obstacle could not repel them from taking possession of a country, not as yet marked out by power, and of course, open to the first occupant. We find, accordingly, that the whole region between the Hercynian forest, the Maine [sic] and the Rhine, was occupied by the Helvetians, and the tract beyond it by the Boians; both originally Gallic nations. The name of Boiemum, which remains to this day, shows the ancient state of the country, though it has since received a new race of inhabitants. Whether the Araviscians, who settled in Pannonia, were originally a colony from the Osi, a people of Germany; or, on the other hand, whether the Osi overflowed into Germany from the Araviscians, cannot now be ascertained. Thus much is certain, the laws, the manners, and language of both nations are still the same. But which of them first passed the Danube? The same good and evil were to be found on both sides of the river; equal poverty and equal independence. To be thought of German origin is the ambition of the Treverians and the Nervians, both conceiving, that the reproach of Gallic softness and effeminacy, which still infect their national manners, may be lost in the splendour of a warlike descent. The Vangiones, the Tribocians, and the Nemetes, who stretch along the banks of the Rhine, are, beyond all doubt, of German extraction. The Ubians, for their services, were made a Roman colony, and, with their own consent, became known by the name of Agrippinians, in honour of their founder; and yet they still look back with pride to their German origin. They issued formerly from that country, and, having given proof of their fidelity, obtained an allotment of territory on the banks of the Rhine, not so much with a view to their security, as to make them a guard to defend the Roman frontier.

XXIX. Of all these various nations the Batavians are the most brave and warlike. Incorporated formerly with the Cattians, but driven out by intestine divisions, they took possession of an island, formed by the river Rhine, where, without any extent of land on the continent, they established a canton in alliance with the Romans. The honour of that ancient friendship they still enjoy, with the addition of peculiar privileges. They are neither insulted with taxes, nor harassed by revenue officers. Free from burdens, imposts, and tributes, they are reserved for the day of battle; a nursery of soldiers. The Mattiaci are in like manner attached to the interest of the Romans. In fact, the limits of the empire have been enlarged, and the terror of our arms has spread beyond the Rhine and the former boundaries. Hence the Mattiaci, still enjoying their own side of the river, are Germans by their situation, yet in sentiment and principle the friends of Rome; submitting, like the Batavians, to the authority of the empire; but never having been transplanted, they still retain, from their soil and climate, all the fierceness of their native character. The people between the Rhine and the Danube, who occupy a certain tract, subject to an impost of one tenth, and therefore called the Decumate lands, are not to be reckoned among the German nations. The Gauls, from their natural levity prone to change, and rendered desperate by their poverty, were the first adventurers into that vacant region. The Roman frontier, in process of time, being advanced, and garrisons stationed at proper posts, that whole country became part of a province, and the inhabitants of course were reduced to subjection.

XXX. Beyond the Mattiaci lies the territory of the Cattians, beginning at the Hercynian forest, but not, like other parts of Germany, a wide and dreary level of fens and marshes. A continued range of hills extends over a prodigious tract, till growing thinner by degrees they sink at last into an open country. The Hercynian forest attends its favourite Cattians to their utmost boundary, and there leaves them, as it were, with regret. The people are robust and hardy; their limbs well braced; their countenance fierce, and their minds endowed with vigour beyond the rest of their countrymen. Considered as Germans, their understanding is quick and penetrating. They elect officers fit to command, and obey them implicitly; they keep their ranks, and know how to seize their opportunity: they restrain their natural impetuosity, and wait for the attack; they arrange with judgment the labours of the day, and throw up intrenchments for the night; trusting little to fortune, they depend altogether on their valour; and, what is rare in the history of Barbarians, and never attained without regular discipline, they place their confidence, not in the strength of their armies, but entirely in their general. The infantry is their main strength. Each soldier carries, besides his arms, his provision and a parcel of military tools. You may see other armies rushing to a battle; the Cattians march to a war. To skirmish in detached parties, or to sally out on a sudden emergence, is not their practice. A victory hastily gained, or a quick retreat, may suit the genius of the cavalry; but all that rapidity, in the opinion of the Cattians, denotes want of resolution: perseverance is the true mark of courage.

XXXI. A custom, known, indeed, in other parts of Germany, but adopted only by a few individuals of a bold and ardent spirit, is with the Cattians a feature of the national character. From the age of manhood they encourage the growth of their hair and beard; nor will any one, till he has slain an enemy, divest himself of that excrescence, which by a solemn vow he has devoted to heroic virtue. Over the blood and spoils of the vanquished, the face of the warrior is, for the first time, displayed. The Cattian then exults; he has now answered the true end of his being, and has proved himself worthy of his parents and his country. The sluggard continues unshorn, with the uncouth horrors of his visage growing wilder to the close of his days. The men of superior courage and uncommon ferocity wear also an iron ring, in that country a badge of infamy, and with that, as with a chain, they appear self-condemned to slavery, till by the slaughter of an enemy they have redeemed their freedom. With this extraordinary habit, the Cattians are in general much delighted. They grow grey under a vow of heroism, and by their voluntary distinctions render themselves conspicuous to their friends and enemies. In every engagement the first attack is made by them: they claim the front of the line as their right, presenting to the enemy an appearance wild and terrible. Even in the time of peace they retain the same ferocious aspect; never softened with an air of humanity. They have no house to dwell in, no land to cultivate, no domestic care to employ them. Wherever chance conducts them, they are sure of being maintained. Lavish of their neighbours' substance, and prodigal of their own, they persist in this course, till towards the decline of life their drooping spirit is no longer equal to the exertions of a fierce and rigid virtue.

XXXII. The Usipians and Tencterians border on the Cattians. Their territory lies on the banks of the Rhine, where that river, still flowing in one regular channel, forms a sufficient boundary. In addition to their military character, the Tencterians are famous for the discipline of their cavalry. Their horse is no way inferior to the infantry of the Cattians. The wisdom of their ancestors formed the military system, and their descendants hold it in veneration. Horsemanship is the pride of the whole country, the pastime of their children, the emulation of their youth, and the habit of old age. With their goods and valuable effects their horses pass as part of the succession, not however, by the general rule of inheritance, to the eldest son, but, in a peculiar line, to that son who stands distinguished by his valour and his exploits in war.

XXXIII. In the neighbourhood of the last-mentioned states formerly occurred the Bructerians, since that time dispossessed of their territory, and, as fame reports, now no longer a people. The Chamavians and Angrivarians, it is said, with the consent of the adjacent tribes, invaded the country, and pursued the ancient settlers with exterminating fury. The intolerable pride of the Bructerians drew upon them this dreadful catastrophe. The love of plunder was, no doubt, a powerful motive; and, perhaps, the event was providentially ordained in favour of the Roman people. Certain it is, the gods have of late indulged us with the view of a fierce engagement, and a scene of carnage, in which above sixty thousand of the enemy fell a sacrifice, not to the arms of Rome, but, more magnificent still! to the rage of their own internal discord, all cut off, as it were in a theatre of war, to furnish a spectacle to the Roman army. May this continue to be the fate of foreign nations! If not the friends of Rome, let them be enemies to themselves. For in the present tide of our affairs, what can fortune have in store so devoutly to be wished for as civil dissension amongst our enemies?

XXXIV. At the back of the states, which I have now described, lie the Dulgibinians and the Chasuarians, with other nations of inferior note. In front occurs the country of the Frisians, divided into two communities, called, on account of their degrees of strength, the Greater and the Lesser Frisia. Both extend along the margin of the Rhine as far as the ocean, enclosing within their limits lakes of vast extent, where the fleets of Rome have spread their sails. Through that outlet we have attempted the Northern Ocean, where, if we may believe the account of navigators, the Pillars of Hercules are seen still standing on the coast; whether it be, that Hercules did in fact visit those parts, or that whatever is great and splendid in all quarters of the globe is by common consent ascribed to that ancient hero. Drusus Germanicus was an adventurer in those seas. He did not want a spirit of enterprise; but the navigation was found impracticable in that tempestuous ocean, which seemed to forbid any further discovery of its own element, or the labours of Hercules. Since that time no expedition has been undertaken: men conceived that to respect the mysteries of the gods, and believe without inquiry, would be the best proof of veneration.

XXXV. We have hitherto traced the western side of Germany. From the point where we stop, it stretches away with a prodigious sweep towards the north. In this vast region, the first territory that occurs is that of the Chaucians, beginning on the confines of the Frisians, and, though at the extremity bounded by the sea-shore, yet running at the back of all the nations already described, till, with an immense compass, it reaches the borders of the Cattians. Of this immeasurable tract it is not sufficient to say that the Chaucians possess it: they even people it. Of all the German nations, they are, beyond all question, the most respectable. Their grandeur rests upon the surest foundation, the love of justice; wanting no extension of territory, free from avarice and ambition, remote and happy, they provoke no wars, and never seek to enrich themselves by rapine and depredation. Their importance among the nations round them is undoubtedly great; but the best evidence of it is, that they have gained nothing by injustice. Loving moderation, yet uniting to it a warlike spirit, they are ever ready in a just cause to unsheathe the sword. Their armies are soon in the field. In men and horses, their resources are great, and even in profound tranquillity their fame is never tarnished.

XXXVI. Bordering on the side of the Chaucians, and also of the Cattians, lies the country of the Cheruscans; a people by a long disuse of arms enervated and sunk in sloth. Unmolested by their neighbours, they enjoyed the sweets of peace, forgetting that amidst powerful and ambitious neighbours, the repose which you enjoy serves only to lull you into a calm, always pleasing, but deceitful in the end. When the sword is drawn, and the power of the strongest is to decide, you talk in vain of equity and moderation: those virtues always belong to the conqueror. Thus it has happened to the Cheruscans: they were formerly just and upright; at present they are called fools and cowards. Victory has transferred every virtue to the Cattians, and oppression takes the name of wisdom. The downfall of the Cheruscans drew after it that of the Fosi, a contiguous nation, in their day of prosperity never equal to their neighbours, but fellow-sufferers in their ruin.

XXXVII. In the same northern part of Germany we find the Cimbrians on the margin of the ocean; a people at present of small consideration, though their glory can never die. Monuments of their former strength and importance are still to be seen on either shore. Their camps and lines of circumvallation are not yet erased. From the extent of ground which they occupied, you may even now form an estimate of the force and resources of the state, and the account of their grand army, which consisted of such prodigious numbers, seems to be verified. It was in the year of Rome six hundred and forty, in the consulship of Caecilius Metellus and Papirius Carbo, that the arms of the Cimbrians first alarmed the world. If from that period we reckon to the second consulship of the emperor Trajan, we shall find a space of near two hundred and ten years: so long has Germany stood at bay with Rome! In the course of so obstinate a struggle, both sides have felt alternately the severest blows of fortune, and the worst calamities of war.

Appendix 6: The Germania of Tacitus

Not the Samnite, nor the republic of Carthage, nor Spain, nor Gaul, nor even the Parthian, has given such frequent lessons to the Roman people. The power of the Arsacidae was not so formidable as German liberty. If we except the slaughter of Crassus and his army, what has the east to boast of? Their own commander, Pacorus, was cut off, and the whole nation was humbled by the victory of Ventidius. The Germans can recount their triumphs over Carbo, Cassius, Scaurus Aurelius, Servilius Caepio, and Cneius Manlius, all defeated, or taken prisoners. With them the republic lost five consular armies; and since that time, in the reign of Augustus, Varus perished with his three legions. Caius Marius, it is true, defeated the Germans in Italy; Julius Caesar made them retreat from Gaul: and Drusus, Tiberius, and Germanicus, overpowered them in their own country; but how much blood did those victories cost us! The mighty projects of Caligula ended in a ridiculous farce. From that period an interval of peace succeeded, till, roused at length by the dissensions of Rome, and the civil wars that followed, they stormed our legions in their winter quarters, and even planned the conquest of Gaul. Indeed we forced them to repass the Rhine; but from that time what has been our advantages? We have triumphed, and Germany is still unconquered.

XXXVIII. The Suevians are the next that claim attention. Possessing the largest portion of Germany, they do not, like the Cattians and Tencterians, form one state or community, but have among themselves several subdivisions, or inferior tribes, known by distinct appellations, yet all comprehended under the general name of Suevians. It is the peculiar custom of this people to braid the hair, and tie it up in a knot. Between them and the rest of the Germans this is the mark of distinction. In their own country it serves to discriminate the free-born from the slave. If the same mode is seen in other states, introduced by ties of consanguinity, or, as often happens, by the propensity of men to imitate foreign manners, the instances are rare, and confined entirely to the season of youth. With the Suevians the custom is continued through life: men far advanced in years are seen with their hoary locks interwoven, and fastened behind, or sometimes gathered into a shaggy knot on the crown of the head. The chiefs are more nicely adjusted: they attend to ornament, but it is a manly attention, not the spirit of intrigue or the affectation of appearing amiable in the eyes of women. When going to engage the enemy, they fancy that from the high structure of their hair they appear taller and gain an air of ferocity. Their dress is a preparation for battle.

XXXIX. The Semnones are ambitious to be thought the most ancient and respectable of the Suevian nation. Their claim they think confirmed by the mysteries of religion. On a stated day a procession is made into a wood consecrated in ancient times, and rendered awful by auguries delivered down from age to age. The several tribes of the same descent appear by their deputies. The rites begin with the slaughter of a man, who is offered as a victim, and thus their barbarous worship is celebrated by an act of horror. The grove is beheld with superstitious terror. No man enters that holy sanctuary without being bound with a chain, thereby denoting his humble sense of his own condition, and the superior attributes of the deity that fills the place. Should he happen to fall, he does not presume to rise, but in that grovelling state makes his way out of the wood. The doctrine intended by this bigotry is, that from this spot the whole nation derives its origin, and that here is the sacred mansion of the all-ruling mind, the supreme God of the universe, who holds everything else in a chain of dependence on his will and pleasure. To these tenets much credit arises from the weight and influence of the Semnones, a populous nation, distributed into a hundred cantons and by the vast extent of their territory entitled to consider themselves as the head of the Suevian nation.

XL. The Langobards exhibit a contrast to the people last described. Their dignity is derived from the paucity of their numbers. Surrounded as they are by great and powerful nations, they live independent, owing their security not to mean compliances, but to that warlike spirit with which they encounter danger. To these succeed in regular order the Reudignians, the Aviones, Angles, and Varinians: the Eudocians, Nuithones, and Suardonians, all defended by rivers, or embosomed in forests. In these several tribes there is nothing that merits attention, except that they all agree to worship the goddess Earth, or as they call her Herth, whom they consider as the common mother of all. This divinity, according to their notion, interposes in human affairs, and, at times, visits the several nations of the globe. A sacred grove on an island in the Northern Ocean is dedicated to her. There stands her sacred chariot, covered with a vestment, to be touched by the priest only. When she takes her seat in this holy vehicle, he becomes immediately conscious of her presence, and in his fit of enthusiasm pursues her progress. The chariot is drawn, by cows yoked together. A general festival takes place, and public rejoicings are heard, wherever the goddess directs her way. No war is thought of; arms are laid aside, and the sword is sheathed. The sweets of peace are known, and then only relished. At length the same priest declares the goddess satisfied with her visitation, and re-conducts her to her sanctuary. The chariot with the sacred mantle, and, if we may believe report, the goddess herself, are purified in a secret lake. In this ablution certain slaves officiate, and instantly perish in the water. Hence the terrors of superstition are more widely diffused; a religious horror seizes every mind, and all are content in pious ignorance to venerate that awful mystery, which no man can see and live. This part of the Suevian nation stretches away to the most remote and unknown recesses of Germany.

Appendix 6: The Germania of Tacitus

XLI. On the banks of the Danube (for we shall now pursue that river, in the same manner as we have traced the course of the Rhine), the first and nearest state is that of the Hermundurians, a people in alliance with Rome, acting always with fidelity, and for that reason allowed to trade not only on the frontier, but even within the limits of the empire. They are seen at large in the heart of our splendid colony in the province of Rhaetia, without so much as a guard to watch their motions. To the rest of the Germans we display camps and legions, but to the Hermundurians we grant the exclusive privilege of seeing our houses and our elegant villas. They behold the splendour of the Romans, but without avarice, or a wish to enjoy it. In the territories of these people the Elbe takes its rise, a celebrated river, and formerly well known to the Romans. At present we only hear of its name.

XLII. Contiguous to the last-mentioned people lies the country of the Nariscans, and next in order the Marcomannians and the Quadians. Of these the Marcomannians are the most eminent for their strength and military glory. The very territory now in their possession is the reward of valour, acquired by the expulsion of the Boians. Nor have the Nariscans or Quadians degenerated from their ancestors. As far as Germany is washed by the Danube, these three nations extend along the banks, and from the frontier of the country. The Marcomannians and the Quadians, within our own memory, obeyed a race of kings, born among themselves, the illustrious issue of Maroboduus and of Tudrus. Foreign princes at present sway the sceptre; but the strength of their monarchy depends upon the countenance and protection of Rome. To our arms they are not often indebted: we choose rather to supply them with money.

XLIII. At the back of the Marcomannians and Quadians lie several nations of considerable force, such as the Marsignians, the Gothinians, the Osians, and the Burians. In dress and language the two last resemble the Suevians. The Gothinians, by their use of the Gallic tongue, and the Osians by the dialect of Pannonia, are evidently not of German origin. A further proof arises from their submitting to the disgrace of paying tribute, imposed upon them as aliens and intruders, partly by the Sarmatians, and partly by the Quadians. The Gothinians have still more reason to blush; they submit to the drudgery of digging iron in mines. But a small part of the open and level country is occupied by these several nations: they dwell chiefly in forests, or on the summit of that continued ridge of mountains, by which Suevia is divided and separated from other tribes that lie still more remote. Of these the Lygians are the most powerful, stretching to a great extent, and giving their name to a number of subordinate communities. It will suffice to mention the most considerable; namely, the Arians, the Helvecones, the Manimians, the Elysians, and Naharvalians. The last show a grove famous for the antiquity of its religious rites. The priest appears in a female dress. The gods whom they worship are, in the language of the country, known by the name of Alcis, by Roman interpreters said to be Castor and Pollux. There are, indeed, no idols in their country; no symbolic representation; no traces of foreign superstition. And yet their two deities are adored in the character of young men and brothers. The Arians are not only superior to the other tribes above mentioned, but are also more fierce and savage. Not content with their natural ferocity, they study to make themselves still more grim and horrible by every addition that art can devise. Their shields are black; their bodies painted of a deep colour; and the darkest night is their time for rushing to battle. The sudden surprise and funereal gloom of such a band of sable warriors are sure to strike a panic through the adverse army, who fly the field, as if a legion of demons had broke loose to attack them; so true it is, that in every engagement the eye is first conquered. Beyond the Lygians the next state is that of the Gothones, who live under regal government, and are, by consequence, ruled with a degree of power more rigorous than other parts of Germany, yet not unlimited, nor entirely hostile to civil liberty. In the neighbourhood of these people, we find, on the sea-coast, the Rugians and Lemovians, both subject to royal authority. When their round shields and short swords are mentioned, there are no other particulars worthy of notice.

XLIV. The people that next occur are the Suiones, who may be said to inhabit the ocean itself. In addition to the strength of their armies, they have a powerful naval force. The form of their ships is peculiar. Every vessel has a prow at each end, and by that contrivance is always ready to make head either way. Sails are not in use, nor is there a range of oars at the sides. The mariners, as often happens in the navigation of rivers, take different stations, and shift from one place to another, as the exigence may require. Riches are by this people held in great esteem; and the public mind, debased by that passion, yields to the government of one with unconditional; with passive obedience. Despotism is here fully established. The people are not allowed to carry arms in common, like the rest of the German nations. An officer is appointed to keep in a magazine all the military weapons, and for this purpose a slave is always chosen. For this policy the ostensible reason is, that the ocean is their natural fence against foreign invasions, and in time of peace the giddy multitude, with arms ready at hand, soon proceeds from luxury to tumult and commotion. But the truth is, the jealousy of a despotic prince does not think it safe to commit the care of his arsenal to the nobles or the men of ingenuous birth. Even a manumitted slave is not fit to be trusted.

XLV. At the further extremity beyond the Suiones there is another sea, whose sluggish waters seem to be in a state of stagnation. By this lazy element the globe is said to be encircled, and the supposition receives some colour of probability from an extraordinary phenomenon well known in those regions. The rays of the setting sun continue till the return of day to brighten the hemisphere with so clear a light, that the stars are imperceptible. To this it is added by vulgar credulity, that when the sun begins to rise, the sound of the emerging luminary is distinctly heard, and the very form of the horses, the blaze of glory round the head of the god, is palpable to the sight. The boundaries of nature, it is generally believed, terminate here.

On the coast to the right of the Suevian ocean, the Aestyans have fixed their habitation. In their dress and manners they resemble the Suevians, but their language has more affinity to the dialect of Britain. They worship the mother of the gods. The figure of a wild boar is the symbol of their superstition; and he, who has that emblem about him, thinks himself secure even in the thickest ranks of the enemy, without any need of arms, or any other mode of defence. The use of iron is unknown, and their general weapon is a club. In the cultivation of corn, and other fruits of the earth, they labour with more patience than is consistent with the natural laziness of the Germans. Their industry is exerted in another instance: they explore the sea for amber, in their language called Glese, and are the only people who gather that curious substance. It is generally found among the shallows; sometimes on the shore. Concerning the nature or the causes of this concretion, the Barbarians, with their usual want of curiosity, make no inquiry. Amongst other superfluities discharged by the sea, this substance lay long neglected, till Roman luxury gave it a name, and brought it into request. To the savages it is of no use. They gather it in rude heaps, and offer it to sale without any form or polish, wondering at the price they receive for it. There is reason to think that amber is a distillation from certain trees, since in the transparent medium we see a variety of insects, and even animals of the wing, which, being caught in the viscous fluid, are afterwards, when it grows hard, incorporated with it. It is probable, therefore, that as the east has its luxuriant plantations, where balm and frankincense perspire through the pores of trees, so the continents and islands of the west have their prolific groves, whose juices, fermented by the heat of the sun, dissolve into a liquid matter, which falls into the sea, and, being there condensed, is afterwards discharged by the winds and waves on the opposite shore. If you make an experiment of amber by the application of fire, it kindles, like a torch, emitting a fragrant flame, and in a little time, taking the tenacious nature of pitch or rosin. Beyond the Suiones, we next find the nation of Sitones, differing in nothing from the former, except the tameness with which they suffer a woman to reign over them. Of this people, it is not enough to say, that they have degenerated from civil liberty; they are sunk below slavery itself. At this place ends the territory of the Suevians.

XLVI. Whether the Peucinians, the Venedians, and Fennians, are to be accounted Germans, or classed with the people of Sarmatia, is a point not easy to be determined: though the Peucinians, called by some the Bastarnians, bear a strong resemblance to the Germans. They use the same language: their dress and habitations are the same, and they are equally inured to sloth and filth. Of late, however, in consequence of frequent intermarriages between their leading chieftains and the families of Sarmatia, they have been tainted with the manners of that country. The Venedians are a counterpart of the Sarmatians: like them they lead a wandering life, and support themselves by plunder amidst the woods and mountains that separate the Peucinians and the Fennians. They are, notwithstanding, to be ascribed to Germany, inasmuch as they have settled habitations, know the use of shields, and travel always on foot, remarkable for their swiftness. The Sarmatians, on the contrary, live altogether on horseback or in waggons. Nothing can equal the ferocity of the Fennians, nor is there anything so disgusting as their filth and poverty. Without arms, without horses, and without a fixed place of abode, they lead a vagrant life; their food the common herbage; the skins of beasts their only clothing; and the bare earth their resting-place. For their chief support they depend on their arrows, to which, for want of iron, they prefix a pointed bone. The women follow the chase in company with the men, and claim their share of the prey. To protect their infants from the fury of wild beasts, and the inclemency of the weather, they make a kind of cradle amidst the branches of trees interwoven together, and they know no other expedient. The youth of the country have the same habitation, and amidst the trees old age is rocked to rest. Savage as this way of life may seem, they prefer it to the drudgery of the field, the labour of building, and the painful vicissitudes of hope and fear, which always attend the defence and the acquisition of property. Secure against the passions of men, and fearing nothing from the anger of the gods, they have attained that uncommon state of felicity, in which there is no craving left to form a single wish.

The rest of what I have been able to collect is too much involved in fable, of a colour with the accounts of the Hellusians and the Oxionians, of whom we are told, that they have the human face, with the limbs and bodies of wild beasts. But reports of this kind, unsupported by proof, I shall leave to the pen of others."(5)

APPENDIX 7 - HYPERBOREI IN CLASSICAL TEXTS

CONTENTS

A7.1   BACKGROUND

Whilst the Hyperboreans who lived, according to Diodorus, in *"an island in the ocean over against Gaul, (as big as Sicily) under the arctic pole,"* could well have been Britons; Hyperborei was a generic term for people who lived 'beyond the north wind'. They occupied the northern parts of Europe to the edge of Asia, well beyond the tribes in contact with the Mediterranean world. No cohesion of clan or culture is recognised among the peoples referred to as Hyperborei.

A number of passages in classical texts contain mention of the Hyperborei, though often no more than a fleeting word. A selection of such passages is reproduced in this Appendix. In addition, references to Hyperborei in literature are found for the Epigoni, whether by Homer or no; Hesiod; Cicero, Nature of the Gods, book 4.12, if it exists; Mela, book 3.5; Pliny, book 6.12; Pausanias, A Description of Greece, book I. c.xxxi. paragraph 1,2; etc. It is reported that some decorated Greek pottery drew upon Hyperborean legends as their inspiration.

The core data is that used to amplify the sanctity and renown attached to the Island of Delos in the Greek world of the Aegean Sea. Diodorus apart, there is little to excite those seeking any insight into the lives and manners of northern folk at this threshold of the written word.

Aristeas of Proconnesus would seem to have lived no later than the sixth century Before Christ. His record of his visits into the northern heartlands may have been the sole source of the earlier statements on the Hyperborei. *"Proconnesus, now Marmora, an island of the Propontus, at the north-east of Cyzicus; also called Elaphonnesus and Neuris. It was famous for its fine marble. Plin. 5, c. 32. – Strab. 13. – Mela, 2, c.7."(4)*

A second source was Hecataeus of Abdera, a contemporary of Alexander the Great. Pliny stated that Hecataeus had written a treatise on the Hyperborei, *Pliny Natural History book 6, chapter 20 - The Seres* (17). Hecataeus was the historian whose works had been perused by Diodorus (46).

A third source would be myth and rumour held in common usage by the wordsmiths contemporary public. An audience appreciates its own thoughts reflected back in elegant fashion.

The following entry occurs in Lempriere.

"Hyperborei, a nation in the northern parts of Europe and Asia, who were said to live to an incredible age, even to 1000 years, and in the enjoyment of all possible felicity. The sun was said to rise and set to them but once a year, and therefore, perhaps they were placed by Virgil under the north pole. The word signifies people who inhabit beyond the wind Boreas. Thrace was the residence of Boreas, according to the ancients. Whenever the Hyperboreans made offerings they always sent them towards the south, and the people of Dodona were the first of the Greeks who received them. The word Hyperboreans is applied, in general, to all those who inhabit any cold climate. Plin. 4, c.12. l.6, c. 17. – Mela. 3, c. 5. – Virg. G. i, v. 240 l. 3, v. 169 & 381. – Herodot. 4, c. 13, &c. – Cic. N.D. 3, c. 23. l. 4, c. 12."(4)

A reference to a chapter, verse or line number in a relatively old publication is not in all cases accurate when applied to later translations and later publications.

A7.2 PINDER

Pindar, a poet of classical Greece, was born at, or near, Thebes in Boeotia, though his family may have come from old pre-Boeotian stock. *"Himself born at Thebes, his parents are said to have come to the city from an outlying north western deme, Kynoskephalai, a high hill overlooking the swamp Hylike. . . . Pindar was twenty years old when he composed the tenth Pythian ode in honor [sic] of Hippokleas of Thessaly."* (48). Pindar was born c.518 BC. He died at some time between 458 BC and 435 BC.

The tenth Pythian ode includes a poetic reference to the Hyperborei. The translation from the Greek is that produced by Gilbert West (1703 – 1756) in about 1749; the quotation is taken from the edition printed at Oxford by Munday and Slatter in 1824.

Pindar: Tenth Pythian Ode [Gilbert West]
Gilbert West Text
" *Page 221. "The tenth Pythian ode was written for Hippocleas, a Thessalian, conqueror in the Diaulic Race. . . . Yet complete bliss cannot befal [sic] men: this he expresses by saying that no one can reach the Hyperboreans. For this nation was the poetic ideal of a race completely happy. The poet is thus naturally drawn into a description of the joys and sweets of the Hyperborean life, 41 – 72. . . .*
[Date of the victory, Pyth. 22 or Olymp. 70, 3. A.C.498.]"(49.1)

A note on page 106 of the Gilbert West's translation identified the *Diaulic Race* as being a total of two stadia in length. It thus had some equivalence with the modern four hundred metres.

Pindar: Tenth Pythian Ode [Gilbert West]
Gilbert West Text
"i.e. of the double stadium. In this contest, the runner, when arrived at the end of the stadium, returned immediately to the starting post." (49.2)

Pindar: Tenth Pythian Ode [Gilbert West]
". . . By such, indeed, heaven's brazen vault is yet
unattained: but in the joys that we mortal race
can approach, in all he reaches to the ocean's
bound; yet neither on ship-board, nor on foot
speeding, canst thou find the wondrous path to
the band of Hyperboreans:-
With whom Perseus, the chief, erst feasted,
entering their mansions, where he found them sacrificing
to god noble hecatombs of asses: in their
feasts ever, and their strains of harmony, does
Apollo greatly rejoice; he smiles too, seeing the
pride of the exulting beasts.
Nor does the Muse absent himself from their estate
in life: but in all parts the choirs of virgins
echo the notes of the lyre and the sound of flutes:
while with golden laurel binding their locks they
merrily feast. Disease nor destructive old-age
reach not that holy race: but void of toil and
battle they live, eschewing vengeful Nemesis – . . . . "(49.1)

These last seven lines are written as a footnote in the translation of Pliny by Bostock and Riley.
Pliny: Natural History book 4, chapters 26 [Bostock and Riley]
[Footnote. Pindar says, in the "Pythia," x.56, "The Muse is no stranger to their manners. The dances of girls and the sweet melody of the lyre and pipe resound on every side, and wreathing their locks with the glistening hay, they feast joyously. For this sacred race there is no doom of sickness or of disease; but they live apart from toil and battles, undisturbed by the exacting Nemesis."](17.1)

The notes for the Tenth Pythian Ode of Pindar written in 1885 by Basil L. Gildersleave, Professor of Greek in the John Hopkins University, Baltimore are given below. They come from the edition published in 1890 by Macmillan.

Pindar: Tenth Pythian Ode [B.L.Gildersleave]
Basil L. Gildersleave Text
Page 350. "Now follows the moral, not other for the youthful poet than for the grey-haired singer, and Pindar prays for Pelinna as he is afterwards to pray for Algina (P.8, end). "Having gained no small share of the pleasant things of Hellas, may they suffer no envious reverses from the gods. Granted that God's heart suffers no anguish, 'tis not so with men. A happy man is he in the eyes of the wise, and a theme for song, who by prowess of hand or foot gains the greatest prizes by daring and by strength (vv. 19-24), and in his lifetime sees his son obtain the Pythian wreath. Higher fortune there is none for him. The brazen heaven he cannot mount, he has sailed to the furthest bound. By ships nor by land canst thou find the marvellous road to the Hyperboreans" (vv. 25-30).

Then follows the brief story of Perseus' visit to the Hyperboreans, a land of feasts and sacrifices. The Muse dwells there, and everywhere there is the swirl of dancing virgins, with the music of lyre and flute. Their heads are wreathed with golden laurels, and they banquet sumptuously. Disease nor old age infests this consecrated race.

The land of the Hyperboreans is a glorified Thessaly, and P. was to come back to it years after in O.3. What Perseus saw, what Perseus wrought, was marvellous; but was he not the son of Danae, was he not under the guidance of Athena? (v.45). And so we have an echo of the duality with which the poem began; and as Pindar, in the second triad (v.21), bows before the power of God, so in the third (v.48) he says . . . .

And now, with the same sudden start that we find in his later poems, Pindar returns to the victor himself. And yet he is haunted by the image of the Hyperboreans, and as he hopes "that his song sweetly sung by the Ephyraian chorus will make Hippokleas still more a wonder for his victories mid elders as mid mates, and to young virgins a sweet care," the notes of the lyres and the pipings [sic] of the flutes and the dances of the Hyperborean maidens (vv.38-40) come before him."(48.1)

A7.3 AESCHYLUS

The Athenian playwright Aeschylus, 524 to 456 BC, included a line in his *Prometheus Bound* on the Hyperborei. The inclusion is of no consequence save it may infer by *"Of daughters born to Boreas:"* that there were priestesses among the Hyperborei. It served to illustrate a poetic bound of the known world. Some authorities doubt that *Prometheus Bound* was a work of Aeschylus on the grounds of style and a lack of complexity.

Edmond Doidge Anderson Morshead, 1849 to 1911, provided the translation from the Greek as given below. The text was made available by Project Gutenberg under "Release Date: August, 2005 [EBook #8714]", Edition 10 on the Internet. It was published under the title *Suppliant Maidens and other Plays.*

Aeschylus: Prometheus Bound [E.D.A.Morshead]
  "Prometheus.
I will not set myself to thwart your will
Withholding aught of what ye crave to know.
First to thee, Io, will I tell and trace
Thy scared circuitous wandering mark it well,
Deep in retentive tablets of the soul.
When thou hast overpast the ferry's flow
That sunders continent from continent,
Straight to the eastward and the flaming face
Of dawn, and highways trodden by the sun,
Pass, till thou come unto the windy land
Of daughters born to Boreas: beware
Lest the strong spirit of the stormy blast
Snatch thee aloft, and sweep thee to the void,
On wings of raving wintry hurricane!
Wend by the noisy tumult of the wave,
Until thou reach the Gorgon-haunted plains
Beside Cisthene. In that solitude
Dwell Phorcys' daughters, beldames worn with time,
Three, each swan-shapen, single-toothed, and all
Peering thro' shared endowment of one eye;
Never on them doth the sun shed his rays,
Never falls radiance of the midnight moon.
But, hard by these, their sisters, clad with wings,
Serpentine-curled, dwell, loathed of mortal men,-
The Gorgons! - he of men who looks on them
Shall gasp away his life. Of such fell guard
I bid thee to beware. Now, mark my words
When I another sight of terror tell -
Beware the Gryphon pack, the hounds of Zeus,
As keen of fang as silent of their tongues!
Beware the one-eyed Arimaspian band
That tramp on horse-hoofs, dwelling by the ford
Of Pluto and the stream that flows with gold:
Keep thou aloof from these. To the world's end
Thou comest at the last, the dark-faced tribe
That dwell beside the sources of the sun,
Where springs the river, Aethiopian named.
Make thou thy way along his bank, until
Thou come unto the mighty downward slope
Where from the overland of Bybline hills
Nile pours his hallowed earth-refreshing wave.
He by his course shall guide thee to the realm
Named from himself, three-angled, water-girt;
There, Io, at the last, hath Fate ordained,
For thee and for thy race, the charge to found,

Far from thy native shore, a new abode.
Lo, I have said: if aught hereof appear
Hard to thy sense and inarticulate,
Question me o'er again, and soothly learn--
God wot, I have too much of leisure here! "(50.1)

The one eyed Arimaspian band appear to be archers who spend all their time in the saddle, while Phorcys' daughters can be thought of as living well within the Arctic Circle, having little daylight in the winter months. Hence, the Hyperborei need not have lived as far north as the Arctic Circle.

The lines describing the annual Nile flood could indicate that the Nile 'delta' had but three outlets in the fifth century BC or that it was then known to once have had but three outlets in the mists of time.

Aeschylus, or Aeschylos, was a playwright not an explorer. He reflected back to his audience the myths familiar in their age. He is not understood to have had any special insight into the geography of outlying regions.

A7.4 HERODOTUS

Aristeas was alive at some time between 900 BC and 580 BC. Aristeas was both a poet and an explorer. No doubts have been encountered as to the existence of a poem that was attributed to him.

Herodotus, circa 484 BC to 408 BC, knew that he himself had little knowledge of North Western Europe.

The full implication of what was signified by use of the term Griffins as guardians of northern gold is not obvious, see Herodotus 3.116 and 4.27. *"A Griffin was an imaginary animal with a lion's body and an eagle's beak and wings; a newcomer in the East, a greenhorn (Anglo-Indian); a pony never before entered for a race; a grimly or fiercely watchful guardian,"* (Chambers). It may be as simple as that the cluster of stars around the north pole was designated by drawing out a dragon in some star system. Hence, the people who lived under 'the Dragon' were far to the north. In *Georgics 1* Virgil states the northern hemisphere is divided into five zones and that the year is divided into twelve signs of the zodiac. He continues as follows, using Dryden's translation and line numbers.

"Around our pole the spiry Dragon glides,
And, like a winding stream, the Bears divides
The less and greater, who by Fate's decree,
Abhor to dive beneath the northern sea."(Georgics 1, lines 334-337 [Dryden], see 51.1)

In a footnote to Herodotus book 4.33, the translator George Rawlinson expressed his opinion on the Hyperboreans. *"Very elaborate accounts have been given of the Hyperboreans both in ancient and modern times. They are, however, in reality not an historical, but an ideal nation. The North Wind being given a local seat in certain mountains called Rhipaean (from ριπη, "a blast"), it was supposed there must be a country above the north wind, which would not be cold, and which would have inhabitants. Ideal perfections were gradually ascribed to this region."(7.8)*

Leonard Schmitz, Ph.D., late of the University of Bonn, wrote the section in *Smiths Dictionary* (46) as follows. *"Aristeas (Αριστεασ), of Proconnesus, a son of Caystrobius or Demochares, was an epic poet, who flourished, according to Suidas, about the time of Croesus and Cyrus. The accounts of his life are as fabulous as those about Abaris the Hyperborean. According to a tradition, which Herodotus (iv.15) heard at Metapontum, in southern Italy, he re-appeared there among the living 340 years after his death, and according to this tradition Aristeas would belong to the eighth or ninth century before the Christian era; and there are other traditions which place him before the time of Homer, or describe him as a contemporary and teacher of Homer. (Strab. xiv.p. 639.) In the account of Herodotus (iv. 13 – 16), Tzetzes (Chil. ii. 724, &c.) and Suidas (s.v.), Aristeas was a magician, who rose after his death, and whose soul could leave and re-enter his body according to its pleasure. He was, like Abaris, connected with the worship of Apollo, which he was said to have introduced at Metapontum. Herodotus calls him the favourite and inspired bard of Apollo (Φοιβολαμπτοσ). He is said to have travelled through the countries north and east of the Euxine, and to have visited the countries of the Issedones, Arimaspae, Cimmerii, Hyperborei, and other mythical nations, and after his return to have written an epic poem, in three books, called τα Αριμασπεια, in which he seems to have described all that he had seen or pretended to have seen. This work, which was unquestionably full of marvellous stories, was nevertheless looked upon as a source of historical and geographical information, and some writers reckoned Aristeas among the logographers. But it was nevertheless a poetical production, and Strabo (i.p. 21, xiii.p. 589) seems to judge too harshly of him, when he calls him an ανηρ γοησ γοησ ει τισ αλλοσ. The poem "Arimaspeia" is frequently mentioned by the ancients (Paus. i. 24. para 6, v. 7. para 9; Pollux, ix. 5; Gallius, ix. 4; Plin. H. N. vii. 2), and thirteen hexameter verses of it are preserved in Longinus (De Sublim. x. 4) and Tzetzes (Chil.vii. 686, &c.). The existence of the poem is thus attested beyond all doubt; but the ancients themselves denied to Aristeas the authorship of it. (Dionys. Hal. Jud. de Thucy. 23.) It seems to have fallen into oblivion at an early period. Suidas also mentions a theogony of Aristeas, in prose, of which, however, nothing is known. (Vossius, De Hist. Graec. p. 10, &c. ed. Westermann; Bode, Gesch. der Episch. Dichtk. pp. 472 – 478.) [L.S.]"* (Smiths, 46)

Herodotus: book 3, chapters 115 to 116 [Rawlinson]
"115. Now these are the furthest regions of the world in Asia and Libya. Of the extreme tracts of Europe towards the west I cannot speak with any certainty; for I do not allow that there is any river, to which the barbarians give the name of Eridanus, emptying itself into the northern sea, whence (as the tale goes) amber is procured; nor do I know of any islands called the Cassiterides (Tin Islands), whence the tin comes which we use. For in the first place the name Eridanus is manifestly not a barbarian word at all, but a Greek name, invented by some poet or other; and secondly, though I have taken vast pains, I have never been able to get an assurance from an eye-witness that there is any sea on the furthest side of Europe. Nevertheless, tin and amber do certainly come to us from the ends of the earth.

[Footnote. Here Herodotus is over-cautious, and rejects as fable what we can see to be truth. The amber district upon the northern sea is the coast of the Baltic about the Gulf of Dantzic [sic], and the mouths of the Vistula and Niemen, which is still one of the best amber regions in the world. The very name, Eridanus, lingers there in the Rhodaune, the small stream which washes the west side of the town of Dantzig. The word Eridanus (=Rhodanus) seems to have been applied, by the early inhabitants of Europe, especially to great and strong-running rivers.]

116. The northern parts of Europe are very much richer in gold than any other region; but how it is procured I have no certain knowledge. The story runs, that the one-eyed Arimaspi purloin it from the griffins; but here too I am incredulous, and cannot persuade myself that there is a race of men born with one eye, who in all else resemble the rest of mankind. Nevertheless it seems to be true that the extreme regions of the earth, which surround and shut up within themselves all other countries, produce the things which are the rarest, and which men reckon the most beautiful."(7.7)

Herodotus: book 4, chapters 12 to 36 [Rawlinson]
"12. Scythia still retains traces of the Cimmerians; there are Cimmerian castles, and a Cimmerian ferry, also a tract called Cimmeria, and a Cimmerian Bosphorus. It appears likewise that the Cimmerians, when they fled into Asia to escape the Scyths, made a settlement in the peninsula where the Greek city of Sinope was afterwards built. The Scyths, it is plain, pursued them, and missing their road, poured into Media. For the Cimmerians kept the line which led along the sea-shore, but the Scyths in their pursuit held the Caucasus upon their right, thus proceeding inland and falling upon Media. This account is one which is common both to the Greeks and barbarians.

13. Aristeas also, son of Caystrobius, a native of Proconnesus,

[Footnote. Proconnesus is the island now called Marmora, which gives its modern appellation to the Propontis (Sea of Marmara).]

says in the course of his poem that rapt in Bacchic fury he went as far as the Issedones. Above them dwelt the Arimaspi, men with one eye; still further, the gold-guarding Griffins; and beyond these, the Hyperboreans, who extended to the sea. Except the Hyperboreans, all these nations, beginning with the Arimaspi, were continually encroaching upon their neighbours. Hence it came to pass that the Arimaspi drove the Issedonians from their country, while the Issedonians dispossessed the Scyths; and the Scyths, pressing upon the Cimmerians, who dwell on the shores of the Southern Sea, forced them to leave their land. Thus even Aristeas does not agree in his account of this region with the Scythians.

14. . . . .
15. . . . .

[Footnote. This date must certainly be wrong. The date usually assigned to Aristeas is about B.C. 580.]

[Compiler. The chapters 13, 14, 15 are identified in a footnote as "Later addition" by J.Enoch Powell in his translation published by the Clarendon Press in 1949.]

16. With regard to the regions which lie above the country whereof this portion of my history treats, there is no one who possesses any exact knowledge. Not a single person can I find who professes to be acquainted with them by actual observation. Even Aristeas, the traveller of whom I lately spoke, does not claim – and he is writing poetry – to have reached any farther than the Issedonians.

What he relates concerning the regions beyond is, he confesses, mere hearsay, being the account which the Issedonians gave him of those countries. . . . .

17. . . .

27. The regions beyond are known only from the accounts of the Issedonians, by whom the stories are told of the one-eyed race of men and the gold-guarding griffins. These stories are received by the Scythians from the Issedonians, and by them passed on to us Greeks: whence it arises that we give the one-eyed race the Scythian name of Arimaspi. "arima" being the Scythic word for"one", and "spu" for "the eye."

28. . . .

32. Of the Hyperboreans nothing is said either by the Scythians or by any of the other dwellers in these regions, unless it be the Issedonians. But in my opinion, even the Issedonians are silent concerning them; otherwise the Scythians would have repeated their statements, as they do those concerning the one-eyed men. Hesiod, however, mentions them, and Homer also in the Epigoni, if that be really a work of his.

33. But the persons who have by far the most to say on this subject are the Delians. They declare that certain offerings, packed in wheaten straw, were brought from the country of the Hyperboreans into Scythia, and that the Scythians received them and passed them on to their neighbours upon the west, who continued to pass them on until at last they reached the Adriatic. From hence they were sent southward, and when they came to Greece, were received first of all by the Dodonaeans. Thence they descended to the Maliac Gulf, from which they were carried across into Euboea, where the people handed them on from city to city, till they came at length to Carystus. The Carystians took them over to Tenos, without stopping at Andros; and the Tenians brought them finally to Delos. Such according to their own account, was the road by which the offerings reached the Delians. Two damsels, they say, named Hyperoche and Laodice, brought the first offerings from the Hyperboreans; and with them the Hyperboreans sent five men, to keep them from all harm by the way; these are the persons whom the Delians call "Perpherees," and to whom great honour are paid at Delos. Afterwards, the Hyperboreans, when they found that their messengers did not return, thinking it would be a grievous thing always to be liable to lose the envoys they should send, adopted the following plan: - they wrapped their offerings in wheaten straw, and bearing them to their borders, charged their neighbours to send them forward from one nation to another, which was done accordingly, and in this way the offerings reached Delos. I myself know of a practice like this, which obtains with the women of Thrace and Paeonia. They in their sacrifices to the queenly Diana bring wheaten straw always with their offerings. Of my own knowledge I can testify that this is so.

34. The damsels sent by the Hyperboreans died in Delos; and in their honour all the Delian girls and youths are wont to cut off their hair. The girls, before their marriage-day, cut off a curl, and twining it round a distaff, lay it upon the grave of the strangers. This grave is on the left as one enters the precinct of Diana, and has an olive-tree growing on it. The youths wind some of their hair round a kind of grass, and, like the girls, place it upon the tomb. Such are the honours paid to these damsels by the Delians.

35. They add that, once before, there came to Delos by the same road as Hyperoche and Laodice, two other virgins from the Hyperboreans, whose names were Arge and Opis. Hyperoche and Laodice came to bring to Ilithyia the offering which they had laid upon themselves, in acknowledgement of their quick labours; but Arge and Opis came at the same time as the gods of Delos,

[Footnote. Apollo and Diana.]
and are honoured by the Delians in a different way. For the Delian women make
collections in these maidens' names, and invoke them in the hymn which Olen, a Lycian,
composed for them; and the rest of the islanders, and even the Ionians, have been taught
by the Delians to do the like. This Olen, who came from Lycia, made the other old hymns
also which are sung in Delos. The Delians add, that the ashes from the thigh-bones burnt
upon the altar are scattered over the tomb of Opis and Arge. The tomb lies behind the
temple of Diana, facing the east, near the banqueting-hall of the Ceians. Thus much then,
and no more, concerning the Hyperboreans.
36. As for the tale of Abaris, who is said to have been a Hyperborean, and to have gone
with his arrow all round the world without once eating, I shall pass it by in silence. Thus
much, however, is clear: if there are Hyperboreans, there must also be Hypernotians. For
my part, I cannot but laugh when I see numbers of persons drawing maps of the world
without having any reason to guide them; making, as they do, the ocean-stream to run all
round the earth, and the earth itself to be an exact circle, as if described by a pair of
compasses, with Europe and Asia just of the same size. The truth in this matter I will now
proceed to explain in a very few words, making it clear what the real size of each region is,
and what shape should be given them."(7.8)

The entry under *Hyperoche* in Smith's dictionary shows the reference in Herodotus
and no other source.
" *Hyperoche. According to the Delian tradition, was one of the two maidens who were*
sent by the Hyperboreans to Delos, to convey thither certain sacred offerings, enclosed in
stalks of wheat. She and her companion having died in Delos, were honoured by the
Delians with certain ceremonies, described by Herodotus (iv. 33 – 35)." (Smiths, 46)

A7.5 CALLIMARCHUS.

Between 260 BC and 240 BC Callimarchus was chief librarian of the library at
Alexandria under the patronage of Ptolemy Philadelphus (13).
His thread connecting the Hyperboreans with the Island of Delos adds little to that
given by Herodotus in book 4.33. Indeed, his lines would prove a puzzle if the
explanation given by Herodotus was lacking.

Callimachus: Hymn to Delos, lines 452 – 474 [Banks, poetry of Tytler]
"But tithes and first-fruits each revolving year,
From distant climes shall on thy shores appear,
And every state beneath the morning ray,
The star of evening, or meridian day,
Shall join the mystic dance; ev'n those renown'd
For length of days shall tread the hallow'd ground
From Hyperborean shores; by whom are borne
The first ripe ears and sheaves of yellow corn.
And the Pelasgi, from Dodona's shores,
Shall first receive the consecrated stores;
The race, that nightly rest along the ground,
Attentive to the caldron's mystic sound;
Consign'd by them the grateful off'rings fill

The Melian city and the sacred hill:
From whence they pass to fair Lilantia's land,
And from Euboea reach thy neighbouring strand.
But Upis bright, and Hercaerge kind,
And Loxo, daughters of the northern wind,
With pious hands the first ripe off'rings bore
To Delos' isle, from th'Arimaspian shore
Fair youths attending, that return'd no more,
But here were bless'd; and hence each hallow'd name
Shall ever flourish in immortal fame."(13.2)

A7.6 DIODORUS

Diodorus of Sicily was alive in 44 BC. A calendar system linked to a nineteen year cycle was reported by Diodorus as that used by some Hyperborians. In this passage he does not name Britain as the relevant island. Other passages in his *History* show that he was familiar with its name and broad locality. In this instance perhaps Diodorus closely followed his source documents.

Diodorus: Histories book 2, chapter 3 [Booth]

"Now, since we have thus far spoken of the northern parts of Asia, it is convenient to observe something relating to the antiquity of the Hyperboreans.

Amongst them that have written old stories much like fables, Hecateus and some others say, that there is an island in the ocean over against Gaul, (as big as Sicily) under the arctic pole, where the Hyperboreans inhabit; so called, because they lie beyond the breezes of the north wind. That the soil here is very rich, and very fruitful; and the climate temperate, insomuch as there are two crops in the year.

They say that Latona was born here, and therefore, that they worship Apollo above all other gods; and because they are daily singing songs in praise of this god, and ascribing to him the highest honours, they say that the inhabitants demean themselves, as if they were Apollo's priests, who has there a stately grove and renowned temple, of round form, beautified with many rich gifts. That there is a city likewise consecrated to this god, whose citizens are most of them harpers, who, playing on the harp, chant sacred hymns to Apollo in the temple, setting forth his glorious acts. The Hyperboreans use their own natural language; but of long and antient [sic] time have had a special kindness for the Grecians, and more especially for the Athenians and them of Delos. And that some of the Grecians passed over to the Hyperboreans, and left behind them divers presents, inscribed with Greek characters; and that Abaris formerly travelled thence into Greece, and renewed the antient league of friendship with the Delians.

They say, moreover, that the moon in this island seems as if it were near to the earth, and represents in the face of it excrescences like the spots in the earth. And that Apollo once in nineteen years comes into the island; in which space of time the stars perform their courses, and return to the same point; and therefore the Greeks call the revolution of nineteen years the Great Year. At this time of his appearance (they say) that he plays upon the harp, and sings and dances all the night, from the vernal equinox to the rising of the Pleiades, solacing himself with the praises of his own successful adventures. The sovereignty of this city, and the care of the temple (they say) belongs to the Boreades, the posterity of Boreas, who hold the principality by descent in a direct line from that ancestor."(11.5)

In Roman mythology Latona was the mother of Apollo and Diana. In Greek mythology Lato (or Leto) was a daughter of the titan Coeus and Phoebe, her father was Saturn according to Homer. Zeus was the father of Lato's twins Apollo and Artemis. The Greek Artemis and Zeus equate with the Roman Diana and Jupiter (4).

Hecataeus of Abdera, a contemporary of Alexander the Great, was the historian whose works had been perused by Diodorus (46). The nub of the data is that a temple existed where the priesthood assiduously kept note of the elapsed lunar months and solar years. A nineteen year period had been determined after which the relationships between the cycles of the moon and sun repeated themselves. The source data used by Diodorus in the first century BC had been written down by Hecataeus between about 315 and 250 BC. Either Britain or Ireland was in all reason the *island in the ocean over against Gaul, (as big as Sicily) under the arctic pole.*

A7.7 CICERO

Marcus Tullius Cicero, 106 BC to 43 BC. The translation from the Latin given below is that by C.D.Yonge, published by Harper and Brothers in 1877 and made available by Project Gutenberg under "Release Date: February 9, 2005 [EBook #1488]" on the Internet. It was published under the title *Tusculan Disputations, also Treatises on The Nature of the Gods, and on the Commonwealth.* Whether or not the American President Benjamin Franklin actually translated this section or not, the possibility is noted for completeness.

In this late work of Cicero, Apollo, son of Latona, went to Delphi. The Hyperboreans who visited the island of Delos worshipped this same Apollo, e.g. see Diodorus above.

Cicero: Nature of the Gods, book 3.23 [C.D.Yonge, perhaps Benjamin Franklin?]
"XXIII. I have already spoken of the most ancient of the Apollos, who is the son of Vulcan, and tutelar God of Athens. There is another, son of Corybas, a native of Crete, for which island he is said to have contended with Jupiter himself. A third who came from the regions of the Hyperborei to Delphi, is the son of the third Jupiter and of Latona. A fourth was of Arcadia whom the Arcadians called Nomio, because they regarded him as their legislator. There are likewise many Dianas."(52.1)

A7.8 VIRGIL

Virgil 70 BC – 19 BC. Publius Virgilus Maro was born 15 October, 70 BC at Andes near Mantua. He flirted with an Epicurian view on life and settled down with a Platonic philosophy. He achieved renown in his own lifetime and was well thought of by Augustus, later to become the first emperor of Rome. The poet Horace was an acquaintance of Virgil. Virgil died 22 September, 19 BC at Brundusium and was buried at Naples.(51) His lifetime included the changeover to the Julian calendar.

By the lifetime of Virgil, Roman armies and Roman merchants had gained a superficial working knowledge that covered much of Europe. Terra totally incognita had shrunk to its northern periphery. Myths had lost their edge.

Lines from *Georgics book 1* identify the *Dragon* as being among the first rising constellations in summer months and that the constellation, so called, circles the north pole. The Roman constellations are set out by Cicero in book 2 of his *Nature of the Gods*, but not included herein.

In this section Virgil sets out that the earth is divided into five climatic zones from the hot torrid zone to the icy northern zone, has two poles, four seasons and the year is divided into twelve parts as the sun moves from one sign of the zodiac to another to complete a circuit of all twelve in a year. Clearly the approximate 'month' attributed to the constellation of *Astaea* embraces the time of the autumn equinox.

The lines 335 to 337 say nothing more than the pole star is visible the whole year long in the northern hemisphere.

> *Virgil: Georgic book 1, verses 295 – 301 and 330 - 339 [Dryden]*
> *"When the Kids, Dragon, and Arturus, rise,*   295
> *Than sailors homeward bent, who cut their way*
> *Through Helle's stormy straits, and oyster breading sea.*
> *But when Astaea's Balance hung on high,*
> *Betwixt the nights and days divides the sky,*
> *Then yoke your oxen, sow your winter grain,*
> *Till cold December comes with driving rain.*   301
> *. . .*
> *Two poles turn round the globe; one seen to rise*   330
> *O'er Scythian hills, and one in Libyan skies;*
> *The first sublime in heaven, the last is whirled*
> *Below the regions of the nether world.*
>   *Around our pole the spiry Dragon glides,*
> *And, like a winding stream, the Bears divides -*   335
> *The less and greater, who by Fate's decree,*
> *Abhor to dive beneath the northern sea.*
> *There, as they say, perpetual night is found*
> *In silence brooding on the unhappy ground:"*(51.1)

Semi domesticated herds of reindeer, pole-axed at the point of slaughter could form the basis of this description by Virgil.

> *Virgil: Georgic book 3, verses 569 - 589 [Dryden]*
> *". . . Of mighty stags, and scarce their horns appear.*
> *The dextrous huntsman wounds not these afar*   570
> *With shafts or darts, or makes a distant war*
> *With dogs, or pitches toils to stop their flight,*
> *But close engages in unequal fight;*
> *And while they strive in vain to make their way*
> *Through hills of snow, and pitifully bray,*
> *Assaults with dint of sword, or pointed spears,*
> *And homeward, on his back, the joyful burden bears*
> *The men to subterranean caves retire,*
> *Secure from cold, and crowd the cheerful fire;*
> *With trunks of elms and oaks the hearth they load,*
> *Nor tempt the inclemency of heaven abroad,*
> *Their jovial nights in frolics and in play*
> *They pass, to drive the tedious hours away,*

And their cold stomachs with crowned goblets cheer
Of windy cider, and of barmy [sic] beer,   585
Such are the cold Rhipaean race, and such
The savage Scythian, and unwarlike Dutch,
Where skins of beasts the rude barbarians wear,
The spoils of foxes, and the furry bear."(51.2)

Dryden chose the word Dutch where others have preferred less specific poetic licence or differed in their translations out of the Latin. The line numbers used by the poet John Dryden in his translation may differ from those in other translations.

A7.9 PLINY

Pliny the Elder, 23 AD to 79 AD, summarises the data available to him in the works of other authors concerning the Hyperborei. *"Behind these mountains, and beyond the region of the northern winds, there dwells, if we choose to believe it, a happy race, known as the Hyperborei, ..."*

Pliny: Natural History book 4, chapters 25 to 34 [Bostock and Riley]
"Chapter 26. - Scythia.   [page 336, 337, 338]
. . . Above them are the Nomades, and then a nation of Anthropophagi or cannibals. On leaving Lake Buges, above the Lake Maeotis we come to the Sauromatae and the Essedones. Along the coast, as far as the river Tanais, are the Maeotae, from whom the lake derives its name, and the last of all, in the rear of them, the Arimaspi. We then come to the Riphaean mountains and the region known by the name of Pterophoros, because of the perpetual fall of snow there, the flakes of which resemble feathers; a part of the world which has been condemned by the decree of nature to lie immersed in thick darkness; suited for nothing but the generation of cold, and to be the asylum of the chilling blasts of the northern winds.
Behind these mountains, and beyond the region of the northern winds, there dwells, if we choose to believe it, a happy race, known as the Hyperborei,"
[Footnote. This legendary race was said to dwell in the regions beyond Boreas, or the northern wind, which issued from the Riphaean mountains, the name of which was derived from ριπαλ or "hurricane" issuing from a cavern, and which these heights warded off from the Hyperboreans and sent to more southern nations. Hence they never felt the northern blasts, and enjoyed a life of supreme happiness and undisturbed repose. . . .]
"a race that lives to an extreme old age, and which has been the subject of many marvellous stories.
[Footnote. Pindar says, in the "Pythia," x.56, "The Muse is no stranger to their manners. The dances of girls and the sweet melody of the lyre and pipe resound on every side, and wreathing their locks with the glistening hay, they feast joyously. For this sacred race there is no doom of sickness or of disease; but they live apart from toil and battles, undisturbed by the exacting Nemesis."]
"At this spot are supposed to be the hinges upon which the world resolves, and the extreme limits of the revolutions of the stars. Here we find light for six months together, given by the sun in one continuous day, who does not, however, as some ignorant persons have asserted, conceal himself from the vernal equinox"

[Footnote. Hardouin remarks that Pomponius Mela, who asserts that the sun rises here at the vernal and sets at the autumnal equinox, is right in his position, and that Pliny is incorrect in his assertion. The same commentator thinks that Pliny can have hardly intended to censure Mela, to whose learning he had been so much indebted for his geographical information, by applying to him the epithet "imperitus", 'ignorant' or 'unskilled'; he therefore suggests that the proper reading here is, "ut non imperiti dixere," "as some by no means ignorant persons have asserted."]

"to autumn. On the contrary, to these people there is but one rising of the sun for the year, and that at the summer solstice, and but one setting, at the winter solstice. This region, warmed by the rays of the sun, is of a most delightful temperature, and exempt from every noxious blast. The abodes of the natives are the woods and groves; the gods receive their worship singly and in groups, while all discord and every kind of sickness are things utterly unknown. Death comes upon them only when satiated with life; after a career of feasting, in an old age sated with every luxury, they leap from a certain rock there into the sea; and this they deem the most desirable mode of ending existence. Some writers have placed these people, not in Europe, but at the very verge of the shores of Asia, because we find there a people called the Attacori, "

[Footnote. The Attacori are also mentioned in B.vi.c.20.]

"who greatly resemble them and occupy a very similar locality. Other writers again have placed them midway between the two suns, at the spot where it sets to the Antipodes and rises to us; a thing however that cannot possibly be, in consequence of the vast tract of sea which there intervenes. Those writers who place them nowhere "

[Footnote. Sillig omits the word "non" here, in which case the reading would be, "Those writers who place them anywhere but, &c.;" it is difficult to see with what meaning.]

"but under a day which lasts for six months, state that in the morning they sow, at mid-day they reap, at sunset they gather in the fruits of the trees, and during the night conceal themselves in caves. Nor are we at liberty to entertain any doubt as to the existence of this race; so many authors "

[Footnote. Herodotus, B.iv., states to this effect, and after him, Pomponius Mela, B.iii.c.5.]

"are there who assert that they were in the habit of sending their first-fruits to Delos to present them to Apollo, whom in especial they worship. Virgins used to carry them, who for many years were held in high veneration, and received the rites of hospitality from the nations that lay on the route; until at last, in consequence of repeated violations of good faith, the Hyperboreans came to the determination to deposit these offerings upon the frontiers of the people who adjoined them, and they in turn were to convey them onto their neighbours, and so from one to the other, till they should have arrived at Delos. However, this custom, even, in time fell into disuse.

The length of Sarmatia, Scythia, and Taurica, and of the whole of the region which extends from the river Borysthenes, is, according to Agrippa, 980 miles, and its breadth 717. I am of the opinion, however, that in this part of the earth all estimates of measurement are exceedingly doubtful."(17.1 part)

It is customary to interpret 'the Seres' as a people of China. In this chapter Pliny informs us that Hecataeus wrote a treatise on the Hyperborei. Hecataeus of Abdera was the source used by Diodorus for his information on the Hyperborians who lived in "an island in the ocean over against Gaul."

Pliny: Natural History book 6, chapters 20 [Bostock and Riley]
"Chapter 20. – The Seres.
. . . The Seres are of inoffensive manners, but, bearing a strong resemblance therein to all savage nations, they shun all intercourse with the rest of mankind, and await the approach of those who wish to traffic with them. The first river that is known in their territory is the Psitharas, "
[Footnote. Ptolemy speaks of it as the Oeshordas.]
"next to that the Cambari, and the third the Laros: after which we come to the promontory of Chryse, the Gulf of Cynaba, the river Atianos, and the nation of the Attacori on the gulf of that name, a people protected by their sunny hills from all noxious blasts, and living in a climate of the same temperature as that of the Hyperborei. Amometus has written a work entirely devoted to the history of these people, just as Hecataeus has done in his treatise on the Hyperborei. After the Attacori, we find the nations of the Phruri and the Tochari, and in the interior, the Casiri, a people of India, who look towards the Scythians, . . . "(17.15)

A7.10 LONGINUS

Longinus, a Greek philosopher, died at the hands of the Romans in AD 273, at Palmyra in the reign of the emperor Aurelian (4). Commentators have observed that the latest author quoted in the text of *On the Sublime* was Cicero, who died in 43 BC. This suggests that the work was written before the end of the first century AD. Both the third century Longinus and the earlier Dionysius of Halicarnassus are each discounted as the author of the work. At the present day, *On the Sublime* continues to be identified as the work of a 'Longinus' for convenience of reference.

There are thirteen hexameter verses preserved in his treatise *On the Sublime* that were taken from the poem *"Arimaspeia"* written by Aristeas. They are reproduced both for completeness and to satisfy any lingering curiosity as to content. They contain nothing of the Hyperborei. This inclusion by Longinus is a demonstration that the work of Aristeas did indeed exist and moreover that it was available to read in some form in the first or third century.

The Latin translation of the Greek is taken from *Dionysii Longini, Greek and Latin, De Sublimate*, written by Jonathan Toup and David Ruhnkenius and published by The Clarendon Press, Oxford in 1778.

Longinus: On the Sublime, chapter 10 [Toup]
"Quo more, opinor, et in tempestatibus describendis ille poeta, sc. Homerus, excerpit maximime terriles circumstantias: Ille enim, qui fecit poema dictum Arimaspia, haec censet grandia esse,
Admirationi nobis hoc magnae fuit, et animis nostris.
Homines aquam incolunt procul a terra in mari:
Iufelix genus sunt hominum; subeunt enim labores improbos:
Oculos in astris fixos, animam vero in ponte habent.
Sanc[c or e] multum Diis suas manus tendentes
Precantur visceribus turpiter rejectis."(53.1)

The translation of the above is taken from *Dionysius Longinus on the Sublime*, translated into English from the Greek by William Smith, 3rd edition, printed for B.Dod at the Bible and Key in Ave Mary Lane near Stationers Hall in 1752. The first edition had been published in 1739.

It is noted that other publications of a similar period refer to Ave Maria Lane and not Ave Mary Lane.

Longinus: On the Sublime, chapter 10 [Wm.Smith, Alexander Pope poetry]
"And it proceeds from his due application of the most formidable incidents, that the Poet excels so much in describing tempests. The author of the poem on the Armaspians doubts not but these lines are great and full of terror.
  Ye pow'rs, what madness ! How on ships so frail
  (Tremendous thought !) can thoughtless mortals fail ?
  For stormy seas they quit the pleasing plain,
  Plant woods in waves, and dwell amidst the main.
  Far o'er the deep (a trackless path) they go,
  And wander oceans in pursuit of woe.
  No ease their hearts, no rest their eyes can find,
  On heav'n their looks, and on the waves their mind;
  Sunk are their spirits, while their arms they rear,
  And gods are wearied with their fruitful pray'r.
                    Mr.Pope."(54.1)

For the purpose of comparison, a translation by H.L Havell, died 1913, made available by Project Gutenberg under "Release Date: March 10, 2006 [EBook #17957]" on the Internet, is as follows.

Longinus: On the Sublime, chapter 10.4 [H.L.Havell, commentator Andrew Lang]
"The poet of the "Arimaspeia" intended the following lines to be grand.
  "Herein I find a wonder passing strange,
  That men should make their dwelling on the deep,
  Who far from land essaying bold to range
  With anxious heart their toilsome vigils keep;
  Their eyes are fixed on heaven's starry steep;
  The ravening billows hunger for their lives;
  And oft each shivering wretch, constrained to weep,
  With suppliant hands to move heaven's pity strikes,
  While many a direful qualm his vitals rives."

All must see that there is more of ornament than of terror in the description. Now let us turn to Homer."(55.1)

ACKNOWLEDGEMENTS

I wish to acknowledge the work of Sally Siddons in bringing this volume to publication.

The range of information made available in the Everyman's Library published by J.M.Dent and Sons was a valuable source of reference data. Great reliance has been placed upon the publications in the Bohn Library series that was begun by H.G.Bohn in 1847 and taken over by G.Bell and Sons in 1864.

The facility to examine books in the public domain at the Project Gutenberg site on the internet at www.gutenberg.org proved useful in checking source data.

The Google Book Search facility at www.books.google.com was a convenient tool with which to seek out information.

It is believed that the substantial quotations reproduced in this volume arise from translations where the copyright has lapsed, but if there are any omissions in tracing the owners of material that might be copyright then please accept this as an oversight.

V. S. White.
Wheathampstead, Candlemas, 2009.

LIST OF REFERENCES

References

References

7 Herodotus : The Histories of Herodotus
translated by George Rawlinson (1858).
Everyman's Library (1910)
J.M.Dent and Sons Ltd.

7.1	Book 4, chapters 93 to 96. Getae, soul immortal.	42, 146
7.2	Book 2, chapter 33. Celts border on Cynesians.	43
7.3	Book 4, chapters 6 to 11, pages 289 to 291. Scythian origin.	73
7.4	Book 4, chapters 100 to 119, pages 327 to 333. Agathyrsi, Budini.	158
7.5	Book 1, chapter 32, pages 15, 16. Calendar year, man's span 70 years.	176
7.6	Book 2, chapter 4, pages 111, 112. Egyptian 365 day year.	177
7.7	Book 3, chapters 115, 116. Uncertain of origin, northern tin and amber.	Ap.7
7.8	Book 4, chapters 12 to 36, pages 292 to 301. Hyperboreans.	Ap.7

8 Xenophon : The Works of Xenophon
translated by H.G.Dakyns in 4 volumes.
Volume 2 Hellenica, books 3 to 7, Agesilaus, The Polities, And Revenues.
Macmillan and Co., London. (1892).

8.1	Book 7, chapter 1.19 to 1.22, pages 191, 192. 369 BC. Celts fight for Greeks against 2nd Theban Invasion.	43
8.2	Book 7, chapters 1.27 to 1.32. 368 or 367 BC. Celts fight for Greeks.	43

9 Thucydides : The History of the Peloponnesian War
translated by The Rev. Henry Dale.
Bohn's Classical Library
George Bell and Sons. Covent Garden, London (1888).

9.1	Vol 2. Book 6.1 to 6.2, pages 377, 378. Iberians in Sicily.	45
9.2	Vol 2. Book 6.90, page 437. Greeks intent to hire Iberians c.415 BC.	45

10 Polybius : The Histories
translated by W.R.Paton (1921).
Loeb Classical Library
William Heinemann Ltd (1923).

10.1	Vol 1. Book 2, chapters 28, to 33, p. 311 et seq.. Naked warriors, torques.	47, 135
10.2	Vol 3. Book 6, chapters 19 to 41. Roman military system.	117

11 Diodorus of Sicily :
The Historical Library of Diodorus the Sicilian in Fifteen Books
To which are added The Fragments of Diodorus and
Those published by H.Valesius, I.Rhodomannus, and F.Ursinus,   48
translated by G.Booth,Esq .
Printed by W.McDowall, Pemberton Row, Gough Square, Fleet Street
for J.Davis, Military Chronicle Office, Essex Street, Strand;
and to be had of the booksellers.
Volume 1 (1814).
Volume 2 (1814).

11.1	Vol 1. Book 4, chapter 3. pages 267, 268. Celts worship Castor and Pollox.	48
11.2	Vol 1. Book 5, chapter 2, pages 308 to 312. Britain	50, 51
11.3	Vol 1. Book 5, chapter 2, pages 313 to 319. Gauls, Celts.	55
11.4	Vol 2. Book 22, page 515. Brennus invades Greece, c.279 BC.	56
11.5	Vol 1. Book 2, chapter 3, pages 138, 139. 19 year cycle, henge?	184, Ap.7

12 Diodorus of Sicily : Diodori Siculi
ex nova recensione Ludovici Dindorfii Graece et Latine
rerum indicem locupletissimum adjecit Carolus Mullerus.
Parisiis Editore Ambrosio Firmin Didot. (1855)

12.1	Vol.2 Book 22, pages 427, 428. Brennus laughs in temple.	56

References

16 Lucan : The Civil War books 1 to 10
translated by Sir Edward Ridley (1896).
Project Gutenberg. – www.gutenberg.org - September 14, 2006.
Pharsalia: Dramatic Episodes of the Civil Wars by Lucan.
E.Text-No. 602. Release Date 1996-07-01.

16.1	Book 1, about lines 445 to 470. Druids.	74
16.2	Book 3 , about lines 462 to 489. Glades of Druids?	75

17 Pliny : The Natural History of Pliny
translated by John Bostock and H.T.Riley.
Bohn's Classical Library (6 volumes)
Volume 1 Henry G.Bohn, Covent Garden. London. (1855)
Volume 3 George Bell & Sons. London. (1904 edition)

17.1	Vol 1. Book 4, ch. 25 to 34, p329 et seq. 5 German races, Gaul.	82, 188, Ap.7
17.2	Vol 3. Book 16, chapter 95, pages 435, 436. Mistletoe and Druids.	82, 182
17.3	Vol 2. Book 7, chapter 57, page 255. Cyclops iron.	83
17.4	Vol 2. Book 7, chapter 57, page 233. British Ocean coracles.	84
17.5	Vol 2. Book 8, chapter 61, page 315. Cross dog and wolf.	84
17.6	Vol 2. Book 8, chapter 73, pages 334, 335. Mattresses.	84
17.7	Vol 2. Book 9, chapter 79, page 468. British oysters.	85
17.8	Vol 2. Book 10, chapter 27, page 499. Goose feather pillows.	85
17.9	Vol 2. Book 10, chapter 5, page 485. 104 BC eagle predominant.	85
17.10	Vol 1. Book 4, chapter 26, page 335. Picts, Agathyrsi.	156
17.11	Vol 1. Book 4, chapter 17, page 299. Scotussaei.	157
17.12	Vol 1. Book 4, chapter 33, page 358. Pictones.	157
17.13	Vol 2. Book 7, chapter 49, page 201. Years among nations.	175
17.14	Vol 1. Book 2, chapter 79, page 110. Days among nations.	175
17.15	Vol 2. Book 6, chapter 20, p.37. Hecataeus on Hyperborei.	Ap.7

18 Voices from the Past, A Classical Anthology,
James & Janet Maclean Todd (1956)
Phoenix House, London.

18.1	Page 409. Mela trans. by A.Golding. On Britain.	88

19 Plutarch's Lives : Volume 2
translated by J.Langhorne and W.Langhorne.
Henry G.Bohn, York Street, Covent Garden, London (1859)

19.1	Caesar pages 766 and 771. Correspondence. Sword.	90
19.2	Caesar pages 760 to 763, 788. Caesar's wife. Shakespeare quotes.	91
19.3	Brutus pages 1029 to 1031. Caesar the father of Brutus.	91
19.4	Caesar page 787. Need for Julian Calendar.	92
19.5	Caesar page 768. Ariovistus, German women prophesy.	92
19.6	Sertorius pages 616, 617. Fawn.	93

20 Plutarch's Lives : Translation called Dryden's. 93, 96
Volume 3
Revised by A.H.Clough.
The Athenaeum Press, London.

20.1	Marius. Pages 57 to 78. Cimbri in 101 BC.	97
20.2	Sylla. Pages 142 and 189.	98

References

References

27 Snorre Sturlason : Heimskringla : The Norse King Sagas   132
      translated by Samuel Laing. (1844).
      Introduction and notes by Rev.John Beveridge.
      Everyman's Library (Volume 847)
      J.M.Dent and Sons, London. (1930).

27.1	The Ynglinga Saga	Chapters 1 to 8. Odin's origins.	136, 145
27.2		Chapter 27. Grave fire ship.	136
27.3		Chapter 29. Sacrifice son.	137
27.4		Chapter 31. Of King Ottar.	137
27.5		Ch. 32. Of King Adil's Marriage. Loot cattle.	137
27.6		Ch. 40. The burning of Upsal. Brage beaker.	138
27.7		Ch. 41. Of Hjorvard's Marriage. Drinking.	138
27.8	Halfdan the Black	Chapter 7.	138
27.9	[839-860]	Chapter 8. Jolner equals Yule.	138
27.10	Harold Fairhaired [860-933]	Ch. 20. Harald the supreme king of Norway. Of the Settlement of Distant Lands.	138
27.11		Ch 21. Of King Harold's Children. Reared by mother's side.	139
27.12		Chapter 22. King Harald's Voyage. Heads hung from horse.	139
27.13	Hakon the Good.	Ch. 15. King Hakon. Christmas, Yule.	139
27.14	[934-961]	Chapter 16. About Sacrifices.	140
27.15		Ch. 17. The Thing at Frosta. Originally burnt dead.	140
27.16		Chapter 18. The Peasants force King Hakon to offer Sacrifices. Horse flesh.	140
27.17		Ch. 19. Feast Sacrifice at More. Horse flesh.	141
27.18		Ch. 27. Egil Uldsaerk's Burial Mound. Ship burial.	141
27.19	Magnus the Good.	Ch 16. Of the Free-Speaking Song and of the Law-Book Grey Goose.	141
27.20	The Sons of Harald.	Chapter 6. The Murder of Bentein [1138]. Lapps Currachs.	142
27.21	Harold the Stern	Ch 59. Footnote. Busse-ship. Page 203.	142
27.22	Hakon the Broad-shouldered.	Chapter 6. Erling's Speech. Page 376. Rooms, 3 men per oar.	142
27.23		Ch 7. Of Hakon's Fleet. Page 377. Battle stations.	143
27.24		Ch. 20. King Olaf's Miracle. Wagon camp.	143

28 Snorre Sturlason : Heimskringla : The Olaf Sagas   181
      translated by Samuel Laing (1844).
      Introduction and notes by John Beveridge.
      Everyman's Library (Volume 717)
      J.M.Dent and Sons, London. (1915).

28.1	Introduction xxvii . Common northern language.	133
28.2	The Olaf Sagas. Laing's Additional Notes page 406. Historic Odin.	146, 154
28.3	The Olaf Sagas. Laing's Additional Notes page 407. 787 AD.	148

29 Northern Antiquities
      translated from the French of M.Mallet by Bishop Percy.
      T.Carnan and Co. at No. 65, in St. Paul's Churchyard, London. (1770).
      Facsimile edition. Garland Publishing Inc., New York and London. (1979).

29.1	Volume 2. Pages 138 to 143. 28th Fable : of Balder. Mistletoe.	144
29.2	Volume 2. Pages 70 to 73. 12th Fable : of the God Balder. Vanheim.	146

References

30 Bede, The Venerable Bede's Ecclesiastical History   151 (2)
  of England and the Anglo Saxon Chronicle.
       Bede translated by John Stevens (1723).
       Edited by J.A.Giles (1840). Bohn's Antiquarian Library
       George Bell & Sons. York St. London (1892).
  30.1   Bede. Book I, chapter 1, pages 5, 6. Eng., Brits., Scots, Picts, Latins.   163

31 Bede, The Venerable Bede's Ecclesiastical History of England   155
  and the Anglo Saxon Chronicle.
       Anglo Saxon Chronicle
       translated by Miss Gurney (1812) and Mr. Petrie.
       Edited by J.A.Giles (1840). Bohn's Antiquarian Library.
       George Bell & Sons. York St. London (1892).
  31.1   Anglo Saxon Chron. 409 AD to 565 AD. Pages 308 to 313.   154

32 Beyond the Highland Line, Caroline Bingham (1991).
       Constable and Company Ltd.
  32.1   Page 32. Orca, Boar folk.   160
  32.2   Page 41. Boar incised on stone at Dunadd in Argyll shire.   160
  32.3   Page 41. Dal Riata Riata's portion.   164
  32.4   Page 39. 2 figures of Picts.   165

33 The Religion of the Ancient Celts, J.A.MacCulloch (1911).
       T.&G.Clarke, Edinburgh.
  33.1   Page 17. Picts called Cruithne by Irish Goidals.   162

34 Bede in Latin : Venerabilis Baedae
       edited by Carolus Plummer.
       Clarendon Press, Oxford (1896).
  34.1   Gentis Anglorum, page 11.   163

35 The Work of Angels : Masterpieces of Celtic Metalwork, 6th - 9th Centuries AD.
       edited by Susan Youngs.
       British Museum Publications for
       Brit. Mus., Nat. Mus. Ireland, Nat. Mus. Scotland (1989).   165

36 Northern Antiquities
       translated from the French of M.Mallet by Bishop Percy.   181
       New Edition by L.A.Blackwell to which is added an abstract of the
       Eyrbyggja Saga by Sir Walter Scott.
       London. Henry G. Bohn, York Street, Covent Garden. (1847).
  36.1   Page 232. Runic.   168

37 Sylloge of Coins of the British Isles   174
       The Hiberno-Norse Coins in the British Museum,
       R.H.M.Dolley.
       The Trustees of the British Museum, London. (1966).

38 Sylloge of Coins of the British Isles   171
       Fitzwilliam Museum Cambridge   174
       Part 1 : Ancient British and Anglo-Saxon Coins
       Philip Grierson.
       The British Academy. (1958).

References

39 Standard Catalogue of the Coins of Great Britain and Ireland   174
        H.A.Seaby and P.J.Seaby.
        B.A.Seaby Ltd., London. (1956).

40 English Hammered Coinage, J.J.North.   174
        Spink & Son, London. (1963).

41 Peoples of Roman Britain   174
        The Carvetii, Nicholas Higham and Barri Jones.
        Alan Sutton, Stroud, Gloucestershire (1985).

42 Plutarch's Lives: Volume 1
        translated by Aubrey Stewart and George Long
        (1844 [G.Long] and 1880 to 1882).
        Bohn's Popular Library (1914 edition)
        G.Bell and Sons, Ltd. London.
    42.1   Page 117. Numa, early Roman calendar.   178

43 Everyman's Dictionary of Dates   179 (2)
        revised by Audrey Butler (4th edition 1964).
        Everyman's Reference Library
        J.M.Dent & Sons Ltd., London.

44 Early Astronomy, W.M.O'Neil (1986)
        Sydney University Press, Australia.
    44.1   Days between equinox and solstice. Page 4.   182
    44.2   Days between equinox and solstice, c.370 BC. Page 56.   182
    44.3   Precession of the equinoxes. Page 71.   186

45 Manetho : translated by W.G.Waddell (1940).   180
        Loeb Classical Library
        William Heinemann Ltd (1971).

46 Dictionary of Greek and Roman Biography and Mythology   184, 186
        edited by William Smith in three volumes.   Ap.7
        Volume 1 1844, Volume 2 1846.
        Taylor and Walton, Upper Gower Street, London.
        John Murray, Albemarle Street, London.

47 Cicero : The Letters of Cicero
        translated by Evelyn Shirley Shuckburgh (1843 to 1906) in 4 volumes.
        Volume 1. B.C. 68 - 52.
        Bohn's Classical Library. George Bell and Sons. London (1908).
    47.1   Page 276. To Trebatius June (54 BC). Waiting letter dated Britain.   Ap.4
    47.2   Page 277. To his bro. Quintus 3rd June (54 BC). Waiting descrip. Brit.   Ap.4
    47.3   Pages 282, 283. To Atticus June (54 BC). British cliffs.   Ap.4
    47.4   Page 287. To Atticus 27th July (54 BC). Suspects Quintus in Brit.   Ap.4
    47.5   Page 289. To Quintus Sept. (54 BC). Had letter from Brit., Soph. banquet.   Ap.4
    47.6   Pages 294, 295, 299. To Quintus in Britain. 28th September (54 BC).   Ap.4
    47.7   Page 327. To Atticus October (54 BC). Quintus - Brit. done with.   Ap.4
    47.8   Page 332. To Trebatius November (54 BC). Treb. did not go to Brit.   Ap.4
    47.9   Page 339. To Trebatius Testa November (54 BC). Refers to Nervii?   Ap.4
    47.10   Page 351. To Trebatius March ? (53 BC). Treb. not gone to Brit.   Ap.4

References

Page in this volume

48 Pindar: The Olympian and Pythian Odes   Ap.7
     Basil L. Gildersleeve, (1885)
     Professor of Greek in the John Hopkins University, Baltimore.
     Macmillan and Co., Limited. London. (1890 edition).
48.1   Tenth Pythian Ode. Page 350, Notes. Hyperborei.   Ap.7

49 Pindar : The Odes of Pindar in English Prose
     translated by Gilbert West. In 2 Volumes.
     Oxford. Printed for Munday and Slatter; and G. and W.B.Whittaker, London.
     Volume 1 (1824).
49.1   Vol 1. Tenth Pythian Ode, p. 221, 223, 224. Hyperborei.   Ap.7
49.2   Vol 1. Page 106. Diaulic race = double stadium.   Ap.7

50 Aeschylus: Prometheus Bound
     translated by E.D.A.Morshead (1849-1911).
     Project Gutenberg. – www.gutenberg.org - January, 2007.
     Aeschylus: Suppliant Maidens and Other Plays
     Release Date: August, 2005 [EBook #8714]. Edition 10.
50.1   Prometheus Bound. Of daughters born to Boreas.   Ap.7

51 Virgil : The Works of Virgil
     translated by John Dryden.
     Frederick Warne and Co., London and New York.
51.1   Vol 1. Georgics 1, pages 364, 365, 366. Dragon star constellation.   Ap.7(2)
51.2   Vol 1. Georgics 3, pages 410, 411. North in winter.   Ap.7

52 Cicero : Cicero's Tusculan Disputations, also Treatises on
     The Nature of the Gods, and on The Commonwealth
     translated chiefly by C.D.Yonge.
     Harper & Brothers, Publishers, Franklin Square, New York. (1877).
     Project Gutenberg. – www.gutenberg.org - January, 2007.
     Cicero's Tusculan Disputations, also Treatises on
     The Nature of the Gods, and on The Commonwealth
     Release Date: February 9, 2005 [EBook #14988]
52.1   Nature of the Gods book 3, chapter 23. 3rd Apollo from Hyperborei.   Ap.7

53 Dionysii Longini, Greek and Latin, De Sublimate
     written by Jonathan Toup and David Ruhnkenius.
     Clarendon Press, Oxford (1778).
53.1   Chapter 10, pages 44, 45. 13 lines from the Arimaspeia by Aristeas - in Latin.   Ap.7

54 Dionysius Longinus on the Sublime
     translated from the Greek by William Smith.
     Printed by B.Dod, the Bible and Key, Ave Mary Lane (3rd edit.1752).
54.1   Chapter 10, pages 54, 55. 13 lines from the Arimaspeia by Aristeas.   Ap.7

55 Longinus: On the Sublime
     translated by H.L.Havell, commentator Andrew Lang.
     Project Gutenberg. – www.gutenberg.org - January, 2007.
     Release Date: March 10, 2006 [EBook #17957]
55.1   Chapter 10.4. 13 lines from the Arimaspeia by Aristeas - English.   Ap.7

INDEX

Index

Index

Index